TO

the Memory of My Grandparents
Edward and Sadie Lee Caperton

The Making
of the Modern Family

THE MAKING

OF

THE MODERN

FAMILY

EDWARD SHORTER

Basic Books, Inc., Publishers

NEW YORK

Library of Congress Cataloging in Publication Data

Shorter, Edward.
   The making of the modern family.

   Bibliography: p.
   Includes index.
   1. Family. I. Title.
HQ734S577   301.42   75–7266
ISBN: 0–465–04327–5 (cloth)
ISBN: 0–465–09722–7 (paper)

CONTENTS

Contents

Contents

APPENDICES

ILLUSTRATIONS

(Following page 128)

The Traditional Family
Plate i
TOP: The Bettmann Archive
BOTTOM: Ullstein GMBH Bilderdienst

From Household to Nest
Plate ii
TOP: The Bettmann Archive
BOTTOM: Culver Pictures, Inc.

Women's Work and Men's Work
Plate iii
TOP LEFT: The New York Public Library Picture Collection
TOP RIGHT: The Granger Collection
BOTTOM LEFT: Robert Gerlack, Black Star
BOTTOM RIGHT: Ivan Massar, Black Star

Courtship and Romance
Plate iv
TOP LEFT: Culver Pictures, Inc.
BOTTOM: Lopez and Medina, Rapho/Photo Researchers, Inc.

Plate v
TOP: Culver Pictures, Inc.
BOTTOM: Niépce, Rapho/Photo Researchers, Inc.

The Onrush of Maternal Sentiment and Concern

Plate vi

    TOP LEFT: Culver Pictures, Inc.

    TOP RIGHT: The Bettmann Archive

    BOTTOM: New York Public Library Picture Collection

Plate vii

    TOP: Dorka Raynor, Rapho/Photo Researchers, Inc.

    BOTTOM RIGHT: Shelley Rusten, Black Star

Towards the Postmodern Family

Plate viii

    TOP RIGHT: B. Freer, Photo Researchers, Inc.

    BOTTOM: Dorka Raynor, Rapho/Photo Researchers, Inc.

PREFACE TO THE PAPERBACK EDITION

WHEN I WROTE this book several years ago, I thought that I would be addressing a somnolent audience of historians picking away at minute quarrels in the remoter reaches of the library stacks. As it turns out, I seem instead to have landed in a hornet's nest of feminists, Marxists, and caretakers of academic prose. I had dimly perceived, from the frosted glass of my ivory tower, that family history was becoming a "hip" subject. This was in part because the nuclear family of our own times seems to be breaking up and people want to know why, and in part because a number of red-hot issues in the general area of "capitalism," "women's work," and "sexuality" seem to run through the filter of the family.

This book has some sharply defined ideas to offer on these subjects, though I hadn't realized when I wrote it just how unpalatable they would be to the conventional wisdom. The book suggests that "capitalism" had on the whole a beneficial impact upon average women from the popular classes, seen at least from their point of view. It suggests that the supposedly repressive nineteenth century liberated many people from the overwhelming sexual repressiveness of traditional village society. And it suggests that high-quality mothering, rather than being some kind of eternal "instinct" slumbering in the female breast, has been very much an invention of the last century and a half.

This news proved unwelcome to the guardians of a number of intellectual bailiwicks. The defenders of "Marxism," an edifice that has towered over university life since the early 1960s, reacted with horror at the notion that anything positive could have come from the dark satanic mills, that young people from the countryside might have drifted into big cities or sought factory work for any cause other than sheer misery. The defenders of "mainline" feminism pronounced themselves appalled at the view that women might have had sex before marriage for any reason save "exploitation," and insisted that the great rush of out-of-wedlock pregnancies at the end of the eighteenth century was most likely a result of rape and prostitution. And the defenders of the Queen's English looked askance at a Canadian professor whose model of literate prose seemed to have been the *Police Gazette*, and pronounced the findings contaminated with "journalism."

Now, in fairness, a number of other slings and arrows have been aimed from quarters with less obvious ideological interests to defend. Some of these shafts have pierced to the heart, such as that calling me the "Helen Gurley Brown" of social history.[1] (Ms. Brown edits an unusually sappy magazine named *Cosmopolitan*.) Some have been just plain silly, such as Joan Scott's charge that I "pitch it low in the trough" in order to appeal to readers who aren't professional historians.[2] (What academic arrogance, moreover, to assume that any effort to address people who don't already have their tenure cards snuggled away must be undignified and without value!)

And some have raised important issues.

Five central problems seem to be emerging for social historians in this debate:

1. *Do patterns of intimate life ever really change at all?* A number of historians have argued that sodomy is to be found in the Middle Ages, that couples held hands in the sixteenth century, and that, while the pendulum may swing from repressive to permissive from time to time, how people feel about such basic matters as romance, infant life, and family solidarity is pretty well a historical "constant."[3]

Here we have a problem untangling the "three examples of bestiality I found in the archives" from what was in fact typical of the large masses of average people. At any moment in time one will observe all kinds of behavior represented in a large group of people. In sex, for example, there will always be a few who remain chaste before marriage and a few who are wildly dissolute, a few who don't masturbate and a few who do, depending on the period under discussion. But the question is, what was typical? And once that has been established, all the deviant little pockets of activity unknown in the daily lives of ordinary people—those sixteenth-century nobles practicing oral intercourse and such—can be dealt with as unrepresentative curiosities. If we do not ask about typicality, the endless citing of isolated examples will make it appear that nothing ever changes in history at all. *Plus ça change....*

The "eternal constant" school heartens visibly, for example, at evidence of a late-sixteenth-century increase in illegitimacy in England, which they take as demonstrating that styles of sexuality swing regularly from repressive to liberated throughout the ages.[4] If a major increase in illegitimate fertility actually did occur just before Puritanism took hold in England, and if it were in fact a result of more sexual intercourse rather than of better birth registration, my own views about a great once-and-for-all sexual revolution at the end of the eighteenth century would be called into question. This school is further encouraged by Jean-Louis Flandrin's notion that masturbation had been a fact of life among French peasants across the centuries, rather than representing (as I argue) a relatively new expression of sensuality which surfaces during the eighteenth century.[5]

The pleasing aspect of these questions is that they are resolvable, ultimately, by evidence. Either I am right or the "eternal constant" people are right. And we'll find out as we ask about typicality. Even if you have one masturbating peasant, how many others existed? Even if parish records show a sixteenth-century-bastardy boomlet, how many young women in village society were likely to have been exposed to impregnation, compared to what was to happen later?

2. *Under what circumstances did women become pregnant before marriage in the years 1750-1850?* Louise Tilly, Joan Scott, and Miriam Cohen have argued that the great increase in illegitimacy took place largely in the cities, as young women who had gone there to work as servants, carrying all their traditional expectations of how men were supposed to behave, suddenly found themselves stumbling about in a confusing new setting, easy prey for cynical employers and silver-tongued seducers.[6] This woman-as-victim approach, so beloved by "mainline" feminist historians, has several inconvenient facts to explain away.

For one thing, many of the impregnators of these women were not powerful men in positions to exploit their subordinates, but other poor devils of the same social class as the women themselves.

For another thing, a simultaneous illegitimacy explosion takes place in tiny villages and hamlets hundreds of miles away from any big city, where prostitutes would have been tarred and feathered and unscrupulous employers charivaried (more about that later on). It is not sufficient to whip out "misery" at this point, to claim that a landless proletariat was growing up in these villages, and that this proletariat merely behaved the way lower-class people had always behaved: sex before marriage. Because that account is incorrect. There had always been landless families in these villages, and their daughters had been chaste before marriage since time out of mind, which we know because they didn't bear any illegitimate children. Then around 1750 these young women from landless families start becoming sexually active and illegitimacy takes off. Of course the number of landless people was rising at the same time, yet some key factor in their "mentalities" was changing as well.[7]

Must we argue that these women were all "exploited"? Or does it not make more sense to think that, in the context of a proletarian subculture which smiled benignly upon sexuality, in the context of new job opportunities in capitalist agriculture that gave substantial personal independence, lower-class women had simply grown tired of waiting until they got married at age twenty-seven for the debut of their sex lives?

3. *Was the ghastly infant mortality of pre-1900 Europe the result of infectious diseases which no one could control, or of poor infant care on the part of indifferent mothers?* Few suggestions have so troubled critical spirits as the notion that all mothers in all times and places have not lavished the same overpowering, self-sacrificing attention upon infants as have twentieth-century mothers. A good portion of traditional infant mortality resulted, it goes without saying, from diseases such as diptheria, the infectiousness of which lay beyond human control. But the more I learn about causes of early infant death in the years before 1900, the more it becomes clear that many babies perished not from smallpox or scarlet fever, but from improper feeding and abysmal care, from being given a mixture of flour and water (rather than receiving a maternal breast), from a brutal obstetrical regime (rather than being attentively delivered by a knowledgeable midwife), and from being left to lie neglected for hours on

end in swaddling bands (rather than receiving playful parental attention while wrapped in warm clothes). We are dealing with a society
where women did heavy field work right up to the onset of labor pains,
where breast-feeding was often sporadic, weaning rapid, and infant
life little valued.[8]

How do we interpret these findings? One school argues that
"misery" obliged mothers to cease breast-feeding prematurely so that
they could resume the struggle for existence. In this view it is the
squalid living conditions of the lower classes that create marasmic
children, not the indifference of mothers. And if occasionally the in-
souciant mother does turn up, the "misery" historians simply argue that
parents benumbed by the shock of previous infant deaths could
scarcely be expected to attach themselves emotionally to subsequent
children. According to this school, mothers withdrew affection from
infants only because a grinding struggle to survive forced them to, not
because of an entire cultural universe that had made lovelessness a
code.[9]

The principal objection to the "misery" interpretation is that a
large chunk of the population, who treated their children with manifest callousness, was not miserable. Those small towns and villages
had a substantial "middle class" of artisans and landed peasants who
in fact possessed sufficient surplus to allow mothers to stop working
for the last month of pregnancy, or to breast-feed attentively during
the neonatal period, or to afford the services of a trained midwife at
delivery. It is an absurdly simplistic view of class structure to see
everyone beneath the level of merchant banker as languishing in
destitution. Somewhere, after all, these butchers and bakers and
Vollbauern got the money for large weddings, dowries, and militia uni-
forms. Yet this village middle class omitted just as much as did the
laborers to breast-feed infants while alive, and to grieve for them
when dead.

4. *What impact did paid-wage work have upon the lives of working-class married women? What consequences for the household
influence of "middle-class" women arose when they ceased contributing to the production of goods?* Here the opposing forces stand poles
apart. A "golden age" group of feminist historians argues that in
traditional society farm women had all kinds of household authority

and prestige.[10] With industrialization those who remained in the labor force found their contributions "devalued," and the vastly greater number who withdrew from productive work found themselves "put on a pedestal," left powerless in their suburban ranchhouses, noses pressed against the glass—when they weren't out buying fine clothes or playing the piano.[11] If true, this account would certainly suggest that industrialization had been "bad for women."

Fortunately, I believe it to be false: (a) because over the long haul the participation of women in the *paid* labor force was enormously increased rather than diminished—a fact that initiated the dismantling of the staggering patriarchy of the peasantry: (b) because it rests on a complete miscomprehension of the real lives of women in eighteenth-century farm-and-craft families, women who were relegated to a status so inferior that those nineteenth-century Victorian heroines would come across as veritable Gloria Steinems by comparison: (c) because it neglects those aspects of late nineteenth-century nuclear-family life which offered a secure emotional nest for both women and infants, in which the vicious brutality of the traditional family had become relatively rare,[12] and in which status relationships between husband and wife had become vastly more egalitarian.

To anyone who argues that women were "on top" in seventeenth-century farm families in France, and "oppressed" in nineteenth-century bankers' families in Mayfair, I shall send a copy of Dr. Moreau's famous tract, "Why reading novels overheats the imagination."

5. *What in the world is happening in family life today?* Is the contemporary Western family undergoing some kind of fundamental soul-wrenching transformation, as I suspect? Or is it just pausing for breath to deal with the onrush of feminism and women working, as a Pollyanna school of sociologists led by Mary Jo Banes has argued?[13] The census and vital-statistics reports pour in daily: breathtaking increases in divorce, in teen-age crime, in premarital nonvirginity and cohabitation, in elderly widows living alone rather than with their children. . . .[14] The nuclear family seems wracked in some kind of final tubercular spasm; the couple family is on the rise, and all the wishing otherwise will not make it different. Thus spake the Helen Gurley Brown of social history.

A codicil. I can feel my vehemence growing as I sit here at the typewriter, "responding to the critics." "What do you think of these bad people who have attacked Your Professor?" I ask my students. But I should try not to be too dogmatic in refuting these alternate views or in pushing my own. The ideas the reader will encounter in this book are hypotheses, not hard-and-fast knowledge. As hypotheses, they are fortified by what other scholars have made known in the published literature and by my own research, but they remain, nonetheless, hypotheses. Which means they can be overturned as new evidence becomes available. And scarcely a week goes by that some important new finding doesn't arrive in the mail: French peasant men fearful of what they imagined to be their wives' raging sexual desires? How interesting. The Bishop of Würzburg banning all winter spinning bees? What a curious thing to do. A massive increase in rickets among lower-class English women"? [15] The mind turns at once to an ominous category of obstetrical literature entitled "Contracted Pelves and Complications of Childbirth."

Now, most of this new work confirms more or less what I had argued in the following pages when I wrote them several years ago.[16] But we're only at the threshold. The whole encounter with love, pain, and death of these millions of anonymous people—inarticulate in life, forgotten thereafter—remains largely unexplored and full of potential surprises. So, you armies of doctoral students and established scholars presently out there in the field, snuffling about for breast-feeding peasants in Oberbayern or sentimental mottoes upon the walls of barrelmakers' homes in Burgundy, command humility. The facts are by and large "in" on Bismarck, on Roosevelt, and on Alexander the Great. We know with reasonable certainty the basic outlines of the story and why war was declared. But we have no such certainty for the enormous, blank panorama of intimate life. There may be surprises.

Which is the point of this little preface, not that I am "right" and my critics invariably, incorrigibly wrong, but that further discovery looms excitingly ahead. The most important accomplishment I could wish for from the pages that follow is not to convince beyond cavil, but to specify the crucial questions, so that other historians can get out there into the semi-legible world of archival evidence, and see what actually happened to young people in these sprawling industrial cities, to weary peasant women pregnant for the ninth time, and to bitter married couples who stop having sex not as a means of birth control, but because they hate each other. Because it is upon these people that all our ideas about how things happen in social history ultimately hinge.

Edward Shorter

April 1977

NOTES

1. A review entitled "What the Doctor Ordered," *New York Review of Books*, 11 December, 1975, p. 53.
2. *Signs: Journal of Women and Culture in Society*, 2 (1977): 192–696.
3. Examples are Peter Laslett's review in *New Society*, 10 June, 1976, pp. 590–591; Keith Thomas's review in *New Statesman*, 28 May 1976, pp. 716–717; Richard T. Vann's review-essay in *Journal of Family History*, 1 (1976): 106–117.
4. Evidence on this late-sixteenth-century rise has recently been presented in Peter Laslett, *Family Life and Illicit Love in Earlier Generations* (Cambridge: Cambridge University Press, 1977).
5. See Flandrin's two recent studies, which can only be characterized as brilliant, *Les Amours paysannes (XVIe–XIXe siècle)* (Paris: Gallimard/Julliard, 1975), pp. 160–165, and *Familles: parenté, maison, sexualité dans l'ancienne société* (Paris: Hachette, 1976), pp. 184–188.
6. "Women's Work and European Fertility Patterns," *Journal of Interdisciplinary History*, 6 (1976): 447–476.
7. An important new contribution to the role of the propertyless in the sexual revolution is J. Michael Phayer, *Sexual Liberation and Religion in Nineteenth-Century Europe* (London: Croom Helm, 1977), chs. 1–3.
8. See Shorter, "Maternal Sentiment and Death in Childbirth: A New Agenda for Psychohistory," in Harvey Graff, ed., *Quantification and Psychohistory*, forthcoming 1978.
9. For statements of this position see Lasch, *op. cit.*, p. 50, and Lawrence Stone, review, in the *Times Literary Supplement*, 28 May 1976, p. 637.
10. "Golden Age" arguments have been made by a whole host of mainline-feminist historians, among them Joan Scott and Louise Tilly, "Women's Work and the Family in Nineteenth-Century Europe," "*Comparative Studies in Society and History*, 17 (1975): 36–64; and Leo Johnson, "The Political Economy of Ontario Women in the Nineteenth Century," in *Women at Work, Ontario, 1850-1930* (Toronto: Canadian Women's Educational Press, 1974), 13–31. For a useful antidote, however, see Patricia Branca, *Silent Sisterhood: Middle Class Women in the Victorian Home* (Pittsburgh: Carnegie-Mellon, 1975).
11. See recently Linda Gordon, *Woman's Body, Woman's Right: A Social History of Birth Control in America* (New York: Viking/Grossman, 1977); and G. J. Barker-

Benfield, *The Horrors of the Half-Known Life: Male Attitudes Toward Women and Sexuality in Nineteenth-Century America* (New York: Harper & Row, 1976).

12. Martine Segalen's new work on French proverbs drives home the unrelenting hostility to women on the part of males in village society. "Le Mariage, l'amour et les femmes dans les proverbs populairres francais," *Ethnologie francaise*, 5 (1975): 119–162 and 6 (1976): 33–88.

13. Mary Jo Bane, *Here to Stay: American Families in the Twentieth Century* (New York: Basic Books, 1976).

14. Paul Glick, a cool headed Census Bureau statistician, recently concluded his analysis of 1974 census data on who-lives-with-whom: "This brief documentation of recent changes . . . leaves no doubt about the general impression that a vastly larger number of young people now than a short decade or two ago are experiencing daily personal relationships in a context quite different from the nuclear family of father-mother-and-children. For older adults . . . the new era takes a great deal of getting used to." "Living Arrangements of Children and Young Adults," *Journal of Comparative Family Studies*, 7 (1976); 321–333.

15. These examples taken from Segalen, *op. cit.*, 6 (1976): 48, 49, 63; Phayer, *op. cit.*, p. 55; Calvin Wells, "Prehistoric and Historical Changes in Nutritional Diseases and Associated Conditions," *Progress in Food and Nutrition Science*, 1 (1975): 729–779, esp. 754.

16. One article which does not, however, confirm the book's findings is W. R. Lee, "Bastardy and the Socioeconomic Structure of South Germany," *Journal of Interdisciplinary History*, 7 (1977): 403–425; David Levine, too, is dubious, in *Family Formations in an Age of Nascent Capitalism* (New York: Academic, 1977), and in Levine and Keith Wrightson, "The Social Context of Illegitimacy in Early Modern England," in Peter Laslett and Richard Smith, eds., *Bastardy and Its Comparative History* (forthcoming in 1977 from Edward Arnold).

PREFACE

I GOT THE IDEA for this book when sitting with Chuck Tilly and Ann Finlayson around the breakfast table one morning. Chuck had said that, in order to really pin down how social change transforms people's lives, what we needed was a general history of the family. Even though the idea intrigued me, I was sure there were some pitfalls I wanted to avoid in making the attempt. I did not want, for example, to pass off a chronicle of court gossip as a history of the family, or to end up writing about that upper five percent of the population who normally monopolize our historical attention. And then, I was absolutely determined to try to find out about the representative experience of the average person, to see what had been typical in the lives of ordinary men and women over the last three centuries. I also wanted to be able to "prove" the various points about family history, insofar as matters in the domain of intimate life are demonstrable at all, rather than just to pile up illustrations, any or all of which might turn out to be totally untypical.

Five years earlier these ambitions would have been impossible. Only the "new social history" of the 1960s and '70s has let us learn systematically about common people's lives in past times. Burrowing through parish registers in dusty provincial archives, putting tax lists on magnetic computer tape, and painstakingly compiling the genealogies of everyone living in a village—only these have made available even the raw material for such a book. The reader will see from my end notes what a great proportion of this evidence has been gathered in the last ten years.

I have, of course, drawn heavily upon my own research. And if it had not occurred to me, as I was digging through the Bavarian State Archives in 1966, to wonder why all these government officials were yelling about "immorality," the question of how the sexual experience of average men and women has changed over the years might never have crossed my mind. But in the 1960s such questions were occurring to many other scholars as well. And to the extent that I've been able to talk about wider areas of Europe and North America over longer periods of time, I've been able to rely upon their work.

I dwell upon the history of this little book only because I want to convey to the reader a massive modesty about its contents. We are talking here about the private lives of anonymous, ordinary people. Many were scarcely able to read. None wrote books about what they did or felt. Reconstructing the record of their family experience is bound to be a chancy business. Very little is certain, and the evidence, far from anchoring indisputably my propositions about sentiment and affection, trembles feebly in the wind. Yet for the time being this is all we know about the history of the average family— the experience of the typical woman or the representative baby, as opposed to the infants of kings and the wives of bankers. I am convinced that my arguments about the onrush of romantic love, family domesticity, and maternal tenderness—which are the core of this book—are correct. But I want the reader to understand how wide the gap is from tentative hypothesis to absolute certainty.

I have some obligations to acknowledge. First, there is Martin Kessler of Basic Books, who taught me lessons about the language I should have learned long ago, and that there is more than one way to skin a cat with statistics. John Demos made a number of valuable suggestions, and my good friend and colleague Michael Marrus obliged me by commenting on an early draft. The Canada Council supported some of the research financially. And Cecile Sydney typed the manuscript.

I should finally like to thank Linda McQuaig, whose questions forced me to return again and again to my typewriter until I got things at least half right.

The Making
of the Modern Family

INTRODUCTION

The Argument

WE MAY THINK of the family in traditional society as a ship held fast at its moorings. From every side great cables run down to bind it to the dock. The ship sails nowhere and is part of the harbor.

Now, in the Bad Old Days—let us say the sixteenth and seventeenth centuries—the family too was held firmly in the matrix of a larger social order. One set of ties bound it to the surrounding kin, the network of aunts and uncles, cousins and nieces who dotted the old regime's social landscape. Another set fastened it to the wider community, and gaping holes in the shield of privacy permitted others to enter the household freely and, if necessary, preserve order. A final set of ties held this elementary family to generations past and future. Awareness of ancestral traditions and ways of doing business would be present in people's minds as they went about their day. Because they knew that the purpose of life was preparing coming generations to do as past ones had done, they would have clear rules for shaping relations within the family, for deciding what was essential and what not.

In its journey into the modern world the family has broken all these ties. It has separated from the surrounding community, guarded now by high walls of privacy. It has cast off its connections with distant kin, and has changed fundamentally even its relationship to close relatives. And it has parted from the lineage, that chain of gen-

3

erations stretching across time: whereas once people had been able to answer questions such as "who am I" by pointing to those who had gone before and would come after, in the twentieth century they would have other replies.

Thus in modern times the family drifted onto the high seas, and the world of metaphor such a voyage suggests started to fix itself in the vocabulary of social analysis. Had the winds always blown so strongly as now? people would ask. Had the currents always been so powerful, the family so little able to navigate a separate course? Was the captain's hand unsteady, or was it that the little ship was carried by such forces as capitalism, anonymous urban life, and the great tides of rationality and secularism over which it had no control? Above all, scholars would wonder, how was it that the family had managed to slip its moorings at the traditional dock?

For many years now, one group has thought that the hawsers were cut by roving gangs of "mass men," bent upon pillaging the established order of things. Other writers, however, have said that the tides sweeping through the harbor became irresistible, and by their sheer force alone parted the cables. I shall argue in this book that it was the ship's own crew—Mom, Dad, and the Kids—who severed the cables by gleefully reaching down and sawing through them so that the solitary voyage could commence.

A number of questions suggest themselves. Why did the family decide to cut the ties that held it within the surrounding social order? Why did it withdraw from the web of interconnections to the small community? Why has it come to prefer friendship with close kin to interaction with the concentric rings of uncles and aunts, neighbors and members of the various peer groups that, as we shall see, were constantly pulling people from the home? Why did the family decide to cut the chain of generations, to no longer follow custom and tradition in arranging its life, to no longer bring up its offspring to perpetuate the patrimony? And why, finally, did its various members decide that other values in life were more important than familial ones?

This book will not supply definitive answers to these questions. Its ambitions are more modest: to point out, among the many factors that will have to be considered before we can understand why the family has changed, the crucial one of sentiment. I shall suggest that a surge of sentiment in three different areas helped to dislodge the traditional family:

Courtship. Romantic love unseated material considerations in bringing the couple together. Property and lineage would give way to personal happiness and individual self-development as criteria for choosing a marriage partner.

The mother-child relationship. While a residual affection between mother and child—the product of a biological link—has always existed, there was a change in the priority which the infant occupied in the mother's rational hierarchy of values. Whereas in traditional society the mother had been prepared to place many considerations—most of them related to the desperate struggle for existence—above the infant's welfare, in modern society the infant came to be most important; maternal love would see to it that his well-being was second to nothing.

The boundary line between the family and the surrounding community. In the Bad Old Days the family's shell was pierced full of holes, permitting people from outside to flow freely through the household, observing and monitoring. The traffic flowed the other way, too, as members of the family felt they had more in common emotionally with their various peer groups than with one another. In other words, the traditional family was much more a productive and reproductive unit than an emotional unit. It was a mechanism for transmitting property and position from generation to generation. While the lineage was important, being together about the dinner table was not.

Then these priorities were reversed. Ties to the outside world were weakened, and ties binding members of the family to one another reinforced. A shield of privacy was erected to protect the foyer's intimacy from foreign intrusion. And the modern nuclear family was born in the shelter of domesticity. Thus sentiment flowed into a number of familial relationships. Affection and inclination, love and sympathy, came to take the place of "instrumental" considerations in regulating the dealings of family members with one

5

another. Spouses and children came to be prized for what they were, rather than for what they represented or could do. That is the essence of "sentiment."

Whether this surge of sentiment was a cause or a result of a change in the family's relationship to the surrounding community is one of the big unanswered questions of this book. Did the terrible shocks of "modernization" shatter the stable community structure within which the traditional family was nestled? Or did these massive social changes first affect the mentalities of individual family members, causing them to embrace one another and block off as an annoying disruption the stream of traffic through the household? In the exchange of peer-group allegiance for emotional intimacy, which came first the chicken or the egg?

If my views on the revolution in sentiment are correct, several aspects of family life today will appear in a slightly different perspective. Part of this perspective is the downgrading of some much-discussed "recent changes in the family." Is there, for example, a growing lack of communication between the spouses? Not at all. As much openness in communication between husband and wife as we're ever going to see was laid down during the nineteenth century in the form of romantic love; spontaneous exchanges between husband and wife were achieved when what I shall call "domesticity" was hammered into place a hundred years ago. And as long as romance continues to be the basic cement binding spouses—as it still is today—the quality of marital dialogue will remain the same. Whatever the vexing dilemmas that Mom, Dad, and the Kids are wrestling with nowadays, they do not include some "new" kind of uncommunicativeness.

And the new liberation of women—has it helped throw the contemporary family into turmoil? While the situation of women is no doubt undergoing some boneshaking changes, I am not convinced that the likelihood that people will form into couples has thereby been much affected. Women are plunging into the labor force with an intensity not seen since the first "cottage" industrial revolution of the eighteenth century. This new access to economic resources has clearly altered the balance of power within the family, as the woman now commands upon unprecedented financial leverage. But it's unclear how—if at all—this recent economic role has contributed to what journalists are wont to call "the breakdown of the family."

This book argues that the reshaping of the family currently underway has two main components: an inherent instability of the couple itself, and a loss of control by parents over adolescent children. As we shall see, among the big surprises modernization has brought for family life is a soaring divorce rate. The chances are good that one in every four marriages now being constituted in North America will end in divorce (as with one in every six or seven in western and northern Europe), a likelihood that contrasts with a virtually non-existent divorce rate in traditional society. This new instability is the result of replacing property first with sentiment and then with sex as the bond between man and wife. It also results from the corresponding shearing away of the traditional couple's ties with the community, kin, and lineage. Formerly, the expectations that these surrounding institutions had of a couple served to keep the partners together throughout life, perhaps (in fact almost certainly) not happy, yet integrated within a firm social order. But then the couple terminated its association with these outside groups and strolled off into the dusk holding hands.

Alas, affection and romantic love have wellsprings in the unconscious, and in the beast's nature lie unpredictability and transitoriness. You're deeply attached to someone one day, the next you aren't. Well, that's the way is goes . . . except that if true love is the only cement holding the couple together, the family will dissolve once it's gone. To be sure, the individuals who pick themselves up from these dissolved unions quickly find new partners and remarry. Our vision of marriage as the ideal state of heterosexual cohabitation hasn't been shaken at all. But this shift in the family's relationship to the surrounding community has had some fairly dramatic implications for the couple's stability. That's one part of the crisis in contemporary family life we might see a bit more clearly.

The other part is the rupture of most of the social controls the couple was once able to exert upon their children. They simply vanished in the 1960s and '70s, not just in North America but as sociologists (normally the last to get the news) are just beginning to discover, in Great Britain, France, Germany, Scandinavia, and other corners of Western industrial society, as well. Why this rupture occurred has been much debated. But if this book is able to contribute anything, it will be the suggestion that the larger lineage—that chain of generations stretching across time, of which individual nuclear families were once a part—has ceased to confer immortality. In the Bad Old Days people learned who they were, and what their place in the eternal order of things was to be, by looking at the progression of generations that stretched behind them—a progression that would extend from them into a future of which one could say only that it would probably be like the present. People in traditional society were, in the last analysis, able to face death so placidly because they knew their names and memories would live on in the lineage of their families.

Today other roads than that of family lineage lead to immortality, or perhaps people care less about the whole posterity business. In any event we have lost interest in the family lineage as a means of cheating death, and we have thus let fall the ties which bind one generation to the next. Adolescents now soon realize that they are not links in a familial chain stretching across the ages. Who they are and what they become is independent, (at least so they believe) of who their parents are. And they themselves are responsible for what their children become only to the point of seeing that they march into the future with straight teeth. The chain of generations serves no larger moral purpose for adolescents, and therewith the moral authority of parents over their growing children collapses.

Other agencies now socialize and control the young. The continuity between the generations falls. No outside institutions at all intrude upon the intimacy of the couple, and men and women come together and wrench apart as freight cars do in a switching yard. If the argument of this book is right, that is the crisis of the postmodern family.

The trouble with writing a history of the family is that the principal characters, the millions of anonymous men and women who populated the everyday world, are silent. Unlike the garrulous aristocrats' wives and the rue St-Honoré novelists on whom social historians so depend, these people failed to put their innermost thoughts

8

on paper. Nor were they terribly communicative with the literate observers on the peripheries of their world. As for their feelings, they maintained a tomblike silence before even their spouses and children, to say nothing of preserving a record for posterity.

But the core of the history of the family is precisely this chronicle of sentiments. The structures that encase a family's life are, after all, fairly visible: the number of people in the household; their relationships with one another; their births, deaths, and marriages. Many constellations of sentiment are, however, possible within any given structure, and because the crisis of the family today is a crisis of emotion—of attachment and rejection—it is incumbent upon the family historian to trace the tale of sentiments.

The easiest way to tell such a story is to string together anecdotes from literary sources—for example, what Balzac's characters say about their neighbors' daughters' pregnancies in Paris, or what Mann's say about their fathers' stifling authority in Lübeck. The charming little stories don't always come from novelists. Social historians are happy to ransack collections of letters, diaries, and memoirs. You pick one amusing story about the banker X's mistress, another about how the chancellor's wife grieved at her husband's death and *voilà*, you've got a social history of the family: love, death, and sex all put together from sources right there on the library shelves. And moreover, fun to do. Historians, being themselves mostly literate people, delight in the literary artifacts of the past. What more entertaining an enterprise than to combine an evening's pastime of memoir-reading with the preparation of a history of the family?

Such an approach has two grave drawbacks. For one, "literary sources" (by which I mean not only novels but the whole range of outpourings of cultivated pens) are largely the work of the upper middle classes and the aristocracy. What kind of people, after all, tended to burst forth in love letters, write novels, or compose memoirs other than a tiny elite at the pinnacle of the social order? Belletristic literature, and the encircling apparatus of diaries and letters, represents the experience of perhaps 5 percent of the population.

The vast bulk of writing about intimate experience comes from people who had very little in common with the classes in which we are interested, the other 95 percent of the population. And while the bankers' wives or salon habitués to whom our library shelves owe so much may have had a nodding acquaintance with the lower orders—greeting their milkmen in the morning, perhaps, or chatting with coachmen in late-night cafés—the patterns of child-rearing, mate selection, and domestic attachment they describe were, in the last analysis, their own. The gulf between upper middle-class life and the experience of the lower orders was enormous in past times. And accounts of the one are not acceptable substitutes for descriptions of the other. The first stumbling block to anecdotes as a way of writing the history of the family, therefore, is their inescapable class bias.

The second obstacle is the problem of representativeness. Let us assume that we clutch in our hands a rare working-class autobiography, or a collection of love letters of popular origin. How are we to know whether their tales of masturbation or handholding are typical? Because one peasant couple exchanged affectionate greetings, does it necessarily follow that all did so? This is the old fallacy of confusing illustration with verification. Representing a general point with an example is not at all the same as establishing the generalization's validity.

The reader will sympathize. We want to lay bare the historical experience of the popular classes rather than of the *haut monde*. We want to establish central tendencies and representative behavior rather than to assume that because a single rustic couple was found walking with little fingers locked together, "peasants showed affection by locking little fingers together." We want, finally, to watch flesh-and-blood people go about their daily lives rather than to stagger through a fog of numbers (for you can always trail the common people with statistical means and medians). We can find out a lot about whether married couples practiced birth control—a crucial problem in family history—by looking at how many children they produced and the intervals at which they arrived. But not only do such investigations make deadly reading, they still leave open to inference what these men and women *felt* about each other as they were generating all these children—and what they felt about the children.

So I attempted a compromise between the narrowness of quantitative analysis and the possibly atypical descriptions of concrete places in fixed times. I tried to find some literate observers—almost by definition upper-middle-class people—who preserved accounts of lives other than their own for posterity, observers close to the people but not of them.

Who was likely to have had good knowledge of the experience of the popular classes while being sufficiently articulate to get onto paper what he saw? Three kinds of observers met these criteria: local medical doctors; minor bureaucrats; and that variety of antiquarian scholar whom the French charmingly call "les érudits locaux." Each kind had his advantages and disadvantages.

The medical doctors of the late eighteenth and early nineteenth centuries often described their little communities in "medical topographies." These were a genre of literature launched by the Parisian Academy of Medicine in 1778 in an appeal to the provincial doctors of France, and carried along by sheer momentum until late in the nineteenth century. Doctors all over Europe imitated the French. In a medical topography, the local practitioner in some village or small town would describe not only the diseases to which his patients were subject and the health hazards of the environment, but often the patients' social lives as well: the condition of women, local child-bearing practices, causes of alarming increases in illegitimacy, or other precious social data the doctor would have absorbed in the course of his daily rounds. And in those days they did make house calls. Being often partially remunerated by the government, they served all classes of the population in their practice. These medical topographies, and the medical literature that appeared with them, thus give us a long look at the social matrix of disease—a final look before medical writers disappear ineluctably into the clinic and laboratory. The problem with the doctors, however, is their imputation of ignorance and superstition to those less enlightened than themselves. Better educated by far than anyone else in the frog pond, they interpret the different cultural norms of local peasants and artisans as an absence of culture. Can men and women who live so closely to barnyard animals be much above them in emotion and sensation? We have to struggle desperately to untangle the doctors' enlightened, urbane, rationalistic prejudices from the reality of a traditional popular culture whose inherent dignity rests upon hundreds of years of accumulated experience.

11

The administrative reports and "statistical" descriptions of lower-level bureaucrats represent a second source. The "cameralist" officials of eighteenth- and nineteenth-century Europe were astonishingly inquisitive about people's private lives. And in those days the state intervened frequently in intimate domains from which it has today, by and large, withdrawn: the chastisement of out-of-wedlock pregnancy, the organization of mercenary wet-nursing, or the according of permission to marry. Even aside from such intrusions, petty bureaucrats were fairly well informed about local affairs, for they had to pass judgment on applications for poor relief, preserve order at the numerous village festivals, or now and then swat at noisy charivaris. Yet one can imagine with what sort of face the local people met *Monsieur le sous-préfet*. The great defect of bureaucratic evidence is the observer's likely inability to get at the core of popular life. If the peasants appeared submissive, stupid, and generally bowed by the weight of centuries, it was not necessarily because they really were that way, but because they didn't want their taxes increased or their eldest sons taken off to military service. In the coming pages we shall be at pains to disentangle officialdom's contempt for the popular orders from the popular orders' efforts to manipulate officialdom.

The final source of evidence is the richest and yet the most explosive for the inattentive scholar: the material prepared by the antiquarians and folklorists. Within every small town and village there hunkered a literate notability, the squire, the parson or priest, the schoolteacher, the landowner who once had been away to Marseille to boarding school. And just as surely as one of them would chronicle local meteorology, noting meticulously barometric pressures and temperatures week after week, another would chronicle local folkways. From the beginning of the nineteenth century, a flood of little "memoirs" and "notes" issued from their pens. These accounts of courting practices and harvest festivals were sometimes privately published, sometimes marketed by a printing house in the regional capital. Often an antiquarian's solemn accounts of local folk sayings, folk dances, or "folksy" practices were prepared as papers to regional scientific societies. Then, toward the end of the nineteenth century, the professional folklorists usurped their role. The contribution of the local antiquarians changed from primitive but nonetheless serviceable accounts of village ethnology to the empty cataloging of forms. In the twentieth century, professional folklorists do not tell us whether the couples held on to each other in the pauses between dances but with what color ribbons the grain sheaves were tied at harvest time.

Unlike the other two sources, the antiquarians supplied discursive accounts of matters intensely interesting to the family historian, such as how individual families participated in the annual cycle of village festivals, or how much group supervision of mating took place. Another difference was that antiquarians were generally smitten with nostalgia, longing for the world they had lost, and tending to see breakdown and disintegration at every turn. Accordingly, they shoved any change in something like sexual behavior into the shoes of "declining morality," and viewed shifts in adolescent attitudes as part of a general "collapse of the father's authority." The most telling defect of antiquarians' evidence for the study of change over time was their tendency to assume a historical changelessness from the days of the Druids until the days of their fathers, whereupon the "great decline of folklore" began.

Now, it happens that in fact they were right. The machinery of modernization was grinding traditional society into piecemeal at the time most of them were writing, the last half of the nineteenth century. So antiquarian sentiments of collapse and disintegration did not come entirely from an eternal human temptation to see in childhood years a gentle idyll guaranteed by the just authority of a wise father, in adult life, by way of contrast, a featureless expanse of anxiety and uncertainty. That may have been present of course, but going on as well was a genuine shift in the structure of the real world. The point is that we want to pursue historical trends from the eighteenth century until the present day. And in the pages ahead, the antiquarian scenario of stability in local culture since time out of mind, terminated by a catastrophic encounter with modernity that happens to coincide precisely with the author's own old age, will serve us poorly.

Because each of these three categories of evidence extends a century or more in time, we may use them as a time series, as data for the study of change. By accumulating the testimony of doctors, bureaucrats, and antiquarians from various periods, we should be able to follow historical shifts. Obviously these accounts will not serve as exacting, quantitative indexes. Manifestly I'm assuming that the biases and preoccupations of the writers themselves did not alter greatly from one era to the next, else we would just have an index of changing views about "x" or "y," rather than an index of change itself. These testimonies will be of little service in differentiating among regions, or even in making very fine distinctions about periods. Yet in a rough way these long chains of medical topographies, "statistiques locales," and tales of "my village" should let us chart the family's movements from the early eighteenth century, when my own interest begins, to the interwar years of the twentieth century, when contemporary social surveys start up.

One more nervous cough about the evidence in this book is in order. The arguments I offer are aimed at all of Western society. Every village in every province in every land has sooner or later undertaken the long trek toward the sentimental family, for the changes in intimate life that modernization fosters are essentially the same everywhere. So what I have to say about the passage from instrumental to emotional behavior in courtship, or about the withdrawal of the nuclear family from the surrounding community, should be true everywhere as well. Once historians start investigating thoroughly, they will (if I am right) encounter these grand transformations in northern Sweden and southern Italy, in the eastern marches of Prussia and the western marshes of France. They should even discover the United States tipping a few degrees, although—because the New World was for the most part "born modern"—this tilt will be undramatic. On the whole, the onrush of sentiment and the cutting of family ties to the community should have been universal within Western society, even though the timing was staggered and the local variation enormous.

Unfortunately, the solid, primary evidence I have to present concerns mainly France, with parts of Germany and Scandinavia thrown in from time to time. And not even all of France or all of Bavaria or Ostergotland are included but only peasant and propertied France towards the end of the eighteenth century, and Bavaria as seen through the lenses of officialdom towards the middle of the nineteenth. This is in the nature of things; a single scholar can never turn up more than a tiny corner of the field, and the earth stretches on endlessly.

Two circumstances cause me to think that the soil I'm uncovering in France and Germany is typical of the West as a whole: the coincidence between my own findings and the preliminary reports of other scholars, themselves busy digging away in little patches far distant from my own; and the similarity in trends that statistical series reveal. Official government data on age at marriage or on infant mortality—to take two examples of the kinds of statistics that shall occupy us later on—are available in uniform series for many places and cover long stretches of time. When the quantitative data for these numerous countries come out as the qualitative, descriptive material for France and Germany suggest they should, the scholar can take heart that many patches are like his own. It is precipitous, of course, on my part, to suggest that all of them are, but I think I'm right.

At the outset, certain terms in this book deserve some clarification. Among them are romantic love, traditional society, and modern society.

Romantic love I shall define as the capacity for spontaneity and empathy in an erotic relationship. Spontaneity is important because it represents the rejection of traditional, community-imposed forms in interpersonal matters. For the couple, romance is a vehicle of self-exploration and self-development. And in this interior search there are no signposts. The couple delights together in the exploration of their individual complexity. Hence all that happens to them, all the gestures they exchange and the forms of tenderness they elaborate, seem to spring from them spontaneously. Now, of course, the surrounding culture offers a series of "models" for expressing affection, and the couple in reality invents very little. But they are not aware of that. Oblivious that they are doing a dance whose steps countless couples before them have already worked out, they believe themselves to be acting spontaneously. How different this is from the couple's behavior in the old regime when, as we shall see, custom wrote the dialogue, and the couple followed forms that a timeless screenplay had imposed since time out of mind.

Empathy, the ability to put yourself in somebody else's shoes,

15

counts because it represents the breaking down of sex roles. Expressions such as "sympathy," "understanding," "communication," images of dissolving oneself in someone else, gestures of eyes and hands locking together—all these belong in the domain of empathy. A major component of romance in Western society over the past two centuries has been the demolition of individual emotional isolation and the locking together of souls. One consequence of such intense emotional exchange has been the dismantling of strict sex-role divisions. Otherwise the emotional encounter would be impossible. People would remain imprisoned within the steel cages their sex roles had fashioned.

Of course sex roles are never completely demolished. Our upbringing, by a system in which sex-role division guarantees social stability, is too thorough for that. But historically, the rigid demarcation of sex roles that prevailed in early modern Europe has given way to far suppler molds within which men and women may define themselves. Such suppleness is kneaded into the texture of emotional life by empathy.

Empathy and spontaneity may run through a variety of human relationships. But only in erotic relationships do they become romantic love. The meeting of bodies is, finally, the forum within which the meeting of romantic spirits takes place. And so in this book we're going to be paying considerable attention to sexuality. Sex can serve a variety of ends: those that concern the attainment of some ulterior, nonsexual objective I shall call "instrumental sexuality"; those that concern the interior search I shall be referring to as "affective sexuality." Without previewing too much of the story, let me indicate here that the instrumental sort of sexual behavior predominated in *premodern* Europe. Affective sexuality, on the other hand, has become paramount in *modern* times. In the first premarital sexual revolution of the late eighteenth century, affective sexuality was linked to romance. In the second sexual revolution of the 1960s, it was linked to hedonism. How all this came about will occupy us later.

Finally, in this realm of the emotions, we have "sentiment." Because so much of the modern family's history is told in terms of the great swath that sentiment cut through the family's ties to the community, we must make sure we'll be able to recognize it when we see it. Sentiment I may define as the willingness to rearrange the objectives in one's life so that emotional ties to other people go to the top of the list, and more traditional objectives get ranked farther down. Sentiment will effect a reordering of priorities in three domains:

1. Partner selection. Sentiment makes personal happiness the most important objective in the selection of a mate, ahead of such traditional criteria as family interest and dowry size. This reordering of priorities is nothing more than "romantic love," a special case of the general category "sentiment."

2. Mother-infant relationships. Sentiment puts the infant's welfare ahead of all other objectives in the mother's eyes, making her limit her traditional contributions to the family economy, such as field work or helping at the loom. Sentiment here becomes articulated as "maternal love."

3. The household. In the course of modernization, families will decide to pull back from their intense involvement with the surrounding community, paying the appropriate price (no more common feasts and such), just as prices had to be paid in each of the other two categories of sentiment. Sentiment in the household means that privacy and intimacy will triumph over the traditional interstitching with the lives of others. Secluded behind closed shutters from the outside, members of the family spin about themselves that web of sentiment the French allude to as *chacun chez soi* and we shall call "domesticity."

Defining sentiment as the reordering of priorities gives us a useful means of "operationalizing" an otherwise abstract notion. When we encounter young men passing up fat dowries to wed their heart's desire, we shall know we're standing before romance. When we encounter mothers setting aside the many forms of industrial work they once did at home, or coming in from the fields in order themselves to wet-nurse their infants instead of leaving them with a paid nurse, we shall recognize maternal affection. And when we see the dissolution of various peer groups that were so much a part of the traditional

17

world, when we observe individual family members renouncing former kinds of extramural social life to remain among loved ones, we shall know this as domesticity.

The way I use "traditional" and "modern" society in this book will upset two kinds of readers: those who believe that everything in *la vie intime* has always been more or less the same and that, accordingly, the Great Transformation of the family never happened; and those who believe that intimate life, while changing, moves in great cycles—a series of alternations between, let us say, repression and liberation. Thus we may, according to this view, point to patches of the sixteenth century that were more "modern" than the nineteenth, and stretches of the twelfth century that seem more liberated than the twentieth.

I wish to make my use of these terms quite clear. "Traditional" denotes a *kind* of attitude that coincides closely with a certain *period* of time. Drawing on a century of social analysis, I would suggest that traditional people are willing to put the demands of the community of which they're a part above their personal ambitions and desires. For modern people, on the other hand, the wish to be free triumphs over the community's demands for obedience and conformity. As Ferdinand Tönnies so neatly explained, the difference between a small traditional community (*Gemeinschaft*) and a large modern social system (*Gesellschaft*) is that, in the former, people are essentially united despite all the particular, differing conditions that appear to separate them; in the latter, people are essentially separate despite all the unifying traits that appear to homogenize them. While this typology is doubtlessly inadequate for Third World countries— primitive Bali not being at all the same thing as "traditional" Upper Austria—I believe it works for the West.

People in traditional families are willing to renounce a number of personal ambitions. They're ready to postpone marriage until late in life, or indeed forego it entirely, so that the farm may prosper under the eldest; they're willing to overcome whatever strivings towards privacy slumber in their breasts, and go to the communal bonfire on St. John's Day; they resolve to fight off weariness in the evening to put right the lace on their bonnets for their neighbor's daughter's wedding. And they are willing to renounce the whole

range of psychosexual satisfactions our social-work manuals guarantee
us in order to keep the family's "honor" intact.

In modern society, on the other hand, individual self-realization
takes precedence over community stability. The careers and happiness
of individual members of the family triumph over the continuation of
the lineage as a whole. The seclusion that romantic love demands,
in order that the egos of the couple may thrive, disperses the crowd
about the bonfire. And fashion snatches the wedding bonnet from a
sartorial affirmation of collective solidarity to a desperate bustle of
individuals determined to outpace one another, or at least not to
be outpaced. As for the right of the individual to sexual gratification—well, we all know about the horrors of "repression."

A mocking note creeps into these lines. How ludicrous we find
ourselves, just as the inhabitants of the world we have lost occasionally found themselves ridiculous too! Yet it would be absurd of me
to appear to reject our own dear world that I am so much a part of.
The point is less complicated: attitudes regarding individualism
vis-à-vis collective duty, were balanced close to the collective pole in
early modern Europe, and close to the pole of egoism in our own
times. In both worlds a minority of the population tiptoed along
all ranges of the spectrum. But the central tendency—the typical
behavior of the average person—was toward one end in traditional
society and toward the other in modern society.

This "traditional" tip towards community solidarity carried with it
several important states of mind. First, a preference for authority as
against free individual choice. Within the household, this meant
patriarchal rule over the other family members. If we discover nothing else in this book, it will be that young people submitted to their
parents in choosing partners and careers, and wives to their husbands
in most matters altogether. And more subtle forms of authority
were to weave themselves through *la vie intime*, such as the blasts the
town fathers could let fly against "immorality," or the local youth
group's censure of wives who beat their husbands.

Second, there was preference for custom over spontaneity and
creativity. These little collectivities, be it the guild, the family
lineage, or the village as a whole, correctly recognized that too much
innovation would ring their death knell; and so they insisted that the

old ways of proposing marriage, curing colicky infants, and organizing the annual fair be retained, to the extent that anyone could remember them. This adherence to tradition in cultural forms, this insistence that human interactions, whose potential diversity is infinite, be cast into unchanging molds, has given us a useful label for the entire social order: traditional.

Finally, there was an abiding suspiciousness of sexuality. Quite rightly, these people realized that what later generations would call the libido contained sufficient dynamite to blow their stable little worlds into pieces. Once the heart began to speak, it would give instructions often entirely incompatible with the rational principles of family interest and material survival on which the small community was ordered. Marry the woman you love, the heart might say, even though your parents disapprove. The traditional system could have survived such mésalliances, even though large-scale marital crossings would have jarringly redistributed property. What it couldn't survive was the heart's insistence upon intimacy and upon the privacy and isolation this would entail. For that reason the traditional world struggled to enforce lifelong monogamy and to impose the rational calculation of objective family interest upon sexual passion, a drive they feared as irrational and that they all knew lay just beneath the surface.

It is possible that European village life assumed these characteristics right from the beginning, or at least from the period when the Franks quieted down. But new research on medieval history suggests to me that the label "traditional" is more properly applied to the three centuries between the Reformation and the French Revolution. In the thirteenth century, movement was to be noted everywhere: there was general prosperity and the population was increasing by leaps and bounds; popular culture was effervescing in bubbles that researchers are only now beginning to pick up. Then, in the late Middle Ages, a long-term regression set in (for reasons much too complicated even to suggest in this short book), and a period of economic, demographic, and cultural retrenchment began which was to continue until the early nineteenth century. It is this epoch of decline and stagnation in the grand sweep of Western life that one might call "traditional." During this epoch the popular values and patterns of doing cultural business were nailed into place that subsequent folklorists would think had begun with the Druids.

Modernization meant the dissolution of this structured, changeless, compact traditional order. One view is that the great social changes of the nineteenth and twentieth centuries simply wrenched everything apart, leaving the tatters to drift about directionlessly in a world without values. Most of the writers who have given us our evidence on family history embrace this view, but I reject it. The second view is that a modern system of values, just as cohesive and with a power to compel behavior just as exacting, has arisen to take the place of the traditional. The content of these modern values is very different, sanctioning individualism over community allegiance and self-realization over collective solidarity. But the players are all clear about the rules and adhere to them.

Where these new rules were first elaborated is unclear. In my view, they surfaced initially as a subculture of the oppressed, as a new code of behavior binding together those lower-class people who were torn from their traditional environment into the vortex of the market economy. Many American observers have argued that these new values turned up most dramatically in the New World, and as we glance at *la vie intime* in the colonies there may seem to be some support for this case. But whatever its origin, the value system that conservative social critics damned as "egoism" made conquest after conquest as the nineteenth century progressed; and although many cultural *forms* seemed still to be "traditional" by the threshold of the twentieth century—peasant wife still standing behind her husband's chair at mealtimes—their *content* was becoming thoroughly modernized.

All this didn't happen, of course, at the same time in every place: Southern England began to scrape against the modern world two centuries sooner than the interior of Brittany, to cite two extreme cases. But sooner or later the Great Transformation would take hold everywhere. How it happened is the story of this book.

21

CHAPTER ONE

Household and Community
in Traditional Society

ONE of the reasons why family life in traditional Europe differed so fundamentally from our own was its physical setting. The structure of the household, the size of the domestic group, the occasions within the community for coming together, the excuses to watch the neighbors—all were unlike the world about us today. Of course, such matters do not in themselves shape people's minds, but they create—and limit—the possibilities to come together and express feeling. A New York existence in the twenty-first floor apartments that overlook the East River differs from domestic life above the tanner's shop in eighteenth-century Memmingen, partly because the one seals out the outside world, while the other is punctured by it at many points. Yet the two milieus also differ because the entire culture in which Manhattan's East Side swingers have been socialized diverges radically from the world we have lost. Just what was this traditional setting?

Members of the Household

One cannot talk simply about "families in traditional society" as an undifferentiated abstraction, since household patterns varied greatly from countryside to city and from middle class to lower class. Pressing these twin categorizations of urban-rural and propertied-propertyless down upon a given population divides it into four parts: the urban petty bourgeoisie, the urban laborers, the landed peasantry, and the rural cottager class. Whether you resided in the city or country would determine, at least in part, how you lived within your four walls; similarly, whether you owned a house (farmhouse, townhouse) or just rented a room or two would affect your domestic lifestyle. The independent urban artisans would be as different from the journeymen, water carriers, and street hawkers who lived in towns as both urban groups differed in their domestic lives from the rural peasantry or rustic *Sternguckhäusler* (cottagers, so called because they could see the stars through holes in their roofs). Each of these groups made distinctive household arrangements, and was likely to experience different degrees of crowding and complexity.

URBAN AND RURAL HOUSEHOLDS

A basic dimension of household life is that of how many people live together. The world of the children, the experience of the couple, life across the breakfast table—these aspects of domesticity will differ according to whether the household contains only the parents and their children, or whether swarms of servants and boarders are also in residence, along with children from a previous marriage, plus the grandparents. Households in traditional Europe were somewhat larger and certainly more complex—in the sense of sheltering more than the simple conjugal unit—than are modern households. And it was this difference in the composition of the domestic group that imparted to the traditional family some of its singularity.

Let us look first at the cities. Here sharp differences in the size and composition of households turn up according to income and social status. The higher the income or the more elevated the social class, the larger and more complex the household. Poverty and wage labor

23

meant that few children would be in residence with the parents, and that kin would be few in number. Servants would be unlikely, both because workers could not afford personal domestics and because, not running their own craft shops or stores, they had no need of employed assistants (also called "servants") to help them with business. The independent proprietors who constituted most of the petty bourgeoisie, on the other hand, had space enough to house spare kin and, more importantly, the means to put them to work. These middle classes also had more children living at home, and in addition needed live-in help—not to bring the coffee in the morning, but to aid in the store or at the big loom that sat in the middle of the living room.

In Paris's Popincourt section around 1795, for example, day laborers had an average of about 1.8 resident children, smallshop employers 2.4. And in the city as a whole during the nineteenth century, these class differences persisted, a third of the wholesale merchants having at least 3 children at home, yet only an eighth of the workers having that many. In early modern Florence the wealthier you were, the larger your household was likely to be; the poor had an average of only 2.5 people at home, the rich 5 or 6. And if you were a craftsman in an important guild you would similarly have more bodies about the household (an average of 5.5) than if you were an unskilled laborer (3.7).[1]

Other continental cities turn up a similar pattern. In Strasbourg we find middle-class homes with an average of 5.1 residents, lower-class homes with 3.8. The same prevailed for the small Schleswig town of Husum near the Danish frontier, and for residents of eighteenth-century Zurich. All these bourgeois homes were larger, partly because the middle classes employed more servants and helpers in family business, partly because they had more children living at home.[2]

Because of my conviction that North American society sprang full-blown modern from the head of Zeus, my fingers tremble slightly to place Salem, Massachusetts, of about 1790 in a chapter on traditional society. Yet the same arrangement prevailed in Salem as in Europe: the higher the status of the head of household, the larger the domestic group. Merchants averaged 9.8 persons per family, master carpenters 6.7, and laborers 5.4. The Salem middle classes

hired more servants and apprentices than did the lower; their fertility was higher, too; for merchants and artisans it averaged 5.9
births per first marriage; for laborers 4.6.[3]

We could catalogue many other places, such as industrial Not-
tingham—where, despite having slightly larger families, the workers
had smaller households.[4] But the point is made: in traditional cities,
"middle-class" life meant a great press of bodies. Only when modernization had really gotten its teeth into the old regime, shaking
out new cities full of people in modern jobs, would "bourgeois"
come to signify small family size and intimacy in household composition. To exemplify this change: Michael Anderson observed
that towards 1850, in the mill town of Preston in the midst of industrial Lancashire, virtually no white-collar or commercial families
shared a house with any other family or had lodgers or kin living
in. Among factory, artisan, and laborer families, on the other hand,
especially those having either no child or just one, lodgers and relatives often turned up. And among all such working people, house
sharing was commonplace.[5]

What distinguished rural from urban life was less the size of households than their *complexity*. More generations would customarily be
present on the farm than in the city (or at least I have this impression,
for virtually no pre-1850 study compares the number of generations in
urban households to rural). But rural life by its very nature also included such "lateral" kin as bachelor brothers and spinster sisters
(for whom there was no land), as well as the aged grandparents.

In many parts of the continent, the peasant patrimony could not
normally be divided. It was not partitioned in practice, at least, even
when permitted by law, because one of the specters haunting rural
society was that of property so fragmented that a family could no
longer live off its inheritance. Thus whenever possible—in Austria,
for example—the land would be settled upon a single child, customarily the eldest son, or in some areas the youngest, to let the
father wait as long as possible before handing over the reins to the
next generation. Other children would receive only money payments
and the right to live in the family home if they stayed unmarried.

Who lived in the typical farmhouse? First of all there was the
rural couple. These were landed peasants or marginal cottagers, but

25

almost never married servants, for the good reason that to marry one had to have a plot of soil and a place to live. Wed in their late twenties, the couple could look forward to perhaps five or ten years together before death would carry one of them away.[6] Widowers were then quick to remarry, widows a little less so. For our present purposes the implication of these frequent ruptures is that any given marriage might well not be the first for one of the partners, and that some of the children in the household would stem from previous unions.[7]

Few children would actually be in residence, seldom over two or three at any given time. In view of the high fertility of traditional Europe, these low figures may come as something of a surprise. If an average woman was likely to conceive ten or twenty times in her fecund years, how did it happen that only a couple of children would actually be on hand? There are two principal reasons, the first being early death. In the modern world infant death is a rare phenomenon (rarer, indeed, in Europe than in the United States). The loss of a child is an almost unheard-of catastrophe, and one that usually happens to somebody else whom we know only distantly. It is hard for us to comprehend, therefore, the devastating rates of infant mortality that once prevailed. In the eighteenth century, the chances were that one in every three children would perish in the first year of life, and that only one in every two would reach the age of twenty-one. This, plus the higher chances that a pregnant woman would miscarry before giving birth, accounts for the "missing" children: they had perished either in the womb, in delivery, or in infancy.

A second circumstance removing children from the household was their early entry into the labor force. In poverty-stricken western France, cottager offspring would leave as early as seven or eight "to work as servants, shepherds, cowherds, or turkey-keepers for a farmer, or as apprentices for an artisan." In Languedoc, even nine-year-old children were doing productive work at home and would, by ten or eleven, "have had experience as lackeys or servants." Even in England, where virtually all children under ten in a given community would be home with their parents or guardians, the great sloughing-off would begin thereafter.[8] First the male children of the poor would leave, because the cottager's plot was too small to need their labor, and no jobs were available locally that would have let them work full time while living at home. Typically, they would go into service under a peasant with a large farm in the neighborhood, later perhaps departing the community altogether for greener pastures. Then, too, the sons of the propertied peasants might take off, not going far and not necessarily leaving for good—going, rather, in the manner of the sons of Flemish farmers, who were sent by their fathers for a year or two to farms in neighboring Artois and Picardy to learn a bit of French and perhaps something of the world as well.[9]

Although the daughters of the cottagers were likely to be sent early into service along with their brothers, the daughters of propertied families tended more to remain home. Until their marriage they would be useful in the household economy, whether spinning, lace-making, or butter-making. Unlike their brothers, they were "perishable goods"; that is, some sexual encounter might take place away from home that would blot the honor of the family for generations to come.

Roger Schofield has written of the chances that adolescents would stay at home in the English parish of Cardington, Bedfordshire, around 1782. A typical Cardington boy would almost certainly live with his parents until his ninth birthday, and was likely to attend school until he was eleven. He had a one-in-four chance of entering service between ten and fourteen, and then an enormously increased four-to-one chance between fifteen and nineteen. There was a six- or seven-to-one chance that in his early twenties he would either still be in service or already be married; by the end of his twenties he would almost certainly be married. In this parish, only a single lad, "the third of a carpenter's four sons, and himself a carpenter, continued to live with his parents after he was married." Girls in Cardington exhibited a different pattern of household life. They had only a one-in-three chance of schooling. Few would leave home before age fifteen. And at fifteen to nineteen, when three-fourths of the boys had already taken off, only a quarter of the girls had done so. Most would leave the parental dwelling only in the arms of their husbands and never have encountered wage work head-on.[10]

The children of the seventeenth-century clergyman–farmer Ralph Josselin, in the little Essex parish of Earls Colne, were a little dif-

27

ferent. There the girls left earlier than the boys, and likely as not went into service:[11]

NAME	DATE OF LEAVING	AGE IN YEARS AND MONTHS	PLACE AND OCCUPATION TO WHICH BOUND
Thomas	25 May 1659	15.5	London, bound apprentice
Jane	21 April 1656	10.6	Colchester, education
John	9 January 1667	15.4	London, bound apprentice
Anne	24 June 1668	14.0	London, bound as servant
Mary	2 February 1668	10.0	White Colne, education
Elizabeth	23 April 1674	13.9	Bury St. Edmunds, education
Rebecka	17 April 1677	13.5	London, bound as servant

But the point is that even within this educated, middle-class family, children of both sexes departed in early adolescence, and to a variety of slots on the social scale.

These two parishes, Cardington and Earls Colne, do not tell the whole story. In the poor areas of France and in the rural industrial regions of Central Europe, youngsters would leave home even before the age of ten to spin or help weave in some nearby household,[12] while in the large farms of southeastern Europe the children might never go away, either remaining single or importing their brides to the large household. But if we contrast the "ideal-type" household of traditional Europe with that of the twentieth century, the chances that adolescents would be at home were very much less than they are today.

Servants were also present in the household, eating at the family table and, in poorer homes, sleeping alongside the family on straw mattresses before the hearth or, in winter, with everyone else in the cow barn. These were the children of neighbors, acquired sometimes in exchange for one's own children and at other times simply because a large farmer needed more hands than his own family could provide. Despite their masters' considerable responsibilities towards them, servant girls didn't have to be dowried at their marriage or servant boys given a piece of the family patrimony. A typical family might have one or two such domestics, engaged on an annual basis, and although housed and fed the year round, desperately needed only from July until October, the time of the big push in the fields.

Modernization would eventually replace these members of the household, for whom the master was responsible the entire year whether anything needed doing or not, with wage laborers hired by the day for specific tasks.

PATTERNS OF DOMESTIC GROUPS

The final group included in the household was that of family relatives. The great variations to be found here force us at the outset to abandon an "ideal" type and to differentiate among countries.

There were three main patterns of kin membership in the domestic group:

First, there was the basic conjugal family, with no other kin living in.

Second, there was the so-called stem family, consisting of mother, father, and children, plus one set of grandparents. The children did not even have to be present to make a "stem" family—just a junior and a senior couple, directly related and living under the same roof or on the same holding.

Third, there was the large multiple family household, extended both "laterally" to the brothers and sisters of either husband or wife, and "vertically" to include a third generation of grandparents. Although the stem family was a "multiple family household" in the technical sense (because it incorporated two conjugal units under the same roof), this third category is distinctive because of the presence of several related couples of the same generation (for example, married brothers living together under the patriarchal rule of their father).

Other family types might be imagined as well, of course: the "extended family," where a single conjugal unit cohabits with unmarried relatives; the one-person household; or the *union libre*, wherein a couple live together outside of wedlock. Yet within the context of Western history, the three types listed above are the most interesting. Remember that servants, lodgers, orphans, and children from previous unions were likely to be found in all three kinds.[13]

The first pattern, then, was the kinless conjugal family. In earlier writings on the history of the family, sociologists acquired the bad habit of assuming that families before the Industrial Revolution

29

were organized in clans or were at least highly "extended." Because any historian with even a passing familiarity with Europe's social history would realize at once the inaccuracy of that assumption, a revisionist reaction developed in the 1960s: the nuclear family was "unearthed" time and again in history, to the accompaniment of loud shouts of discovery. As often happens to revisionists, these writers fell over backwards attempting to overturn the conventional wisdom; instead of merely correcting the sociologists' fantasies about clans and sprawling patriarchies, they tended to proclaim that at most times and places it was the conjugal family—mother, father, children, and servants—that had prevailed. The revisionists thus proceeded to create a little fantasy of their own: the nuclear family as a historical constant.[14]

Now, many kinless families did exist; indeed, they often represented a majority of all households. But to get a sense of the typical experience of the average person, we must ask what kind of household a child would most likely have been socialized in: extended (stem), or nuclear? And there is a good chance that in better-off households as opposed to poorer ones, and in East Europe as opposed to West Europe, the average child was raised in a dwelling that contained many relatives besides his mother and father.

North America and the British Isles were the principal bastions of the kinless domestic unit. In colonial New England, for example, households tended to be quite large, but this was owing to the number of children rather than to the number of relatives living in. David Flaherty puts typical family size in Massachusetts Bay and Rhode Island, towards 1700, at an average of 5.8. The additional house-sharers, plus assorted servants and lodgers, increased the average household size by roughly one person again. (One-third of all homes had servants; a third of all houses were shared with other people.)[15] Peter Laslett has demonstrated the virtually complete absence of uncles and aunts (lateral kin) and the sparseness of grandparents in English rural households.[16] It is possible that Anglo-Saxons preferred to live in the same neighborhood with their relatives rather than in the same household; there are hints in traditional England that residential proximity figured prominently in family life.[17] In colonial New England, certainly, many related settler families wound up side by side.[18] But in no wise may we argue that extended families (conjugal groups with other kin living in) were important in rural life before the nineteenth century. (Paradoxically, the lower mortality rate attending modernization increased the chances that grandparents would at least survive to live with their children.)

Conjugal groups *minus* kin also turned up frequently enough in rural Europe. There were, for example, the pastoral regions of the Netherlands, where the grandparents seldom lived with the farmer and his wife. In Norwegian villages relatives co-resided with propertied peasants only about a fifth of the time, and the percentage was even lower among the cottagers. Across much of Lower Austria and in at least two well-documented villages in Salzburg province, three-generation households were unusual. While it happened not infrequently that a senior couple (or the surviving member thereof) would live under the same roof as a junior farm couple, by the time the junior couple's children were born, the senior couple would no longer be alive. (In these parts of Austria fathers waited until late in life to pass the torch, because the holding could support two couples only with difficulty.) For the farm village of Isbergues in France's Artois province there was only a one-in-six chance that any household, at any given moment in time, would contain grandparents or other relatives. The same proportion prevailed for the Perigordian commune of Montplaisant toward the middle of the seventeenth century.[19] Yet we must still consider the possibility that in such communities many households might, at some point in time, have contained several generations, but that death snatched away the grandparents before the census-taker arrived. Thus in the census they appeared as single-family units, whereas they might actually have been, for a period of years, stem families.[20]

However, in many other areas of western and central Europe, the stem family was commonplace and the kinless family an anomaly. Frédéric Le Play, the nineteenth-century French sociologist, coined the term *famille souche* to denote families that passed on a given farm undivided from one generation to the next over long periods of time.[21] The inheriting son brought his bride right into the parents' household, either taking command of the holding with his marriage, or living with his new family in subordination to his father.

31

(The other sons, of course, received no land and might not marry at all.)

Consider the problem of the aging peasant farmer. His principal objective in life was to pass on—undiminished and if possible, even augmented—the land he had received from his ancestors to the next generation. He knew that his son would more than likely not treat him well once he relinquished control and so he delayed doing so for as long as possible. Yet if the father waited too long, the son (now a grown man in his late twenties or thirties) might become vengeful against the parents once they did retire. Even more important, a peasant who clenched the reins past his prime might do harm to the *maison*, causing a slackening in the fieldwork and thus transmitting a reduced patrimony to posterity. Worst of all, if the wait seemed interminable, the son might just pull up stakes and take off. So the old peasant had to perform a delicate moral and material calculus in handing over the farm to the next generation.

Once the son had the title, he was obliged to support his retired parents, allot them a bit of land on which to grow their potatoes or flax, furnish them with half a slaughtered pig every year, grant them foraging rights for their cow, and provide them with any of the other little perquisites that the old folks needed to maintain themselves. The parents lived right at hand, perhaps in an adjoining lean-to, nearby cottage, or even a separate room within the main house.

Given the high mortality rate, this aging peasant couple was likely to have had more than one son; the death of an only child would have brutally uprooted the stem. On the other hand, if the eldest survived, the other siblings would be denied access to the land. How, then, were they to be provided for? The customary arrangement was to pay them off in cash; not, to be sure, an equal portion of the market value of the farm, but enough, often, to force the inheriting son to go into debt. The eldest son in any event had to accord them the right to live in the big house until the end of their days—if they remained single and were willing to work. The daughters would be similarly paid off, a part in dowries when they married and a later part, perhaps, at the time the estate would be handed over or at the father's death.[22] All these payments constituted a heavy burden.

And so, for various reasons—the sheer number of people living in the household, the having to look at someone across the breakfast table day after day who was not a member of your immediate family, the sexual rivalries—the emotional patterns of the stem family would differ from those of the "nuclear" family. In practice, three generations meant that the old father would work alongside the married son in threshing grain or the elderly mother alongside the daughter-in-law during the evening's spinning bee. Presumably the son's own children would be raised by the grandmother as much as by their mother. Presumably the interaction of husband and wife would be different from the kinless group, for even in the "intimacy" of the family dinner table the older couple would scrutinize the goings-on minutely —or even insist, as in medieval Béarn, upon pride of place (to say nothing of the field hands' silent gaze).[23] I say "presumably" to all this because in fact we know little of the emotional climate that prevailed within such stem families. But if the whole question has any title at all to large investments of research time, it is for that very reason: household arrangements ultimately affected how people thought and acted.

What *do* we know about the stem family? An example or two may make things clearer. In the Austrian Waldviertel, where stem families were the norm during the eighteenth century, peasants actually sold the farm to the inheriting son and staggered the payments to make a lifetime annuity for themselves.

When Joseph and Anna Maria Pichler decided to retire in October 1784, for example, they drew up a contract with their son Johann and his bride Gertraud, selling them their house and fields for 100 florins. Joseph deducted 20 florins from the price as a wedding gift to his son, and asked that the rest be paid in installments of 20 florins every Michaeli (September 29). As a retirement settlement they reserved the right to live in the *Stübl* [a room built onto the house] rent-free for the rest of their lives, the use of a small piece of meadow and a section of the garden to grow cabbage and potatoes, and a yearly supply of seven bushels of wheat, 32 batches of hay, and two piles of wood.

Lutz Berkner, the source of the above description, has studied this population carefully and speculates that "severe psychological strains" must have been present within these families—the young couple impatient to take over, the elderly anxious about security in their declining years. A Waldviertel folksong that Berkner quotes from the beginning of the twentieth century gives a clue:

> Voda, wann gibst ma denn's Hoamatl,
> Voda, wann loszt ma's vaschreibn?
> s'Dirndl is gwoxn wia's Groamatl,
> Lede wülls a nimmer bleibn.

> Father, when ya gonna gimme the farm,
> Father, when ya gonna sign it away?
> My girl's been growin' every day,
> And single no longer wants to stay.

> Voda, wann gibst ma denn's Hoamatl,
> Voda, wann gibst ma denn's Haus,
> Wann gehst denn amol in dein Stüberl ein,
> Und grobst da bra Eräpfoln aus?

> Father, when ya gonna gimme the farm,
> Father, when ya gonna gimme the house,
> When ya gonna retire to your room out of the way,
> And dig up your potatoes all day?[24]

Elsewhere in Europe the stem family made slightly different arrangements for passing on the farm. In France after the Revolution it was unusual to actually sell the holding to the son. Instead, a legal agreement would allot to the children their various portions. The eldest gained the right to manage the homestead and provide for the parents; or else the eldest would bring his bride into the parental household, while the parents would retain legal control of the farm until the father's death. Abel Hugo, Victor Hugo's brother, describes what happened in the (classic stem-family) department of the Corrèze early in the nineteenth century:

In most of the well-off [peasant] families the eldest of the male children, or of the females too if there are no sons, takes in advance a quarter of the inheritance and then receives of that which remains another portion equal to that of each of the other inheritors. He has in addition the privilege of living in the ancestral home when he marries, with his wife and children at the expense of the others up to the moment when the death of the father gives him the largest share. Thus one sees a large number of Limousin families embittered by lawsuits and divided by hatred. The siblings regard their eldest brother as a *natural* enemy. And following this enmity among brothers is the reciprocal enmity of their children after them. Thus the spirit of the family is lost.[25]

How numerous were these stem families in comparison with the two-generational variety? Only after a closely-woven net of research has been cast upon Europe will we be able to say for sure. Yet in Germany south of the Main River and in France south of the Loire they seem to have been the rule. Alain Collomp discovered that in eighteenth-century Upper Provence it was rare for the married son to live apart from his parents if they were still alive. But the parents retained the economic reins; the father held control even of his daughter-in-law's dowry. Only the father's death would grant the married son economic independence and the other siblings their portions. Until then, several different conjugal units were literally "living from the same pot, under the same roof." Raymond Noel found records of many *familles élargies*, or three-generation families, in Mostuejouls, another village of southern France, where nearly half of all households contained two or more conjugal units (and in those that didn't, many of the parents had presumably died early).[26]

I shall forego trotting out other local studies that also point to numerous three-generational households, whether the senior couple actually sold the holding to the junior couple (on the Waldviertel model) or kept control itself. The point is that in central and western Europe, children commonly had close exposure to their grandparents and that parents would have to contend with the grandparents for at least a few years before death brought its radical simplification to the household structure.[27]

The third principal domestic arrangement was the large extended (multiple) family of eastern Europe, called the *zadruga* in Yugoslavia and the *Gesind* in Kurland along the Baltic coast. The Serbian zadruga is probably more familiar to Western readers: households containing three or four conjugal units, administered by a patriarch, with all work done in common, and all profits retained collectively by the group. Zadrugas might be communities of married brothers, or they might embrace three generations of the same family, with lateral outriders of uncles, aunts, and married brothers and sisters. A typical zadruga might include from ten to thirty members, with the couples sleeping separately in their own quarters but eating together around a common table. Once the patriarch's grandsons began to grow up, however, they split off to form their own zadrugas, using the inheritance they received from their fathers as a base. The zadruga thus had a life cycle of its own, seldom extending over more than three generations and rarely exhibiting much complexity of kin ties.[28]*

The enserfed peasantry of the Russian province of Kurland had living arrangements similar to those of the zadruga, yet the chief peasant, or Wirth, had only the produce of the land that the lord owned, and his children could claim no automatic inheritance rights. In these Baltic *Gesinde* the landless would marry, move into a chief peasant's household to eat and sleep, and receive a money wage from him. Andrejs Plakans, to whom we owe an excellent study of this little-known region, describes the allocation of space there:[29]

. . . only one half of the main building was in use [for continuous human habitation—people slept in outbuildings during the summer], the other half being a combination storeroom and baking room. The inhabited half contained one large common room, the center of the daily activities of the farmstead's people as well as their main sleeping quarters. Doors from the common room opened into a much smaller *Wirth* room occupied by the head and his wife, and sometimes to yet another small room reserved for some of the relatives of the head or older farmhands. Privacy in the main house was apparently a prerogative of high status and seniority. No special dwelling place, house, or room seemed to be set apart for the retired parents of the current head. . . . [Living arrangements were] highly flexible. People slept where space was available, on pallets on the floor or permanent beds, sometimes with more than one person per bed, on the stone shelf behind the oven which had been warmed during the day, or on the floor. Infants stayed in cradles or in their mother's bed, while older children slept in the common room with everyone else. Preparation of food took place at the single facility. Eating involved turns at the table by adults first and then children. Separateness

*I have been discussing the zadruga as part of "traditional" society, even though it is alive and well today in Yugoslavia. Yet let me add as a parenthesis that ever more Yugoslavians have escaped its grasp since the Second World War. A decline in fertility and the migration of young sons to the city has reduced the number of fraternal zadrugas; and even though increasing life expectancy elevates the number of three- and four-generation households, the lifestyle revolution which has come even to this corner of the world takes single people away from their parental homes once they grow up. (See Halpern and Anderson, cited in note 28.)

as a fixed condition for individuals or conjugal family units apparently was the exception.

The average number of people living in such a farmstead was fourteen: the *Wirth's* own family, consisting of the couple and maybe three children, then three or four of the *Wirth's* other relatives and possibly their spouses and children, plus a melange of non-family farmhands, herders, unrelated couples, orphans, and foster children.[30] These large households would thus contain several conjugal groups.

Our modern minds are barely able to encompass the zadrugas: sisters-in-law laboring at the same kitchen sink, refraining from tearing out one another's hair only because they are related; mothers and daughters-in-law at each other's throats over the sexual affection of the men (and possibly the other way around).[31] But the Baltic *Gesind*, with couples tied only through the cash nexus, living and sleeping in the same stuffy room—this is a different ballgame.

Household arrangements differed from class to class with wealthier peasants having larger domestic units. In the Bavarian village of Neudroschenfeld, for instance, married houseowners around 1836 had an average of 2.6 children living in, while married tenants had only 1.5.[32] The same pattern appeared in the nineteenth century Norwegian communes that Michael Drake studied: propertied farmers averaged between 5.4 and 7.7 persons per household, while marginal crofters averaged only between 3.0 and 4.8. This difference derived from larger family sizes among the propertied, their bigger staffs of fieldhands, and the other kin for whom the farmers, but not the crofters, had room.[33] The same differences, for roughly the same reasons, were to be found in Bedfordshire's Cardington parish in 1851: 6.4 persons in the average farmer's household, 4.9 in the average laborer's; 3.5 resident children for the farmer, 2.8 for the laborer, and so on.[34] In the village of Sennely (Loiret) during the eighteenth century, the households of the poor contained just the couple plus several young children. Households of wealthier peasant *métayers* ran to perhaps a dozen members: the couple and their two to three children, three or four domestics and fieldhands, and one or two orphans taken in on guardianship, plus perhaps a junior couple (the inheriting son and his wife); but the junior couple would seldom

37

have to wait more than a year or two before the senior couple died, turning a stem family into a nuclear one.[35]

We have encountered larger numbers of children among both the urban and rural middle classes than among the lower classes. Is this not simply because child mortality was higher among the lower orders, who otherwise as we know, breed like rabbits? The answer, to put things simply, is no. It is true that infant mortality was higher among the propertyless, but it is also true that the propertied had *more* children. Among the local studies listed in Appendix I which make available fertility data by social class, occupation, or income level, only in two (those being where the data are especially shaky to boot) do the poor have higher birth rates. In those German and French communes where the data have been accumulated through exacting "family reconstitutions" with large statistical bases, the propertied classes show higher fertility; in three studies no difference appears at all between the classes.

Propertied families may have reproduced themselves more amply than did lower class people for any number of reasons. Perhaps they were more apt to conceive, or had sex more often, or practiced contraception less often and less efficiently, or had few fetuses die in the womb. It is my feeling that greater likelihood to conceive and lower fetal mortality were the chief factors. One may seriously doubt that the married middle classes had intercourse more often than the lower classes. And as for contraception, the middle classes almost certainly practiced it more reliably and regularly than the lower (see Appendix I). In the last analysis, if these middle-class mothers had more children swirling about their knees it was because they ate better than lower-class women and were thus healthier: their better physical condition made it more likely that they would get pregnant and not have miscarriages.

The essential point to retain from this barrage of statistical data is that households in earlier times were very complex structures. A much more numerous and varied crowd of people witnessed or disrupted intimate life in those days than in our own times. Anyone doubting this should compare the kind of people who live in the tiny state-subsidized apartments that dot the Paris region today with house number 32 in the Bavarian village of Neudroschenfeld in 1836, where lived:

—Georg Hermsdörfer, sixty-three years old and still a journeyman mason, "totally unable to work," with his two children; he was the homeowner.
—Georg Frühaber, a thirty-two-year-old agricultural laborer, with his wife and one child.
—Margarethe Hermsdörfer, probably Georg's spinster sister, age sixty.
—Muh Lauterbach, age thirty-four, married with a single resident child, an agricultural laborer who owned half a Tagwerk of land.

Dwelling within this large farmhouse, therefore, were two conjugal units, which included two wives and two children, one single woman, her widower brother, and his two children. Each little nuclear unit had, presumably, its own living space. Yet growing up or negotiating with one's spouse about spending money in that big farmhouse must have been very different from growing up in the world of, say, Sarcelles, in the twentieth century.[36]

Privacy in the Household

One important historical aspect of household structure is the scope that it provided for sexual privacy and emotional intimacy. As a general rule of thumb, over the period being studied, opportunities for sexual privacy diminished as one went down the social scale and as one traveled from west to east. A wealthy couple could more easily withdraw from contact with others than could a poor couple—although before the seventeenth century it is difficult to demonstrate that couples of any description, well-to-do or impoverished, thought to take advantage of such seclusion as the structures of their homes may have allowed. And couples in North America and England would have access to more private space than would couples anywhere in Continental Europe.

Let us first examine territorial variations in the opportunity for privacy. Among the lower classes of France and Germany prior to

1850, the chances were very high that all members of the family would sleep within the same room, that at least one person not a member of the immediate family would share this sleeping space, and that in this room would take place all the other activities of the family as well. Such dwellings were either farmhouses in which no more than a single room was given over to living (the rest being used for equipment, storage, and sheltering animals), or apartment houses in which most tenants also got along with but a single room, to which perhaps was added a small kitchen.

Here is a typical peasant dwelling in Germany's Spessart region:[37]

> Wherever you go you find relatively small houses, composed of a single family room with a small side chamber and a small kitchen. You climb up stone steps to a tiny entryway, straight back from which is the kitchen and on one or both sides living space; above is a garret for storage. . . . Inside such a dwelling there invariably lives a family of numerous offspring. Sometimes several generations are on hand, sometimes as well several unrelated families. Especially common in these rooms are lateral relatives, who also have children. The household's few beds, always very dirty and sometimes thick and sweltering, are found both in the main room and the dark, fetid side chamber, so that normally 2–3 people, even of different sexes, sleep in the same bed.

Very little of what took place in these peasant homes would be *unter vier Augen,* as the Germans say. But if cramped housing took away the married couple's opportunity for intimacy, it also brought the unmarried into close physical contact—with the opposite results. So bad had the overfilling of domestic space become, reported the provincial government of Würzburg in 1839, that "the hired hand and the farmer's son sleep often in the same room, and in the same bed, as the farmer's daughter and the maid." The result was illegitimacy.

Overcrowding was even worse in rural Switzerland, especially where the population, responding to the employment opportunities of the eighteenth-century domestic system, had been increasing. One writer invited his readers to imagine a small room with a stove and a few windows, collapsible tables in two corners, and two further tables against the far wall, so that each of the *four couples* that inhabited this single room would, at least, have its own table. "In addition there come, as I have seen with my own eyes, two or three children for each couple. What crying, what noise. . .!"[38]

Nor were city dwellers in central Europe much better fixed. Nineteenth-century social statisticians collected data to demonstrate the great overcrowding that urbanization had caused. But their figures also indicated how unusual it was to block off separate sleeping space for the couple from the rest of the dwelling. In the 1880s—data are not available before this late date—23 percent of Frankfurt-am-Main's population lived in one-room households, 28 percent of Hamburg's population did so, 49 percent of Berlin's, 55 percent of Dresden's, 62 percent of Breslau's, and 70 percent of Chemnitz's.[39] But even earlier, by all descriptive testimony, the crowding could not have been much less. In 1801, Hamburg's Doctor Rambach attributed the poor health and fractious disposition of that city's lower classes to the jamming together of several families in one-room apartments. Even the petty bourgeois of small-town eighteenth-century Germany, better lodged in dwellings that were typically of two rooms plus kitchen, were able to listen at night through the thin walls and narrow passageways to young couples making love.[40]

In Scandinavia, a curious variant of the above living arrangements created emotional privacy for adolescent girls while denying it to the rest of the family. In summertime the daughters of peasant farmers would sleep in outlying cowbarns and granaries rather than in the main house. The economic rationale for this isolation was the girl's dairy work. The social reason, however, was to permit young men to come and court their sweethearts without disturbing the rest of the family at night. In wintertime the girls might sleep near the cows in the barn or in the loft of the big house where, again, suitors could come courting without waking the entire family. We shall return to these courtship patterns in a later chapter.[41]

In France, peasant life lacked even this adolescent-privacy arrangement. Although French farmhands might sleep year round in the stables, the peasant family would eat, recreate, procreate, and slumber all in the same single room or two. For the rustics of Bourbon–Lancy canton, three or four beds would be lined up in a row, either with no separation or a paltry curtain between them, and the childrens' cradles gathered around. In the poorer regions of western France, a single bed more commonly received the weight of the entire family, the straw mattress being placed upon a wooden block and covered over with several feather quilts. Even when a member of the family fell sick, he continued to share the bed with others.[42]

Nor were the lower classes in French cities better housed. The small artisans of eighteenth-century Lyon usually had just one large room (weavers sometimes had a second one for their looms) in which to live and work. Space would be sectioned off at night by partitions of planks. More than half of these families had outsiders in residence, such as apprentice weavers or servant girls from the provinces. In eighteenth-century Paris it was the same story: heterogeneous households crowded into space that was not separated by function.[43] For a nation in which conjugal privacy and the isolation of *chacun chez soi* from the outside world were later to take on pathological proportions, these housing conditions were still quite "traditional."

It was in England and colonial America that arrangements differed; here domestic living space was partitioned by function, and sexual privacy was assured for perhaps a majority of the common people. Whereas the reconstruction of rural French dwellings—with the replacement of stone by wood and the insertion of a second floor with bedrooms into previously undifferentiated space—commenced only in the nineteenth century, the rebuilding of rural England was already underway in the sixteenth. W. G. Hoskins attributes the living-space change to a new desire for privacy and to the new availability of heating coal and window glass. Both resulted in "more rooms, devoted to specialized uses: so we get in the Elizabethan yeoman's house (the equivalent of the wealthy French peasant) the kitchen, the buttery, the best parlor, two or three separate bedrooms, the servants' chamber, besides the truncated medieval hall now shorn of many of its functions; and to achieve all this in a house of moderate size we have two floors instead of one."[44] Admittedly, these were prosperous farmers, but by the sixteenth and seventeeth centuries even agricultural laborers were moving toward more segregated living arrangements. Between 1560 and 1640, the number of laborers' houses having three or more rooms rose from 56 to 79 percent.[45]

Perhaps reflecting the English origins of their designers, colonial

American homes were enclaves of domestic intimacy. Spacious and specialized by Continental standards from the outset, they tended to become larger and even more partitioned over the years. Whereas in the late seventeenth century the average rural home in Suffolk County, Massachusetts, had 4.3 rooms, the figure was 6.0 a century later. Solid walls came to replace blankets in the subdivision of sleeping space. By the time of the Revolution, colonial men and women could, to a far greater extent than was possible elsewhere in the West, lead sexual and emotional lives that would not be monitored by outsiders.[46] Well, almost. For Boston's Ann Leonard, who in 1743 accused her husband of "beating her and entertaining lewd women," the nuclear family's architectural isolation was not quite complete. Her neighbors, John and Rebecca Milliken testified at the trial:

Q. Do you know anything of said Henry's beating or striking his Wife?
A. [John Milliken] The said Henry had made Shutters to his Windows, but I have often heard a Quarreling and after that have heard a noise which I apprehended to be a Striking a person against a Wall. . . .
Q. What do you know of his frequently having Bad Women at his house?
A. [Rebecca Milliken] I have seen with said Henry Severall Women of bad Characters . . . and this at late Hours of the night—but said Henry made Window Shutters and Stopt up all Cracks least he should be seen or overheard as I verrilly believe.[47]

Privacy decreased from west to east, and the idea of privacy descended from higher to lower classes. The rich were the first to carve up the undifferentiated living space of the Middle Ages into separate rooms with distinct functions. They divided the kitchen from the scullery and removed the family's entertaining to a salon and its meals to a dining room. It was among the rich that it first became expected that ladies would receive in drawing rooms and not in their bedchambers, that husbands would retire to read in separate studies, and that both sexes would have private sleeping quarters in which to conduct independently amorous adventures.[48] The rich, that tiny handful at the summit of the social pyramid, do not interest us here. But by the early nineteenth century the lower middle classes were aping this specialization of space, with Parisian shopkeepers withdrawing to studies that contained no books,[49] and English farmers eating apart from their field hands and servants. In the five-story houses of Paris, the master artisan who inhabited the second floor would sleep and eat in different areas of the apartment. But for his employees, who lived in upper floors of the building, single rooms had to serve all their purposes.

In part, of course, this class difference in space utilization merely reflected the fact that the rich had more space than the poor—you can't further partition lodgings that are tiny to begin with. But it was also a matter of desire. As we shall see in Chapter 6, the revolution in domesticity started first among the upper classes, spreading only relatively recently to poorer people. Differentiating the conjugal family from the servants required hallways, for example, so that the evening's serenity would not constantly be interrupted by employees trooping from the front of the house to the back. (In the Middle Ages you would have had to march through every room, since there would have been no central passageways.)[50] Intimacy for the couple demanded a bedroom in which only they slept, and in which tender expressions of sentiment would not leave onlookers slackjawed. Thus one aspect of the revolution in sentiment would depend upon changes in domestic architecture. Yet other parts of the surge of sentiment originated in the lower classes—for example, the infusion of romance in courtship—even without changes in traditional space arrangement.

Community Controls

It is the central argument of this book that the history of the family is the story of a shift in the relationship between the nuclear family and the surrounding community. Setting the scene requires us, accordingly, to cast a glance at the traditional community, or at least at those features of it that are of relevance to family life.

Most people in traditional Europe lived bunched fairly closely together, in villages or hamlets, rather than on the isolated farmsteads that so characterize rural North America. In southeastern Iowa, the part of the country where I grew up, a farm boy might easily pass an entire day without talking to anyone beyond his immediate family and maybe the hired help. And as a rich tradition of American literature and popular culture gives us to understand, this part of the country was not exceptional; farm lads in Manitoba and Mississippi would have similar tales to tell. In most of Europe this would be unthinkable. The rural population clustered in settlements, and life, as they said in the *shtetl*, was with people.

In areas where the population was tightly grouped however, interactions between family and community differed from those in areas where the population was relatively dispersed. Regions of dense settlement include inland southern France, the French Mediterranean coast, western Germany, and southern Italy. Dispersal into hamlets and isolated farmsteads, on the other hand, is found in western and central France, Flanders and northwestern Germany, Alpine regions, and much of southeastern Europe. Northeastern Germany is characterized by "street villages," the houses adjoining each other by extending along a road rather than grouped in a cluster. In the southern regions of Sweden, Norway, and Finland, settlement was "nucleated." In northern Scandinavia, it was dispersed.[51] For generations scholars have speculated about the differing impacts on social and cultural life that these variations in settlement have had. It seems reasonable to claim that the proximity in which the houses were clustered mattered in two ways. First, and most obviously, the sheer level of surveillance would be higher in thickly settled communities, for the simple reason that people who live close together have many opportunities to watch and overhear one another. The whole community will know that Marie-Claude returned late one night with Jean-Pierre simply because all the dogs barked as they strolled by (and all the family fathers leaped from bed to look out the window). Around Roussillon in the Vaucluse—where most of the peasant population lived clustered in relatively large villages—perhaps ten dogs would bark; around Remiremont in the Vosges, where farms were spread out singly or in small clusters, maybe only two dogs would have sniffed the tardy couple. At that obvious level such variations in settlement patterns make themselves felt in family life.

[handwritten margin note: Essay / Economic]

Traditional
Essay
Economics

Second, and more interestingly, the arrangement of houses affected the family by conditioning the general array of community controls upon individuals. Where houses were clustered together, the open-field system normally prevailed and much work was done in common. In open-field agriculture, large areas of decision-making were deemed beyond the individual and placed in the hands of the collectivity: what should be sown when, the date of the harvest's beginning, arrangements for grazing a herd that was sometimes collectively owned, etc. Where, on the other hand, individual holdings were self-contained and fenced off from one another by hedgerows, agricultural individualism was more pronounced. Because the farmer's strategic decisions affected only himself, he did not need to consult or cooperate with others in the community.

Now, it seems that where community controls have been exerted over cropping and livestock, they have had a habit of spilling over to other, nonagricultural domains of life such as migration, morality, and the annual cycle of ceremonies. In the nuclear-village regions of Europe, many aspects of existence having nothing to do with getting the crops in and out of the ground were regulated by the community as a whole, not by individual choice. In regions of dispersed settlement, the hand of the collectivity gripped with less force.[52]

What evidence exists that any of these assertions about the relationship between settlement patterns and cultural forms are true? Because social historians and ethnologists have worked so resolutely at the level of single regions or language groups, cross-national data on the charivari or on community pressures upon would-be seducers are about as rare as evidence that the soul is lodged in the pineal gland. We have plenty of speculation, cast mostly as debates between nationalistic French and German cultural geographers, but little solid information. According to one historian, communal enforcement of premarital chastity was stronger in the villages than in the hamlets of traditional France.[53] And from my own comparative work on the charivari, I have the strong impression that there was more community toleration of all the uproar that such demonstrations entailed in nuclear-village than in dispersed-hamlet Europe.[54] The various traditional bonfires—important occasions in France for vil-

46

lage supervision of courtship—were more common in the densely settled regions of the north and east than in the isolated farm country of Brittany and the West.[55] Finally, within those areas of Europe where bundling was to be found at all, we see the hand of the community preventing sexual irregularity. Where settlement was dispersed, local youth had to constitute themselves in *formal* organizations to supervise the bundlers; where settlement was concentrated, such organizations were unnecessary and youths went night-courting individually, because the community as a whole was able *informally* to supervise the goings-on.[56] Thus the proximity in which families were thrust together would affect in several ways the nature of their relationship to the surrounding community.

A second feature of traditional communal life was its stability. Le Play's organic metaphor—the stem family with roots deeply planted in the soil of France—was the product of conservative romanticism. Yet a certain reality had given rise to it. England seems to have been exceptional. The great city of London circulated the kingdom's population vigorously, and much of the land was worked by tenant farmers, by nature a mobile breed; hence the chances of the average person's dying in a place different from where he was born were fairly good.[57] But on the continent the vast majority of the population stayed firmly in place. While peasants might, for reasons of consanguinity or property, have to reach outside their natal village for marriage partners, it would not be far outside; and farmers who moved from their parents' homesteads seldom went more than a few kilometers before coming to rest.[58] There were, of course, specialized nomadic populations, men who for much of the year would be on the roads of France, selling knives and thread or looking for buildings to build. Yet there is no evidence that their households as a whole were any less stable than any other kind. There were people who moved to the big city seeking work and the chance to save up a nest egg, with which they would later return home and buy a bit of land. And folklore had it that still others who had in youth left for Lyon or Paris would return in their declining years to the perched villages of the Var, to spend the end of their days sitting on the stoop in the sun.[59]

This massive stability had several implications for the life of the family, some fairly obvious, some less so. Clearly you will act differently in the presence of people you have known all your life, whose parents your parents associated with, and with whose children your children are likely to grow up, than you will around people whom you have known only for three months, who before that time had never heard either of you or of the bog you crawled out of, and who three months from now will never again lay eyes on you. The web of rules that binds together acquaintances of long standing is much more extensive and subtle than the web bringing together relative strangers who associate with one another in a largely instrumental way. Among people long familiar, the realm of privacy is much reduced and the realm of public interaction vastly expanded—with all that that implies about dos and don'ts. For old acquaintances ("friends" would be precisely the wrong word for much of Europe's village population, with its hatreds and rivalries), the unformulated conventions were even more commanding than the formulated ones, so numerous were the threats to one's respectability, so varied the possibilities of diminishing one's standing in the community. A family's good name was compounded of many half-articulated factors— not just wealth or political position, but also cleanliness, probity, and qualities such as being well gotten-up on public occasions and running an orderly household.[60] Thus, occasions for loss of status were not limited to the handful we have today—arrest, bankruptcy, noisy domestic battles on the doorstep—but extended into every nook and cranny of daily life: how the children were sent to school (after the late eighteenth century), how presentable the bed linen was that one boiled every spring in the large communal kettle, whether the husband took his purse from his pocket easily in picking up a round of drinks with the boys at the bar. For people who had known one another a long time, such matters were of great importance. And such was the tyranny of this communal scrutiny that a family's interior life would be mobilized to the all-consuming purpose of preparing a face to meet the faces they would meet in the surrounding community. When people know one another for short periods only, or when large chunks of familial privacy have been carved from the realm of communal interaction, these small points become trivial.

But the stability of Europe's farm villages would leave a certain kind of imprint upon the interior lives of their families.

This village stability served to maintain the larger fabric of popular culture. To know the unwritten rules of a complex social system, full of informal face-to-face contact, one must be around for a long time. It helps to have been born in a place and to have absorbed its norms as children learn such things in growing up. It is essential to have spent some time in the little community, or one will remain at the margin as an outsider. Even today, in France, families count as "strangers" anyone who has not been in the village for at least a generation or two.[61] But a great deal of long-distance migration makes it impossible to learn the village's rules. With huge segments of the population churning from one district to another, the previously valid, unwritten prescriptions for getting along are never learned by many, and fall into disuse. They are replaced by formal rules, laid out in the Prussian Allgemeines Landrecht or the French Code Napoléon, enforced not by public opinion but by justices of the peace and gendarmerie.

In all the remaining niches of social interaction, hitherto covered by the web of custom, no further regulations of any sort prevail. As we are about to see, the nineteenth-century family would withdraw from these numerous sociable contacts into its private nest. Whether, however, it was an increase in migration that broke down this informal web of rules, or whether the massive moving of modern times began as a *result* of the breakdown, is a question I shall leave aside for the moment.

A final point: if these little communities were stable, it wasn't simply because of an absence of pressures from outside. Towns and villages were able, to some extent, to deflect those forces that bore in upon them. Municipal government had sufficient legal power to reduce population turnover, to control the arrival of outsiders, and to meliorate dire poverty that might otherwise drive local people away. Although French communes possessed relatively few such controls, a wide range stood available to Central European municipalities. Village assemblies had the right to reject strangers who wished to buy land, providing a local purchaser could be found—and even then the neighbors had to approve the "foreigner's" settlement.[62] In the

49

towns the power to license craftsmen was either directly vested in the guilds or indirectly controlled by them via their representatives on the town council.

Established craftsmen exerted every effort to exclude outsiders and advance local sons—as August Watter, a tailor from Lauba in Saxony, discovered in 1837 when he applied for permission to practice his trade in the Swabian town of Lindau. Town officials had rejected this "foreigner," but royal bureaucrats at the province level overturned their decision upon Watter's appeal. Contesting the provincial decision, Lindau argued that "given the crowding in the tailor occupation, Watter can succeed only at the cost of older masters, who will be driven to poverty. Two of these men, healthy yet too old to change jobs, have already gone on poor relief since Watter's license was issued." A provincial investigation revealed, however, that the real reason for Watter's rejection was Lindau's plan to wait until some of the local journeyman tailors, then traveling in their wanderyears, could return and themselves be granted licenses.[63] Multiply the Watter case by dozens (or in Germany as a whole, by tens of thousands), and one gets a sense of what these localities could do to protect their economic and demographic stability.

Every society makes arrangements for ensuring that private behavior will conform to public morality. So it will come as no surprise that traditional European communities regulated such matters as marital sexuality or the formation of the couple. What may be startling, however, is the extent to which these affairs were removed from informal regulation by public opinion and subjected to public policy. What may also appear foreign to our own libertarian times is the extent to which people were prepared to submit to these controls. Traditional European communities possessed, of course, a whole array of informal levers upon private morality; we shall examine these much later. Here our concern is with municipal government's formal administration of *la vie intime*.

In no country was collective morality absolutely helpless in the face of individual deviance, but it was unquestionably in central Europe that the community's legal authority reached its peak. While precise arrangements varied greatly from place to place, some kind of "fornication penalty" (fines and punishments levied by the town

fathers or by a seigneurial court against women pregnant out of wedlock) was virtually universal. In theory, all unmarried women who
had intercourse were liable to prosecution, but in practice only those
whose sexual activity had been confirmed by pregnancy were likely
to be punished. Both Catholic and Protestant churches were eager to
reinforce public law sanctions with their own interdicts: no white
bridal crowns for pregnant brides, humiliating scoldings from the
pulpit on Sunday mornings, and the like. In some Bavarian counties,
women who were pregnant out of wedlock had to carry about "a wood-
en contrivance shaped like a fiddle" for fourteen days, unless they
bought an exemption.[64] An edict of France's Henry II in 1556 obliged
women to declare premarital pregnancies to a judicial official—mainly
in order to reduce infanticide, but this *recherche de la paternité*
doubtless inhibited sexual adventurousness as well.[65] Moreover, such
controls have limits; after the middle of the eighteenth century,
young women became increasingly inclined to go ahead with what-
even personal plans they had in mind, with the legal consequences
thrown to the winds. But for a long time such collective sexual repression helped to keep the unmarried woman chaste.

Central European governments promulgated regulations of domestic service (*Dienstbotenordnungen*). These defined the obligations
and rights of servants and farmhands vis-à-vis their masters, permitting
aggressive officials to control free-time activities, clothing and expenditures. Similarly, the wages of servants and laborers were often administered, and were kept deliberately low on the assumption that
poorly paid hands would have little money to spend on corrupting
"luxury." Local officials could also restrict dancing and staying out
late at night, both harmful as incitations to premarital sexual activity.
Also, servants and workers who did not get enough sleep were useless
the next day.[66]

Other social agencies joined the town fathers in their fight against
immorality. Central to the guild ethos was the notion of "honor-
ability," by which was meant, first and foremost, sexual propriety.
And because German guilds in particular were imbued with all kinds
of public powers, they acted in the community as a mighty force
for right. The guilds insisted not only that a man himself not be
illegitimate (or even conceived before marriage), but that his parents

51

be respectably born as well. This criterion was not uniformly enforced upon everyone. That was indeed part of the point: you could pardon the people you knew. But the legitimacy requirement was often invoked against men coming from outside the community.[67]

Community law touched the family *foyer* at less obvious points, too. Before the mid-nineteenth century, central European towns could forbid outsiders from establishing residence if there was anything morally questionable attaching to them. A "good reputation" meant abstaining from such morally dubious enterprises as dancing in private or staying out late at night; it also meant not being a known adulterer or fornicator. The town of Amberg, for instance, attempted to keep one Leonhard Tafelmaier, a day laborer from Unteramersricht, from becoming a resident because his character was bad. We know about this tiny episode only because the municipal council's decision was overturned, on appeal, by higher authorities, on the grounds that, among other things, Tafelmaier had started living with his bride-to-be only *after* he had submitted his application.[68]

Of all public actions to reach into the family's intimate life, however, the most radical was the community's power to halt marriages. While this prerogative reached its most awesome extension only in the early nineteenth century in states such as Bavaria, strictures against undesirable unions had long been present in most areas. The saving of community poor-relief resources was the ultimate reason behind such bars, for the town fathers thought it better to have just the couples seek public assistance as individuals in hard times, rather than their numerous progeny in the bargain. So for each prospective pair the authorities would weigh their likely risk of impoverishment, guided in principle by universalistic criteria, but in practice more by the good principle of letting in people whose families you knew and keeping out those you did not. If the probity, industriousness, and economic prospects of the couple were found wanting, the community's veto would strike down their alliance. One Bavarian case shows what difference this power made in the lives of the common people. An old man presented himself in 1840 to a state official, desperate because his only child had become pregnant out of wedlock. The seducer had declared himself ready to marry the girl, but the commune had exercised its veto right, blocking all hope. The old man had a fit in the office after learning that the bureaucrat could do nothing, and began pulling out his hair and beating his head against the wall. He died a short time later "because of the shock of dishonor."[69]

It goes without saying that in the public law of our own times, all such powers are inadmissible. Any government that presumed to meddle with the sacred natural right of matrimony, to reprimand the sexually indiscreet, or to evaluate the general moral uprightness of individual family fathers would soon be toppled by an outraged citizenry. All these matters are today still subject to informal community regulation, of course, but they have ceased to be the objects of legislation or public law. That is because in the twentieth century the family occupies a basically different relationship to the community than it did in the eighteenth. Nowadays the dividing line between private and public spheres is clearly drawn, and efforts to blur it are seen as offenses against civil liberty. In traditional society the community and family interlocked at many junctures, and a web of regulation was necessary to ensure the stability of both.

The physical matrix within which the traditional family found itself discouraged intimacy. Too many curious faces thrust themselves into *la vie intime*; too many heterogeneous elements swirled through the household. The community's informal surveillance was omnipresent, thanks to the arrangement of space, and the formal restrictions that the social authorities placed on sentiment and inclination were too powerful to let close emotional ties arise. The evolution of the modern couple would require a dissolution of this intense collective life. The layers of generations within the household would have to be parted, nonfamily members removed to arm's length and the sentimental unit itself restructured, made smaller and less disparate in age. And the couple would have to acquire sufficient autonomy to control their own destiny, to tune out that babble of voices insisting that the urgings of the heart not be heeded. Before we can understand how the modern couple formed, however, we must have some sense of the relations between men and women within this traditional matrix.

CHAPTER TWO

Men and Women
in Traditional Society

ALEXANDRE BOUËT, in his classic, early nineteenth-century description of Breton peasant society, alerts us that something unfamiliar is going on. The husband in every sense "ruled the roost" in that region. His wife had authority over nothing. "Most often she doesn't even know how much money there is in the house. And if she's permitted to buy or sell something, she has to render an exact accounting. Not only does she serve her husband at the table without herself being seated, and speak to him respectfully as though to a superior person, but she is only the chief servant even to her sons and the male farmhands." And why at harvest time did the husband stand idly by while the wife heaped and piled the hay atop the wagon? It was because, explained Bouët, if the husband were to climb up there he might fall and have a "regrettable accident." If the wife fell, "it matters little."[1]

We have to ask what emotional relationships prevailed within those chilly farmhouses and dank huts. How did husbands and wives, surrounded by morose servants and ill-kempt infants, actually get on? Were they a happy yeomanry, perhaps, going about their tasks with a brave whistle and then tender affection among loved ones round the evening fire? Or should we more probably think of them as like those Swedish peasant couples in which "the man precedes, the woman falls back. However wide the path may be, the woman won't walk alongside him but behind. Thus a fifteen-year-old servant lad will precede a servant woman, though she be thirty, and will walk ahead of the farmer's daughter herself. Indeed one might even see the farmer's wife behind the lad."[2]

In this chapter I shall argue that popular marriage in former centuries was usually affectionless, held together by considerations of property and lineage; that the family's arrangements for carrying on the business of living enshrined this coldness by reducing to an absolute minimum the risk of spontaneous face-to-face exchanges between husband and wife; and that this emotional isolation was accomplished through the strict demarcation of work assignments and sex roles. Whereas the modern couple would brim over with expressive behavior, hand-holding, and eye-gazing as they embarked upon the interior search, the traditional husband and wife were severely limited: "I'll fulfill my roles, you fulfill yours, we'll both live up to the expectations the community sets, and *voilà*, our lives will unfold without disorder." It would never have occurred to them to ask if they were happy.

Here I have a confession to make. While for the larger purposes of this book I shall argue that this lack of affection characterized most couples in traditional society (excepting, of course, the handful of upper bourgeois and noble families), I shall be able to document my case for only a relatively narrow group, within a comparatively short span of time, in the confines of a single country: the landholding peasantry of France in the years 1750–1850. And this documentation will be closer to subaudible taps than to the hammering down of irrefutable data. This is in the nature of things, for we are auditing the intimate life of a semiliterate population two centuries ago who didn't talk about what they did, and about whom the literate classes, on whose testimony we are obliged to rely, had only the vaguest ideas. In the next few pages I shall do the best I can: I shall present some of the available evidence on everyday relationships between husbands and wives in France, indicate—with still less adequate material—the possibility that similar patterns prevailed in other countries, and remind the reader of my conviction that this lack of emotional expression among French peasants was archetypical of traditional society.

Affection in Marriage

Dr. Brieude, describing the life cycle of the peasant family in eighteenth-century Haute Auvergne, strikes the keynote: "Our young peasant lads, confident that their strength and industriousness will carry them through, take a spouse to satisfy their sexual needs. But the cold climate plus the precautions they fail to observe soon give them a numerous family. Becoming members of the community, they are burdened with taxes. As youths they were rich, as married men impoverished, because after taxes they have to feed and clothe a wife and children. The children languish and waste away for want of bread; the woman suffers in silence; the husband, unable to rise to so many demands, falls into melancholy and apathy. One must actually witness this cause of rural depopulation in order to comprehend it."[3] Thus, according to this intelligent young eighteenth-century doctor pining away for the City of Light in his provincial isolation (he says as much), lovelessness among the rustics stemmed from the crushing burden of daily existence, of brutalization by *la force des choses*.

But the systematic subordination of women by peasant men that we commonly encounter surely had deeper roots than mere misery. The Bretons described by Abel Hugo, for example, were not living on the margin of existence, yet there could scarcely be talk of emotional intimacy for these couples: "The wives are the first servants in the household: they plow the soil, care for the house, and eat after their husbands, who address them only in harsh, curt tones, even with a sort of contempt. If the horse and the wife fall sick at the same time, the Lower Breton peasant rushes to the blacksmith to care for the animal and leaves the task of healing his wife to nature."[4] Nor did couples seem any happier in the Bourbonnais, in the middle of the French hexagon. Although his testimony comes a bit late in time, we might listen anyway to Dr. Bernard-Langlois: "There are happy marriages here. Yet for an overly large number wedlock is only a yoke, without any exchange of kindness, without attentiveness or tenderness. And there have recently been angry separations, highly deplorable domestic quarrels."[5] So contemporaries recorded neither romantic love as such among these peasants—we will have to wait much later for that—nor even the sense of privileged intimacy, already present among middle-class urban couples, which we shall later encounter as "domesticity." On the farm, man and wife got along in quiet hostility and withdrawal.

But, the reader may object, surely these people were moved by death. Would not the loss of a partner break through this emotionless facade to reveal such familiar modern sentiments as bereavement? On occasion, the loss of a partner would in fact shatter the carapace of immobility. Dr. Maret tells the following story:[6]

I was sent in 1760 to the village of Ruffey [Côte d'Or]. A malignant putrid fever had been epidemic there. In my round of the sick I was taken to a woman of perhaps thirty whose husband had just died several days earlier. She had been attacked by the same disease. I was accompanied by the curé of the place and a surgeon, but our arrival scarcely seemed to interest the woman; she kept a profound silence. I approached her, interrogated her, tried to raise her spirits. . . . Succumbing to my importunities she turned and said in a tone that fairly broke my heart, 'I thank you kindly but I don't want no medicine. My husband is dead. We was poor but we loved each other a lot.' After that moment she never again spoke to a soul, took neither food nor medicine, and died on the morrow, the sixth day after the death of her husband.

Yet such deeply felt loss was not typical. The prospect of death seemed to arouse no deep sentiments between spouses. Among rustics to the east of Paris (Seine-et-Marne), special testamentary provisions were seldom made for spouses in a will.[7] And so much more firmly did economics rather than emotion bind together the peasant couple that when the wife fell ill, her husband commonly spared the expense of a doctor, though prepared to "cascade gold" upon the veterinarian who came to attend a sick cow or bull.[8] That was because, in the last analysis, a cow was worth much more than a wife. According to the prefecture of the Charente: "The loss of a stable animal grieves a peasant more than the loss of his wife. The first

57

may only be recuperated with money; the second is repaired with another woman, who will bring with her some money and furniture and who, instead of impoverishing the household, will increase its wealth."[9] And when the peasant finally did call a doctor for a dying member of the family, the following drama was to be expected:[10]

[The peasant] is more interested in his cow than in his wife; he might have exchanged his cow for a couple of shiny dollars [*belles pistoles*]. But for his old father or his poor sick mother he temporizes; he calculates; he fears expense. They've had their years, he says, if death prolongs its arrival; then he gives in to the insistence of neighbors and the remonstrances of the curé; he goes into town to get the doctor; but this visit will be the only one; nobody even gives the doctor reports on the progress of the illness. If he loses a child, the peasant expresses his grief in terms of the expense involved: 'It would be nothing,' a father told me whom I was attempting to console for the loss of his son, 'if it were only necessary to pay the expense of the sickness, but Monsieur le Médecin, last year I laid out 1700 francs for his substitute for military service! And that's what hurts, and will continue to hurt for a long time.'

In a study of eighteenth-century Anjou, François Lebrun contrasts the grief of upper-class men at the loss of their wives with the "indifference" of the popular classes, men who would spare nothing upon the veterinarian to save sick livestock, "but it's different for wives, here today, gone tomorrow" (*une perdue, une autre retrouvée*).[11]

The permanence of the peasant's affection for his property and the transience of his attachment to human life are revealed in several proverbs:[12]

—"Mort de femme et vie de cheval font l'homme riche." (Brittany)
(Rich is the man whose wife is dead and horse alive.)
—"Deuil de femme morte dure jusqu'a à la porte." (Gascony) (Your late wife you so deplore until you enter your front door.)
—"L'homme a deux beaux jours sur terre: lorsqu'il prend femme et lorsqu'il l'enterre." (Anjou)
(The two sweetest days of a fellow in life are the marriage and burial of his wife.)

In one of demography's little ironies, these peasant husbands who cherished their cows more highly than their wives, would likely be the first of the couple to expire, since death rates for men above forty were considerably higher than for women. In mourning, the widows gave back in like coin, at least according to one observer of eighteenth-century Provence: "If it is a woman who has just lost her husband, she emits cries of lamentation [at the wake] capable of bringing the very stones to tears before each newcomer. She's obliged to play the wife *qui avait de l'amour.* She strikes her head against the wall, omitting nothing to persuade all of the immensity of her grief; tears and contortions cease immediately as soon as no one is about, but begin again with the next arrival."[13]

The rituals of daily life sanctified the wife's subordination to her husband. We learn something about deeper patterns of interaction from observing how people act at the table, for example. Among the peasants of traditional France, the wife did not join her husband at meals. She stood serving him at his side and would take her own food only after he had finished. In the Deux-Sevres, wives were more the *premières servantes* than the *compagnons* of their husbands. (Note that this account was composed by middle-class bureaucrats, to whom alone could the idea even have occurred that the wife might be a comrade to the husband.) "Before she dare be seated at the table, he must give permission."[14] More commonly the peasant women would not find themselves at the table at all, as in the Ain: "At mealtimes the mistress of the house, her daughters, and the female servants never sit down, remaining constantly afoot, cooking spoon in hand to ensure that each person is served, during which the master and all his farm help down to the little shepherd lads are putting the food away."[15]

These customs had a larger significance: they were ritual signposts of the wife's subordination to her husband. This was not lost on contemporaries. Dr. D. Monnier, after explaining that women in the Jura seldom joined the men at table—never, when strangers were present—explained that "in general the peasants don't have the same ideas on the fairer sex as people who've been educated; they regard them to some extent as a defective part of the human race, to the point of excusing themselves when speaking of women. More than one time I have heard people say . . . in talking of females "begging your pardon [*sauf votre respect*]."[16] The only other subject on which peasants commonly asked their middle-class interlocutors' indulgence was barnyard animals!

And if we may glimpse into people's interior lives by noting what they call one another and what they insist on being called, peasant France did not exactly stand out as a stronghold of the companionate marriage. In the mountain commune of Saint-Romain-en-Gal (Rhône), for example: "The wives have a certain respect for their husbands. They call them *notre homme, notre maître, notre gros*, never tutoyer them, and remain standing behind them during meals."[17] Other testimonies concur on the rarity of tutoiement among the peasants, so that on their wedding day even women who had addressed their mates previously in the familiar "tu" would change over to the polite "vous."[18]

This sort of ethnology soon reaches its limits. We have no way of knowing whether these peasant couples held hands before the evening fire, caressed each other tenderly as the night wind whipped down from the Alps, or delighted in the mutual joys of discovering each other's complexity—the sort of spontaneity and empathy we would expect from romantic love. But it seems unlikely. The emotional distance separating the couple appears unbridgeable, and if more than a few escaped the iron cells which their social and sexual roles had cast for them, our sources do not record it.

Although the nuances of this marital lovelessness may have varied from one social stratum to another and perhaps from town to country, the fundamental outlines of the couple's emotional life remained constant in the years before 1800. "Traditional" behavior undoubtedly prevailed at that time for virtually everyone other than the upper middle classes and intellectuals. The few shards of evidence available for city dwellers suggest that the same was true for them. Regarding the small-town bourgeoisie of the Haute Auvergne, Dr. Brieude explained that provincial society has drawbacks: the absence of "arts and sciences," the moribund condition of commerce, the mediocrity of private wealth. "Pressed for money at every turn, [the provincials] are preoccupied with their neighbors' standard of living; they are envious, obstructionist and spiteful, which gives rise to constant feuds and ruinous suits. . . . It is therefore scarcely surprising that lives are passed in bitterness since people dedicate themselves to doing malice to others or to fending off others' assaults. *L'amitié*, that delicious sentiment, is scarcely known. There are in these little towns only marriages of convenience; nobody appreciates that true happiness consists in making others happy, who always reward us in kind."[19]

Within France's great cities all remained still cool formality among bourgeois couples. The one Lyon husband who willed all his goods to "my dearest wife, the object of my most tender affection and to whom I owe my life's happiness," was not a Lyonnais.[20] And Louis-Sebastien Mercier's cutting remarks about couples who smiled radiantly at each other in public but who didn't speak for weeks at a time in private, though aimed at the upper-middle classes, were doubtlessly valid for the lower-middle class as well.[21] The great surge of sentiment begins earlier in the cities than in the countryside, and sooner among the middle classes than the lower, but before this secular unfolding commences, relations between men and women in the household seem to have been affectionless everywhere in France.

Perhaps there is something peculiarly French about this absence of affection in marriage. As we shall discover, the French depart from European family norms in several important respects; perhaps they do so as well in their dearth of marital romance. So thin is the evidence on which we depend for the rest of Europe that a resounding answer would be foolhardy. Yet the bits and pieces of scholarship available on traditional family life elsewhere suggest that France is, after all, typical rather than exceptional, and that lovelessness was a common feature of the petty bourgeois and peasant marriage everywhere.

In 1748, the little weekly paper of the small Prussian town of Halle attempted a statistical estimate: scarcely ten marriages in a thousand were happy ones, while in all the others "the spouses cursed and bemoaned their choices." The figure itself, of course, is fanciful. But the tendency to which the Halle *Gesellige* pointed was probably correct.[22] We may take more confidence in Helmut Möller's recent study of the German petty bourgeoisie, based on an exhaustive survey of the literary and ethnographic sources of the eighteenth and early nineteenth centuries. Möller was able to discover scarcely a reference to romance within marriage for this class before 1820. In the preceding period he encountered only fathers emotionally isolated from their wives and the rest of their families—men who were brutal, domineering, obsessed with external forms, prudish, and (with the increasing disappearance of their power over journeymen, who were moving out of the masters' homes in droves) frantically authoritarian.[23]

It wasn't so much that the petty-bourgeois husbands were all beasts and that their wives were brutalized, but rather that each had strictly defined roles to perform. Should either partner fail, insufficient affection existed within the marriage to permit communication and compromise. That's what happened to Georg Zöll, a miller in the Bavarian commune of Zolling, and his wife Theresa. Zöll's father, it seems, had never trained him properly in the miller's trade, and then several floods and military campaigns exacerbated the problems to which the man's basic incompetence had given rise. His wife, on the other hand, was an indifferent housekeeper, a poor cook, and useless to Zöll in his work. (Present-day readers may read this with derision, but remember, it was precisely for such qualities that women were married—those were their roles.) Things had apparently gone poorly between the two from the start. In 1750, ten years after the wedding, Theresa's angry step-father was complaining to the local bishop about his son-in-law's outrageous conduct: he slept late in the morning, he was at the tavern too much, he was lazy at his work. The civil court in Freising attempted to judge the case. Witnesses were called:

———Georg Krazer allowed as how the miller had been poor at his work at the outset, but had greatly improved over the years, and that the fault was Theresa's, "who was always on at him, even though she herself was no great shakes as a housekeeper."

———Sebastien Veichtner, the miller's helper, related how one day at the luncheon table Theresa had started to nag her husband "for doing nothing other than eating and drinking. If he really wanted to succeed, he would have long since gotten the horse out of hock." When she persisted, the miller gave her a couple of "not all too big" slaps, which only made things worse. Thereupon the miller rushed from the kitchen and seized a stick of firewood to beat her with. The other men present at the table grabbed him in time, however, and the wife fled.

————Veith Saufüssl testified that the wife never ate together with Zöll, "and because she never gives him a kind word indicates clearly she doesn't care for him."

————Maria Widenmayr, who had served previously in the miller's home, told the court how the wife always started to nag when the miller came back from the bar, "on account of which he would usually give her a few slaps." Furthermore, the wife prepared better dishes for herself than for her husband and in general considered herself superior to him. Were it not for this attitude, Widenmayr observed, peace would prevail in the home.

We in the modern world might find our sympathies torn in the miller's case. The court sentenced him to a short jail term not because he beat his wife or came home drunk on occasion, but because his attendance at Mass was irregular and because, in being away so often, he had abandoned the administration of his household to his servants. And in the scale of values of eighteenth-century Germany, those were the major offences. That men should whack their wives about and eat at separate tables was normal in the eyes of the court. (As for the villagers, they felt Theresa was falling short in her domestic role.) Of love, tenderness, or affection, not a word was ever said. The case dragged on for over thirty years, with Georg living at home with his wife for most of the time. And even her death at age fifty did not end the war, for Georg next attempted to prevent his twenty-three-year-old daughter Kathrina from taking over control of the mill (which the court had denied him), on the grounds that she was too much like her mother![24] What counted for the burghers of Zolling was not the quality of the couple's intimate life—not eating together, combined with regular physical assaults, must have somewhat limited that—but how well the couple performed the tasks that life imposed on them. What was important was doing the essential work of society: grinding the grain, transmitting the property from generation to generation in an orderly way, clothing and feeding the members of the family sufficiently so that they wouldn't become a burden to the rest of the community. *This* was what marriage was all about for the Zollingers; it was not a means of finding personal happiness.

Not only are detailed studies lacking in general for England, there is no consensus among the handful of scholars who might be expected to have some impression of the subject. Peter Laslett, in a sensitive reconstruction of village society, refers to the time when "the whole of life went forward in the family, in a circle of loved, familiar faces, known and fondled objects . . . ," but he refuses to say more.[25] Alan Macfarlane, who analyzed the seventeenth-century diary of clergyman Ralph Josselin, alludes to a "joint-role relationship" that might be described as an "emotional success," but he admits that the evidence behind this inference is little more than the couple's long cohabitation. (There was talk of physical attraction at the beginning, but within the context of courtship rather than of established marriage.)[26] Another side of the English coin, one supporting the argument I am trying to establish about affectionlessness, is offered in Frank Huggett's portrait of the family life of a Victorian agricultural laborer. It is admittedly a portrait embarrassingly late in time for my case, and half-fanciful, yet impressive for the author's learning on the minutiae of daily life. Here, with Mr. Strudwick off at the local inn, is the laborer's wife at the end of a typical evening:[27]

Meanwhile, back at home, Mrs. Strudwick had washed up and put the children to bed. She sat huddled round the dying embers of the fire, finishing the last gloves by the spluttering light of a stump of candle. [Ascending at 9 o'clock to retire], she soon fell asleep. Some time later she was awakened by the sound of her husband clattering up the stairs. He staggered as he came into the room and knocked against a chair. She hissed to him to be quiet. She heard him undressing. He got into bed and settled down to try to get warm. Soon all she could hear was her husband's heavy breathing in the dark.

Suddenly, from the direction of the village, there was a great din of kettles and pans being banged with sticks, and much shouting. . . . Some of the men in the village were giving John Ford the 'rough music' for giving his wife a black eye again. It served him right. Mrs. Strudwick smiled to herself, turned over, and settled down to sleep.

With Mr. Strudwick coming in drunk and waking his wife, we could be in some Long Island bedroom in 1954, but not with the charivari in the background. If we peer closely at English rural society, even towards the mid-nineteenth century, it does not look entirely familiar.

But the Puritans in the New World do. There was something about coming to the colonies in the eighteenth century that gave family life a new quality. Perhaps the easy availability of land set aside the whole psychology of *intérêt* in forming alliances.[28] Perhaps the sprawling restless communities of the New World lost their ability to impose collective morality upon individuals who wished mainly to be free. Perhaps there was something about the shock of migration. . . . In any event, references to romantic love as an active force in the life of the couple began with the Puritans and never ceased thereafter. John Demos believes it impossible to say anything conclusive about companionate marriage in Plymouth Colony, but talks anyway—and convincingly—about the "instinct of love." Edmund Morgan is forced time and again to use the word "love" in describing the Massachusetts Bay settlement, a *consequence* rather than a cause of marriage.[29] And anyone tempted to think such marital sentiment a peculiar product of Puritanism might consider the following passage from a letter of the (supposedly) Anglican Theodorick Bland to his wife, while away from his native Virginia in the service of General Washington:[30]

> For God's sake, my dear, when you are writing, write of nothing but yourself, or at least exhaust that dear, ever dear subject, before you make a transition to another; tell me of your going to bed, of your rising, of the hour you breakfast, dine, sup, visit. . . . Fear not, my Patsy—yes, 'you will again feel your husband's lips flowing with love and affectionate warmth.' Heaven never means to separate two who love so well, so soon; & if it does, with what transport shall we meet in heaven?

Sexual Roles

In contrast to the strict segregation of labor and of sex roles in traditional society, in the modern world empathy intervenes to blur the boundaries: being able to put yourself in someone else's shoes increases your willingness to share that person's tasks. For the traditional couple the sex roles were absolute, and the community punished with ridicule those who attempted to break them down. As Dr. Perron tells us of the Franche-Comté: "Public opinion forbids the husband to milk the cows, to fetch the water, to wash the dishes. . . . He would be scoffed at and called a *quenillot*, a *fouille au pot*, a *coquefredouille*, and even made a laughing-stock among the women themselves."[31] Today sex roles blend together, approaching interchangeability. What brought this state of affairs about was "a coincidence in sexual and affective exchanges," as an anthropologist puts it.[32] To understand these exchanges we must first learn how roles and jobs were segregated in the past.

One of the principal questions of the new women's history is that of how much power women ever did have in times past.[33] For best effect, the answer is supposed to be zero, the history of women being a history of black-as-night repression and all. But it turns out, in fact, that *within their particular domains* women were all-powerful. A watertight division of sex roles and tasks meant that the housewife would run her little kingdom as she saw fit; even if she didn't choose to rebuke a meddling husband, other friends and neighbors would. Today, on the other hand, women's individual "power" is considerably less because they are obliged to share all their traditional spheres of control with men. In the companionate marriage, husband and wife consult about and cooperate on everything imaginable, accordingly reducing their respective domains of absolute autonomy. Of course, that doesn't necessarily mean that women's control over societal, familial, or personal resources has diminished with modernization.

The question is more complicated. Rather than asking uncategorically about women's "power" in traditional society, we should inquire what specific realms lay in their hands, and then ask what difference control over these made in the larger sexual roles they were persuaded to adopt. We should ask how the wife's fierce grip over the interior of the ménage affected (if at all), the domains such as sexuality in which she had to negotiate directly with her husband. The larger argument I shall be making is that women's control over certain domestic spheres, which were isolated from the economy as a whole, did not free them from subordinate social *roles*. Only direct access to the market economy would ultimately spring them from this kind of role subordination.

What, exactly, was women's work in traditional times? The daily routine of a typical Basque farmwife sets the stage. She rose at 5 A.M., with the sun in the summer, in pitch-black darkness in wintertime. Only after she lit the kitchen fire did the men get up (the hired hands lived in). She served them their breakfast *soupe* and they departed for the fields. Then she had to rouse the children, wash, feed, and dress them, and sent them off to school. Then came the beds, sweeping up, and putting things in order. She next picked vegetables from the garden for the noontime meal, washed and peeled them, and put things on the stove to cook. The men returned and she served them lunch, standing behind her husband's chair when not waiting table. Afterwards she herself ate, seated on the hearth or standing with the plate on the mantel. And we have only reached the day's halfway point, for in the afternoon this average farmwife was out in the fields, and in the evening she did her spinning by the lamp. She went to bed towards 11 P.M., some time after her husband.[34]

Similarly, in the division of financial responsibilities, the Basque farmwife had certain well-defined tasks. Whereas the husband would handle the buying and selling of livestock, the woman cared for dairy and poultry products. Even more importantly, "[the women] retain the key to the granary, often however abusing their privileges; they filch from the supply to get sweets or cloth from the store-keepers. Woe to the mistress of the house who has gotten into the habit of stealing wheat! She starts giving life to her fantasies, buying on credit. She goes into debt and ruins the family."

Interestingly, consultation between spouses took place over the big economic decisions. "The husband polls his wife when buying or selling. He gets her approval for all business matters. Before making a decision he wishes to have her advice." But it turns out that all this apparently modern harmony stemmed from the circumstances that the wife was likely to be the owner of the farm. In Basque country a daughter might inherit if she were the eldest—and her husband would, at least in the Middle Ages, have taken *her* name! Elsewhere in France control over big decisions seems to have been less well apportioned between the spouses.[35]

Our best documentation happens to be for France, and the Basque example highlights several general features of the rural division of labor between sexes in that country. Farm women were active in the fields as well as within the house; the spheres of men and women intersected not at all (with the wife, for example, behind the husband at meals rather than before him, and rising and retiring to a different rhythm); and control over resources was carefully differentiated: the husband was master of some, the wife of others. The following chart represents the general apportionment of labor likely to prevail between men and women there, and distinguishes between work inside and outside the farmhouse.

Thus within the house, French farmwives would be responsible for the three "C"s: child-rearing, cooking, and whatever cleaning

TABLE 3–1

Division of Labor by Sex in Traditional Rural French Households

	WOMEN'S WORK	MEN'S WORK
Inside House	child-rearing cooking cleaning household accounts cottage industrial work	lighting oven farm accounts
Outside House	wood-gleaning water-carrying vegetable garden poultry-dairy care poultry-dairy marketing larding hay-tossing weeding	wine storage cattle-feeding (varies) cattle-marketing care of agricultural implements spading plowing scything pork slaughtering

Note: This table rests on observations from many different sources, but of special interest are: d'Abbadie d'Arrast, Mme Charles, *Causeries sur le pays basque: la femme et l'enfant* (Paris, 1909), pp. 50–56 and *passim*; Louis Caradec, *Topographie médico-hygiénique du département du Finistère* (Brest, 1860), p. 67 (the author was a doctor); Deribier-du-Châtelet, *Dictionnaire statistique ou histoire . . . du département du Cantal*, 5 vols. (1852–57), vol. II (1853), pp. 132–133; Guy Thuillier, "Pour une histoire des travaux ménagers en Nivernais au XIXe siècle," *Revue d'histoire économique et sociale*, 50 (1972), pp. 238–264, esp. 239–240; and Henriette Dussourd, *Au même pot et au même feu: étude sur les communautés familiales agricoles du Centre de la France* (Moulins: Pottier, 1962), pp. 4–39.

was to be done. Now, the reader should keep in mind that relatively little cleaning as such went on in these peasant farmhouses, with their thatched roofs and dirt floors, for the simple reason that things were always dirty and little could be done to make them clean short of putting in flooring, rebuilding and plastering the walls and ceilings, keeping out the farm animals, separating the stable from the living quarters, and so forth. So cleaning for traditional peasant women was not at all the floor-waxing, dusting, and cobweb-removing that consumes so much of the modern housewife's energies in her security-sealed, solidly-built bourgeois home. As far as cleaning was concerned, only laundry would be likely to take much time, and the huge washes of peasant France, with boiling cauldrons and lye, happened only a few times a year.

"Child-rearing," too, must be qualified. While the care of infants and the socialization of children was indeed women's work, in these large peasant households this work would not necessarily fall on the mother. If a grandmother were still alive and living there, she would be charged with infant care. In the large multifamily households of central France (*communautés familiales*), one woman would specialize in child-rearing, leaving the others free for field work.[36] Thus, of the 3 "C"s, only cooking loomed as a considerable burden to the average woman. But that was strictly her province. Men who donned aprons would get charivaried.

Also bulking large in the world of women's work were the cottage industrial tasks to which wives would apply themselves during the day, when winter kept them away from the fields, and in the evening on a year-round basis—except in the exhaustion of the big harvest push. The spinning, knitting, glove-stitching, and lace-making that were done at home were strictly female tasks. In all the chronicles of the *veillées*, for example, I have not seen one in which men do industrial work. When men bestirred themselves at all in the evening, it would be for rope-making or for repairing tools. In addition, preparing the yarn for the family's own clothes fell solely to the women: this included drying, hackling, and sorting the flax to have thread for infant garments and household linen, and combing, carding, and spinning the wool. These home-prepared yarns would then be given to professional weavers and tailors to be made into shirts, bonnets, and sheets. Or sometimes these were woven and sewn at home, except that the fingers of many peasant women were so stiff and swollen that sewing, knitting, and darning were impossible for them.

Women also had a large array of responsibilities outside the home. Everything touching the farmyard fell into their province: slopping the swine in the event they didn't forage freely; feeding the chickens and gathering the eggs (if the family had any poultry); and milking the cows and making cheese and butter, in regions where this was not a specialized activity. Gleaning firewood was also a female responsibility. The actual amount of work women did in the fields depended on the form of agriculture. If the soil were tilled directly, the men would probably shoulder most of the spading and plowing because they were stronger. Yet other kinds of work such as weeding and hoeing or, where grapes were grown, trimming the young vines in early summer, could be done by women. Where livestock raising predominated, there was little outside labor of any kind for women— except perhaps the young girl's shepherding—and so they worked more about the house and barns, making cheese or pitching hay.[37] Although the frantic push of harvest time broke down the sexual segregation a bit, hay tossing and straw piling remained woman's work and reaping remained man's. In the Lot-et-Garonne department, for example, "it is the women who climb on the cart and do the heavy work of pitchforking down the bales of straw, during which the farmer merely stands in front of the team looking on; he is there to give orders. . . ."[38]

The list of jobs for men is much shorter than for women. In truth, men had more disposable time. Male daily routines permitted at least the possibility of bar-sitting several times a week, although not all men did so. In contrast, observers thought farmwives so rushed with their work that virtually no disposable time remained—which is why sociable occasions for women were simultaneously work occasions. Yet we must not forget that the jobs allocated to men involved grinding physical labor, often leaving them physically wrung out by the age of forty. Within the house the man had virtually nothing to do—save, perhaps, lighting the fire, in homes fortunate enough to have a baking oven. Outside the house some ancillary tasks would fall to him, such as slaughtering the pigs or procuring and storing the wine. Before the nineteenth century, however, few peasants besides the vintners themselves were sufficiently well off to afford wine routinely at the table. The wife's job was to make paté and butcher the lambs. Then came the care of field implements, including the repair of spades, rakes, harrows, and the rest of the primitive equipment by which the earth was scraped and scratched. But the main male tasks were sowing, spading, plowing, and harvesting. These were the heart of the peasant's day.

Getting the cows to market and buying and trading horses was the husband's responsibility, as was marketing the grain, and with those revenues he paid the family's external obligations: taxes and rents. Even at the marketplace itself this division between the sexes was maintained: the cattle market would find itself in one part of the village square, and only men would congregate there; the goose market would be located at the opposite end of the square, and only women and children would cluster there.[39] The income from each market was allotted within the household to the responsibilities; of each sex; failure by either partner would bring down bitter recriminations.[40]

France is a land of endless regional diversity. The broad brushstrokes I have drawn in here would surely be modified in passing from one locality to another. The main lesson is that peasant women were not without considerable authority in their own households. Just as a "separate but equal" pattern of domestic control applies today in Serbia[41], so did women in traditional France reign over well-defined spheres of life. Yet because the woman's spheres were largely removed from contact with the outside market economy, she had little leverage upon her husband. She imported new resources into the household. The roles she was obliged to perform in relation to him and the outside world were all inferior, subjugated ones, in which the autonomy she enjoyed within the domestic sphere did her no good. Only when wives gained direct contact with the market economy—by means of cottage industry and later by means of factory work—did they seize hold of a solid lever with which to pry themselves loose from these subordinate roles. But this jumps ahead of our story. A

71

profile should first be drawn of the differing roles husband and wife felt obliged to assume in traditional society.

The wife's roles were all subservient. It was not merely that she occupied roles calling for her to be different from her husband. This would not necessarily have ruled out emotional equality. It was that in several important realms she was expected to be the *inferior*.

In the realm of external relations, for example, the husband was to take the active role, the wife the passive. In every point at which the household's life touched that of the surrounding world (with such customary exceptions as egg marketing), the woman was expected not to initiate démarches. It was the husband who was responsible for dealing with state officials or the seigneur and for handling external threats to the family's interest from any quarter.[42] Women who stepped from their passive places to discharge this role would, according to the principle of "feminine irresponsibility," be condescended to as minors. During a drought in France's Vivarais region, for example, a miller's wife stoned a group of workers who were trying to dam the creek. Although she told the court that she had acted "alone and spontaneously," witnesses testified that the husband gave her orders nearby all the time. By sending his wife out he had hoped to escape prosecution, "for the culpability of a woman is that of a minor, and inclines the courts to exact only compensation for damages caused, without punishing either the act of violence or malice aforethought."[43]

I do not wish to exaggerate the "confinement at home" of these peasant women. The annual cycle of festival and ritual provided numerous occasions for them to come into contact with other people. But aside from sorties for work, such as fetching water or firewood; aside from religious occasions, such as attendance at mass; and aside from ceremonial occasions, such as the St. John's fire or the village fair, women did not venture beyond their holdings. They did not arbitrarily or impulsively decide to "go visiting"; they would not leave their homes just for the sake of sociability. But men did. Men would seize every chance to take off for the local tavern or café and sit around drinking and talking with their friends.

A host of folk sayings on women and the outside world express this view of female passivity, and male dynamism:[44]

—"Les femmes à la maison, comme les chiens, les hommes à la rue, comme les chats." (Gascony)
(Women belong at home, like the dogs; men belong in the streets, like the cats.)
—"Femme fenestrière et courrière n'est en rien bonne ménagère." (Gascony)
(If you hang out the window or run around, you'll have the sorriest home in town.)
—"Jamais femme ni cochon ne doivent quitter la maison." (Dauphiné)
(Never let go out the doors either the women or the boars.)

This passivity of women in external relations was woven into a larger passivity in their relations with men in general. The moment she stepped into some domain of life outside her own household, the peasant wife ceased to shape events. As far as men were concerned, she did not make things happen; they happened to her. This little lesson in relations between the sexes was acquired first in courtship. Here is the scenario for picking up the bride on wedding day in the Mayenne department: "Accompanied by his father, the bridegroom arrives at sun-up to get the girl, invariably finding her in working clothes and occupied with domestic duties. 'Weren't you expecting us?' he asks. 'But how could I have known that you hadn't changed your mind,' the young girl humbly responds, only then going to get ready for the wedding."[45] Even before the wedding day, no other boy would think of approaching a girl someone else had already chosen, and it was necessary to ask permission for a dance, not of the girl herself, but of her boyfriend.[46]

Within the household itself the notion that the man proposes, the woman disposes, turned up in numerous ways. Proverbs, for instance:[47]

—"Le chapeau doit commander la coiffe." (Brittany)
(The hat gives order to the headdress.)
—"Quand la femme est maîtresse à la maison, le diable y gouverne." (Provence)
(When the wife is mistress at home, it's the devil who's in charge.)

73

In some places it was improper for the farmer's wife to give orders to the male hands—a curious, precapitalist notion that sexual authority weighed heavier than economic authority.[48] Finally we note, as exceptions that tend to prove the general rule of passivity, the few ritual occasions on which women had the right to order men about. On Ste-Agathe's Day (5 February) in the Champagne, for example, "the husbands were charged with cooking and housekeeping. After mass the women, and especially the young marrieds, rang the midday chimes, and then took off for the café. In the afternoon and evening they played cards [loo] in someone's home, thus engaging in masculine recreations."[49] In other places the entire month of May was devoted to a sexual turning of the tables, in which women avenged themselves against wife-beaters and the like.[50] But these were just little flickers in an otherwise black night of female domestic passivity. That was woman's place.

Self-abnegation and personal sacrifice for the family represented a second specifically feminine role. Women of the petty bourgeoisie were supposed to put aside the beautification of their own bodies, the pursuit of stylish clothes, or any other vain, "egotistical" distractions that might have impeded them from serving the *maison* with less than total dedication. The world of the German middle classes abounded with phrases such as *Treue, Häuslichkeit,* and *Eingezogenheit* (loyalty, domesticity, and seclusion), all of which connote an expressly feminine responsibility to others. This loyalty was not necessarily to the woman's own children, as modern notions of feminine self-renunciation were to demand, but to the household in general. Petty-bourgeois distrust of female beauty and makeup, for example, may be laid at the feet of this self-abnegation.[51]

It may be objected that such renunciation of self was expected not just of women but of everybody in the little community, which feared egoism at the societal level as it did plague at the biological, and took comparable steps to isolate the contagion. Yet the pathetically thin documentation on collective mentalities does hint that women were expected to do more giving-up than were men. Men, after all, had numerous little socially-approved pleasures: the arrival of the silver tankard of beer on Sunday; playing cards with the boys at the bar; and fooling around with the servant girls, in the event that these burgher husbands had chosen abstinence with their wives as a contraceptive measure. In the world of women one is at a loss to point out counterparts to these customary delights. The little punctuation marks of self-indulgence that ran through the man's week in this ritual manner are absent from the woman's. The knowledge that others would thrive through her sacrifice was supposed to suffice.

Finally, women's work was found in sex and reproduction: sleeping with their husbands on demand and producing babies up to the limits set by community norms.[52] But is that not the way nature meant it? the reader might ask. After all, only women are biologically equipped to bear children; so the assertion that birthing belongs to their special tasks, while true, is unstartling. The really intriguing questions here are (1) whether the reproductive role was divorced from the erotic role—that is to say, whether wives were supposed to provide their husbands with sex *independent* of childbearing—and (2) whether husbands were supposed to reciprocate for their wives, assisting them to orgasm in coitus. These questions matter; for should it turn out that husbands imagined themselves to be responsible for their wives' sexual gratification—that is, if men thought that pleasure in intercourse should properly be a two-way street—my views on the long emotional distance between man and woman in traditional society would be called into question at this very fundamental level. Conversely, if husbands imagined sexual pleasure as merely one of many duties to which their wives were obligated, while they themselves owed nothing in return, the whole dimension of reciprocity and mutual exchange, so important to companionate marriage, would seem to have been lacking.

We shall return to the first question—whether sex for recreation accompanied sex for procreation in the Bad Old Days, in Chapter 6. Here we shall briefly treat the question of reciprocity in erotic matters within peasant marriage. The problems we normally encounter in "proving" any assertion about *la vie intime* of times past, always enormous, are almost insuperable in this particular domain of the sexual relations between husband and wife. From these sprawling rural populations, so homogeneous in some matters and so diverse in others, we have only flashes of light on this least accessible of all subjects—more fireflies to illuminate the obscurity of intimate life.

Of course, many people who did not know what they were talking about were willing to declaim confidently about peasant sexuality: witness the *oeuvre* of Restif de la Bretonne.[53] But finding someone literate who *did* know is another matter. The local doctor of Puy-en-Velay (Haute-Loire), writing in 1777, seemed to have some knowledge of his rustic patients:[54]

The peasant returning home in the evening, harassed by weariness and misery, thinks only of the food before him, which is normally not terribly abundant. Badly needed rest coaxes him away from sexual delight that would not refresh him anyway. The woman, for her part, is exhausted with the worries and struggles of the day, and after a frugal meal from which her nursling will take most of the nourishment, falls asleep at the side of her husband rather than in his arms. I state with confidence that their embraces [by which he means coitus] are confined to the natural, arising from their basic needs. . . .

Dr. Balme was writing to assure anxious mothers that the peasant women to whom they confided their infant children as nurslings were little stimulated by erotic fantasies. Contemporaries feared that the excitation accompanying foreplay and afterplay would harm the wet nurse's milk, but—said the good doctor—there's none of that among the rustics.[54]

A similar perfunctoriness characterized coitus among the married petty bourgeois of Germany, if Helmut Möller's sources are to be trusted. He writes of "the low level of masculine erotic accomplishment" and tells the story of Händler the tailor who, feeling "neither inclination nor affection for the older woman who had been forced upon him as wife," nonetheless produced ten children by her in fourteen years. One can imagine the quality of their sexual rapport, especially Ms. Händler's views on "the joy of sex."[55]

Nor, if we may trust the thirteen-year rural experience of one German pastor, was there peasant reciprocity even in masturbation. "When couples quarrel, the wife often reproaches the husband for not sleeping with her yet expecting from her that she. . . ." (Left blank in original text.)[56]

These peasants and petty bourgeois in fact regarded their wives as baby-machines and treated them as one would treat any machine: mechanically and without affection. Female sexuality served only the production of standardized merchandise—in this case not widgets but male inheritors. This was precisely the image that one author selected in describing the peasant masons of the Creuse department: "The haughty egoism of the men makes them view their wives as *une machine à enfantement,* unworthy of solicitude, as an inferior being incapable of development."[57]

The apparent casualness with which men were willing to give their wives venereal disease confirms this masculine indifference to the affective side of sexuality. Towards the end of the eighteenth century, a substantial increase in syphilis seems to have taken place in the French countryside. Some of this was the result of passing armies infecting innocent peasant lasses, of diseased nurslings infecting their wet nurses, and of prostitutes infecting soldiers who would then infect their sweethearts—in short, the standard causes. But a prime additional source seems to have been husbands returning from seasonal labor to bestow upon their wives what they had received from the prostitutes of the big cities. The seafarers of St. Malo, for example, were said to be passing venereal diseases acquired abroad on to their wives. M. Mallet de la Brossière believed the phenomenon to be increasing.[58] The Royal Society of Medicine broadcast the following information to provincial doctors in 1788:

> Although hitherto unknown in the countryside, venereal disease has recently become in some localities quite common, the result of the [sexual] needs of workers and especially of the masons who contract employment in the Parisian construction industry during the summer months. These thoughtless unfortunates find so many occasions inviting them to sexual release that they give in and contract the disease. Then they communicate it to their wives when they return, either because they are in ignorance of their own precise condition or because some hasty treatment at the hands of a charlatan gives them a sense of security just as dangerous as the disease itself.

Dr. Brieude commented of the Haute Auvergne in 1787 that VD was becoming "common" in the countryside, despite a continuing purity of morals. Husbands who worked elsewhere seasonally were at fault. "Our industrious Auvergnats, whose constitutions are so vigorous, satisfy their sexual needs without running any risk when they are in the bosom of their family. But when far away their appetites take control and occasions are present. It is this ease which poisons them. Once returned to their wives, these men live chastely enough because they no longer feel driven [to go outside the marriage]. But the wives are given the germ."[60]

And a good sixty years later, when you might think people would have finally caught on, the same mechanism was still operating. According to two Strasbourg doctors in 1864, "the worst cases [of VD] were those women who voluntarily confined themselves to the hospital. They are ordinarily peasant women, infected by their husbands and unaware of the nature of the sickness; not daring to speak of it to a doctor, they let the disease take root. . . ."[61]

Thus we have the spectacle of husbands, who spend part of the year in agriculture and part of the year away working, coming home to give their wives syphilis. What could have been going on in their minds? Was it perhaps genuine ignorance, the false belief that the infection was not contagious? Popular consciousness about the nature of venereal infection was sufficiently developed among men (witness the substantial sales of condoms, expressly for the prevention of VD) to make this unlikely. Granted, the disease's full life cycle was as yet incompletely understood, and people did not realize what relationship tertiary syphilis bore to the initial manifestations. But anyone who contracted the disease realized that he had a severe medical problem, something more than a case of athlete's foot. Despite such knowledge, these men continued to infect their wives. We might conclude only that for them women were a sexual convenience and if, as their wives performed their "conjugal duties," certain disagreeable consequences resulted, *tant pis pour elles.*

These fragments of information about rustic sexuality fit into a larger mosaic of silence and affectionlessness between husband and wife. Each had his or her own tasks to perform in this world, and each would be judged by the community on the basis of how well these work assignments were carried out. Each had his or her own roles to act out before the opposite sex: the men were to be domineering, overawing in their patriarchal authority, selfish, brutal, and unsentimental; the women were to be loyal, self-effacing, and submissive. It is both this extreme segregation of work tasks and this emotional inequality of sex roles that justifies us in speaking of an unbridgeable sentimental distance between the couple.

CHAPTER THREE

The Two Sexual Revolutions

AT THE END of the eighteenth century, young people began paying much more attention to inner feelings than to outward considerations, such as property and parental wishes, in choosing marriage partners. They began to court those whom they liked rather than those whom their parents thought best. In the 1950s and 1960s people of all ages—but adolescents in particular—began to strip away the sentimental layers from the romantic experience to get at its hard sexual core, thinking eroticism most precious in what human relationships have to offer us and impatient with the delays that feeling once imposed. Both of these historic changes of mind were sufficiently massive and full of consequence for the rest of the social order to be considered revolutionary. And so I have called this chapter "the two sexual revolutions."

After such a thrilling beginning, I'm afraid the reader will find what follows rather boring. The challenge in writing a book like this is not in making grand assertions but *proving* them. Consider the concept of sexual revolutions. Many people believe that in the domain of sexuality, nothing ever really changes. Now who is right? In the variety of history I prefer, "proof" means numbers—that is, data on the representative experience of the average person: how many were doing what, and when? Thus, to establish that changes in sexual behavior are indeed real, we shall have to accumulate great piles of numbers—on illegitimate births, on women who become pregnant before marriage, on how many sexual partners young girls have, and so forth.

How people get along sexually before marriage is central to the story of the family. For one thing, the onrush of eroticism in courtship would spill over into the lives of the mature couple, modifying their subsequent relationship. For another, these libidinal drives would drive apart the generations within a family, straining the links in the lineage.

A small leap of faith will be required of the reader at this point, for the material that follows concerns only premarital sexual activity. And of course, even if people *did* start fooling around before marriage, it doesn't necessarily mean that they also rearranged their entire personal hierarchy of values and priorities. They could have continued to think traditionally about how to choose a partner while at the same time beginning to make love. I do not think that that is what actually happened. But in this chapter we shall content ourselves with getting into place the figures on coital activity and the like for the unmarried. This duty done, we can turn in the next chapter to those affairs of the heart that are less easily quantified.

The Great Increase in Illegitimacy

The central fact in the history of courtship over the last two centuries has been the enormous increase in sexual activity before marriage. Before 1800 it was unlikely that the typical young woman would have coitus with her partner—certainly not before an engagement had been sealed, and probably not as a fiancée, either. But after 1800 the percentage of young women who slept with their boyfriends or fiancés rose steadily, until in our own times it has become a majority. And recently there have been large increases especially among adolescents, in intercourse by *un*engaged women (if one can imagine such a thing).

Illegitimate births and premarital pregnancies give us the most reliable data for determining the incidence of sex before marriage. Of course, not all women who are sexually active before marriage bear children. Some practise contraception—at least to the extent of saying, as in France's Vendée, "Look out!" before their partners ejaculate. Others force an abortion or miscarry spontaneously, and still others are not yet entirely fecund. But assuming such factors remain more or less equal, there will be at least a general coincidence between the level of coitus among unmarried women and the rate at which they become pregnant. Provided that the other "intervening" variables (such as contraception) remain unchanged, we should be able to infer from a long-term rise in premarital conceptions a similar rise in sexual activity before marriage. That, at least, is the assumption behind Figure 3–1, in which the solid line represents children con-

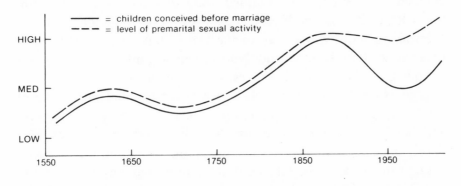

Figure 3-1

ceived out of wedlock (illegitimate births and "legitimate" children born within eight months of marriage) and the broken line the probable level of premarital sex. The point at which these two lines diverge is the point at which all other things cease to be equal—that is, when unmarried couples begin practising contraception.

A caveat: there are some things that Figure 3–1 does *not* say. It does not say, for example, that every commune or region in western Europe and North America underwent the same development, with identical timing in the shifts and similar leaps in the increments. It does not say that Belgium saw the same late-sixteenth-century rise in illegitimacy that did France, or the same post-World War II increase in intercourse before marriage that Britain did. We don't know the status of illegitimacy in sixteenth-century Belgium. And after the Second World War, sexual activity among the unmarried Belgian population appears to have undergone nothing like the increase that happened across the channel. So Figure 3–1 homogenizes the vastly divergent experiences of various regions and countries, and infuses the reader with false confidence that solid information is present for many parts of the West, when in fact little is known. On the other hand, it is possible to present average or "representative" developments in those areas for which data exist, as well as to find the central tendencies in movements wildly divergent from one locality to the next. Mind you, central tendencies *were* present: if illegitimacy rose, between 1750 and 1820 in thirty local districts and declined in only four, we are justified in writing "On the average illegitimacy climbed. . . ." But the historian will want to know about those other four villages as well, and Figure 3–1 makes it easy to forget *them*.

Speaking broadly, we may divide the history of sex before marriage in western Europe and North America into the four major periods given below. (For sources, see Appendix II.)

1550–1650. A brief, relatively insignificant rise and fall in out-of-wedlock pregnancies took place, most likely caused by a similar rise and fall in premarital intercourse. Of all periods, this is the most poorly documented; exactly what was going on in the *vie intime* of young Europeans in the late sixteenth century remains largely a mystery. Various charts of illegitimacy show an unmistakable peak in the 1590s, especially in England.[1] Evidence is present that premarital pregnancy underwent the same uphill-downhill course. There is nothing to indicate that more sexual intercourse caused this increase. We have neither qualitative testimonies (other than the usual lamentations that the young were becoming more "immoral") nor sufficient data on such "intervening" variables as fetal mortality or female health (fecundability) to let us point to intercourse by process of elimination. As for the years that followed, the notion of the Counter-reformed, Puritanical seventeenth century as a time of sexual repression is so firmly entrenched that I shall give it a respectful nod here as the probable explanation for the charted decline between 1600 and 1650.

1750–1850. There was an enormous rise in illegitimacy and premarital pregnancy in the years of the French and Industrial revolutions. Late in the eighteenth century, the number of out-of-wedlock pregnancies began to skyrocket in virtually every community we know about, often reaching three or four times the previous levels. In case after case, from interior Massachusetts to the Alpine uplands of Oberbayern, the number of infants conceived before marriage increased markedly. Indeed this is one of the central phenomena of modern demographic history.[2] In a moment I shall suggest that this huge upsurge in part reflected a decline in abortion and an improvement in female health and hence reproductive biology. Primarily, however, it was the result of increasing sexual activity.

Then, towards the middle of the nineteenth century, a plateau was reached; the incidence of both bastardy and premarital pregnancy leveled off, or even began to decline slightly. The stage was set for the third period.

1850–1940. During this period, the rate of out-of-wedlock conceptions—at least those leading to illegitimate births—plummeted; cases in which the woman married before the child's birth declined much less swiftly, if at all.[3] In some countries this trend began towards the middle of the nineteenth century, in others not until the end. This precipitous drop in illegitimate fertility extended to virtually every province of every country in Europe, save Bulgaria. (What was happening in Bulgaria, nobody knows.) Illegitimacy declined as well in Canada and the United States.

Did premarital pregnancies fall off because people had sex before marriage less often in these years (Victorian repression and all that) or because unmarried couples began to practice contraception? While many scholars choose the former explanation, the simultaneous decline in *marital* fertility suggests to me it was the latter.[4] If people had fewer and fewer children within marriage, it was probably not because they were making love less often but because they were practicing birth control. The simultaneity in the timing of the marital and nonmarital fertility downslides is so close as to suggest that contraception caused the drop in nonmarital conceptions as well.

There is no reliable evidence on the actual incidence of premarital sex before the First World War; moral laments had by this time discredited themselves as a reliable indicator of behavior, and survey data had not yet been gathered. Yet I am convinced that the torrent of literature on sexual purity that descended upon mid-nineteenth century women was written and read by only a tiny elite at the summit of the social order, and that such doctrines made no difference in the lives of the millions of anonymous women from the popular classes. Moreover, we know of no social or economic processes at work at the time that would have reduced the propensity of unmarried women to intercourse.[5] Quite the contrary, as we shall see.

1955–1970. Illegitimate fertility having reached bottom during the Great Depression, it rebounded after the Second World War. Rates of both bastardy and premarital pregnancy climbed in Anglo-Saxon and Scandinavian countries after 1945 principally as a result of the improved biological capacity to conceive, which in turn came from a better diet.[6] Not until the late 1950s were actual patterns of sexual behavior among the unmarried to change. In the 1960s and early 1970s, the proportion of young women willing to have intercourse before marriage rose significantly. Being young, many of them did not take precautions and hence became pregnant. Increasingly, they did not become engaged to the men with whom they slept. And with time these new patterns of behavior spread to younger age groups to include teenagers.

It is ironical that out-of-wedlock pregnancy rates soared just as genuinely efficient contraceptives were becoming available. Just think to what extent the accelerating contraception that did take place masked the true proportions of the second sexual revolution! In terms of "quantitative behavior" the revolution was just that. Late in the eighteenth century, an initial premarital sexual revolution had occurred; in the 1960s, a second revolution would make sex before marriage a part of the representative experience of the average person.

To sum up, the course of premarital pregnancy since 1500 might be subject to two differing interpretations. The "grand oscillations" school says that sexuality moves in long cycles. The "linear increase" school sees shifts in *la vie intime* as essentially the consequence of a once-and-forever change in the history of Western man: that of "modernization."[7] I subscribe to the second school.

Accounts of a high illegitimacy rate during the Middle Ages, combined with the late-sixteenth-century "bulge," appear to support the grand-oscillations interpretation, which holds that human sexual behavior, like so much else, marches historically in large cycles. One century the pendulum will swing towards liberality, the next towards sexual conservatism. T'was thus ever so; t'will thus ever be. I am dubious of this view. For one thing, medieval "illegitimacy" must be viewed in the context of a definition of marriage considerably different from our own. In the eyes of medieval society, a couple who plighted their troth without undergoing the formality of a legal ceremony would still be considered as married by the surrounding society, even though the offspring might be recorded as illegitimate. A strict separation between marriage and engagement was not laid down until the Reformation, by a Catholic Church desperately eager to complete the sacramentalization of marriage and by a Protestant Church militantly watchful against "immorality."[8] Thus only after the Reformation does the notion of "illegitimacy" acquire much cultural meaning. And the 1590-ish "bulge"—the other fact on which the grand-oscillations interpretation rests—was so overshadowed by subsequent increases as to make it a minor, perhaps even localized, fluctuation rather than a massive upheaval in the premarital practices of Europe's common people.

I prefer to see the giant rise in out-of-wedlock pregnancy in the late eighteenth century as the principal phenomenon to be explained. It changed the lives of more people than any fluctuation in premarital sex had previously or has since ('before the 1960s, at least). And it accords perfectly with a larger notion of social change that I am advancing here: that there was, once upon a time, such a thing as traditional society, which endured relatively unaltered for a number of centuries but which was finally destroyed and replaced by something else we call "modern society." I see our own dear modern times as entirely different from this world we have lost, especially in everything touching intimate life, and I believe this huge one-time change in premarital sexual behavior to be part of the transition from one to the other.

Is Sex the Villain?

Let us focus upon the period of the great increase in illegitimacy, 1750–1850. On what grounds may we conclude that a rise in extra-marital sex produced this illegitimacy explosion? Suppose we assume that illegitimacy rates were available from the very outset (which they were not) and that the propensity of the average unmarried woman to bear children really was increasing. (See Appendix II on some technical problems of measurement.) Would we be entitled to infer automatically a corresponding rise in sexual activity from such an increase? In a word, no. Other variables could have "intervened" to increase the number of illegitimate births per 1000 unmarried women; we must rule them out before we are justified in concluding that changes in illegitimacy mean changes in sexual behavior. Seven alternative arguments are presented below.

1. If the illegitimacy rate rose, it could have been because a greater number of unmarried women had become fecundable, thus increasing the likelihood that sexual activity would result in conception. This suggests two possibilities: (a) that a lowering in the average age of first menstruation increased the adolescent population available for intercourse; or (b) that an improvement in diet enhanced across the board the ability of women to conceive. I think we may rule out the first possibility simply because unmarried women customarily didn't start engaging in intercourse until long after puberty had arrived.[9] The typical French or German girl would have started menstruating towards sixteen or seventeen around the mid-eighteenth century; yet the mean age for the birth of the first illegitimate child was the mid-twenties.[10] Thus at least five years and possibly as many as ten would pass between the time when a girl could become pregnant and when she actually became pregnant.

We must take the second possibility—a general enhancement of fecundity—more seriously. The capacity for conception is a function of diet and general physical condition, and this does appear to change over time. In the United States, female fecundability—to the extent that such things may be measured by the proportion of married women who remain childless until age forty-five—seems to have decreased during the late nineteenth and early twentieth centuries, rising again after the Second World War.[11] But what the course of fecundity was in the *eighteenth* century, and whether Europe saw a rise in the chances that intercourse would lead to pregnancy, remains a dark mystery.

There are glimmers of light. The end of the terrible seventeenth-century famines apparently restored regularity to women's cycles of ovulation, which would tend to have improved their ability to conceive.[12] Although historians debate fiercely exactly what happened to popular standards of living during the eighteenth century, the most reasonable position, in the case of France, seems to be that they rose a bit. If so, we would expect a simultaneous improvement in the average woman's fecundability.

But how much difference did these elusive trends in human biology make in the illegitimacy explosion? In view of the sheer size of the increase in bastardy, I am reluctant to ascribe strategic importance to changes in the ability to conceive. It strains credulity to argue that all these women had been leading active sex lives since time out of mind, but had not become pregnant simply because their constitutions were so weak.

2. If the illegitimacy rate rose, it could have been because couples came to practice contraception less efficiently or not at all. If so, sex before marriage had not increased; instead, the very same people who before had contraceived well were simply now omitting to do so. I find this most unlikely. It is implausible that the young and unmarried could have been practicing contraception at a time when married couples were demonstrably not practicing it. We know in general that contraception begins first for older married couples; its adoption then passes downwards to younger people.[13] And we know that systematic contraception did not begin to lessen illegitimacy until late in the nineteenth century after its initial acceptance among the married. Logically, therefore, it seems unlikely that around the year 1700, young people were the only ones in the population to use contraceptives effectively. More probably nobody was doing so except the prostitutes and the aristocrats. (One also asks why these supposedly "Malthusian" youths would have failed to take with them into marriage the dark arts of contraception that they

were practicing outside of it.) And it is implausible that one generation of youth would fail to transmit its contraceptive lore to the following generation. Let us assume—though this is manifestly false—that before 1750 young shepherdesses away on the hillsides commonly had sex before marriage. Why would the following generation of shepherdesses have suddenly failed to take precautions their former co-workers had long followed, thus becoming pregnant?

Finally, our three series of descriptive sources make almost no mention of contraception before marriage, although alluding from time to time to its practice within marriage. Among the texts I have seen, only the officials in the Gers prefecture even acknowledged the practice of contraception among the unmarried around 1800, and then only to say that "it happens in the big sinful cities, not here." The next reference after that comes from Dr. Baudouin, writing just before the First World War, who opined that only within the preceding twenty years had young folks in the west of France started making it before marriage, the girls exhorting their swains to "watch what you're doing" [faire attention] and to have their orgasms "extra muros."[14]

Rather than a shift in contraceptive practice, then, it is a change in sexual activity that caused the illegitimacy explosion. Even today, in our own enlightened times, the young are breathtakingly naive about precautions against pregnancy.[15] How much more so was this the case two hundred years ago, when all those unknowing young lasses began sleeping with their boyfriends, and a wave of premarital pregnancies swept across Europe and North America.

3. If the illegitimacy rate rose, it could have been because there were fewer *spontaneous* abortions than before. If more premarital conceptions survived to term, illegitimacy would have increased without any change in intercourse having taken place at all. We cannot summarily rule out this possibility. Even among today's healthy populations, as a general rule, for every 100 live births among unmarried women there are an additional seventy fetuses that perish. The rate is higher among black single women, where there are more spontaneous fetal deaths than live births.[16] Thus even a small change in fetal deaths will exert considerable leverage on illegitimate fertility.

Fetal loss among the unmarried of traditional Europe must have been enormous. The doctors of the time were aware of the problem but probably underestimated it. Among the 8,700 pregnancies reported by women sampled at Manchester's Lying-in Hospital in 1845–46, 14 percent had miscarried.[17] In eighteenth-century Rouen, "there are a number of sterile women, not from nature but from disease; abortions and miscarriages are common."[18] But how did these levels change, if at all, over time? Let's leave it at this: when local studies begin to document substantial increases in the living standards of these populations before, say, 1820—and especially when the documents indicate better nutrition and thereby better physical condition—I will have to concede that much of the illegitimacy explosion could have been a fecundity explosion instead. But to my knowledge, only one writer has yet made this case.[19] In no continental community have we been able to see the average person's physical condition improving markedly before the mid-nineteenth century. Thus the inference that fetal wastage rates did not alter significantly before that time may remain in court.

4. If the illegitimacy rate rose, it could have been because fewer women were *deliberately* aborting themselves. Here we confront the major competitor to my explanation of increased sexual activity. The decline in illegitimate births late in the nineteenth century was almost certainly the partial result of more induced abortion.[20] Could not the earlier rise in illegitimacy have been due to a similar decline in abortion? Possibly. As one might imagine, data on deliberate abortion for these historical periods are rare and unreliable. We are reduced to a few tatters of speculation. Let us distinguish, to start with, between the eighteenth and nineteenth centuries:

Eighteenth century. On the basis of church evidence, Jean-Louis Flandrin has conjectured that induced abortion among unmarried women may have declined. He sees newly established foundling homes as having given premaritally pregnant women an alternative to the dangers of abortion or the abomination of child-murder.[21] Also, several Central European writers of the time believed that the abolition of "fornication" penalties towards the century's end lessened the incidence of premarital abortion and infanticide.[22] So there are hints that abortion among the unmarried may have declined slightly during the eighteenth century. In any event there are, to my knowledge no complaints that it was rising.

Nineteenth century. Induced abortion among the unmarried seems to have undergone a major increase throughout the century. There are evidences of this in France. Thus Dr. Coutèle, writing in 1809 of his practice in Albi (Tarn), said that all the local midwives were complaining how empty their lying-in houses had gotten, "although because of the relaxation of morality, pregnancies are becoming ever more numerous. Pregnant women simply aren't coming; no more deliveries are taking place, so popular have abortionists become and so numerous their operations." Then the doctor conducted a mini-survey. "A number of young folks from here, getting together at the last carnaval for a working-girls' dance [bal de grisettes], put at twenty-four the number of them who had become pregnant. They told me later that only six had carried to term."[23] Dr. Bérenguier, discussing the nearby commune of Rabastens (Tarn) nearly fifty years later, said that abortions continued to increase—a result, in his opinion, of the abolition of the revolving hospital door in which mothers previously had been able to abandon unwanted infants without being tabbed.[24] The child welfare inspector of the Pas-de-Calais complained in 1873 of the increase in very premature stillbirths among the unmarried, and he linked this source of "depopulation" to the immoral young lasses "who abort their deliveries when they don't suppress the infants entirely."[25]

As the nineteenth century closed, abortionists started running ads in newspapers, offering services which, one supposes, were greatly in demand. A big Parisian daily trumpeted "Postponements, payment after results, success guaranteed in all cases. Write to. . . ." In the Berlin papers, abortionists crouched behind paramedical titles: "Mesmerist, Frau Keyer, Wartburgstrasse 1" or "Footcare specialist, Annalie Zimmermann, Feilnerstrasse 6."[26]

Even into the twentieth century, the doctors continued to complain about abortion. In rural parts of the Seine-Inférieure, unwed mothers were willing to bear their children and then see them perish in the first few days of life; but in the cities "women kill instead of letting die; instead of allowing the infant to come, all traces are made to disappear. . . ." This particular observer believed abortions to have doubled since the Great War.[27]

This chronicle may be duplicated for the other European states and for North America—where, too, a wave of abortions seems to have taken place towards the century's end.[28] For the earlier part of the century, however, the fragmentary testimony yields little more than a handful of smoke. Yet I have seen no indications that induced abortions *declined* after 1800. There is no warrant for assuming that a lessening in their incidence created an illusory rise in illegitimacy from 1800 to 1850.

5. If illegitimacy rose, could it have been because fewer pregnant women were getting married before the child was born—a change, that is, in courtship practices? This possibility, too, is a powerful contender, for in those places where illegitimacy went up and pre-marital pregnancy fell (or the other way around), we are manifestly dealing with little more than a change in attitudes towards "saving the honor" of the prenuptially pregnant. The proportion of pregnant women who managed to get married before the child was born rises, the proportion who married afterwards (if at all) falls; but the total number of women sexually active before wedlock remains constant. If this happened often, the intercourse variable would be called seriously into question as an explanation of the bastardy explosion.

But it did not happen often. In the great majority of local studies where the two series (illegitimacy ratio and percent of first children born within eight months of wedlock) are simultaneously available, they rise together.[29] More engaged women were getting pregnant before marriage—we assume they were already engaged, because the honor-saving marriage followed so quickly—and more nonengaged women were getting pregnant, as well. Thus a shift in the dividing line between the engaged and nonengaged populations, or a shift in popular notions about the "sinfulness" of bearing a child outside of wedlock was not responsible for the huge increase in illegitimacy, although these shifts may also have been going on.

6. If the illegitimacy rate rose, could it have been because of a decline in the illegitimate stillbirth rate? Stillborn children com-

monly did not find their way into parish registers, at least not in France and England. If there are fewer stillbirths, more illegitimate children will be registered (the number of conceptions outside of wedlock, however, remaining constant). Here the timing of Europe's great decline in stillbirths is crucial. At some point after the mid-nineteenth century, the proportion of stillborn among both legitimate and illegitimate deliveries sinks everywhere. Could that drop have begun soon enough to account for the illegitimacy increase?

To go by the German experience, I think not. German and Scandinavian localities assiduously registered stillbirths before 1800, and several long-term time series are available. In each of these the proportion of stillbirths *rises* during the eighteenth century: in Stuttgart between the years 1700 to 1811, in Königsberg between 1769 and 1802, in Breslau between 1687 and 1727, in Berlin between 1746 and 1792, and in Sweden as a whole between 1751 and 1900 (though an improvement in birth registration may have been partly responsible there).[30] Because these births are already included in the German illegitimacy figures, they are eliminated as an intervening factor. If stillbirths rose in France and England as well, which we don't know because such births were infrequently registered, they would sooner have concealed than magnified the true size of the illegitimacy explosion.

One last word about stillbirths. Many writers of the time suspected that children born dead from apparently natural causes had in fact been the victims of infanticide or abortion. The possibility is intriguing as a solid statistical means of apprehending a shadowy phenomenon. Yet the foremost nineteenth-century student of the question, Bernard-Benoît Remacle, thought that most stillbirths were just that: fetuses whom nature, rather than a cynical or desperate mother, had victimized.[31] In this view, the considerably higher rates of stillbirth for illegitimate than legitimate children would be attributable to poorer prenatal care or inadequate childbirth procedures rather than to malice aforethought.

7. If illegitimacy rose, finally, could it not have been because official birth registration procedures improved, and children whom previously the pastor or mayor had not recorded were now being

caught in the reporting net? For reasons too technical and boring to go into here, I suggest that the answer is no.[32] Such explanations appeal to the timid who are reluctant to believe that anything important changes in *la vie intime*; but such improvements in reporting as did come about could not possibly have accounted for a phenomenon of this magnitude.

Figure 3–2 reviews the logic over which I have hauled the reader

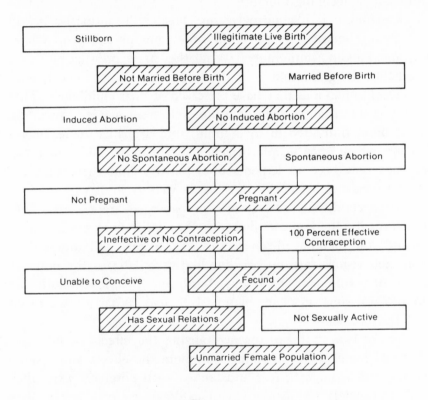

Figure 3-2

In Phillips Cutright, "Illegitimacy, Myths, Causes, and Cures," *Family Planning Perspectives*. 3 (January 1971): 27.

in the preceding pages. It shows the systematic elimination of the other "intervening" variables that could have caused a rise in the illegitimacy rate. But how many possibly crucial variables remain question marks! The logical chain at the end of which the sexual revolution dangles seems fragile indeed. Is there no proof other than this demographic exegesis?

As it happens, there is some additional evidence to confirm the conclusion already suggested by this process of elimination, that an increase in premarital sexual activity caused the illegitimacy and premarital pregnancy explosions. This evidence consists of complaints about declining morality.

Such evidence is like nitroglycerin. Treated incautiously, it will blow up in the user's face. At all times and places, people have complained about "immorality." What they are expressing by this is in part that the grim realities of their adult lives accord poorly with the innocent memories they have preserved of their childhoods. That is to say, a transition in their own life cycle from naiveté to worldliness becomes translated in their minds into a change in real-world behavior: where once people in general were moral and honorable, they have now become serpents of depravity. And then there are dirty old men and hysterical spinsters, as well as adult writers of all shapes and conditions who record on paper, as statements of an external reality, the fantasies flickering through their minds. Some of these dirty old men have been doctors, bureaucrats, and antiquarians —and their visions turn up two hundred years later in the notes of eager young American historians, burrowing in the Bibliothèque Nationale for some evidence of sexual change. What are we to do about this problem?

There are two strategies for neutralizing the effects of nostalgia and sexual fantasy. One is simply to ignore the effects and assume that, however riven with fear and fantasy such observers were, they hadn't completely lost contact with external reality. Thus if they said, "Many more young people are making it together nowadays than when I was growing up," maybe something was in fact changing. The second strategy is to assume that while a background rumble of fear and anxiety about sexuality is a historical constant, if this rumble suddenly rises to a shriek, we have independent warrant for assuming that something was changing in the real world—else why this acceleration in the tempo of complaints? Neither of these solutions is really a good one; but then, in working with historical materials, there are no perfect solutions. We find ourselves with noses constantly pressed against the window of subjectivity in our sources; any description of an external reality transmitted to us will have passed through some observer's fantasy life, and scholars who can't live with this should find another field of work.

In point of fact, the years 1750–1850 witnessed a crescendo of complaints about immoral sexual activity among the young. This amount of lamentation was unprecedented since the Reformation— before that time my knowledge falters—and it was not again to be attained until the 1920s. Doctor after sober doctor, senior administrator upon administrator, would turn from their normal weighty concerns about infant hygiene or local self-government to comment upon the sad state of sexual morality. What could have been going on in their minds? Had all these observers been seized by some collective delusion, some secular millenarianism dormant since the fifteenth century? Or were they in fact picking up, even in their self-inflated, self-righteous ways, a shift in the fabric of intimate life about them? I believe the second.

Observe some German examples.[33] Bavarian administrators early in the nineteenth century became alarmed about dancing because they thought the walk home customarily meant a stopover for sexual intercourse. Women would appear unescorted at dance locales and wait there until they had been asked to dance or had found a male partner to escort them home; nine months later the fruits of these casual couplings would appear.[34] But the good Bavarians didn't need dancing as an excuse for coitus, as Joseph Hazzi discovered around 1800 in an administrative tour of Oberbayern. In the Seefeld district: "Both sexes are so inclined to debauchery that you scarcely find a girl of twenty who's not already a mother." Around Marquartstein County this interest in sex nestled within a larger rebelliousness. The proverb "We'll have no lords" was popular among people who "get married enthusiastically and very early, produce lots of children, among whom sufficient illegitimate ones that this is considered much more a beneficial than a sinful deed."[35] Officials in Oberfranken testified in 1833 that communities full of deflowered maidens were commonplace. "In the countryside a girl who has preserved her virgin purity to the age of twenty counts as exceptional, and is not at all esteemed for it by her contemporaries."[36] In Unterfranken even the "middle classes" in rural areas, and certainly the laborers in cities, had by 1839 concluded "that the natural satisfaction of the sex drive is neither legally forbidden nor morally very reprehensible."[37] By 1854 premarital sex had apparently become so commonplace that provincial officials were hand-wringing: "Every time single boys and girls go out dancing or to some other public entertainment they end up in bed. In places where male and female servants work side by side, sexual intercourse is a daily phenomenon; and Altötting County reports that it's not seen as sinful at all to have produced children before marriage."[38] These are droplets in a torrent. Literate observers were shaken in southern Germany during the first half of the nineteenth century by what they deemed a sexual revolution, first among the youth of the lower classes, and then finally even among those of their own class.

In France it was the same story.[39] To give the flavor of such cultural criticism, here is the flowery Doctor Louis Lépecq de la Cloture, on a medical trip through Normandy's Caux district late in the eighteenth century. Although feminine beauty was, to be sure, somewhat disadvantaged by missing teeth and overly large thighs, "nature gives [to young women of the district] a taste for vanity and a penchant towards romance, a double attraction for vice, which lurks ever ready for justifications to modify the integrity of local morality. Add to that their reputation for good looks, that ominous stumbling block to innocence, and you'll be obliged to rank the Caux district among the great cities."[40] (Eve proferring Adam the apple, in other words.) But Doctor Lépecq was not an idiot. His observations about local hygiene have passed into the standard sources of French social history; and illegitimacy in Normandy was climbing rapidly during these years. The historian asks himself: what, exactly, was going on?

To take another little puzzle: why, wondered Dr. Hécart in Valenciennes, had observance of the festival of Ste.-Catherine (25 November) declined so in recent years? The *fête* had formerly been such a lovely occasion for young women to get dressed up and go to church to light an enormous taper, covered with flowers and ribbons, in honor of the pure unmarried. "Nowadays ever fewer attend, be it for the same reasons that have destroyed family reunions, or because young women are less concerned to honor their holy patron, or because finally, knowing the science of good and evil, they are ashamed to put themselves in evidence."[41]

As a final example: what, the historian ponders, could have prompted the mayor of the mill town of Amiens to decree in 1821 that "in view of the fact that girls [at the spinning mules] frequently take boys as thread-knotters, and that boys in their turn often take girls for the same purpose, and that it is accordingly very much in the interests of good morality to forestall the problems which arise from contact between the two sexes, above all for young men, we decree that both men and women are expressly forbidden to have as assistants members of the opposite sex." The statistician Louis-René Villermé, who reported this ordinance, was not at all surprised that sexual intercourse in Amiens frequently began around the age of fifteen for both boys and girls.[42]

Now, bear in mind that none of the Frenchmen or Germans whose observations I have reported were writing for the purpose of censuring immorality. Their chief purposes were invariably hardheaded, and these remarks about how young folks so often ended up in bed together were made in passing. These were not thin-lipped pastors, aching for fire and brimstone to fall upon Sodom and Gomorrah; these were not crackbrained moralizers in the fastness of some provincial nest. Nonetheless they were convinced that young people were participating in premarital intercourse more often than before. I think we must give their testimony some credence—and not only theirs, but the enormous body of comparable literature to be found elsewhere in northern and western Europe.

My argument for a premarital sexual revolution rests thus upon three supports, each rather spindly in itself, but together sufficient to maintain the case. (1) There is the evidence of the illegitimacy ratio alone, which is a rather ambiguous demographic indicator. (2) There is the evidence of premarital pregnancy, the percentage of first children born within eight months of marriage, which in itself is an indicator of little else than sexual behavior within courtship. (3) There is the evidence of middle-class observers who sensed the groundswell to be changing in popular life, but whose testimony, alone, might reflect little more than the libidinal preoccupations of the observers themselves. Taken all together, these three indicators point to a massive change in premarital sexual morality in the years 1750–1850.

Were Young People Ever Really Continent Before Marriage?

If illegitimacy was only 2 or 3 percent in traditional society, the implication is that young people stayed chaste before marriage, or at least before engagement. And because the average marriage age was in the late twenties—indeed, more likely the early thirties for the eldest sons of largeholding peasants—we are obliged to conclude that men and women abstained from intercourse for ten to fifteen years or more after puberty. Can that be right? modern people ask themselves. Is it possible to imagine a population the great majority of whom have not experienced coitus before their lives are more than half over? Here we thought the sex drive a universal constant, and sexuality in most times and places the rough mirror of what we know today! If my logic holds up, and if unmarried people in ages past did indeed abstain from intercourse until their late marriages, some of the conventional wisdom on the social dimensions of human sexuality will require recasting.

Or will it? Eroticism embraces more than just genital intercourse between the sexes. People who do not have coitus on the standard model can still experience a rich libidinal life. So even if young adults in times past did not have plain old straight-up-and-down sex before marriage at age twenty, perhaps they found other ways of relieving their sexual longings and giving life to their erotic fantasies. Jean-Louis Flandrin has recently argued that, even if the adolescents of traditional France did not make love before marriage (and he is unwilling to concede this), they used masturbation and homoerotic sexual contacts of various kinds—possibly bestiality, possibly affairs with married women as well—to get through the long, fallow years. The sex drive, for Flandrin, is a universal constant. And if eroticism doesn't surface in one way, it will in another.[43]

We pause for a moment, therefore, to consider these young

peasant lads in their late teens, presumably fully informed about the facts of life but faced with a ten-year wait before marriage. If they didn't make love with their sweethearts, what did they do with them? And if they didn't even have sweethearts (their parents having not yet accorded permission for an engagement), what did they do in general? I shall very tentatively advance the argument that Flandrin is wrong, that before 1750 the lives of most young people were resolutely unerotic, and that traditional society succeeded quite effectively in suppressing (sublimating, if you prefer) the sex drives of the unmarried.

It seems to me unlikely that masturbation, for example, was practiced on a wide scale before the premarital sexual revolution. Flandrin, relying upon clerical sources, conjures up the image of a nation of frantic masturbators.[44] But in the medical and ethnographic sources, a different image emerges: a rural society premaritally almost as pure as the driven snow. The keystone of this position is, alas, the argument of silence. Before 1750, masturbation is rarely mentioned in nonclerical sources. After that date a wave of concern about "solitary practices" rolls across the medical and pedagogical literature. Because the doctors and teachers suddenly became so upset about young men and women masturbating, may we conclude that only at that point did youth in fact begin doing so?

The protests in the medical literature are certainly not conclusive. The regular local doctors who discuss masturbation at all do so in passing, usually in veiled allusions that leave the reader in doubt about exactly what is going on. What are we to make, for example, of Amien's Dr. Maret, who in 1772 discerned an increase in "premature pleasures" among boys, "which rendered their practitioners incapable of ever becoming useful to society," and in "secret desires" among girls as well, "who in seeking on their own to quench them, merely redouble the fire."[45] What was happening in eighteenth-century Chambéry to make its local doctor expostulate against the boarding homes which had made masturbation "so frequent among our own youth and in general everywhere"?[46] The specialized literature on the horrors of masturbation, from Simon-André Tissot's *Onania* (1758) onwards, has a sort of crackbrained quality that discredits its authors as reliable judges of change over time. Yet the silence that prevailed beforehand (the English pamphlet *Onania*, ca. 1710, was actually the first widely read tract) would indicate that, in the late eighteenth-century flood of literature, something must have been moving in the real world. That is unless we are to accept the hypothesis of a collective hysteria in the fantasy life of doctors.[47]

More intriguing are the differentials in the incidence of masturbation that these various writers believed they were singling out. For if it was the "modern" sectors that offered the leading edge of adolescent eroticism, we may at least seriously entertain the hypothesis that as more and more people became involved with urban life or secondary education, the incidence of masturbation increased correspondingly. Writers were convinced that urban boys masturbated earlier and more often than rural boys. "In the countryside, where I lived for thirteen years, I never heard from the parents or thought from my observation of the children themselves that there need be cause for alarm. It's my impression that this vice is extremely rare in the villages." The anonymous "respected cleric," whose letter Christian Salzmann published in 1787, explained that rural mores were so pure because rural lads were raised with such rigor, ate so little, and had to do hard farm work "even in school years," and because stimulation and temptation were so lacking.[48] Even a century later German observers were still amazed at the apparent lack of interest in autoeroticism among peasant youth. It was pronounced by a doctor in the Allgäu as "extremely rare. As a grammar-schooler in the countryside I never heard a word about it. Nobody talked about it, not even the adults. I learned about the art only when I went off to school."[49]

The Allgäu's Doctor Grassl has given us a clue about the second important social differential in masturbation: those who attended secondary school versus those who did not. A red thread in the antimasturbation literature of the late eighteenth century was how the vice proliferates among school lads. According to Salzmann's correspondents, they were doing it under their long coats, beneath their desks, behind the stoves, about the toilets. Of 94 pupils in one school, forty-nine confessed to masturbating, most of them ages ten to thirteen. In other schools "everyone" was said to be masturbating, some of them so taken with the vice as to persist even with Tissot's book in hand! What's worse, the pupils would assemble to masturbate in unison. "When I once visited one of my older school comrades, I found a small group of his friends gathered together, who very soon steered the conversation towards this disgusting subject, the usual object of their discourse. But things didn't remain there, and instead, after heating up their imaginations with the most indecent pictures and stories, they began to unite these immoral images with actual physical sensations. . . . As soon as they noticed my own inexperience in these horrors and identified my hesitation about following their godless example, they began to ridicule me and to declare me unworthy of their company."[50]

Self-defilement was, indeed cutting down the very flower of the nation itself: the cadets in the military academies. Dr. Guillaume Daignan in 1786 related this tale of a young man's road to ruin:[51]

Joining his uncle, captain in a regiment of four battalions, he was supposed to take up the first available post. He was very well received by his numerous comrades and soon imitated all their follies, which in this profession are not always in the direction of prudence and sagacity. He had been very well raised, polite and agreeable. These qualities, which should have preserved him from seduction, served only to draw him in all the more, because of his intimacy with his mates. Remorse was not delayed. First, he experienced violent cramps whenever he excited himself to such acts [one contrasts the elegance of these French accounts with their maddening indirectness] which his whole mode of thinking should have made him detest, if he had not been swayed by the example of the multitude. . . . I encouraged him to break completely with this detestable habit, and he assured me that he wished to do so all the more because he felt not at all tempted by it. But he didn't know how to avoid the occasions. Having as yet no functions to fulfill, he could scarcely sequester himself from his comrades without appearing unusual. Upon learning that this variety of orgy took place only in the evening, I counseled him to absent himself on the pretext of a migraine headache. The excuse worked for a time, but the damage was already done. The cramps returned frequently. . . . And sure enough, the lad's health turned out to be permanently ruined, a "nervous degenerate, deprived of the sweetness of life and the charms of sociability."

The final social line across which the incidence of masturbation seems to have varied was class: middle-class youth manipulated themselves earlier and more frequently than did lower-class ones.

With the phenomenon in general on the increase, it was especially the leaders of tomorrow who invited ruin upon themselves by self-manipulation, often instructed in the devilish art by servants. But as for the boys of the "lower orders," even if they were a bit rough and undisciplined, they nonetheless knew to keep themselves from defilement when "the passion for certain pleasures rears itself in their breasts and separates the wheat from the chaff."[52] Which means simply that while middle-class Viennese youths were off in their rooms with dirty novels, lower-class lads had already started making out. Which is what the general argument of this book leads us to expect.

The evidence for an increase in the frequency of masturbation late in the eighteenth century is not exactly irrefutable: a burst of hysteria on the subject from doctors and educators, combined with reasoning which says that if the phenomenon was to be encountered chiefly among urbanites, middle classes, and secondary-school youth, it must have increased as these groups expanded. But more than that, about this particular domain of *la vie intime*, we may never know.

What about "petting"? Even if young folks didn't actually have premarital intercourse before 1750, perhaps they made out pretty heavily? Or, as with masturbation, did nongenital sexual activity become commonplace in courtship only during the eighteenth century? For large parts of Europe we simply have no answers to these questions, but in one area at least—Scandinavia—information on "collective nightcourting" permits us to zero in on the pre-engaged couple and see exactly what they were doing. Nightcourting, or what was known in North America as "bundling," put a young man and woman in an intimate situation. The historian then must ask: to what extent did the couple take advantage of this privacy for love play, and how did their hesitancy to violate community norms about nightcourting change over time?

First, a word about how nightcourting functioned in Sweden and Finland.[53] On Saturday nights a group of youths, aged perhaps seventeen to twenty-five, would gather in the village square, have a drink or two, tell a couple of dirty jokes, and then set off together on the rounds of the girls' houses. Arriving before an outlying storeroom or the loft of the main house (where, the reader will remember, Scandinavian girls slept), they would recite various "endeavor" rhymes, prescribed by tradition, trying to persuade the girl to open the door to the boy they had selected to spend the night with her. Or perhaps custom demanded that she open to them collectively, with the negotiating over exactly who, if anyone, would stop off with her being done as they all milled about her bed. Then the group, minus one member, would proceed to the next house, losing yet another boy to its occupant, and so on until all its members had been deposited at the homes of various girls. Then the remaining two boys might well spend the night at the home of the last girl on the list.

Once inside, the boy would remove his coat, hat, and shoes before getting into bed with the girl. If it were his first visit, he would probably spend the night atop the covers; if he knew her well, he would climb beneath the covers, yet retain socks and certainly shirt and pants. Only if the couple had informally agreed upon an engagement would he take off all his clothes and make love to her.

In the absence of an engagement, little intimacy was permitted. They would lie in bed, her head atop his outstretched arm, or perhaps with arms wrapped about each other, yet no skin touching. Custom required that he not fall asleep, and if his arm did so (that heavy weight upon it and all), he was permitted to change sides with her, observing rules of propriety. Now, this lying together was not completely without eroticism, for tradition permitted that she kiss his neck, perhaps, or that they rub bodies together. Yet the unengaged couple's legs were not to touch, and under no circumstances was coitus permitted. The real purpose of the visit was not sex but conversation, permitting the participants to make some personal assessment of a series of potential partners.

For couples who got carried away there were sanctions. Should the group return and discover the boy had removed more than the minimum, the offending article of clothing would be displayed, and he would be chased out. For girls who became intimate or had intercourse with more than one lad, group sanctions were rigorous: exclusion from nightcourting and public humiliations of various kinds.

The logic of the nightcourting system was a balancing of the freedom of individuals to get acquainted with the community's need for sexual probity. In theory, every Saturday night of the season a different boy would see a different girl, until all the candidates in the community had got to know one another. So girls might have forty or fifty boys in their beds before deciding on a husband. The group arranged the mechanics of pairing off; the group supervised the proceedings in bed, to guarantee that individuals were not transported by passion into making love before the parents had approved the match or before a farmstead was available in which to set up house. But once a couple had decided for each other, all was permitted.[54] Thereafter the young man would stop off only at that house, if indeed he still bothered to go out with the group at all. And he would stay to have breakfast with the parents in the morning, rather than stealing away in the dawn. But until the engagement was sealed, the participants behaved decorously.

What erotic contact did take place within the nightcourting system (before engagement), happened in the presence of other people. In Sweden, if a girl were reluctant to take on a boy for the night, the group might entwine the couple's arms about each other. (When boys and girls bedded down in the hay together at big weddings, a number of couples were together in the same loft; nonengaged couples did not sneak off to the woods.) The presence of a third person in the girl's bedchamber was considered quite acceptable —typically one of the boy's buddies or the girl's sister—because the couple had no need of sexual privacy.

This, then, was the traditional nightcourting system, as practiced in Scandinavia and parts of Germany until perhaps the mid-nineteenth century:[55] a host of community norms surrounding the process of getting acquainted; all kinds of ritual sayings for approaching the girl and then later for proposing marriage; and ruthless peer-group discipline against those who violated the rules by courting on their own or being promiscuous. If the scholars who have studied this are right, an absolute minimum of actively erotic contact between the sexes occurred: no kissing on the mouth, no rubbing the genitals against the other person's body, and—heaven forbid—no mutual masturbation among the nonengaged.

With time this system collapsed; and when it did, all kinds of erotic practices rushed across the shattered community defenses. In Sweden the appearance of such men in the village as loggers, men who were not part of the system and who could remove themselves without having to marry the impregnated locals, brought it to an end.[56] In Finland the bicycle gave individuals sufficient mobility to break off from the group, expand their wooing radiuses, and travel swiftly through the cold night.[57] Other factors were doubtlessly at work as well. For present purposes, however, it suffices to note that sex play did come to occupy the empty shell of the old nightcourting system, as evidenced by the upsurges of illegitimacy toward the end of the nineteenth century wherever it was practiced.

In other kinds of contacts between the sexes in Sweden and Finland, eroticism also took over. Finnish youth, for example, long played a wide variety of ritual games, such as folk dramas in which the clearing of land, the building of boats, or the hauling in of fish was acted out. Innocent folkloric practices. . . . but in the nineteenth century these traditional games were pushed out by a host of sexual and mating games, in which couples ended up together under blankets, inspecting each others' bodies ("Doctor, I have this . . ."), whipping each other's palms, playing marriage, or whatever. "Sexuality was referred to quite openly," we are assured.[58] So, ultimately, Finnish rural courtship did become sexualized, and all those erotic impulses that the traditional courtship system had so effectively repressed were given free rein. But that happened only late in time.

An important aside: even though erotic play was a relatively recent development in Scandinavia, premarital intercourse had gone on there since time out of mind. A couple's sexual life customarily began before marriage. But this was coitus for people who were already engaged, who were absolutely certain they would marry each other, and for whom promiscuity would have been as unthinkable as anal intercourse. In fact Scandinavian "marriage" began with engagement, and before the seventeenth century the popular classes were close to indifferent towards nuptials in church. I suspect, however, that a recent student of current premarital practices in Denmark has been too hasty in writing, of the eighteenth century, "Young people continued to live together as they had done in the Middle Ages and as they do still today."[59] The difference here is that youths in the 1970s may change sex partners once or twice before marriage, coitus begins considerably before engagement, and a higher proportion of couples are premaritally active than in any previous era. At any given time, the custom of betrothal license makes Scandinavia quite different from France or Ireland. But Scandinavia has undergone the same historical evolution towards liberality.

What about France, Germany, and England? What kind of pre-engagement erotic contacts between the sexes took place there? The curtain of ignorance parts for a moment upon the west of France— specifically, a corner of the department of the Vendée called the *Marais*, where there prevailed, towards the beginning of the First World War, a curious erotic practice called *maraichinage*, the essence of which was doing what we used to call in Iowa—appropriately— "French kissing" in public. The technical term for such contact is the intrabuccal embrace, in which the partners touch tongues, or put their tongues inside each other's mouths. The local peculiarity of the *marais* was to practice this embrace openly, perhaps in the back rooms of taverns, perhaps lying upon the grass on Sunday afternoons, genteely secluded from direct observation by the girl's large black umbrella. The custom's foremost student, Dr. Marcel Baudouin, assures us that people often passed beyond intra-oscular embraces to mutual masturbation, with the aid of specially constructed clothing (skirt and pants "pockets" without bottoms, and the like). Once events reached this stage, the two were already affianced. Yet among the mere French kissers, no kind of permanent relationship was required at all, and partners might freely change.

This account centers on the *belle époque*, yet Baudouin argues that the custom had existed since time immemorial, going back to the lost island of Atlantis. If he is right (!), my argument adducing that there was no erotic contact among courting peasants before they became engaged would suffer a setback. Yet Baudouin is unable to document intrabuccal kissing before the 1880s, and my conviction is that we have instead in *le maraichinage* a colorful local variant of the sexual revolution of the nineteenth century.[60] The Vendée's illegitimacy rate was quite low early in the century, which strikes me as incompatible with a practice as erotically explosive as deep kissing. Then, in the period 1876–1896, Vendée's illegitimacy suddenly leaps upwards, suggesting that only then was *le maraichinage* being diffused.[61]

There is a final way out for those who insist that youths did not remain premaritally chaste in traditional society: namely, to say that the youths resorted to prostitutes, especially to some village-model "loose woman." Were prostitutes indeed available to these young lads, permitting them to relieve sexual tensions without defiling the local beauties? The fact that systematic sanctions against loose women existed in local folkways suggests that the village prostitute, or the "promiscuous" young woman, paid or not, did exist. There was, for example, the fellow who went with Marie Francoise Fourre to a cafe in Cambrai in 1719. He said he wanted to sleep with her, but she replied that she "had a husband to keep her warm at night." So he then offered to pay her a crown (*une pistolle*). She refused. But how would the idea have come into his head in the first place—a nice girl like Marie and all—unless the concept of prostitution had been clearly established in local culture.[62] In Badenese villages, a local loose woman would commonly find a bale of straw strewn between the door of her house and the stall of the village pastor.[63] In the small French town of Dôle, a doctor complained about a local youth visiting the prostitutes, but suggested that the phenomenon was a recent one.[64] It is not clear, from Scandinavian nightcourting accounts, whether public humiliation of "promiscuous" women, such as nailing their scarves to the church door, was directed merely against those who slept with more than one man, or against semiprofessionals. (The Lutheran Church did not tolerate prostitution as such in small-town Scandinavia.) Unfortunately, the considerable historical literature on prostitution concerns mainly the large cities and focuses upon the prostitutes' own backgrounds rather than the composition of their clientele. We know, of course, that in seventeenth-century Paris, Grenoble, Berlin, and other big cities, organized prostitution was to be found.[65] But was it equally present in the heartland of traditional society, in the small town and village? The night closes in again over our pathetically inadequate knowledge; but in contemplating a map of illegitimacy in Europe towards 1900,[66] I find simply implausible the explanation that bastardy was low—across vast reaches of inland

Spain and central France, all of Ireland, and most of the British Isles—because youths in these places had prostitutes available and so could leave the local women in purity. I believe the local lads themselves remained in purity, for a long time.

The Second Sexual Revolution

There are really three things to keep in mind about sex-before-marriage in the twentieth century: (1) premarital intercourse is now much commoner than in any era since the Middle Ages; (2) although the period 1900–1950 is thoroughly "modern" in comparison with past centuries, little change took place within these years; and (3) the 1960s and early 1970s have witnessed what amounts to a second premarital sexual revolution (the first having occurred at the end of the eighteenth century).

Some of this news may come as a shock. Many people have considered any period before World War II "traditional." Since part of this book's message is that truly traditional society had broken up by 1850, we might wish to find another expression for the days of our grandfathers; in sexual behavior they were indeed much like our fathers. Other people have drifted into the habit of seeing 1900 as the beginning of the end for western society, the teeter-point of a spectacular Spenglerian collapse of values and morals. Yet this dating of change is equally inappropriate, because in sexual relations between young men and women little was altered. For the general populace, the burial of chastity before marriage commenced in 1750, not 1900. A final group of observers, peopled heavily by worldly-wise academics, should (if what I say is right), stop pooh-poohing the great shifts in adolescent sexuality of the 1960s as an optical illusion or an unimportant ripple in the tide of history.[67] Rather, we are now living through a transformation of sexual behavior whose proportions are dramatic and whose implications will long be felt.

What evidence is there that premarital intercourse stayed at a constantly high level in the period 1900 to 1950? There were, for one thing, few changes in premarital pregnancy—that is, in the proportion

108

of legitimate children born within eight months of marriage. Even in our days this is a fairly sensitive indicator of levels of intercourse, because engaged women (who are the chief contributors) do not practice contraception as efficiently as women who are not engaged (and who thus cannot rely upon honor-saving marriages to cover slip-ups). In the United States there was a seven percent chance that a white woman married in 1900–1909 would already be pregnant as she advanced to the altar; in 1945–1949 there was a ten percent chance—not a big change.[68] In Sweden in 1911, a one-in-three likelihood existed that a woman would already be pregnant when she married; this was the same as in 1948.[69] And in German industrial cities before World War I, a third to a half of all marriages began with the bride pregnant. Thirty years later the same state of affairs persisted.[70] In many cases prebridal pregnancy was higher at the end of the eighteenth century than in the middle of the twentieth, because contraception outside wedlock had increased substantially in the intervening 150 years.

Keep in mind that in the years 1900–1940, illegitimacy fell off precipitously in every country. A group of us have already described this decline in another publication,* and I see little reason to rehearse the statistics and graphs here. But after an extensive technical analysis, much too tedious to reproduce in these pages, we concluded that illegitimacy had decreased not because there was less intercourse but because people were practicing contraception more often.[71]

Finally, a number of sociological surveys have been conducted for the period 1900–1950 on the incidence of intercourse before marriage. Alfred Kinsey's was the most famous, but others also exist. Do they show significant increases in premarital sex in the first half of the century? The answer is ambiguous. In the United States such statistics illuminate only a fairly specialized population: the educated middle class. And in France, the only other country for which survey data over time are available, some liberalization took place, but only in the years after 1940.

Kinsey saw the 1920s as the major turning point in the United States. Women in his sample who were born in 1900–1910, and who therefore had come of age after the First World War, experienced

* "Decline of Non-Marital Fertility in Europe," *op. cit.*

premarital intercourse more than women born before 1900. He discovered, however, no later changes in premarital intercourse levels. (For men he found no trends.) So, according to Kinsey, America passed through its sexual revolution in the Roaring Twenties, thereafter reaching a high but stable rate.[72]

The second part of Kinsey's conclusion is congenial to my analysis; the first part is not. Things did level off after the 1920s, but they began considerably before then, if my argument is correct. Defects in the construction of Kinsey's sample appear to save the Shorter Hypothesis. Kinsey relied heavily upon volunteers—and what kind of people would answer questions like *that*, one interjects—and overrepresented the university-educated middle classes in his survey.[73] What probably happened was that Kinsey got hold of the very last social group to participate in a liberalization of premarital morality: the daughters of the American midwestern bourgeoisie. If illegitimacy and premarital pregnancy statistics are any guide at all to *popular* behavior, a majority of the population had lurched towards liberality considerably before the 1920s, probably at some as yet unspecified point in the nineteenth century.[74] After the 1920s, the rates of premarital intercourse within this population of the daughters of small businessmen and insurance salesmen leveled off, doubtless as did everyone else's.[75]

If Kinsey was the principal scholar to report change over time before 1960, a number of other researchers have tried to get pictures of sexual behavior at given moments by interviewing college students. By lining up this series of "snapshots" we should be able to discern trends—on the risky assumption that the surveys were reliably done and the populations comparable. But no trends emerge. Of the coeds one scholar interviewed in 1929, 11 percent reported themselves sexually active. Of those another researcher interviewed in the same year 35 percent testified to the same. While 47 percent of the college and high school girls interviewed in 1953 declared themselves nonvirginal, only 14 percent of the college students interviewed in 1959 said they had already "made love," or words to that effect. These sample populations are, in short, too varied from one interview to the next; the findings are unstable; the controls on class, urbanity, region, or whatever are insufficient. The results are not very dependable, and in no event do they point to an increase in premarital intercourse even among university women in the 1930s, 1940s, and 1950s. They say nothing about the great masses of other people living in the real world.[76]

The premarital sex lives of French women changed somewhat more rapidly in the twentieth century than did those of American women. Here are the results of two public opinion polls, one on sexual behavior and another on premarital pregnancies.[77] The parallels are striking:

TIME IN WHICH WOMEN REACHED MATURITY	DID YOU HAVE INTERCOURSE BEFORE MARRIAGE? (PERCENT ANSWERING "YES")		PERCENT OF ALL MARRIAGES IN WHICH CHILDREN WERE BORN WITHIN SEVEN MONTHS
	IFOP POLL	"SIMON" POLL	
1925–29	—	—	12
1930–34	15	} 11	13
1935–39	20		13
1940–44	32		17
1945–49	33	} 33	17
1950–54	38		19
1955–59	37		19
1960–69	—	55	19 (1960–61)

Between 1925 and 1959, with every advance in the French Institute of Public Opinion's (IFOP) nonvirginity series, there was an advance in premarital pregnancy. The first two years of premarital conception in the 1960s, however, fail to reflect the large increase in sexual activity, probably because by this time contraception had broken the link between intercourse and impregnation. Most interesting in the above table is the enormous leap in intercourse during the 1960s, with over half of all women having sex before marriage—a fivefold increase over those who spent their twenties in the Depression years.

Thus various kinds of data give us a tentative sexual portrait of young people in the first five decades of the twentieth century. They indicate a fairly high exposure to premarital sex as early as the beginning of the century, as well as a slow rise in coital experience for women. But only the 1960s would see major discontinuities in the erotic life of the average unmarried woman. One of the little ironies of modern demography is that precisely at the time when sophisticated contraceptive information was being diffused, illegitimacy and premarital pregnancy rates began to shoot upward. So rapid was the sexual activation of the unmarried in the 1960s that not even the pill, not even the eased access to abortion and the machines that sold condoms in filling-station toilets, could lower the soaring curves of out-of-wedlock conception. In the 1950s in some countries, and in the 60s virtually everywhere in the West, premarital pregnancy took a new upturn, the likes of which had not been witnessed since 1800. Late in the 1960s, the spread of the pill finally did lower these surging levels of pregnancy. But until the pill began its work, the revolution in postwar sexual behavior would leave unmistakable pathmarks in the official demographic statistics.

Virtually every Western country saw major rises in illegitimacy after the Second World War. Australia's illegitimacy rate, for example, increased by seven "points," from 12 births per 1000 unmarried women in 1950 to 19 in 1965. England's rate doubled from 10 to 20 per 1000. Swedish illegitimacy climbed from 20 to 28. Only in West Germany, France, and Finland was the likelihood of the average woman's having an illegitimate child *not* significantly higher in 1965 than in 1950. And in France, a new rise in bastardy began after 1965.[78]

In the United States we can identify some of the dynamics of these huge leaps. One factor partly responsible for the rapid postwar rise in American illegitimacy was an improvement in the health of the average woman, as better diet and a decline in venereal disease (especially among blacks) made it easier for her to become pregnant. But as American illegitimacy continued to soar, increasing every year from 1961 to 1968 (the last year for which data are available), it became clear that other factors were operating as well, most notably an increase in intercourse.[79] In the mid–1960s, contraception and abortion would finally reduce illegitimacy among older unmarried women. But the teenage rate has continued to climb. Over half the illegitimate births in the United States are now produced by adolescents. And because teenagers are so naive about contraception, they remain the only group whose sexual activity we can follow with the contrails of illegitimacy.[80]

Premarital pregnancy also increased dramatically between the end

of the Second World War and the mid–1960s. Other countries underwent the experience of France that we discussed a moment ago. In
Switzerland, a bride's chances of being pregnant on her wedding day
increased from 24 percent in 1955 to 29 percent in 1965; in the
Netherlands from 17 to 19; in England from 13 to 20. Indeed, in
the United States her risk of premarital pregnancy actually *doubled*
between the mid-1940s and mid-1960s.

With the contraceptive revolution after 1965, however, premarital
pregnancy everywhere began to drop. In no country except France
were 1970 levels above those of 1965; in Scandinavia, rates had been
cut almost in half (but Scandinavian illegitimacy had risen accordingly).[81] With the Pill, out-of-wedlock conception had ceased to be
a reliable indicator of sexual activity. But in the pre-pill period, which
is to say before 1965, illegitimacy and prenuptial pregnancy data point
to a major change in the sexual patterns of the average woman.

Surveys abound to confirm this increase in intercourse, if we may
assume the college students polled in the 1960s to be at all typical
of the general population. Unfortunately, almost no sociologists
thought to ask any group outside the university about its sexual
behavior, and the few investigations of representative cross-sections
that did occur failed to include different ages. Hence we can't get
directly at the matter of change over time.[82] Yet among university
students throughout Western society in the 1960s, virginity fell away
like the chrysalis about a butterfly.

———At Uppsala University in Sweden, the percent of women
who had "participated in intercourse" rose from 40 percent in 1960
to 65 percent in 1965, an annual increase of 5 percent. At church-
related schools the rise was even more stunning: 38 percent to 77
percent in one, 80 percent to 87 percent in another. The ceiling was
approaching.[83]

———Among Danish university women, the ceiling had in fact
been reached by 1968. In 1958, fully 40 percent of them declared
themselves yet virginal; ten years later, only 3 percent remained.[84]

———A series of surveys unearthed rapid increases in American
nonvirginity rates. Within a typical cross section of adolescent women
polled in 1971, almost half had had intercourse by age nineteen (compared with less than 20 percent in Kinsey's day).[85] Students had been

especially libertine. Intercourse experience had increased by 60 percent in universities that Vance Packard surveyed in the mid-1960s (almost half the female students non-virginal).[86] Another investigation, in which just over half of the women students as a whole were sexually experienced, distributed the classes as follows:[87]

Freshmen (women) non-virginal:	15–20 percent
Sophomores	30–35
Juniors	40–45
Seniors	50–60
Graduate students	60–70

Other writers found that coeds in 1968 made love much more often within the context of dating and going steady than they did in 1958.[88] One final flagstone in this pathway to Sodom was a survey that indicated a modest increase in sexual activity from 1958 to 1968 among women at a midwestern university (from 21 percent to 34), but that registered a *tripling* of intercourse among women at an anonymous western Mormon university (from 10 to 32 percent).[89] Students everywhere were doing it more, having more fun, and feeling less guilty about it afterwards. (The survey data for various countries dutifully confirm these observations.) It remained for the Gallup Poll to expunge any remaining doubt that a sexual revolution was in progress: the percent of Americans who believe "it is wrong for people to have sex relations before marriage" fell from 68 percent in 1969 to 48 percent in 1973—a 20-point collapse in four years' time![90]

Here within English Canada, my adopted country, the sexual revolution has proceeded apace among university students. According to an unpublished survey of University of Toronto women, 68 percent had never made love in 1968 and only 62 percent by 1971, which works out to a 2 percent average annual increase in nonvirginity.[91] This was nothing like the Swedish church schools, of course.

If Jean-Louis Flandrin is right that premodern youth, kept by opprobrious parents and censorious communities from heterosexual intercourse, turned massively to masturbation, we should expect to find the incidence of adolescent autoeroticism dropping over time.

To the extent that young men and women started coitus, they should have abandoned their "solitary practices." If Flandrin is correct, the youth of the past should have given up mutual masturbation, oral–genital contacts, and sodomy—to which in theory they had had recourse in order to relieve tension—as genital intercourse with members of the opposite sex became available to them.

Now I, of course, believe that Flandrin is wrong. I believe that none of these things happened on other than an infinitesimal scale, in the Bad Old Days, and that it is only our modern times that have witnessed widespread autoeroticism and sexual experimentation among unmarried youth. Masturbation and polymorphous sexuality are the *creations* of modernization, rather than its victims.

The delineating of "periods" for the progress of masturbation and innovative sexual styles among the youth is impossible. We have nothing comparable to the demographic statistics that permit us to carve up the last four hundred years into neat half-centuries. We have already noted the sources' deafening silence on masturbation before 1750, and the display of medical censure thereafter. The only remaining question is whether it was late in the eighteenth century that high levels of masturbation and coital inventiveness were reached among the young, or in our own times. I opt for the latter. A multitude of postwar sociological surveys have turned up rates and kinds of premarital erotic activity that could simply not have existed, I am convinced, in the older world.

There is no doubt that masturbation was fairly extensive in the Europe of 1900. We may glean this from demands that the toilet walls be painted black and that boys be forced to take their hands from their pockets; and from the apparent casualness with which the lower orders treated the whole subject—for example, the young German worker who at the mid-morning break reclined upon his workbench and masturbated "without concealing himself in the least from the many younger people standing around."[92] In any event, autoeroticism among German workers had reached its maximum possible extension in the 1960s. Four fifths of the men masturbated by age fifteen and nine tenths by age twenty; in the case of women, one third by fifteen and nearly 60 percent by age twenty. Nor was such diffusion peculiar to the working class. German students, in fact, began a bit earlier in life, but women workers did it more than women students.[93]

Elsewhere in the 1960s, youthful masturbation was virtually universal for males, somewhat less so for women. Alfred Kinsey, for example, found that 80 percent of American men had begun masturbation by age fifteen, but only 20 percent of the women.[94] A 1964 study of Swedish high schools found that four fifths of the boys and one third of the girls masturbated.[95] Similar results turned up in a 1970 survey of a sample French population: three quarters of the men had masturbated, but only one fifth of the women. All were over twenty when asked, and some skeptics believe a number of the women lied.[96]

Such surveys uncovered small increases over a period of time in masturbation. In the Kinsey data, for instance, American women born after 1900 were 10 percent more likely to masturbate than women born earlier. And the above-mentioned French study learned that masturbation was more frequent among the more recent generations, especially among men.[97] Whether such snippets point to an ongoing twentieth-century trend towards autoeroticism is unclear; but it is manifest to me, in any event, that these staggering incidents did not occur in the small towns and villages of eighteenth-century France, Germany, or England.

Sexual styles among the unmarried have also changed with modernization. Of the many variations of erotic activity that men and women can undertake together, let us single out oral–genital contact. In societies that tabooed kissing, and where intertwining little fingers counted as a grand public display of passion,[98] I just don't believe that much embracing of one's partner's genitals and the like went on. Today, by way of contrast, Kinsey found that roughly a quarter of adolescent American men had experienced some variety of oral–genital contact. And while he did not make directly comparable data available for women, it appears that nearly half the unmarried females with substantial sexual experience "had attempted to stimulate the male genitalia orally," and that the percentage increased over time.[99] Nearly half of the teenage women polled among the German working classes in 1968 had taken part in oral–genital sex, 33 percent of them performing the active role. And 64 percent of the female students had experienced such activity. Interestingly, scores for men in both groups were lower.[100]

Finally, a third of the English adolescent girls in a mid-sixties survey had manually fondled a boy's genitals, and a higher proportion had themselves been fondled; but oral–genital contacts as such were very rare.[101] It appears that the distinguishing feature of England's unmarried is not oral sex but the insistence upon "whipping or spanking before petting or other intimacy;" for in one survey, 17 percent of British men expressed this preference, as opposed to 8 percent of the Americans and 5 percent of the fine young Canadians.[102]

It is inconceivable to me that things were like this in traditional times.

At this point, the serpent of social class rears its head briefly. There were significant differences from one class to another in the spread of illegitimacy, differences we shall continue to encounter in other domains of sentiment. The illegitimacy explosion and the premarital sexual revolution began first among the lower classes; it seized the middle classes only much later, and then in reduced measure.

When illegitimacy became rampant in eighteenth-century France, virtually the only women to get pregnant were domestic servants, laundresses, seamstresses, spinners, and other such proletarian creatures. Out-of-wedlock pregnancy simply did not happen to nice girls from good families; or if it did, almost none of them carried to term a live-born infant subsequently registered as illegitimate. Of the women who bore illegitimate children late in the century in the Artois village of Isbergues, for example, fourteen were the daughters of laborers, eight were spinners, four servants; for three the occupation was unknown.[103] So bastardy was not an affair even of the substantial peasantry. Among women pregnant out of wedlock in Lille during the eighteenth century, scarcely a single one came from the upper classes.[104] And in the 1820s a German doctor informs us explicitly that while working-class girls do not even regard premarital pregnancy as immoral, "bourgeois daughters are sharply opposed to this view. Here a virgin's undamaged reputation counts for a great deal; a moral false step dishonors her and her family, usually shattering her emotional security and happiness.[105] Among the 339 illegitimate mothers

117

whose occupations were known in several parishes of London during the 1850s, only three were "gentlewomen," and the largest share by far were domestic servants.[106] Example could be piled on example.[107] Old-regime illegitimacy struck almost exclusively the lower orders.

With time, however, the daughters of the middle classes were drawn in—not to the same extent as the proletarians, yet in rising proportions. Several late nineteenth-century German social surveys show more than traces of bourgeois bastardy; as, for example, in Dresden:[108]

Origins of women pregnant before marriage
in Dresden, 1890–94

worker	56
petty bourgeois	28
merchants, industrialists	10
artists, writers	3
high officials	3
Total	100 percent

The *propensity* of the average middle-class young woman to bear an illegitimate child, as well as the absolute number of such women, had probably also increased by the turn of the century. Proletarian industries such as textiles continued to have higher illegitimacy rates, but female white-collar employees in education, health, and office work did not follow all that far behind. In Baden during the 1890s, for example, the proletarians might have three or four births annually per 100 unmarried women, and the white-collar types perhaps one per 100.[109] None of these scattershot statistics replaces a good time series of illegitimacy rates, broken down by social class. But it seems undeniable that by 1900, intercourse had become a significant reality in the lives of unmarried, middle-class women, whereas a century earlier it was not.

In the contemporary world, premarital pregnancy and illegitimacy have reached very substantial proportions among the middle classes, although the lower classes continue to have higher rates. Countless statistics point to extensive white-collar sex before marriage; were it not for greater middle-class sophistication about contraception and abortion, the gap between the two social classes would probably by now have closed entirely.[110]

We shall see a similar pattern in the advent of other aspects of sentiment: one class begins the trend with a big headstart, and the other then follows later, at a lesser speed. With premarital sex it is the lower orders who kick things off, the middle classes who tiptoe behind. But with child care and a new fondness for the hearth's warm glow, as we shall see, the situation is reversed.

To conclude: the larger message of this barrage of statistics is the trend to liberation of the young from sexual controls imposed by the family and the surrounding community. Sexual activity has changed from a dangerous and marginal aspect of relations between the unmarried, to a central part of mating and dating. This unleashing of sexuality to destroy all competing passions (such as avarice or familial egoism) in the arena of courtship, occurred in two steps— two separate sexual revolutions.

First, there was the initial incursion of premarital intercourse into the lives of the unmarried, late in the eighteenth century. Before that time we could not say that any couple more than a step or two distant from the altar was close to coitus. After that date there was a good chance that engaged couples would begin having intercourse fairly early in their courtship; and with time, even couples who were not engaged but were simply going out on a casual basis would sleep together.

Second, there was the generalization of intercourse to encompass the majority of the unmarried after the mid-1950s. In the 1960s the chances were very high that young people who felt attached to each other would extend their relationship into the sexual domain. Even those who did not feel very attached would probably do so as well. The chances were good that they would advance their experimentation considerably beyond the "missionary position." As we shall see in a later chapter, the chances, finally, were overwhelming that if things did not go well in either the quantitative or the qualitative realm of sexuality in the 1960s the couple would dissolve and the dance of courtship would recommence with someone else. And *that* would have been unthinkable in times past.

CHAPTER FOUR

Romance

OF COURSE, if people have sex together, that doesn't necessarily mean they love each other. Courtship could have become sexualized without any changes in basic emotional ties. But that is not what, in fact, happened. At the same time that premarital erotic behavior was loosening up, a rush of sentiment swept over mating and dating, replacing familial and prudential considerations with "inclination," "affection," and finally "romance."

Property-oriented courtship had been possible only as long as the community intervened actively in mating. Left completely to their own devices, young people would never have chosen to behave in the "traditional" way, for sexual desire, physical attractiveness, and mutual sympathy tend inevitably to assert themselves. The young had to be *socialized* to act instrumentally in these matters, not just by their immediate families (many of whom were poor and had no patrimonies to protect through marriage) but by the entire surrounding community. Traditional courtship could work only in the context of the controls that the peer group and the larger adult society exerted upon the young.

The transformation of courtship from an instrumental to an expressive mode of behavior was to embody two features. One was the decision of young people themselves to replace a value system that emphasized allegiance to the chain of generations and responsibility to the community with a value system that exalted personal happiness and self-development. The other feature was the cutting of the strings by which the larger society had formerly made the couples do their little courtship dances, the ending of community controls upon young men and women trying to find each other. Now we'll start finding ourselves, they said. It was the wish to be free, to develop one's personality, and to realize one's personal ambitions that drew shut the curtains between private courtship and public behavior. Only when mating and dating had become "privatized," was sentiment able to take hold and romantic love to blossom forth.

For the larger narrative of family history, this transformation of courtship is both an element and an index. The sudden infusion of romance into courtship could not fail to leave a mark upon the mature couple. In short order, the arrival of true love outside the family would affect what happened within as well. That story we shall treat in Chapter 6. But the transformation of courtship *indexes* as well a larger transformation of intimate life. Once people disappear inside the house, their *vie intime* disappears to all intents and purposes from the historian's view. Whether the popular classes held hands before the evening fire and so on we just don't know, because they themselves didn't talk about it; and the literate middle-class observers on whom we so depend wouldn't have known about it either (the couple having stopped holding hands when the doctor came to call). Couples remain visible, however, as long as they are outside the home, wheeling and dealing with one another in public view, associating within the context of long-established, familiar institutions. We can see them arm in arm on Sunday evening walks in small German towns, and bicycling along the little lanes of rural France. Perhaps, then, there was a progressive spillover into marriage, so that by the time of our own era the couple would—in theory— behave romantically until the end of its days.

Traditional Courtship: Occasions for Getting Together

Under traditional courtship, all situations in which boys and girls met for the first time were monitored by some larger group. In some cases it was an organization of the youth themselves; in other cases it was the larger community. In either case there would be collective supervision. Young women simply did not encounter young men without other people around. Of the youth-controlled occasions, Sundays offered most. People from outlying farms would come into the village for church services or to sit about in the cafés; then, in the afternoon, encounters with the opposite sex commenced. One common format in German villages was the Sunday evening walk (*Abendmarkt*). The young people would pair off and parade up and down, singing until late in the night. Afterwards the couples might well go off and make out. But the community had monitored the selection process.[1]

For western France we have a somewhat clearer notion of the disposition of forces in these encounters. On Easter Monday after church, the youth of the district *marais de monts* (Vendée) would pour by train into its capital, Challans. The boys would roam about in bands, and the girls would align themselves along a wall, facing the street. "Who will turn up?" they asked themselves (according to the chronicler), "Mr. Right, or a creep?" Towards two o'clock the boys would start to collect in small clumps before the girls, their expressions studies in indifference. The battle lines would be drawn thusly:

Point of departure for meeting of young men and women in Challans-Ville, 1906.

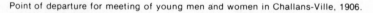
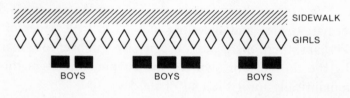

Figure 4-1

Marcel Baudouin, *Le Maraichinage*, Paris, 1932, p. 52.

"The girls divide themselves soon into six groups, and I count from left to right: nr.1, four; nr.2, three; nr.3, a girl standing alone; nr.4, four; nr.5, two; nr.6, two. . . . A boy, as we see below, is talking with group nr.4; two boys with nr. 5, and two with nr.6. It's evident that in a few seconds the girls of groups 5 and 6 will be provided for [*casée*] and have gotten what they wanted."

How the young men approach the young women.

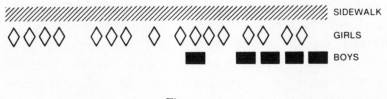

Figure 4-2

° Marcel Baudouin, *Le Maraichinage*, Paris, 1932, p. 56.

While Baudouin's somewhat martial account of proceedings comes embarrassingly late in time for my purposes (all the more so because these couples were going off to practice "French-kissing," *(le marai-chinage)*, the participants seem to have been animated by thoroughly traditional considerations. "I'm looking at three lads who pause some distance away to contemplate the exposition as a whole, discussing the qualities of the goods. One would think them already farmers, selecting on the cattle market a pair of oxen they need for their plows."[2] Whether the stock thus selected was just for the afternoon or for life is unclear from the account. In any case, what is important for our purpose is the public nature of the entire enterprise.

Elsewhere, rather than assembling in a central square, a group of fifteen or so young men would go from house to house to see the marriageable daughters. "Thus mutual likings are formed, and the fellow who intends to marry makes a choice."[3]

The need to do certain kinds of rural work collectively offered youth another occasion to get to know one another while remaining among themselves. In early modern Finland, for example, young people would assemble at night in the threshing sheds to brake and scutch flax, with boys and girls choosing partners and holding little competitions to see who finished first. Or they would meet in the saunas to dry the malt, or in the fields to burn in a tar pit, or in various outbuildings to watch over the boiling of laundry, the curing of sausage, the distilling of liquor, or the birthing of calves. All of these situations were "watches," for which people had to be present over long hours.[4]

Among the various occasions for acquaintanceship controlled by the youth themselves, the most important in large parts of Europe was nightcourting. Nightcourting, the reader will recall from the previous chapter, had two components: going collectively from house to house to see the girls (called *Kiltgang*), and stopping off one by one with an individual girl to spend the night chastely ("bundling"). Of interest here is how widespread the collective side of nightcourting was outside Scandinavia. In western Europe, collective visiting and monitoring were to be encountered mainly along the Baltic coast, Germany's North Sea coast, and in German-speaking Alpine regions. In France there was virtually no group night visiting, but local youth would organize themselves for a number of ends to be later discussed, one of which was courting. Formal organizations of young men (including not just adolescents but older bachelors as well) would establish themselves with a "captain" at their head and with enforced dues. (Lads who didn't pay up weren't permitted to go courting at night.) In general, however, the further one travels westward from Germany, the more courtship is supervised by the community as a whole, rather than by the youth in particular.[5]

Intriguing though such youth-controlled institutions for acquaintanceship may be, those run by the village as a whole loomed larger in the experience of the typical adolescent. Now, by the "village" I do not mean that the community council actually convoked the young folks and supervised their pairing off. I mean merely that persons of all ages and conditions were present when acquaintanceship was in progress, observing what transpired and ensuring—through gossip, scorn, and advice—that the youth did as they were expected.

For France and Germany, the principal community-run arenas of courtship were work evenings, the *veillées*.* As I sit at my typewriter in Toronto it is hard for me to imagine anything more foreign to the modern, urban experience, or at least to the world I live in. The French expression "veillée" (its German counterpart is

* Pronounced "vay-yay."

124

Spinnstube or *Rockenstube*) means simply an evening's working bee for spinning, knitting, or sewing, and in my North American frame of reference that conjures up the image of a rural barn dance, with lads and lasses in checked gingham do-si-doing. But for the world we have lost, different images are appropriate. We encounter a peasantry who lived closely enough together to share three or four evenings a week and, in so doing, make the private destinies of its members everybody's business. These gatherings were an integral part of popular life in almost every part of continental Europe, although less so in England (which is why we don't really have a good corresponding English term for these evening "bees."

In the veillée, women from the surrounding farms, or from houses in the village, would gather at eveningtime in someone's barn to spin or sew. There were many variants: sometimes the men would come, sometimes not. Often there would be dancing or some form of recreation at the end, but not invariably. Sometimes the veillée season would begin with All Saints' Day on November 1 and sometimes not until Saint-Catherine's Day on November 25. The veillée season might conclude in mid-January after Epiphany, or perhaps not until the carnival season in March. The evening might be over at nine, the women trooping home early to bed in their cold houses (or more likely, stables); or it might last until twelve—indeed to the wee hours if dancing and merriment were involved. So completely was the veillée woven into the fabric of popular life that it will occupy us at a number of points in this book. But what concerns us here is how the skeins of courtship wound about it.[6]

The veillée facilitated the operations of mating by bringing together marriageable girls. Groups of five or six boys would go from barn to barn, looking over what was available in each and then making tentative approaches.[7] All kinds of ritual procedures existed for these preliminary negotiations. The girl might drop her distaff to see who would scramble to pick it up. Finnish girls who wanted to be courted would wear empty knife sheaths, and boys who wanted to get things going were supposed to stick in their knives.[8]

One can imagine the attentiveness with which others in the barn followed these maneuvers. The first pairings were bathed in publicity, as in the Maconnais, where the suitors found themselves

". . . a little embarrassed by the presence of so many people and by the jokes of which they were sometimes the butt. Courage to exchange a few low, tender words would come only when the general conversation became very noisy and animated, permitting them to spend a moment unobserved." Now at this point they weren't necessarily engaged, not being yet of age. But in the setting of the veillée, every subsequent step toward the altar was minutely observed: the approach to the girl's parents through an intermediary, the wooing of the bride-to-be. . . . "The whole village was informed of the ups and downs of the suitor's offer, of the girl's attitude, of the behavior of the parents, so that once the outcome was known nobody was surprised. And the bitterness was all the more galling when, should the suitor finally be rejected, everyone knew he had been 'given the flush' (avait reçu son chaudron)."[9]

How did things actually go between the couple at the veillée? Decorously, in rural communes of northern France. In the evening perhaps ten women would get together in some locale rented for the purpose. All would bring along chairs, and the daughters would share theirs with their boyfriends. "The young girls have their pockets filled with nuts, which they hand out or let be taken."[10] In Savoy, people told stories in the work evenings, or the young women sang, with "the hilarity increased by the presence of the young men. It's in the veillées that normally the first attachments are formed." (The author added that in cities and small towns, card games were taking the place of these working bees.) The evening would end with a dance or two.[11] In western France, after several hours of subtle negotiation to see who one's admirers were, and after the participants had chilled themselves with tales of ghosts and werewolves, there would be gavottes and minuets and the branle of Poitou. The girls would dance to the point of exhaustion, and then presumably go home with their mothers.[12]

These evening work bees were ostensibly for purposes such as the saving of precious firewood by congregating in a barn, the people profiting both from one another's warmth and that of the animals and the steaming manure. And to be sure, throughout the evening, womens' hands were busy spinning wool or knitting socks. But the supervision of courtship, the submission of youthful friendships and inclinations to the eyes of the older women, was not the least of these functions. In some parts of France, indeed, veillées were held expressly by people who had daughters to marry, and the "fiddle or the fife which carried far into the night" was beating the time of the courtship dance.[13] The veillée permitted the community to monitor the "formation" of the couple; and when individual young men and women finally refused to subject their intimate lives to this kind of community supervision, the institution fell into desuetude.[14]

Other forms of the veillée were to be found outside of France; and although the literature is meager on how things worked before the nineteenth century brought its great changes, we do have hints. The Finnish veillée incorporated a stronger component of play and dancing. It also permitted the participants to pass the entire night in whatever house (not barn) they happened to be gathered, for the rigors of the Finnish winter made homeward journeys at 11 P.M. uninviting. In Russia, the partners in such overnight stays were chosen by lot.[15] Swiss veillées appear to have been controlled more by the youth than the community, and despite repeated efforts of the Protestant Church at suppression, peasant youngsters continued to use spinning as an excuse for courting and racing about at night. To what extent older people were present at these occasions is unclear.[16] So the French form of the veillée comes across in a European context as more domesticated, with the passions of the youth more bridled by the community. Yet everywhere there is a standard net of mothers spinning woolen yarn to enmesh youthful libidos. That is an expressly "traditional" arrangement for putting work into the service of repression.

A second arena for acquaintanceship which the community as a whole oversaw was dancing. Although the great explosion of popular enthusiasm for the dance would not come until the nineteenth century, even in traditional society numerous occasions presented themselves; and the youth who participated were closely watched. In Göttingen, for instance, it was illegal for girls who had not yet been confirmed (that is, around the age of sixteen) to attend dances unaccompanied by their mothers.[17] And although French girls were permitted to visit the local café or tavern for afternoon dances, those who went in the evenings would go with their mothers, who knew the score. The mothers would align themselves along the walls of the hall "like a string of onions," while the courters and courted dueled with each other on the dance floor. "And when, towards 11 or midnight, the modest *soirée dansante* concluded, the village scolds all riveted their attention upon who would pair with whom in the darkness on the homeward trek behind the carts of watchful mothers. The hopeful young man arrived finally, after numerous calculated delays, at the girl's home with his arm about her waist; and the gossips later strained to know if he were sent away without further ado, or indeed if things were sufficiently advanced for him to be invited in for a nightcap, a customary offering to a suitor one wanted to encourage. . . ."[18] The point is that there was little opportunity for girls to fool around with uncouth young men.

What happened in the Ardennes shows the extent to which these dances were part of larger networks of organization. On the evening of the annual festival the boys would go from house to house "with a huge basket filled with ribbons of all different colors." Each girl got one, "which floated elegantly upon her left shoulder, like dainty wings." These ribbons were the admission tickets to the following day's dancing; one can imagine with what attentiveness the proceedings were followed and how carefully they had been prepared. And there's more: on the day after the big dance, it was the girls' turn to invite the boys. In dancing that lasted from morning till evening, they were able to "renew former attachments, make new ones, encourage prospects they wanted to see blossom, and avenge themselves for neglects and slights of the previous day, or of all the preceding year. For them it's a true day of emancipation."[19] Similarly in Switzerland traditional youth organizations ran village dancing. In Elm (Glarus canton), for example, the local lads delegated "dancing masters," with ribbons and flowers on their hats, to get together the music, invite the girls, and pair off individuals as they saw fit.[20]

Unfortunately, most of this evidence dates from the mid-nineteenth century, when traditional courtship patterns were in full dissolution. Already in these testimonies we are picking up substantial romantic-love effects that I suspect would have been absent a century earlier. Yet compare these local dances—the focal point of a considerable community effort of organization, the cynosure of all eyes—with the

The Traditional Family

Extended Family

and Stable Nuclear Group

From Household to Nest

Kitchen of farm Household in eighteenth-century Landes in south-west France. Note diversity of people, animals, and activities.

A modern home (circa 1950) houses only the nuclear family.

Women's Work and Men's Work

Then—Sex Determined Work Roles

Men's work outdoors.

Women's work indoors (with men watching).

And Now—Men and Women Freely Adopt Any Role

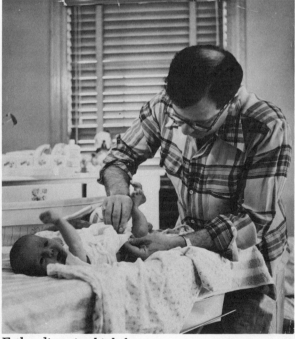

Father diapering his baby.

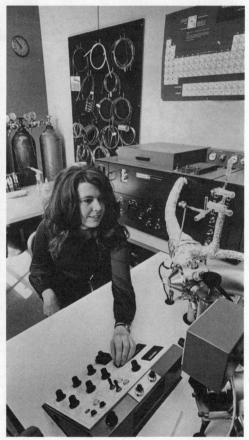

Woman engineer at work.

Family Interest . . .

The Marriage Proposition.
(From a print by Cornelius Troost, 1697-1750.)

and Decorum . . .

Picnic group in Bornarville, France.

and Romance

Give Way to ...   **Intimacy ...**

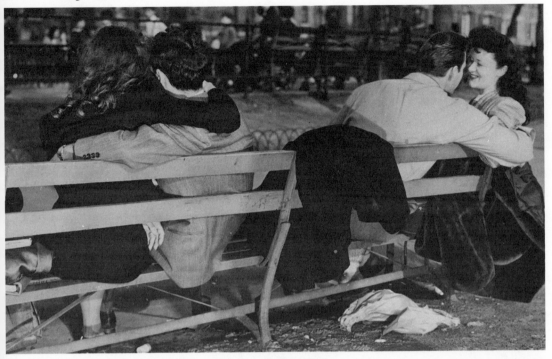

Dating couples 1940s.

and Spontaneity

Contemporary French youth at beach party.

The Onrush of Maternal

From Child Abandonment . . .

In a New York tenement . . . or French foundling Hospital (infants would be placed in a revolving box and be received in hospital after the bell was rung) . . .

or with wet nurses (Spanish wet nurse is leaving her own infant to nurse another woman's child.)

Sentiment and Concern

to the Celebration of Motherly Love

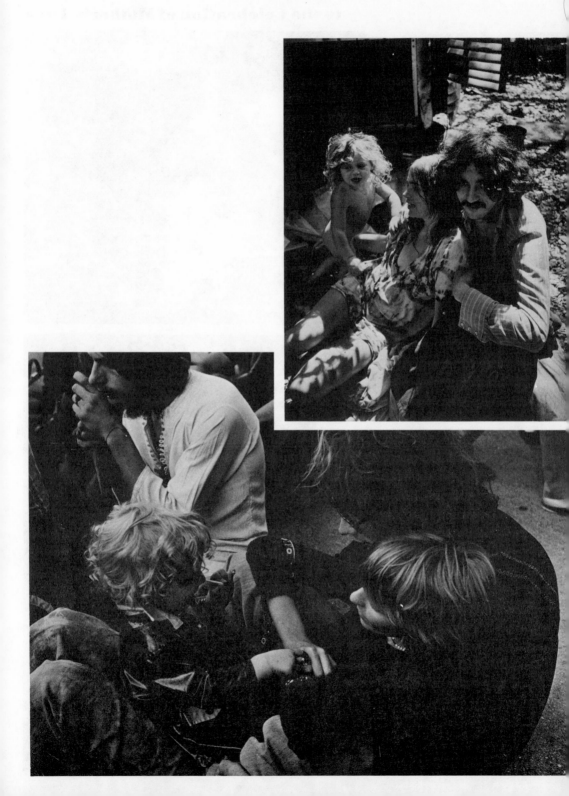

discothèque scene a hundred years later. Forming a couple was still a public event.[21]

A third community-run occasion for courtship was the village festival, several of which dotted the year. Unlike our own times, when the calendar year is largely homogenized and the days indistinguishable, the march of the days in traditional society was paced by fêtes, some of them religious (such as Lent and Christmas) and others secular in nature and tied to the agricultural calendar (such as May Day or the harvest home). Because most of these festivals involved costuming, partying, drinking, dancing, and even eating together, they provided superb opportunities for getting acquainted. But even on these occasions, when the youth could presumably weave in and out amidst the babble of their drunken elders, community supervision prevailed. We know about these village feasts and rituals largely from the folklorists. And for the orderly mind, folklore is a jungle. Customs vary wildly from one district to the next, and the subject's masters all display a magisterial contempt for chronology and historical development.[22] We shall simply have to keep in mind that, despite local diversity, a rough similarity existed in the outlines of the traditional calendar; and that the center of gravity of the customs we shall be examining was the early nineteenth century.

What follow are the high points of courting in the French traditional calendar.

Carnaval. The week before the beginning of Lent was given over to partying, especially the three days that led up to Shrove Tuesday (Mardi gras, the last of the big celebrations). Then came Ash Wednesday and forty days of supposed solemnity until Easter.

Carnaval brought boys and girls together in various ways. Games were traditionally played in many villages, the lads and lasses bouncing one another on teeter-totters affixed to logs in barns, throwing hammers blindfolded, or engaging in egg races.[23] Or the young men and women would join together to put on little farces and dramatic representations, composing in advance texts that would satirize the stupidity or cupidity of some local citizen. In a Burgundian village, for instance, some poor woman who, not knowing just how to treat her husband with leeches, had fried some for him to eat, was made the object of a cavalcade the following carnival. One of the group's members paraded about with a huge "pan for frying leeches," the others singing verses about the woman's naiveté.[24]

Even more propitious for courting was all the dancing at carnival time. Unlike the nineteenth century, when dance opportunities were to spread themselves throughout the year, dancing clustered in traditional society about a small number of festival events. But at those times it was pursued frenetically. Here are the occasions carnival presented in Prats-de-Mollo (Pyrénées-Orientales):

—The "bear dance" of Candlemas (February 2), the kick-off of the carnival cycle. As the customary prelude, bear dances had several locals disguise themselves as bears, burst into homes, smear lampblack on the women, and fondle a breast or two.
—The "cuckholds' dance" on the Thursday preceding Shrovetide, staged by the drapers' guild.
—Friday, masquerades, a bull chase, in the evening a snake dance for the men, and thereafter what was presumably a general dance for everyone.
—Saturday, a special dance for the serving maids of the village (whose mistresses would loan them some finery), followed by another dance for couples about to become engaged.
—Sunday, first some youth-group raiding parties to gather provender from each house for the carnival feast, then a couples' dance about the village square, then a showering of candies upon everyone by the spectators.
—Monday, more of Sunday's activities, but dancing only by married men.
—Tuesday (Mardi gras), dancing of all kinds.
—Wednesday, the burning of the carnival scarecrow, then a folkloric dance by the young men alone—the women abstaining because, after all, Lent had begun.[25]

One can imagine how often the marriageable population of the village came together in these eight days. Yet note that the dancing was invariably in public settings, attended by people of all ages and conditions.

Carnival's major courtship occasion, however, came five days after Mardi gras, on the first Sunday of Lent, in a set of linked folk customs known as the *dônages* (collective matchmaking) and *brandons* or *bures* (evening bonfires and torchlight parades). Although local variations were considerable, it was a standard pattern for all the young people of mating age to assemble before one of their number who played the role of "announcer." The group would call out "To whom do you give Jean-Pierre" (or Marie-Claude, or whomever), and the announcer would pair that person with a member of the opposite sex. Or better yet, the group would answer its own question, "We give Jean-Pierre to. . . ." This gathering might happen in the village square, in the street, or in front of someone's home. The speaker, a fellow with a strong voice and a quick wit, would be up on some kind of stand before his peers.

Couples thus thrust together would not yet be engaged or going steady, for everyone already knew about them. It was more fun to link up people one knew were vaguely interested in each other but too timorous to declare themselves. Even more amusing was to link up obvious mismatches, such as the poor hunchback with the village belle, or a girl already ardently pursued by one fellow to another fellow. (This kind of humor, indeed, brought the custom to an end in one village, where the police had to suppress it because of the fights that were always breaking out.)[26] But most of the linkups were appropriate. The dônages were the peer group's way of making sure that the suitable people found each other, a collective intervention in the otherwise chancy mechanism of finding partners.

There was nothing binding about the unions thus proposed. A fellow might buy the girl to whom he had been linked a glass of wine, and then not see her again. Or she might accept a dance with him later on, and therewith terminate her obligation. So this custom has nothing to do with group marriage, or the collective auctioning off of brides, or any of the other heavy folkloric baggage authors often heap upon it. It represented merely a gentle collective hand in the delicate process of couple formation.

The dônages were a community- rather than a youth-run intervention, because such matchmaking happened in full earshot of everyone. In the Franche-Comté, for example, the young men would divide into two groups on opposite sides of the village and then propose alliances to each other, shouting across the rooftops "I fix X up with Y. Whom do you want to fix up?" ("Je dône, je dône, qui dônes-tu. —Un tel à une telle." This happened, however, on Saint-John's day and not at the beginning of Lent.)[27] Afterwards they would pick up the girls at their homes and there would be dancing.

The second phase of matchmaking on that first Lenten Sunday was the bonfire. Either the village would assemble about some central fire, for which the youth had laboriously assembled the wood in the course of the preceding week, or individuals would light up torches and parade about with them. As the fire burned, circle dances would take place; when only the glowing embers remained, young men and women who wanted to marry in the course of the year would jump over them. In villages of eastern France especially, the practice had established itself of wrapping a wagon wheel with straw, setting it ablaze, and then rolling it down the hill, to the admiration of onlookers. Responsibility for furnishing the wheel fell to the husband most recently married, but the War of 1870 had cut such swaths among the young men of one village that there were no more marriages, and the same fellow had to furnish wheels from his wagons seven years in a row. The custom was abandoned when he finally refused to give up any more wheels (his barnyard full of wheel-less wagons), to the consternation of the unmarried women, who looked at the fiery-wheel festival "as a sort of matrimonial institution, a husband fair, whose disappearance could augment the ranks of spinsters in the village."[28]

Mating about this lenten bonfire was not merely a French custom but was known throughout traditional Europe. In Finland they were more for children, in Germany more perhaps for couples already engaged.[29] The role of communal suggestion seems to have been stronger in France than elsewhere. Yet everywhere, these bonfires and assemblages let everyone who belonged to the village watch the couples coming together who would perpetuate the collective life.

Walpurgis Eve and May Day (April 30–1 May). We must strive to expunge from our minds images of merry maids in Sherwood Forest or crêpe-paper pole dances when we turn to May celebrations. The reality was simultaneously simpler and more complex; simpler because the purpose of the festivities was just the declaration of attachments, complex because the two-day period offered scope for collective discipline—and ensuing ugliness and bad feeling—as well as for mating negotiations.

The cycle would begin with an April 30 bonfire. And though once upon a time this blaze might have had all sorts of magical significance, by the time our sources begin it's nothing more than another opportunity for boys and girls to get together and dance around. What happened after the fire was out and the girls had gone home was more interesting. The boys, working either singly or as a group, would affix to the house of each marriageable girl in the village a clump of greenery, or perhaps plant a stripped tree trunk in her yard. To this vegetation could be attached either lovely ribbons and flowers, in the event the lad (or lads) wanted to say something nice about the girl and begin serious courting; or bones and goats' heads in case the boy wanted to rebuke her for past putdowns or the group, in their collective wisdom, wished to reproach her as promiscuous, fickle, lazy, or whatever. This affixing of bones and detritus represented a deadly threat to the reputation of a girl's entire family and might engender hatreds that would last for generations. In the Lot department, "Such a *mai* is a serious insult and is never forgiven, exposing its victim to the most vicious raillery."[30]

The arboricultural "vocabulary" permitted some fine differentiations of sentiment. Vegetation mounted on a girl's house at Walpurgisnacht could have the following meanings:[31]

Birch branches: friendship, attraction (*sympathie*)
Boxwood: innocence or, with ribbons, love
Cherrywood: marriageable girl
Hornbeam (*charmille*): "you charm me"
Hazeltree: reconciliation
Fir branches: "I love you" (if with needles); dubious virtue (if without needles); spiteful (if painted black)
Spindle tree: whore
Beech tree: hatred
Holly tree: hard hearted (but in some places, "I love you")
Elder tree: disgust
Sycamore: enduring friendship

But let's assume things had gone well, and on the morning of May 1 the girl had found no nasty messages before her home. Next step was the May dance, with perhaps a maypole in the village square. She would affix the ribbon she found upon her own *mai* to her shoulder, and wait at the dance for the cavalier who had put it there to identify himself, offering to buy her a drink. If she wanted to discourage his further attention (providing she knew who it was), she would simply leave the ribbon at home and face would be saved all around.[32] May Day was thus yet another opportunity for bringing the behavior of individuals into line with community norms, and for facilitating the formation of couples of whom the community as a whole would approve.

St. John's Day (Midsummer), 24 June. Several mating and dating themes ran through the cycle of festivities that commenced on the eve of St. John's day and lasted until the day of St. Peter and St. Paul (June 29). For one thing, there was all the dancing, singing, and appraising that went with the bonfires, torchlight parades, and fiery wheel-rollings of the evening of the 23rd. In the Gironde the young men and women, participating in their usual groups, would turn up, the girls to parade about the glowing log, the boys finally to take them in their arms and hold them over the embers a bit, counting "one . . . two . . . three. . . ." The boys would appear to dangle the girls' feet in the coals and then a saving embrace would complete the rite.[33] Or in Alsace the boys would construct little pinwheels of wood that would be set alight and flipped spinning into the night. "Each young lad presents one of these disks to the girl he loves. It's a good sign if she accepts. There are cries of delight when people display clumsiness. The crowd all return arm in arm to the village. . . ."[34] None of this differs greatly from any of the other periodic bonfires that dot the year, save perhaps for a greater number of wheels rolling downhill—the fireworks displays of early modern Europe.

What did distinguish St. John's Day from the other courting occasions was the servant-hiring fair. In some parts of Europe, servants were engaged on an annual basis, starting with All Souls' Day (November 1); in other places the annual contract would begin with St. John's; in still others, hiring would take place biennially—for a four-month period on St. John's Day (the period covering the big push in the fields), and for eight months on All Souls. Hiring day meant the convergence of the district's servants in the town square, where they could be inspected and picked over like cattle at market, with drinks afterward to seal the deal. They would have money in their pockets from their previous job, and there would be dancing and partying throughout the day, not just for those in the job market but for everyone. This festival was the sexual highpoint of the annual courting cycle, and many would share the fate of the maidservant of Bozas (Ardèche) who, tipsy from so much dancing about the bonfire, was swayed by her seducer's repeated promises of marriage (a journeyman baker) and "weakened enough to permit herself to be sexually known by him, the eve of St. John's Day 1775."[35]

The Parish Holiday. In the autumn, the last of the great courting festivals took place: the parish holiday, known also as the village holiday, the wake, *Kirchweihtag,* or the *fête patronale*—the multiplicity of phrases indicating the diverse origins of what was essentially a harvest home. Theoretically a religious ceremony commemorating the day on which the village church had been consecrated (or the saint's day of the church, or the day of the village saint), in practice this huge blowout had been moved to the end of the harvest season and retained little spiritual character. It was in fact a great release from the ardors of harvest work, an occasion for the commercial fairs of the year, and a perfect opportunity for mating and dating. Parish holidays, more dispersed in France throughout the calendar year, were concentrated in the autumn in Germany and Scandinavia, perhaps near St. Michael's Day (Michaelmas—September 29) or perhaps arbitrarily assigned to a given weekend, such as the third Sunday in October, which Joseph II of Austria designated for the *Kirchweihen* of his realm.[36]

Here is the courtship side of a typical parish holiday in southwestern France: "On the day consecrated to the festival of the patron saint of each parish, the inhabitants of neighboring communes flock there in crowds, less for pious reasons than to get in on all the entertainment which goes on in the afternoon. After having spent several hours in the tavern, the young lads, emitting horselike neighs, go to the village square carrying a cake ornamented with ribbons that their girlfriends have given them. Frequently each commune has a cake with its own colors, and it forms the post about which each delegation will dance, to the sound of the bagpipe or the hurdy-gurdy. Sometimes the girls take part in these noisy pleasures. Thus are born rivalries between the young men of the diverse villages, and it's rare that the holiday ends without a serious fight."[37]

In northeastern France other stratagems existed for directing the public eye to the formation of the couples on the parish holiday. The lads of a given commune would form a committee to organize the festivities, each contributing enough to pay for a barrel of wine and a fiddler. This public-spirited act gave them, however, first right to invite the girls, and any girl who showed up with another "cavalier" after having rejected a committee member's invitation could be excluded. Or better yet, the committee member could simply direct the fiddler to stop playing in mid-dance, pointing to the outsider as the fellow truly responsible for stopping the music. Any intruder who continued dancing thereafter would be exposed, the chronicler tells us, "to a severe correction."[38]

The trouble with these accounts, as with the flood of similar parish holiday accounts I have seen for Germany, is their nineteenth-century origin. The German tales especially suggest that the boys and girls of such backwoodsy districts as Niederbayern could be compared only with those of ancient Nineveh for sexual permissiveness.[39] Yet this was a time when the sexual and romance revolutions were already in full gallop. We have been victimized by the folklorists' occupational blindness to evolution. For these writers, any point in the nineteenth century before the Great Decline of Folklore was just like any time in the fifteenth century, and so they neglect the careful differentiations among sources that are required to unearth distinctively early-modern traits. Yet potsherds of information indicate that, whereas parish holidays had served since time immemorial as arenas for matchmaking, only late in time did they come to facilitate lovemaking as well.[40]

The folkloric origin of these descriptions has given a powerful peasant bias to our view of traditional society. And while it is true that most people lived in small towns and villages during those times, perhaps 10 percent of the population on the continent did inhabit larger cities. Were their mating and dating patterns much different?

Urbanity altered at least three facets of the dating scene, to go by a handful of recent studies of eighteenth-century France. There was, for one thing, less community pressure for sexual responsibility. Urban bridal pregnancy was higher, and so was urban illegitimacy, indicating both that couples slept together more often before marriage and that the seducer would be more inclined—more able—to take off once his deed became known. In fact the standard reaction of men who had impregnated their girlfriends in eighteenth-century Grenoble was flight, and in eighteenth-century Lyon fully 70 percent of the men deemed responsible quit the city before their bastard's birth.[41]

These differences in sexual responsibility are surely attributable to different degrees of social control. In the city, young men and women would be more likely to encounter each other in solitary settings, or at least not at community activities. While urban young people would observe the same calendar of festivities as did rural people, what they did on, say, St. John's Day would be different. An urban "date" would consist of a walk—in Grenoble, on the "champs Elysées" or just beyond the Bone or Trois Cloîtres gates—or perhaps an unchaperoned, unsupervised visit to the girl's lodgings. (Most of Grenoble's fallen maidens had been seduced in the kitchen, in their quarters, or in the man's quarters.)[42] So wild was the drinking and dancing at Lille's annual worker festival in 1821 (the *fête du Broquelet*) that poor old Dr. Dupont thought the moral order had altogether collapsed. "A woman lace-maker was singing a love song next to a male spinning-worker who was completely in the clutches of Bacchus. A filter-worker was declaiming fidelity to his wife, who kept mysteriously pressing the knee of a young journeyman. . . ." Afterwards the merry-makers all jammed into coaches for the trip back back to town.[43] How much collective supervision of these goings-on could there have been? Or as Susi's mother said to Mary's, "I thought she was at *your* house. . . ."

If community control was less effective in the city, so also was community matchmaking. The point of village *dônages* was to bring together couples whom the collectivity felt were "right" for each other, not just emotionally (if at all that) but socially and economically. In the city, chance encounter played a greater role. Thus, a large proportion of the seducers of urban women turn out to be

137

other servants working either in the same household or in the same neighborhood.[44] Employers are also heavily represented among the ranks of the seducers at the beginning of the eighteenth century, as we shall see in a moment. While we do not know whether similar situations prevailed in the countryside, it seems unlikely, given our general knowledge of the communitarian context of rural court-ship, that the community's interest in avoiding *mésalliances* would have permitted casual encounters to reach the proportions they did in the city. And it seems improbable that the watchful neighbors would have permitted the employers to sexually exploit their em-ployees to a comparable extent.

Prudence and Affection in Traditional Courtship

Even though couples were formed in public, sooner or later they would go off in private. Once that happened, did affection arise be-tween these young men and women? Is there evidence of spontaneity and empathy, or were their face-to-face relations just cooly instru-mental? Did people come together to find personal happiness—or to safeguard the material interests of the lineages, kin groups, and communities of which they were a part?

The surest evidence of emotionless courtship would be the ar-ranged marriage. If the wishes of the young people were completely neglected and they were matched to whomever in the village best suited their parents' dynastic ambitions, affection and sentiment would by definition be absent.[45]

In part, the selection system depended on the social class. Among the wealthy peasantry the parents themselves were likely to make the match, often while the couple were still children; marriage then followed puberty. To one observer's horrified eyes, "People are mar-ried very young in the Bresse. The children are affianced before the age of nubility. . . . I saw in a tavern at Coligy a meeting of two families who had come to link their children by promise of marriage. The bridegroom had been put at the table beside his future bride and neither had much of an idea what was happening to them. After this solemn occasion they were to be parted, to reunite definitively only after becoming nubile. The ages of the two fiancés added together could scarcely have been more than 20."[46] On the other side of France, in the Limousin, it was the same story: early engagement with matrimony after nubility. The bride's servitude would then continue as she moved into her father-in-law's house, where she enjoyed about the same status as a domestic servant.[47] In the Nivernais before the nineteenth century, the patriarchs of clan-like extended families would dispose of their marriageable daughters in the house's best interests. "And though [the patriarch] tried to take account of the sentiments of those involved, if by another marriage the family community could acquire an advantageous piece of land, the person had to obey." Women thus married away received a money dowry, but renounced forever their succession rights to the property.[48]

The offspring of such premature unions were said to be "underdeveloped and puny."[49] The arrangers were indifferent to the welfare of the young brides themselves, who, sometimes subject to intercourse before reaching puberty (in places where first menstruation arrived only towards sixteen or seventeen) would sustain actual physical harm and be able to bear children "never or very late."[50] The age at wedlock even in such bastions of arranged marriage as the Limousin was generally in the twenties, and so we know that early, forced matches were not the norm.[51] Yet for a substantial minority of France's peasant population, the welfare of the individuals and the happiness of the couple were subordinate to larger familial considerations.

For most couples, however, marriage was not arranged. The individuals chose their partners freely. To what extent may affection be observed in the courting behavior of these people? At the outset we must remind ourselves that our own forms of expressing sentiment may not be universal. People in other cultures may feel just as powerfully the emotions we feel, yet express them in forms completely different from our own. So as we gaze at these vanished peasant populations of the eighteenth and nineteenth centuries, we must be constantly on the alert for unfamiliar external expressions of an internal emotional life. The following vision of twentieth-century peasant love in the Auvergne should by itself give our culture-blinkered minds pause for reflection:[52]

L'amour paysan is almost mute. There's a greeting, a look, a morsel of a sentence. "So you came." A silence. The next time the boy will put his arm around the girl's shoulder. But it's true as well that he knows how to chat up and entertain his sweetheart!

There was a fellow from Mollanges, Angélique told us one evening, who said to his girl, "You love me?" She replied, "Ummm," as if she had responded that she loved potatoes. "Will you always love me?"—"Ummm." After that the fellow had nothing more to say. Then it was her turn: "Do you love me?"—"Ummmm."—"Will you always love me?"—"Ummmm." They understood almost nothing about making love in the evenings together. How we laughed at those two!

Nonetheless—after a pause and several deep breaths—I argue that romantic behavior, even in the terms of that particular time and culture, was by and large missing from *traditional* peasant courtship.

Our sources confine us to France. Likely as not, a go-between rather than the young man himself would make the proposal of marriage. Prestige and family honor were riding so heavily on the outcome that a direct refusal would cost painfully. Much better to have someone else conduct preliminary overtures to the girl's family and hammer out the rough outlines of the dowry settlement. Only when agreement in principle had been reached would the boy's parents and the lad himself (trailing behind this team of negotiators) appear on the scene. The go-between would then receive a place of honor at the wedding, a special jug of wine, and perhaps some monetary consideration.[53]

Yet even if the fellow himself made the offer, a host of conventional formulas for proposing and rejecting would crowd out any possibility of a direct emotional transaction. These French peasants—reciting little rhymes to each other, turning the firebrands this way and that—seem light-years distant from the twentieth-century scenario of looking one's partner in the eye and saying "Wanna get married?" In the department of the Gers in the 1830s, "The young farmer pinches the arm of a girl and there you've got his proposal. Some time afterwards the girl plops down in a familiar manner upon his knee and you've got the acceptance. To go further than that the consent of the parents is needed, above all of the boy's."[54] In the Charente it all happened very quickly, starting with an at-home dance the girl's peasant parents would stage for her. "In dancing, one of the young men might set his cap for the girl. He manages to announce his intentions by seating her upon his knee familiarly, whispering sweet nothings and *propos d'amour*, and giving her an embrace or two. Success is assured if her father discreetly asks him to stay behind afterwards for a nightcap."[55]

The script for saying no was supplied by tradition rather than impulse. After his big interview with the grandparents (who ran the family) in the Morvan, the young suitor had only to look at the brands in the fire for his answer. If they were placed together and burning brightly, the bride's family had accepted; if they were separated at the ends of the hearth and the blaze extinguished, he had been rejected.[56] Aprons rolled up, inverted silverware, an empty sack for the hopeful lad, or a pocketful of oats—all meant refusal.[57] These were nice ways of doing matrimonial business because they resolved affairs without a lot of screaming and crying. But that's just the point: no histrionics of any kind accompanied courtship in the world we have lost. Exaltation and despair had to await the surge of sentiment.

A final sign of the lack of romance in peasant courtship can be seen in the way the couple acted together in public. Interpreting the language of gestures is riskiest of all in this emotional reconstruction of traditional society, for the meaning of body talk may shift dramatically from one culture to another. It is, however, safe to say that peasant notions of demonstrativeness were not the same as our own. How young men and women felt about public displays of affection may be glimpsed from this account of a local festival in the Landes:[58]

After services were over the parishioners assembled in front of the church, perhaps 150 strong. The men were on one side, the women, squatting on their heels in a circle, on the other. The young people of both sexes were together in a group, each holding his partner and leaping up and down to the voice of a shepherd, who called out the time from a perch. This sort of dance tune had nothing melodious; there were just his voice inflections, brusk, raucous, primitive and without rhythm. The

curé and the notary, who like me were attentively observing their movements, told me that several matches were being made, that they spied
the handshaking which was the infallible sign. And in fact I saw three
young locals leave the group successively, each pulling abruptly his dancing partner. After looking at each other and exchanging a couple of words
and mutual slaps, they went to their parents to declare that they had
'agreed' [*s'agréer*] and that they wanted to get married. The parents gave
their consent, since "agreement" had been reached, and after discussing
matters among themselves, summoned the notary and the curé. Then
the day was set for signing the marriage contract, for the nuptial bene-
diction, and for the wedding.

Not all couples were as immobile as these Landais. Here are
fiancés at a dance in the Deux-Sèvres: "Any girl who shows up at
a *ballade* without a young man clinging to her fingers is condemned
by her peers. Between dances you see the swain standing in front
of his girlfriend, one elbow resting heavily upon her shoulder, the
other hand slid artlessly underneath her corset, which no outer gar-
ment covers. They look at each other saying nothing, and remain in
this posture for hours on end."[59] This is actually fairly amorous behavior by peasant standards. The norm was much less demonstrative.
"Our robust Chloes," wrote Dr. Bogros of the Morvan, "willingly
renounce tender confidences for rude thrusts, and our hardy Daphnes
substitute for sweet embraces energetic hand twists which seem to
come less from the province of romance than from that of gymnastics."[60] Rubbing together cheeks and thighs, twisting arms and smash-
ing shoulders, crushing fingers and striking knees, spitting in mouths
and exchanging eaten apples—this was peasant romance.[61] Clearly
feeling is not completely absent from their lives. Some sort of affection binds the young couple together before marriage, but neither
in intensity nor form was it what the modern world was to call
"romance."[62]

One last test of the heart's resolve is its willingness to overcome
all obstacles. And here the peasant heart fails decisively; confronted
with the obstacle of parental refusal to a proposed union, the young
couple would renounce each other. Make no mistake: the parents
of the couple *had* to approve, because to spite parental will was to
risk disinheritance, and in a society where capital was inherited, not
accumulated, exclusion from your patrimony automatically con-

signed you to a marginal existence—not to mention having to endure the anguish of community opprobrium if you started keeping house without the proper sanctification. Thus a couple could decide nothing until the boy had asked the peasant parents for the girl's hand: "The supreme moment has arrived. He puts on his Sunday best, including his leather shoes [otherwise he would have worn wooden clogs], takes his staff, and accompanied by his father presents himself of an evening at the home of his beloved. It's clear from the solemnity of his deportment that something big is afoot. 'Good evening to you all,' they say upon entering, a salutation which is appropriately received, and then according to the hospitable customs of the region they are invited to share the family's evening meal. But the boy's father refuses: 'We are here neither to drink nor eat, but to ask the hand of your daughter.' And the young man himself, at pains to point out his love and the purity of his long association with her, hastens to add: 'We have been in love for a long time, together from morning to evening. But I have never suggested to her anything that I shouldn't have.'" Which was probably true on his part, for in fact the Cantal had a quite low illegitimacy rate.

Nothing can be decided on this evening, however, for it's necessary for the girl's father to inspect the holdings of the boy's father. And on the following Sunday both families troop about the latter's fields, carefully looking over the crops, the barns, the quality of the cattle. "He [the girl's father] doesn't even leave out the manure pile, the height of which is a sure gauge of peasant prosperity. The investigation then continues inside the house, where the father makes sure that plenty of bacon and lard is hanging from the rafters, that the chests are full of linen, that the cupboards contain ample crockery, and finally that the attic is well stocked with provisions. But this inspection offends no one. Business is involved here, and in the Cantal people believe you take that kind of thing seriously." At the end the girl's parents might accept the offer of the boy's parents and a marriage contract be drawn up. Or, uneasy about the lack of provender and the small holdings of their prospective in-laws, they might reject the offer, and so call off the engagement. The girl's heart, of course, would be broken, "but her pride would remain intact, for it is business matters that have caused all the trouble."[63]

143

Two observations are suggested by this little account: one, that the couple itself recognizes the need for family matters to take precedence over affairs of the heart; two, that these relationships have a remarkably ritualistic quality to them. The form of contact between young man and woman is determined by custom, the intricate dance of "the offer" (with the men having clearly in mind their fixed speeches the son's affirmation of purity and devotion—all this is set dialogue, lines from an old play that all the players learn as they grow up and then repeat to one another throughout their lives. The scope for spontaneity in interpersonal ties, the realm of creative transactions between individuals, is kept at an absolute minimum.

This youthful fidelity to parental wishes persisted well into the twentieth century, although by World War I patterns of sentiment themselves had changed greatly among the peasants. A story was told of an Auvergnat village just before the Great War, where a young man was wildly in love with a girl of fifteen. "Des grandes, grandes amours." But his parents wouldn't hear of it because her parents weren't sufficiently well off. "The couple would go to her place together, to the veillées, into the fields. They were seen frequently seated together, kissing a bit. That was allowed. But they went no further." The fellow went off to the trenches, returned wounded in thirteen days, and was invalided out. Again he asked his parents for permission and again they refused. "They said their goodbyes one evening just before nightfall behind a hedge which is not far from the village. They cried in each other's arms, and cried and cried. . . ." She married another lad, and he danced at her wedding, without being able to look into her eyes.[64] Now *that*, folks, is romantic love. But in the 1960s the story would most likely have had a different ending.[65]

Certainly physical attractiveness was relatively unimportant. As the peasants of Baden warned, "You look at the pocketbook, not at the face."[66] Dr. Charles Perron assures us that for his countrymen in the Franche-Comté, youth and beauty were decidedly "accessory" qualities, and trotted out some appropriate folk sayings to prove his point:

—"You can't eat beauty with a spoon."
—"It's better to be able to say, 'Hey ugly, what's for dinner,' than 'Tell

144

me, my lovely, do we have anything to eat tonight.'"
—"If you've got a pretty wife, you won't have pretty hogs." "Why's that, Fred?" "Because instead of eating, the hogs spend all their time looking at the wife!"[67]

The need to marry big, strong women able to shoulder their full share of work may have blinded peasants to the delicacy of line and fineness of feature that constitute our modern ideal of feminine beauty. (The same would be true for peasant men in the eyes of the women.)[68] But to what event was inclination of any kind permitted to override purely economic and prudential considerations in choosing a mate? Would these peasants sacrifice any material advantages at all in order to end up with partners to whom they felt attracted?

If income occasionally gave way to inclination among these propertied farmers of traditional France, our sources do not record it. Comments from scattered districts indicate that wealth conquered all. In the Franche-Comté, "You chose the richest person, of course, because there with the money were generally also to be found frugality, savoir-faire, and good manners. Aside from that, the morality and health of the parents were taken into account." Thus the absence of varicose veins (one index the peasants associated with good health) mattered more than mutual attraction.[69] In the opposite corner of France, as well, everyone acknowledged that peasant marriages were "affairs of convenience."[70] Inclination rarely figured.

And the same seems to have been true of German peasants. In Griesbach County—where the world of passion was not unimportant, given the high incidence of illegitimacy and adultery—"nothing is more comical than matchmaking, and nothing counts aside from the desire for money."[71] Whether the personalities of the couple are compatible is irrelevant, explained Altdorf County's doctor. What matters is whether the parents are content after their inspection tours of the other family's farm. "People then assume that afterwards the newlyweds will get accustomed to each other."[72]

As for Finnish society, in order even to be permitted to go out socially you had to pass a number of community-ordained tests. Boys had to lift heavy stones or sharpen stakes as evidence of their ability to provide for families, and girls had to be able to make a man's underwear or to "mend the knee of his trousers." "Don't hope for a man before you can shear the sheep's neck, knot the ends of the homespun, and sew a man's shirt," cautioned the villagers.[73] Nowhere does it say anything about pimples or sex appeal or liking each other, and we may guess that as the Finns chose each other for marriage they didn't think much about these things.

It would be an exaggeration to suggest that wealth, large dowries, and the merging of neighboring fields were decisive factors in most rural marriages, because many rustics were virtually landless and would not have dowries to exchange. What I think was true for all, however, was a preference for prudence in making alliances. The families of agricultural laborers had to get on in the world just as those of the peasant aristocracy did, and this meant that a woman able to endure the harsh cycle of rural work and capable of keeping her domain running smoothly was absolutely essential for the family's survival. That was why "passion plays little role in alliances" among the peasants of northern France. "People want wives simply to have children, to have a housekeeper who can make a good stew and bring something to eat out to the fields, and who can spin for the shirts and mend the clothes."[74] In the sheer struggle for existence, such prudential considerations finally had to count more than all others.

With the urban bourgeoisie, we are light years away from these peasants in their barnyards. Yet we find the same lack of romance in courtship. True, things would change after the mid-nineteenth century. But before that, references to *"calcul"* and *"intérêt"* predominate in the genesis of the petty bourgeois couple, and there is little mention of "inclination" and of "following one's heart."

To begin with, there were "technical" reasons for the passionless character of the petty bourgeois. Whereas the lower classes had ample opportunity to "frequent"—that is, to go out together unchaperoned (dating, or going steady, being the modern equivalents of *se fréquenter*)—young bourgeois women led a cloistered existence. Daughters of the "lace-curtain bourgeoisie" (*bourgeois gênés*) were not permitted to go out alone socially. Because their parents had to be with them, they were denied all the frenetic socializing their brothers enjoyed in the company of upper-class friends, for the simple reason that their parents were unlikely to be invited to such homes.[75] For the petty bourgeoisie, dating risked "sullying the merchandise," for in the big city a seducer might easily escape into the fog, leaving his pregnant girl friend stranded in a way that a peasant lad would not have been permitted by the community to do. For both classes, marriage meant a fundamentally commercial transaction; dowries were seen as an immediate commodity and status as indirectly convertible into cash. And when *intérêt* is at the wheel, the pitter-patterings of the heart take a back seat.

Yet the absence of romance in the petty bourgeois couple involved more than a lack of opportunity. Even if the chance to go out with young men and to exchange soulful looks had been present, these youth had internalized values sufficiently antipassion to have rejected "fooling around." Even *risking* pregnancy would have been seen as an unthinkable betrayal of the economic mission the family and the community had assigned to young women. So they didn't think about it.

Louis-Sebastien Mercier describes how couples were formed among the Parisian petty bourgeoisie:[76]

Pursuing a woman in bourgeois style means trying to marry her. The lad shows up on Sunday after mass and plays a few hands of loo. He loses but grumbles not; he asks permission to come back, receiving it in the presence of the girl, who pouts prettily.

The next Sunday he sets up a little walk, in the event that the weather is nice. Acknowledged as a suitor, he now has the liberty to chat with his bride-to-be fifty straight steps in front of the parents. Emerging from the woods he makes the vital proposal, scarcely a surprise to the belle.

The suitor is always well groomed and charming, and so the girl ends up a little attached to him. It's because she realizes that for her marriage is the sole avenue to freedom. The whole house is constantly after her about honor preserved, a family tradition since time immemorial.

But a small problem crops up. The lad's parents have located a more attractive partner for him. The engagement is broken. The girl is put out but consoles herself, for it is the third time this has happened. Outfitted with her mother's preachings, a nobility of spirit arms her against the inconstant.

Other suitors present themselves. But the difficulty of arranging a marriage contract is always in the way. The girl is, however, heading for her *twenty-first birthday*; there can be no more delay, for merchandise kept on the shelf loses its value, and accidents can happen.

The girl becomes sullen; the next one who comes along is accepted and things are wrapped up in three weeks. She will be able to boast of having been sought by five young men, omitting to add that four of them dropped her.

Mercier is amusing. But what a sad little world from our modern perspective, in which *calcul* dominates *la vie intime*, and sentiment counts for nothing in the vital decisions of life. *Calcul* is another word for endogamy. That like tends to marry like shouldn't surprise us, for even today people from the same general social class customarily marry one another. Yet as we decide exactly which woman (or man) to choose from a pool of thirty or so approximately equal candidates, a fine calculus of sentiment and compatibility guides us—to say nothing of the wild pulls of passion. In traditional society, economic interest narrowed the pool of "possibles" to such an extent that the heart's felicific calculus never had a chance to go into action. You simply married the fattest dowry you could find; and if by chance a choice of equally generous dowries presented itself, the youth group—with a sensitivity to social appropriateness honed by generations of accumulated experience—would help you find Ms. Right.

The Transformation of Courtship

The most important change in nineteenth-and twentieth-century courtship has been the surge of sentiment. Two things happened. People started to place affection and personal compatibility at the top of the list of criteria in choosing marriage partners. These new standards became articulated as romantic love. And secondly, even those who continued to use the traditional criteria of prudence and wealth in selecting partners began to behave romantically within these limits.

This important change lies at the center of the relationship between romantic love and community control. For when we talk of romance, we are speaking of spontaneity and empathy: the couple's ability to create their own little forms of tenderness and affection, and to place themselves in the other's shoes. Both dimensions of romantic love entail radical departures from tradition: spontaneity, because it involves substituting extemporaneous dialogue for traditional scripts; and empathy, because it beats down the sex roles, the entire sexual division of labor that had customarily separated the lives and emotions of men and women. In order to realize this romantic ideal, the couple would have to distance itself from the surrounding community, for the community was the great enforcer of tradition. Moreover, privacy—seclusion from curious eyes—was needed for experimentation and innovation in hand-holding and the other games of love. The romantic revolution which began late in the eighteenth century, sweeping across vast reaches of class and territory in the nineteenth to become, in the twentieth, the unassailable norm of courtship behavior, thus carried two components: a new relationship of the couple to each other; and a new relationship for them, as a unit, to the surrounding social order.

To begin with, what evidence do we have of the infusion of romance into courtship before 1900? For one thing, people either started to say they were in love or to act in ways consistent with no other interpretation. After 1730 there was a big jump in the use of such words as "amour" and "passion" in the explanations that unmarried women gave to municipal officials in Grenoble.of why they were pregnant, and there was a decline in the use of such terms as "amitié" that suggests a limited commitment.[77]

In a small town in western France, to take another example, a young journeyman cabinetmaker impregnated the daughter of his employer in 1787, a banal event and in every way "traditional"—save for the young man's remaining in contact with the girl after his flight to avoid prosecution (the traditional seducer would have vanished without a trace), and save for the tenderness of the love letters he wrote. "My dearest, I embrace you with all my heart. I am unable to forget you. Everyday I think of you and hope you do the same for me. Tell me how you feel, if you want to make me happy. I remain your close companion. . . ."[78] Note that the young man was not a peasant but an artisan; for as we shall see, it was outside the agricultural middle class that the revolution begins.

Towards the mid-nineteenth century we learn the following of the coastal town of La Ciotat (Bouches-du-Rhône): "The young men are constantly letting partners with handsome dowries go begging. When they marry, it's ordinarily for inclination and not for advantage. They would be incapable of feigning sentiment they did not feel. Such is the case above all for the young lads who go to sea."[79] So seafaring people, at least, were willing to sacrifice their pocketbooks for their affections. And if it wasn't love, how else may we explain that in a Gascon village, around 1911, "three mailmen became needed instead of two because the posts got so cluttered by all the magazines and postcards the young men and women were in the habit of sending one another"?[80]

These are illustrations, not verifications. And they concern only France, rather than the larger realm of Europe and North America that I would encompass in my arguments. Are these testimonies, then, sufficiently representative? Any imaginable case could be "documented" by scissoring together quotations culled from two hundred years of time. How can we capture the *central* tendency, the *representative* experience that the *average* young person had with romance?

One kind of data permitting the verification of larger hypotheses is who marries, or impregnates, whom. Throughout this book we use the "sacrifice" test to gauge the intensity of emotion. And if it is true that romance was replacing such nonsentimental criteria as property in choosing partners, we should be able to witness the renunciation of material advantage, or at least some form of flaunting community pressure. I argue that the willingness to abandon endogamy—marrying within one's own social bracket or village—represents such a test. Social and territorial endogamy were highly prized by public opinion because they concentrated the wealth: dowries wouldn't escape the village if marriages took place only within it, and fortunes wouldn't leave the family if sons and daughters married only people from other equally wealthy families. Traditional peasant-marriage strategies aimed at guaranteeing to each son the amount of inheritance he would have received had he been an only son, by snagging for him a compensating dowry. Now, to achieve this kind of social and territorial endogamy, the individuals involved must be prepared to renounce partners outside their social bracket or village so that the larger strategies of the collectivity may be accomplished. For people who defied the collectivity's aims there were costs: charivaris and ostracism hit those who married outside the village; disinheritance and family bitterness struck those who married outside their social rank. Therefore, to the extent that endogamy decreases and people begin marrying those *un*like themselves, we can speak of the advance of true love: the sacrifice of community approbation for personal happiness, the sacrifice of money for self-realization.

One interesting decline in endogamy took place along occupational lines. By "occupation" I mean not just class or status, but also the intermarrying of young men and women whose families were in the same business, be it viticulture, weaving, or barrelmaking. The daughters of, say, small-town merchants could choose among numerous potential marriage partners whose parents, though not merchants, occupied approximately the same status and income rank. So if these girls expressly chose the sons of other merchants, it must have been because they were subject to a whole battery of familial and communal controls on whom they selected.

Such occupational endogamy was very strong within traditional Europe. I happen to be looking at an "intermarriage index for communities of southern Anjou" for the late eighteenth century that tells us how likely it was that people within a given community would marry their own kind. Thus, the chances were eight times higher that the son of a large farmer would marry within a similar family than within a family of artisans, ten times higher than within a merchant's family, and three times higher than within a family of smallholding peasants. The children of vintners were so much more likely to marry other vintners that most other rows of the table just have zeroes; and so on.[81] Similar eighteenth-century data for a coastal district of Normandy show that the sons of fishermen married the daughters of fishermen two-thirds of the time; the sons and daughters of artisans intermarried three-fourths of the time; and the siblings of agricultural laborers, peasant farmers, and bourgeois married within their own circles more than half the time.[82] Similar findings turn up elsewhere in western France during the eighteenth century, and in other regions of Europe as well.[83]

Social change dissolved this traditional occupational endogamy. Explaining why this was so would involve us in questions outside the scope of this book. But part of the answer lies in the declining importance of work (one's "job") in the way people define themselves. This decline affects the extent to which modern workers are willing to band together in professional "guilds" and to make the various nonoccupational threads of their lives pass through this little circle of colleagues. For example, if you work at IBM, whether or not your children marry the children of other IBM workers is probably one of your lesser worries. Even in the small village of Vraiville (Eure), the choice of marriage partners today has become unrestrained. But early in the nineteenth century, day laborers in a village mainly married day laborers, large peasants mainly large peasants, and so forth. Today, only the peasants with large holdings have managed to retain their solidarity.[84]

Still more interesting is a probable decline of class and status endogamy that has taken place over the years. (And let me rush to furl the red flags that readers who have taken first-year sociology courses are likely to be waving at this point! Yes, class endogamy in our own time is still quite high.[85] There is still a tendency for like to marry like. The huge U.S. family sociology industry has succeeded in demonstrating that you are not likely to marry someone whom you haven't had a chance to meet, and that the forums for mating and the mechanisms of introduction continue to run along class lines.) One way to establish the extent of this tendency is to ask how much the actual distribution of endogamous couples improves upon chance. For some groups it does so considerably. In Belgium, farm families are three times more likely to marry among themselves than chance would allow. French agricultural laborers are even more endogamous. But such "middle-class" types as artisans and salaried employees intermarry only slightly more frequently than would happen by luck. The same is true for factory workers.[86] So while like still tends to seek out like today within such broad categories as "salaried employees," people don't try all *that* hard.

In any case, the really important question is how the tendency to marry within one's general social bracket has changed over the years. One long-haul study of a number of English villages finds the tendency for people to marry outside their class considerably higher in 1901–1967 than in 1837–1900.[87] In the Baden village of Wollbach, much more interclass mating took place in the twentieth than in the nineteenth century.[88] Surely the diversity and pace of larger cities, where most people have come to settle in the twentieth century, assure still higher levels of class crossing. The paucity of research ambitious enough to take on long stretches of time leaves us unable to pinpoint the change's beginning and diffusion.[89] But the indisputable fall-off in occupational endogamy illustrates the extent to which other people have ceased to intervene in the individual's choice of partner. And the probable decline in class endogamy illustrates the extent to which individuals have come to follow Cupid's arrow in mate selection, which in its descent is as likely to pierce a proletarian as a Brahmin heart.

Similarly, there has been a decline over the years in the tendency to marry people within one's own village. For Englishmen in a group of Northamptonshire parishes, the turning point came towards the mid-nineteenth century although the women there followed only later.[90] In a series of West Dorset parishes the percent of marriages between local people started to tumble downwards in the 1880s, starting around 81 percent in the 1830s and ending at 32 percent a hundred years later.[91] And in the Wurttemberg village of Weilimdorf it was in the 1820s and 1830s that both sexes began to take outside partners; whereas in the 1760s only a handful of peasants there were marrying women from elsewhere, by the 1860s over a third were doing so. The same trend existed for women.[92]

In France, local marriage was the general rule. In the towns, people even married within their own parishes.[93] Then the change began. Whereas, in the seventeenth century, over four fifths of all the men marrying in the village of Soudeilles (Corrèze) were born there, by the mid-nineteenth century only half of them were. And in the Eure's Vraiville, only 2 percent of the men marrying in the early 1700s were nonlocal; by the early 1900s, 20 percent were. Comparable figures for women show a rise from 2 to 58 percent.[94]

Now, who will be surprised when I announce that in today's world many, many people take marriage partners from outside, and that the chances that either bride or groom will marry in the place they were born are diminishing? What sociologists call "residential propinquity" continues to play a role in mate selection, perhaps more so than common sense might suggest.[95] But even in France, for example, where there is still a one-out-of-five chance that both husband and wife will have been born in the same locality, a fifty-fifty chance of their being from the same arrondissement, and a three-out-of-four chance of their coming from the same department,[96] these figures are almost certainly much lower than in traditional society.

In addition to occupation and residence, age is a third basis of endogamy. Yet here it is increasing *equality* in the ages of the partners that points to romantic love, increasing *disparity* that points to instrumental considerations. I suggest that there are two reasons for this. (1) People who marry at the same age will grow old simultaneously, obviating messy problems of exhausted elderly men with still-spirited wives. In traditional society the potentially adulterous restlessness of the younger wife didn't create difficulty, because such women simply repressed their sexuality, having internalized absolutely ironclad prohibitions against adultery. (2) At the level of daily routines, romantic love means conversation. The companionate marriage implies a steady discourse with one's partner. And to feed conversations, people must have experiences in common. The experience of belonging to the same age cohort contributes powerfully to this commonality.

Over the last two centuries, age disparities between partners have declined dramatically. The chances of a younger man marrying an older woman have gone from four or five to one, to ten or twenty to one; and although the likelihood that a younger woman will marry an older man has not declined as much, here too there has been a drop. Our longest time series comes from France, where in the traditional times up to a quarter of all husbands took brides five or more years older than themselves, and about half of all women took considerably older husbands. By the twentieth century, only 8 percent of first marriages involved older women. But the percent of marriages with older *men* had changed relatively little—indeed, up to 1900, it had increased. Other countries also show this downdrift in marriage between younger men and older women. The precise figures are available in Appendix III. By the 1970s it had become unusual for a fellow to marry a woman five years or more his senior; in traditional Europe, it was a standard pattern. And that represents a major change.

It is worth speculating for a moment why this change occurred. In traditional Europe there were three good reasons for marrying an older woman. First, she would have had time to acquire experience in farmwork, buttermaking, spinning, gardening, and other skills that made the difference between getting along and being miserable.[97] Second, she would have fewer fecund years before her and so would bear fewer children; and in societies where contraceptive practice was still hit-and-miss, this could be an important technique of family limitation.[98] Finally, she would have had time to accumulate a nest egg. The scenario Dr. Murat gives us for Vaud Canton in the eighteenth century probably played itself out in many places. Young peasant girls would come to the city, go into domestic service, and spend long years arduously eking out a little nest egg. Finally, such fortyish women would seek to marry and, on the basis of their *pécule* of accumulated capital, would be able to attract younger husbands.[99] Or there are accounts of master craftsmen's elderly widows marrying younger journeymen: the widows needed someone to run the shop; the young men were desperate to establish their independence in a society where an ossified guild system had choked off all possibility of advancement; and so the *mésalliance* was made.[100] All three varieties of June-December unions entailed strictly instrumental motives: you marry someone as a means to an ulterior end.

Note that in the contemporary world, two of the three motives for contracting June-December marriages have disappeared. The family economy now produces few goods, and wifely efforts to economize involve common sense and thrift rather than learned skills. And almost all couples now practice contraception efficiently enough to dispense with the age differential as an aid to birth control. As for the third motive, I shall argue that other emotions have in our own times triumphed over the desire to capture nest eggs.

Still, these "contemporary" circumstances do not explain why the shift toward younger brides began around 1800 (if we may rely on the Meulan series). For at that time birth control was not well known among the popular classes, and most people still got their living from peasant farming, where female domestic skills counted enormously. I suggest that we are here encountering, statistically, the impact of romantic love, which created a climate wherein older men were perfectly acceptable for younger women but where the reverse was not true. The revolution of romance in Western society has rendered unacceptable the older woman and the younger man, because the psychological mechanism of romance is fundamentally Oedipal: love at first sight means that you are falling in love with your mother. (You couldn't possibly have had time to cherish and appreciate the woman herself in front of you; you've only known her for three minutes.) As any psychoanalyst will be happy to explain, an unconscious attraction to maternal images produces their *conscious* rejection, and so as men become caught in the sway of true love they acquire a horror of spouses who recall their mothers in any way. So they stop marrying older women.[101]

A final sort of like-marrying-like turns up in the social distance between the mother and father of an illegitimate child. Whereas a growing gap in status is the mark of romance among legitimate couples, an increasing *convergence* in status is the mark of romance among illegitimate ones. In traditional society women who slept with men outside marriage did so mainly because they had to. The man used his economic or political power over them to achieve sexual access, and they went along to avert worse consequences, such as dismissal from their jobs. The traditional disparity in status between seducer and seduced is the result of sexual exploitation, the opposite of inclination and affection. Among the unwed mothers in late seventeenth-century Grenoble, for example, more than half were servant girls bedded by their bourgeois masters: the wood merchant who had his maid substitute for his absent wife; or the notary who

156

profited from his wife's departure to "pay a visit to his servant, a naive child of seventeen."[102]

Then, as time progresses, the status gap lessens. The servant girls and washerwomen of Europe end up increasingly with men who are their social equals and who therefore have no economic or political authority with which to extort sexual concessions. If, therefore, women didn't sleep with these men because they had to, it must have been because they wanted to. This, at least, is the lesson of a study of "pregnancy declarations" during the eighteenth century in Nantes. Early in the century, "sex-on-the-side" (*amour auxiliare*) represented the archetype of illegitimacy in that city, with masters exacting their traditional sexual rights over domestic servants. Then two developments took place: the masters themselves turned increasingly to kept mistresses in separate apartments, women for whom—unlike their domestics—they appear to have had some tenderness of sentiment; and the lower-class women who previously had slept chiefly with their social superiors under obvious duress, turned to men of their own class and attempted with them a rather precarious domestic life. Thus, among illegitimate mothers in Nantes, the percent of employees seduced by employers declined from 36 percent in 1737–1746 to 9 percent in 1780–1787. The seducers of women who bore more than one illegitimate child came increasingly from the lower classes. On the whole, however, these "repeater" mothers came to be greatly overshadowed by the "one-shot" unwed women. Seduced women reported more often at the end than at the beginning of the century that marriage had been promised them. All this involved a tremendous increase in illegitimacy.[103] The trend in Nantes was thus toward the romantic couple and away from the exploited "auxiliary," towards social endogamy and away from the victimization of class by class.[104]

There is one other kind of statistic that may help us pin down the progress of romance in premarital matters: the enumeration of the differences in levels of intercourse from one month to the next. If we, like the gossips, count backwards by nine, we may discover from statistics on the seasonal distribution of births at what time

157

of year the conceptions took place. Assuming seasonal variations in miscarriages and contraception to be minor, the distribution of conceptions from month to month should directly mirror the distribution of intercourse. If my argument that sex has become linked with romance is right, shifts in seasonal sexual patterns should tell us something about the commonality of romance in everyday life.

In traditional society, premarital intercourse—to the extent that it happened at all—occurred unevenly in the course of a year. Appendix IV shows the statistical pattern. Late spring and early summer offered the most frequent occasions, while the months from August through December were less favorable. This should not surprise us, for we have just reviewed the string of courtship festivals that punctuated the first half of the year, and the absence, after St. John's Day in June, of anything more exhilarating than an occasional harvest festival. The point is that in traditional society, premarital sex marched to the rhythm of the holidays. It happened on exceptional occasions, during discontinuities in the passage of the days, and therewith it was not a part of normal life.

As modernization progresses, these seasonal fluctuations flatten out. Rather than taking place during any special period, intercourse becomes evenly distributed throughout the year, so that any given month will see approximately as much sexual activity as any other month. If the experiences of Liège and Montpellier (see Appendix IV) may be generalized, during the eighteenth century we already see the beginnings of a decline in monthly variations in premarital conceptions. Most impressive, however, are the declines that take place within whole countries, such as Germany, from the nineteenth to the twentieth century. In the United States seasonal fluctuation in premarital sex is now barely discernible: the drumbeat is steady throughout the year.

What these figures show, I think, is how sex and romance have become woven into the fabric of popular life. Unlike traditional times, sex in the modern world blends into the normal, ongoing routine of unmarried people. The annual calendar has slackened its grip. No longer does each part of the year bear its particular mood and flavor, with a set time to live and a time to die (seasonal fluctuations in mortality having been reduced as well). The passage of the days becomes homogenized. Each season is like the next, save for the single great discontinuity of the annual vacation, whose sexual effects remain the sole feature distinguishable in the American seasonal profile. What in statistical terms is a lesser "amplitude of seasonality" is, in the real world, the normalization of romance. That is, the less that any one season is the "season for lovers," the more intercourse becomes a routine part of unmarried life. Although such statistics do not say that the chances of young men and women finding each other have increased, they do say that when people get together in bed, the decision will be timed by their own desires and circumstances rather than by the cycle of life of the community of which they are a part.

If the annual cycle of festivities lost its hold upon the courtship of the young, it wasn't necessarily because of some general breakdown in village folkways; rather, it was because the young in particular had deliberately decided to remove their intimate lives from subjection to communal supervision. At some point in the nineteenth century, the youth of Europe made a massive decision to withdraw courtship from collective control—and that means collective control of any kind. There is a kind of received sociological wisdom which says that courtship systems have passed from being community-run to being run by peer groups. But things didn't stop there. In the end, young men and women were no longer subject in their amorous lives to either the larger adult community or the subcommunity of their peers. Courtship had become privatized.

A quantitative verification of this argument seems to me impossible. I cannot imagine systematic data, to which the historian might reasonably have access, that would prove the case one way or the other. Yet the wind of discontent that whips out of nineteenth century ethnographic literature sets plenty of leaves to rustling, and the attentive historian will pick these up.

Here are some rustlings that suggest the couple's retreat from community:

———Once upon a time, we are told, the youth of sunny Brignoles (Var department) spent their "moments of leisure" playing ball together and having races. In the lovely summer evenings they would gather in the fields to picnic and sing, make music and dance, and "amuse themselves with decency and modernization [you may guess what's coming]. Boys and girls of all ages, motivated and united by ties of family, *intérêt*, and friendship took part in these gatherings, upholding for the good of all a spirit of harmony, politeness, and sociability that our new ways have caused to evaporate." Whatever really *had* happened, it is clear that when the nostalgic Dr. Amic penned these lines in 1837, this behavior had come to an end.[105]

———If courtship in Baden towards 1900 was escaping communal supervision, it was, as one local antiquarian explained, because the veillées, which formerly had performed their role, were falling into disuse. The veillée's decline was partly the result of a shift from homespun to store-bought clothing, and partly the result of prohibitions by the police, who saw in the institution a "spawning ground of tattle, superstition, mischief and immorality." But another reason was that youth itself had come to shun this forum in favor of "party night" (the *Dorfkasino*), "to which not only the girls, but boys, and men and women all come in order to flirt [*artig mit einander verkehren*]."[106]

———Whereas before the turn of the century boys and girls in France's Vendée had at least had the good sense to neck in groups, gathered, perhaps, in the main hall of an inn or upstairs in a room (the reader will recall the above discussion of deep kissing, termed in that area *maraichinage*), "these days couples are isolating themselves, seeking out some remote corner of a field or a thick hedge."[107]

———On the eve of the Second World War, one nostalgic old man in the Isère department dwelt lovingly upon the courting customs of the good old days, the village dances, the groups of young men going from house to house to serenade their sweethearts, the beribboned maypoles, and the bonfires on the last Sunday of carnival. "Alas, our youth today no longer know how to entertain themselves in such a simple and poetic manner. . . . They believe themselves great derring-doers in racing about at sixty miles an hour on their motorcycles. It's too bad that they no longer have the time for amusement, for in this manner comraderie and solidarity have given way to envy and egoism, the two great defects of our epoch."[108]

Such testimony, from old men curdled by bitterness and aliena-
tion, swarms with defects. We cannot know if they told true; we
cannot be sure if their little villages were typical; we are at a loss to
say, even at the beginning of our own century, what the reality of
courtship was in the big cities and among the industrial workers,
the new centers of social gravity. But I maintain that such laments
are straws in the wind. The nineteenth century was removing mate
selection from group hands and easing collective pressures upon individual choices. Guys who raced about on their motorcycles were
pretty hard to keep track of, after all.

Courtship in the Contemporary World

A major argument of this book is that there is a close connection
between sexual and sentimental patterns. Thus changes in premarital
behavior towards the end of the eighteenth century went hand-in-
hand with a new orientation towards feeling. Similarly, another
major change has occurred in the twentieth century that we described in the preceding chapter as the second sexual revolution of
the 1960s. The principal theme of the first sexual revolution was the
primacy of affection in mate selection; by the twentieth century,
romantic love had triumphed almost everywhere (except such isolated groups as the French upper bourgeoisie) over *intérêt*. The two
themes of the second sexual revolution were to be the couple's
definitive rejection of pressures from surrounding social networks, be
they the family, the community, or the peer-group—and the unlinking
of coitus and "lifelong" monogamy.

Here again my impression of the premarital couple's growing isolation from both peer-group and community controls is not rigorously
empirical. Family sociologists, obsessed with "conflict resolution"
and "predictors of marital satisfaction," have not troubled to accumulate systematic data on whom the couple see when they go out
together, on whether they are likely to spend the evening anony-
mously or whether they criss-cross larger networks of friends. The

entire social context of premarital behavior is critical, yet the huge social-work and family-sociology industries have neglected it in favor of trivia whose unimportance boggles the mind.[109]

Still, we're not flying entirely by the seat of our pants. Several large-scale studies have inquired where the spouses met. In Sweden, for example, one third had met at dances. In France almost one half—more so among younger couples, less among older—had encountered each other in such anonymous situations as movies, dances, vacation trips, and fairs, or just in the street. And three fourths of a sample population of American teenagers polled in 1972 bravely reported, "So far as sex is concerned, what other young people do doesn't have any influence on what I myself do."[110] In comparison with what we know of acquaintanceship historically, the role of family or friends in introducing and monitoring people has thus been reduced and anonymity enhanced.

As we have seen, historically, the peer group exerted powerful pressures upon the premarital couple to stay together, so that in early nineteenth-century France other fellows had to get permission before dancing with someone's girl; and even in the 1940s and 1950s, American women would lose respectability if they hopped from boyfriend to boyfriend.[111] Consider, then, the evidence of one study of Denmark in 1967: the chances were three in five that young men having their first sexual experiences would, after a subsequent date or two, not see their partners again.[112]

By the 1960s young people had rejected parental intervention in mating. In the United States, the young had begun to fly in the face of parental courtship wishes long before that, of course. Daniel Smith argues that the tendency of daughters to marry in the order in which they were born is a fairly good indicator of parental control over courtship, the parents dealing with each daughter as she comes along in the line. The percentage of daughters marrying *out* of their position in the birth order rose from 8 percent in the mid-seventeenth century in Hingham, Massachusetts, to 18 percent in the mid-nineteenth.[113] And by the time another researcher came along to look at parental supervision of mating, among college-trained married women in Ohio in the late 1940s, things had deteriorated much farther: 31 percent of the first generation of women reported that their parents had been opposed to the man they married, 45 percent of the second generation women reported parental opposition, and 55 percent of the third generation did so.[114] All of which means that women have tended increasingly to go out with men even if their parents disapprove. By the 1970s, one half of all the girls aged 16–19 and three fourths of all the boys were boldly rejecting the proposition that "When it comes to sex, my attitudes and my parents' attitudes are pretty much the same."[115] Some of their testimony was enough to make the hair of any mother curl. One seventeen-year-old girl complained:

"Lately they [her parents] have gotten into a thing with any guy who asks me out: 'Oh, I think he really likes you.' It's just garbage I don't feel I need. If he likes me, I can tell. I don't need my parents to say 'I think he really likes you.' 'Oh good, he wants to take you out.' . . . I don't feel it's any of their business whether I date or not. I don't feel they should push me one way or another."[116] Oh, true words. And here's another sixteen-year-old sweetheart whose testimony would turn the directionist parent to stone:

"Parents should acknowledge that people do fuck, which was hard for me to realize because my mother didn't acknowledge this. And just because you have to be home by one doesn't mean you can't fuck from eleven to one. . . . Well, I really hope I'll be a lot closer to my daughter than my mother and I were."[117]

The second major development in courtship during the 1960s was the transition from "only one sex partner ever" to "serial monogamy." Previously, young people had been willing enough to begin intercourse before marriage but—and this applies to women especially—only with a single person, the man they were going to marry. In the 1960s the chances improved considerably that a typical young woman would sleep with several different men before marriage, yet have only one boyfriend at a time. This passage to a *series* of intimate relationships is not to be confused with the famous unlinking of sex and love which, although much discussed in the popular press, never actually happened. People would continue to feel passionately about their sex partners, each one a *grand amour*. But it became accepted that, during one's single years, a number of *grandes amours* might pass by.

Having several sex partners before marriage began in a number of different countries during the 1960s. In the United States, for example, the 1960s saw a sharp acceleration of the drift towards multiple coital partners that Alfred Kinsey's survey had already picked up among women. Among those born before 1900, only 44 percent of the sexually active had slept with more than one man before marriage; about the same figure prevailed for women born in 1900–1909; for those born in 1910–1919, it rose to 52 percent (again, the phenomenon of the "roaring twenties" among the predominantly middle-class women whom Kinsey interviewed).[118] These were all women who were already married when polled, and thus who had completed their premarital experience. How much more striking it is, therefore, that among the teenagers Robert Sorensen interviewed in 1972, half of the sexually active ones had *already* had more than one sex partner: two fifths of the nonvirginal girls thirteen to fifteen (and more than half of those aged sixteen to nineteen) had slept with several fellows. Just imagine how high those scores may be by the time these women marry. (Of the girls interviewed, 30 percent of those aged thirteen to fifteen were nonvirginal, as were 57 percent of those aged sixteen to nineteen.)[119] Note, however, that within these manifold coital relationships, romance was still vigorous: only an eighth of the girls described their relationships to the fellows they slept with for the first time as less than affectionate, and fully three-fourths of the girls polled said, "I wouldn't want to have sex with a boy unless he loved me."[120]

Droplets of data gathered in other lands in the 1960s and 1970s also point to that combination of partner-changing plus romantic involvement that we call "serial monogamy." Among a sample population of married Frenchwomen polled in 1970, only 4 percent of those over fifty had slept with their future husbands *and* with one or more other men before marriage, but 9 percent of the thirty-to forty-nine-year-olds, and 16 percent of the twenty- to twenty-nine-year-olds had done so. These scores are not very high, but the trend is evident.[121] Although only one-third of the adolescent female German workers polled in 1968–1969 had actually had more than one coitus partner in the preceding twelve months (their cumulative scores would of course be higher), a large majority refused to morally condemn "women who change partners frequently." And nine-tenths agreed that it was all right to have sex before marriage if you loved the fellow.[122]

The German data are silent about changes over time, but a 1968 survey of the Danish female undergraduate population shows a big leap over the preceding ten years in the proportion of unmarried women who had slept with more than one man. Whereas in 1958 only 43 percent of them had experienced coitus with more than one partner, 75 percent had done so by 1968. Their initial adventure, by the way, was much less likely to have been with a steady boyfriend in 1968 than in 1958.[123]

English teenagers polled in the early 1960s had a comparatively high number of sex partners (2.3 for the sexually experienced girls, 6.2 for the boys), but otherwise they conformed to the pattern of serial monogamy. Fewer than a quarter of the sexually active girls had had coitus with more than one fellow in the twelve months preceding the survey, and virtually everyone agreed with the notion that "There is more to sex than just having a good time."[124]

These figures are flashes of light upon a world otherwise in the shadows. If my thesis that premarital serial monogamy is possible only within an anonymous courtship system is correct, this handful of surveys points toward adolescents casting themselves adrift from the supervision of their neighborhoods, their parents, and their peers in mating and dating. If further research shows the contrast between 1905 and 1965 to be as powerful as I believe—in terms of average number of coital partners and the seclusion of acquaintanceship— we shall be justified in speaking of a second sexual revolution in the 1960s and 1970s.

Let us try to draw together—in a manner inevitably far too schematized and general to do justice to any particular time and place—the main developments in courtship over the last three hundred years in Western society. We may usefully distinguish between the uses of sex in the individual's mind, and the individual adolescent's image of his relationship to the surrounding community.

The uses of sex. In traditional society, sexuality mainly served instrumental objectives. That is, it helped the participants to achieve

ulterior goals of a nonsexual nature rather than serving the exploration of the personality. For traditional unmarried women, especially,
intercourse was a means to an end (such as having peace with the
employer, or ratifying a marital alliance between two families) rather
than an end in itself (sex as personal fulfillment). The testimony
we have reviewed suggests that in Europe before 1800, people seldom had sexual intercourse before it was absolutely certain they
would marry, and that sex served for them the larger ends of procreation and the continuation of the lineage, rather than being in itself
an object of joy and delight. Otherwise the emotionless, passionless, affectionless courtship rituals we have observed would be
incomprehensible.

With the first sexual revolution came a breakthrough in intimacy,
a dismantling of the sex-role barriers that had hitherto kept men and
women locked in watertight compartments with little hope of emotional exchange. The libido unfroze in the blast of the wish to be
free. In the years after 1750, lower-class young men and women
awakened to the fact that life involved more than just doing your
duty in the eyes of the local social authorities and doing your work
in the same way that your father had done it, and his father before
him. People had personality needs that might conflict with the surrounding community's need for stability. Among these needs was
"happiness," and among the cardinal ways of becoming happy was
undertaking an emotional relationship with a person of the opposite
sex. Such a relationship, of course, meant fooling around, for sex was
an obvious extension of emotional intimacy. And so the first sexual
revolution would be danced out in the stiff, awkward manner of
people who had spent eons in immobility and who were just beginning to create for themselves a sympathetic world of symbols and
signs, a culture congenial to romanticism.

Although the Beautiful People would scoff at this, such romanticism was not unhorsed in the second sexual revolution of the 1960s.
"True love" had become a permanent saddlemate of intercourse in
modern society. It is possible that intimacy assumed new dimensions in the second sexual revolution, tugging coital partners towards
the "interior search"—which would be unsurprising, in view of the
drug-related inward turning of the adolescent subculture in the

1960s. But here we risk confusing cultural fads with genuine long-term historical shifts; we are so close to these phenomena that our vision blurs.

The courting couple's relationship to the surrounding community. In traditional society, many different social networks and a variety of peer groups took a hand in guiding the couple's formation and its behavior. There would be no *mésailliances*, no fooling around in a way that would endanger the orderly transmission of property or make individuals slough off the staggering weight of their responsibilities to the collectivity.

The first sexual revolution of the late eighteenth century shifted supervision of courtship from the community as a whole to the peer groups of youth itself. Barriers to promiscuity there had to be—firewalls against the fulmination of all this erotic nitroglycerin that the onrush of sentiment had started agitating—but barriers within the context of a subculture generally sympathetic to self-discovery and intimacy. So there was a lot of sex, and because the youth organizations lacked much of the coercive power of the larger village networks, accidents happened, suitors jumped ship, and illegitimate children were born. Yet the coital partners were doubtless anxious to follow the standards of the larger peer groups of which they were a part.

The second sexual revolution of the 1960s seems to have removed even this feeble peer-group control over adolescent mating and dating. The wish to be free has frayed all the cables that used to tie the couple to surrounding social institutions. Self-realization—accomplished through sexual gratification—has taken command of courtship.

CHAPTER FIVE

Mothers and Infants

GOOD MOTHERING is an invention of modernization. In traditional society, mothers viewed the development and happiness of infants younger than two with indifference. In modern society, they place the welfare of their small children above all else. That is the story of this chapter.

Perhaps I should explain why the evolution of the mother–infant relationship deserves to be discussed here. At first place it has little immediately to do with the larger narrative of family ties to community. Yet mothers and infants have a claim to our attention, if only because the rush of maternal sentiment into the family circle was part of the larger surge of sentiment that is the basic subject of this book. But then too, we won't be able to fully understand the formation of "domesticity"—that mesh of privacy and intimacy encircling the family as a whole—without understanding how the new relationship between mother and baby came into being.

Please note that babies, rather than "children" in general, are the subject of this chapter. Our concern here is with the crystallization of maternal love for infants, love in the sense of spontaneity and empathy. This gave the entire family a new emotional base and introduced a rationale, independent of romantic love (which after all, didn't survive the wedding ceremony all that long), for withdrawing from community life.

The little band of scholars that for some time now has been arguing that in traditional society mothers didn't love their children very much has met with stark incredulity.[1] Mothers not attached to their babies? Indifferent to their welfare and resigned to their squalling, usually fatal "convulsions" and "fevers"? Impossible, says the twentieth-century spirit. But in fact, among the general populace, life was that way. Mothers in villages and small towns across the continent from Cornwall to Lettland seldom departed from traditional—often hideously hurtful—infant hygiene and child-rearing practices; and this is what lacking "spontaneity" is all about. Nor did these mothers often (some say "never") see their infants as human beings with the same capacities for joy and pain as they themselves. Parents were not, in other words, able to put themselves in their infants' tiny shoes, to imagine the world from their viewpoint, and thus to make it as agreeable and delightful a world as possible—which is what we mean by "empathy."

These millions of traditional mothers were not monsters. They had merely failed the "sacrifice" test. If they lacked an articulate sense of maternal love, it was because they were forced by material circumstances and community attitudes to subordinate infant welfare to other objectives, such as keeping the farm going or helping their husbands weave cloth. We will be able to spot the emergence of maternal love only when all these millions of mothers consciously decide to reorder their priorities and put the life and happiness of their infant above everything else.

Traditional Indifference

It was the pioneer social historian Philippe Ariès who first argued that maternal indifference to infants characterized traditional society.[2] With the aid of portraits and family reference books, he concluded that small children were seen in the Middle Ages as creatures apart from people. Barely possessing souls of their own, they came at the Will of God, departed at His behest, and in their brief mortal sojourn deserved little adult sympathy or compassion. Ariès argued

169

that among the upper bourgeois and noble groups, on whose evidence he depends, this pattern of indifference started to give way towards the sixteenth and seventeenth centuries. And he is probably right about those classes. But among the ordinary people who are my concern, this traditional insouciance persisted until at least the last quarter of the eighteenth century and, within some classes and regions, considerably later. That is one modification that this book hopes to bring to Ariès' classic analysis.

In the eighteenth and early nineteenth centuries, parental indifference to infants was still firmly implanted among all segments of the popular classes, and among all kinds of communities. A number of indicators suggest that the great transformation Ariès saw as already long underway among the upper bourgeoisie had not yet filtered down. At least, that is what we must infer from the way these mothers *acted* towards their children.

It was not so much a question of brutality, child-beating, and the like. Although physical violence certainly abounded in both large city and small village,[3] it has persisted into our own day and in any case is not a good inverse indicator of affection. Children were brutalized by the daily routines of life as much as by savage outbursts of parental rage.

There was, for example, the cradle, in peasant hands a benumbing contraption. Wakeful children were commonly *knocked* into the sleep of insensibility. "Most pernicious is the rural practice of . . . forcing children to go to sleep through immoderate rocking, through swinging and shaking, through lugging up and down and loud singing, methods which are sooner appropriate to effect . . . stupidity and idiocy" (of Schesslitz near Bamburg).[4] Nor was violent rocking confined to peasants; in Vienna, "the dumb, harmful custom of calming children with benumbing shaking and rocking, although abandoned by the upper orders, is still widespread among the lower."[5] The same was true of Stuttgart: upper-class renunciation of the cradle for the crib, lower-class persistence in "forceful shaking."[6]

More serious for the infant's welfare was the well-nigh universal practice of leaving it alone for long stretches of time. All the doctors complain about how parents permit children to stew in their own excrement for hours on end, tightly wound in swaddling clothes;

about how children left unattended before the hearth perish when their garments catch fire; and about how unguarded infants would be attacked and eaten by the barnyard hogs.[7] In the mountains of the Vosges, peasant women would spend hours away from their cottages in the summer, leaving their babies crying "with all their might" in the cradle (in the observer's view, a cause of hernias).[8] Around Montpellier, especially in the season of silkworm growing, filth and lack of care were thought to be more important causes of infant death than epidemic diseases: "It's common knowledge how much assiduity this sort of pursuit demands: the women are constantly busy with gathering mulberry leaves or with the worms themselves. The children are neglected, suffer, and die. The habit of seeing such a great number perish in this season has given rise to a proverb which says that 'in the time you see the silkworm rise, the most kids go to paradise.' "[9] In the valley of the Morienval (Oise), infants died in especially great numbers during the hemp and grain harvests because—according to "Citizen" Cambry, prefect of the department—their mothers neglected them to work in the fields.[10] (In fairness, harvesting also coincided with the time of year in which the risk of contamination and infection were greatest—witness the late-summer peaks of infant diarrhea in both city and countryside all over Europe.)

Industrial work had the same results. Mothers in Budapest often left their small children at home during the day with another child just a few years older, thereby "giving rise to accidents of all sorts and delaying the arrival of medical attention for sick infants whose condition is subject to quick deterioration." (Even worse than leaving the children at home was taking them along, however, for mothers who had to earn their living as day laborers would "even in foul weather just wrap the infants in a blanket and lay them on the ground nearby, through which many go under.")[11]

Such material inattentiveness could be explained by economic necessity alone, though the reasons were doubtlessly more complicated than that. Even when mothers were *with* their children, however, we note little of the affectionate concern, the playful efforts to help the infant develop as a person, that characterize the modern mother. Traditional babies were left pretty much to themselves, and

171

we have no reason to think the following account of mothers in and around the town of Laval (Mayenne) untypical: "Here they care for infants only with this phlegmatic tranquility characteristic of the pituitary temperament. If they hold them in their arms, if they walk them, it's in stillness, the silence of resignation to their duties, which the mothers and servants execute with exactitude but seldom go beyond. They don't sing; they don't talk to the infant; they don't try to awaken its senses; they make no effort to develop the child's sensations through merriment or through the little coquetries of maternal tenderness."[12]

And what kind of mothers, we ask ourselves, refer to their children as "it" (or often, *la créature*) without distinguishing the sex, forget their offspring's ages (one French mother believed her son "six or eight months," another "eleven or fourteen years"), give the name of a dead baby to one newly born, or can't remember how many children they've had? In eighteenth-century Languedoc, from which these examples are taken, "one looks in vain for the evolution Philippe Ariès postulated in the attitudes of parents towards their children."[13]

The apparent absence of bereavement in the face of an infant's death further underlines our point. If they bore the loss of their children with equanimity, how much affection could these traditional mothers have felt? Mothers would simply leave their dying babies "lying in the gutters and rotting on the dung-heaps of London," a sight which horrified Thomas Goram, the patron of a hospital for foundlings.[14] Dr. Johnson's Mrs. Thrale was said to have "regarded the death of various daughters at school with great equanimity." And Sir John Verney "cheerfully remarked when two of his fifteen children died that he still had left a baker's dozen."[15] In southern France bands of robbers groping their way along a path would say, "It's a dead kid," and pass on.[16] It often happened in one parish of Anjou that neither parent would attend the funeral of a child younger than five, and in others that only one would show up, sometimes the father, sometimes the mother.[17]

There were, of course, circumstances in which infant death was received with less equanimity, as when the mother would perish along with her first child at the delivery, for this would require that the husband return his wife's dowry to her relatives.[18] But especially with the third or fourth child, death would be perceived as a blessing for both children and parents. In Bavaria's Haidau County "people are generally pleased with the quick death of children, and say 'they're well provided for.' "[19] Francois Lebrun writes of eighteenth-century Angevin peasants: "The death of a small child, provided it had been baptized, is considered on the religious plane as a deliverance, for the infant has had the grace of acceding directly to paradise without knowing the bitterness of this life and of risking his [spiritual] health. On the human plane infant death is almost a banal accident, which a subsequent birth will recuperate."[20] In the modern world a child's death sears a couple for life. What kind of people were these, in traditional society, who did not even attend the funerals of their deceased infants?

Clearly visible at the tip of this iceberg of traditional indifference were the divorcing mothers who left their children. In marital separations in the diocese of Cambrai during the eighteenth century, for example, there were almost no squabbles over the custody of children: women were quite happy to surrender them to the husband. To persuade his wife Marie to agree to a divorce, Abraham Pluchart, a merchant in Valenciennes, offered to "take on the child and care for him to permit her to live more tranquilly."[21]

Or consider the willingness of parents to abandon legitimate children, to deposit them in the still of night at the door of some local charitable institution that would see to it that the children were raised by a mercenary nurse. Were it a question of abandoning Baby Billy to be raised by rich industrialist Fink, that would be one thing. But the chances were excellent that the infant would die in the hands of the paid wet nurse; such abandonment was tantamount to infanticide.[22]

Exactly what percentage of the enormous number of foundlings was legitimate is not clear—one scholar believes it to have been negligible among the abandoned infants of the Ardèche department during the eighteenth century.[23] But another puts the proportion as high as four-fifths of the total in the nearby Limousin around the same time.[24] Roughly 15 percent of all foundlings deposited at Paris's General Hospital in 1760 were legitimate, the same proportion as a century later.[25] To get a general order of magnitude, keep in mind that towards the middle of the nineteenth century in France, around 33,000 children were abandoned every year. Any foundling more than a month old was likely to be legitimate (on the logic that unwed mothers would abandon the child as soon as possible), and little ribbons and notes attached to the garments of many gave supplementary clues, so authorities had some basis for guessing at legitimacy status. We might reasonably estimate that between a tenth and a quarter of all foundlings were legitimate. This means that in a given year perhaps five thousand children would be abandoned by their families.

What moved their parents to abandon them? In the first place, desperate poverty. Whenever grain prices rose in the eighteenth century, so did the number of foundlings, showing that the cost of living was forcing many parents to rid the household of a child or two. Moreover, the higher the prices, the higher was the age of the foundlings, which indicates that parents were ridding themselves not just of the newborn but of older siblings too.[26]

For some the separation was heartrending. "The times," reads a typical note pinned to an infant's clothing, "are so hard and so unfortunate and the misery so great that we've been forced despite ourselves to abandon our dear child of three years. We ask the good sisters of the hospital kindly to try to keep our poor girl apart by means of some mark and by the time of day of her abandonment, so that we shall have the joy of recognizing her and taking her back." But the parents seldom returned.[27]

For others the separation seems to have been a matter of indifference. Although we must allow for the tendency of middle-class observers to believe factory workers by nature depraved, it does appear that proletarians were quick to abandon their legitimate children. The prefect of the Nord conjured up for his great textile cities the spectacle of women squandering their household budgets upon brandy, then kicking out their children, who would "run about in bands of three and four, at the mercy of public charity."[28] And observers of Lyon's married workers were convinced that at least a fifth of those who gave birth at the Hôtel-Dieu exposed their infants in this way. A typical story is that of a master weaver being asked by a friend about a relative who, it was said, had abandoned her second child. "Your sister-in-law is well settled," said the friend, "and her husband too. That's what surprises me. I thought her an upstanding woman." "Well, yes she is," said the weaver, "but her child got in the way of her daily routines, and moreover, she exposed her first one as well."[29]

The grim misery behind these accounts makes abandonment something less than a perfect mirror of indifference. And the many factory workers who exposed their children show that the phenomenon was not just "traditional." It is when we turn to mercenary nursing that the separation of mother from young infant stands out as a systematic practice of all classes, poor or not. And the rise of maternal breast-feeding shows that abandonment, whether to a mercenary nurse or a charitable institution, was indeed a traditional practice.

Paid Wet Nurses and Breastfeeding Mothers

One of the remarkable phenomena of European social history was the large number of mothers who sent their infant children away to be cared for by mercenary wet nurses in distant places. Just after baptism the child would be taken from the mother and whisked away over long roads to some peasant cottage where, if it survived the trip, it would spend the next two years.

This custom of boarding out legitimate infants should not be confused with bringing a nurse into the home to feed the infant under the mother's watchful eye. It must also be distinguished from hand-feeding—giving the infant pap, animal milk, or a mixed diet instead of a pure regime of mother's milk. Nor, finally, should we confuse the phenomenon of married women sending away their children with the efforts of unmarried mothers to disembarrass themselves of illegitimate offspring, or with the desperate attempts of foundling homes all across Europe to find rural families to take in the wave of abandoned children that was inundating them in the eighteenth century.

Just how widespread this boarding out of legitimate children was, remains something of a mystery. It varied widely by country and by social class. Mrs. Jane Sharp recorded in her *Midwives Book* (1671) that in England "the usual way [is] for rich people to put forth their children to nurse.[30] But it was most often the English public authorities and not the couple who sent away children, and only the offspring of unwed mothers or of families shattered by poverty were affected.[31] In the American colonies, extramural wet nurses were employed occasionally, such as the Pennsylvania woman "with a good breast of milk" who in 1782 announced in the paper that she was "willing to take a child in her own family. Enquire at Robert McGoogen's near the three-mile stone."[32]

Town dwellers in Central Europe seem to have boarded out infants on a fairly widespread scale. The statistician Johann Peter Süssmilch commented in 1742 on the many wet nurses in the cities, and on how their ministrations made urban infant mortality rates higher than rural. Only wet nurses living in the homes of the rich were exempt from the rule that "nurses are not the same as mothers, and the lack of tenderness is the cause of many a fatal omission." In rural areas, on the other hand, women nursed their own children (for such long periods that, according to Süssmilch, breastfeeding amounted to a contraceptive technique).[33] The first half of the nineteenth century saw enough references to the use of wet nurses by city dwellers to let us conclude that "boarding out" stretched considerably beyond illegitimate babies and foundlings.[34]

It was in France, especially, that married women commonly sent their infants to rural nurses. Buffon, on the basis of mortality data from the Paris region, estimated in 1777 that a sixth of all infants were boarded out.[35] And if we may go by recent work on the Beauvais district, the figure may have been even higher. In some regions of old-regime France, a majority of families may have been involved in the boarding out of small children, either by sending their own away, or by taking in other people's children from outside.[36] Class differences were considerable. Only among the landed peasantry would women almost always breast or handfeed their own infants, and then only because in the time thus liberated they couldn't earn enough to pay a wet nurse. Among other classes, women whose earnings would cover the nurse's wages, or whose husbands could foot the bill, boarded out their children in large numbers. Poor women in rural areas, for example, would put their own children out at very low rates in order to take a better-paid nursling from elsewhere.[37] The wives of small storekeepers and artisans also boarded out their infants in order to help their husbands in the shop. Maurice Garden has recently shown in detail how common the practice was among silk-weaving families in eighteenth-century Lyon. But whatever the occupation, if we are to go by testimony from places like Montpellier, Puy, and Chambéry, urban mothers seem generally to have sent out their babies to rural nurses. Of Chambéry, for example, it was said, "The mothers of the city have still not been able to accustom themselves to nursing their own children; this concern is unfortunately still entrusted to women in the countryside, where many of these nurslings die of convulsions. . . ."[38]

It is significant that the one group that never either boarded out its own infants on a large scale or took in nurslings from outside was the factory workers, the spearhead of modernization. Although women in industrial plants often used day nurses, or handfed their infants, they did not send them from home for long periods. Margaret Hewitt writes, for example, of Lancashire, "There is no evidence that the married (nor, indeed, the unmarried) operatives put their infants out to nurse for a longer period than that of a working day."[39] Though aghast at the way female mill-hands in Lillebonne treated their small children, Arsène Dumont never claims they sent them from home. And working mothers in Landshut rushed to take advantage of an employer's offer of a six-week, paid maternity leave, thereby decreasing the mortality of their babies during this period by one fourth.[40] If despite the direst poverty and the sorest temptations to fail the "sacrifice test," proletarian women kept their infants at home, it must have been because their attitudes were already "modern."

How did the system of mercenary wet nursing work? Our evidence is most complete from France, where boarding out had become a highly organized form of cottage industry. In the big cities, private agencies would most often serve as intermediaries between mothers and peasant nurses. Alongside the municipal Nursing Control Board of Paris (*Direction municipale des nourrices*) there flourished a number of hole-in-the-wall bureaus that unscrupulously exploited both nurses and natural mothers. They would advertise, as fountains of lactation, women whose own breasts had long dried up and who could do no more than handfeed their charges. Or the nurses themselves would fool both mothers and agencies by borrowing (or renting) other people's healthy babies and pass them off as their own. Another ruse was to have the local mayor falsify the baptismal certificate of the wet nurse's own child so as to make it appear that her milk was the same "age" as her nursling-to-be. (People thought it important that the milk correspond to the child's age, another of the items of medical misinformation in which this domain abounded.) Yet even though the whole wet nursing industry was vitiated by fraud, Parisian families resolutely ignored the official agency and flocked to the private bureaus, confident that their offspring would thrive in the pure country air. In a given year the official agency would send out 2,000 to 3,000 legitimate children from Paris, the hole-in-the-wall agencies perhaps 12,000.[41]

Once the infants had been boarded out, their parents seldom visited them. Oh, to be sure, they would ascertain by mail every now and then that all was well. And the nurses had what amounted to a standard form letter for supplying reassurance that normally was totally unjustified:[42]

Dear Madame,
  I'm writing to give you news of your precious dear, and at the same time to ask how you yourself are getting along. The little darling is fine. He has just had a touch of rickets [!], but I took him on a pilgrimage which cost me three francs and now he's doing much better. It's astonishing how much he resembles your husband. Might I ask you to send me booties, for he'll be walking soon. It's also soon going to be time to get him into clothes. His toothing has been so difficult that I've had to put sugar into everything he takes. Would it be convenient for you to send along a bit of sugar and some soap. My regards to your husband.

                                                              Your nurse, . . .

A standard closing was to invite the mother out for a visit, but had these mothers actually traveled to whatever dark hole their child had fallen into, they would have been stunned. The wet nurses, drawn from the agricultural laborers, marginal peasants, and unwed mothers (who often got pregnant in order to lactate and thus market themselves) were desperately poor, harried creatures who generally lived in rural hovels. In the Eure-et-Loir "the dwellings of many nurses are badly aired. Several have only a single room, in which are crowded together a number of beds and chests. Some have but a single bed, and three nurslings."[43] And in a typical wet nurse's dwelling in the Nièvre, the occupants most often just dumped their water on the dirt floor, "unable to take the trouble to throw it outside." The domestic livestock of pigs, goats, sheep, and poultry lived right with the family. The great hearth "gave off as much cold air as heat," and to ventilate the smoke the door had to be left ajar anyway, which sent "mortal" drafts racing across the infant. In addition to the two or three huge beds, there would be several cradles suspended hammock-like above one another. Right at the door was the fertilizer pile, and rotting straw was stuffed about the place in nooks and crannies. Underfoot there squished "a sort of black water, greenish, and fetid."[44] Just the place for a baby, in other words.

The terrible poverty that had motivated the rural family to take on a nursling in the first place created an environment that was in every way inhospitable to good mothering and even to physical survival. In one department the nurses' shacks were even "without a fire in the winter, and the children's feet freeze in their soaked clothing."[45] This was from a report of a commission on foundlings, but in that region foundlings were supervised by the state, often receiving better care than the boarded-out legitimate children. "The women [who work for the private nursing agencies] are the poorest of the district, the most badly housed, and the most deprived of everything. They take one, two, or three little Parisians whom they obtain from several agencies or direct from the families. These children, thus deposited in the countryside and isolated from any kind of medical or administrative surveillance, become the victims of ignorance, cupidity and lack of attention. For the nurse, staggering under the work of her own household and the burden of her own children, can pay but little attention to the cleanliness and physical exercise of which these children are in such need."[46]

But bad housing and filth were, after all, the lot of poor country children in general. It was the nurse's inattentiveness that was so

179

dangerous. There were horror stories of neglect: "The nurse was drunk, and carried the infant with its head downwards. I saw what the fate would be of the poor, innocent creature. Assigned several months later by the police commission to investigate the death of this nursling who had arrived at Nogent so fresh and rosy, I found in the shack which the woman inhabited a dessicated little form, its features shriveled, laid out upon a foul, stinking straw mattress without sheets. The poor child was dead of hunger and misery. In the nurse's absence, an absence which had lasted the entire morning, the neighbors had finally been moved by the plaintive cries, which all of a sudden had stopped. They had to break in the door to ascertain that the infant was dead."[47] Yet if we are to trust the scandalized nineteenth-century rural doctors who practiced among these people, neglect and indifference were the norm. In the Morvan, for example, wet nurses didn't change the bedding from one infant to the next, and the feather bolsters, "impregnated with sweat, urine, and fecal matter, exhaled an odor of foul ammonia."[48] Impatience, weariness, and indifference finally led the nurses to try to silence bawling infants with alcohol, or with such opium-based tranquilizers as "Godfrey's Cordial," a mixture of treacle, laudanum, and sassafras.[49] Observers thought it strange how silently the infants lay when they came to call, and soon of course the infants would go under.

Ironically, the "wet nurses" were likely to be dry, their careers having long outlasted their milk supplies. Indeed, it often happened that even lactating nurses would not have enough milk for all the nurslings, giving their own children first go (in the event that they hadn't abandoned them), and then supplementing the milk remaining to the outsiders with hand food. Or even worse, the more destitute nurses, who had neither a cow nor a goat, would have to offer their charges "pap"—a mixture of flour, water, and sugar which, devoid of protein and vitamins, gave them starches far too soon and in general deprived them of any natural immunities they might have received from human milk. In the countryside around Budapest, "a baby farmer takes sometimes two or three children from outside as nurslings, continuing meanwhile to suckle her own. Of course she gives the strangers her breast only when her child is full, and actually then only *pro forma*, for in fact they're fed with cheaper and usually

unsuitable foods, simply to keep them quiet."[51] Rural nurses near
Bremen gave most of their milk to their own children, then sup-
plemented what they had left with surrogates for the outside nursling.[52] For infants several months old there would perhaps be bits
from the family's dinner table, premasticated by the nurse.

We are told that English nurslings were "fed on meat before
they have got their teeth, and what is, if possible, still worse, on
biscuits not fermented, or buttered rolls, or tough muffins floated in
oiled butter, or calves-feet jellies or strong broths yet more calculated
to load all their powers of digestion."[53] For the sooner the infant
could be weaned to solid food, the sooner the nurse could get another
to breast-feed. And if, in the pell-mell race towards weaning, the infant died—well, then she could easily get another too.

The reader will not be surprised to discover that under these
circumstances, the mortality of legitimate children boarded out was
ghastly. Whereas the normal mortality of legitimate infants who
stayed with their mothers was 19 percent in eighteenth-century
Rouen, that of legitimate infants sent to rural wet nurses (subsidized by the city) was 38 percent. (The mortality of foundlings
sent to the rural nurses around Rouen was 90 percent!)[54] Of the
2,400 nurslings sent from Paris to the arrondissement of Nogent-le-
Rotrou in 1858–1859—most of whom seem to have been legitimate—
35 percent died within the first two years of life; of the infants born
in that arrondissement of local parents (most presumably breastfed
by their mothers), only 22 percent died.[55] In the city of Erfurt
around 1870, 17 percent of all infants nursed by their own mothers
perished before age one; 30 percent of those confided to wet nurses
did so.[56] It is thus clear (and was surely so to the people of the
time) that giving a child to a mercenary nurse appreciably increased
the chances that its parents would never see it again.

If maternal breastfeeding made the difference between life and
death, perhaps we might use it as an indicator of the advance of
maternal sentiment. We submit the mothers of late eighteenth-
century and nineteenth-century France to the "sacrifice" test: to the
extent that they were willing to abandon mercenary nurses in favor
of breastfeeding, they were placing the welfare of their infants above

other criteria. Because traditional mothers had to sacrifice income in order to breast-feed, we have in maternal nursing a clear sign of the valuation they placed upon their child's health: no nursing equals low value. But how about all those peasant women who had nursed since time out of mind? The other part of our breast-feeding index is the proviso that to be considered "modern," the nursing mother must suckle *only* her own child, refusing to take in others because their presence would either endanger her child's life by reducing the available milk supply, or because such nonfamily members would intrude upon the new-found privacy of the domestic unit. So the hordes of breast-feeding peasant women do not get classed as modern.

After 1800 a great decline in mercenary extramural wetnursing took place. Whereas the Parisian municipal wet-nursing board was sending out 5,000 to 6,000 infants a year in the Napoleonic Period, by the 1830s the figure had dropped to 1,000.[57] But the argument I wish to present here has a twist: it was among the middle classes that the practice first came to a halt. Only later did the lower classes catch up. And while by the beginning of World War I the boarding-out of legitimate infants of any class was vastly reduced, this class lag in the diffusion of maternal nursing should tell us something about the reasons behind it.

It has been customary to date the triumph of maternal breast-feeding from Jean-Jacques Rousseau's *Emile* of 1762. Although the date may serve as a useful landmark in intellectual history, it is unlikely that *Emile* itself played much part in initiating the movement, partly because such ideas had long been circulating, and partly because in the 1760s we find the switch to maternal nursing already well underway among the middle classes.[58] Well-to-do women of La Rochelle, for example, shaken by a wave of deaths among infants they had sent out to peasant nurses, by 1766 themselves commenced to breastfeed (and outraging society by doing so in public). Artisans' wives, on the other hand, had undertaken exactly the opposite course. Whereas formerly it had been they who suckled the children of the wealthy, these wives were now sending their own babies into the countryside, in order to revel in *luxe* and idleness;

or so explained Doctor Destrapierre, the dean of the Royal Medical College of La Rochelle.[59]

Doctor Destrapierre has probably supplied the key to the movement's initial growth: the hideous mortality that struck nurslings sent to the countryside, a death rate that became higher as the century progressed.[60] To save the lives of their children, mothers were forced to keep them at home. It was, for example, an epidemic of syphilis among rural nurses that compelled mothers of Saint-Malo to begin wet nursing in the 1780s. Venereal diseases had spread from the sailors and soldiers of the port to the surrounding countryside, "and it is the fear that mercenary nurses may be infected which has constrained local mothers to listen to the voice of nature and themselves to nurse their infants. This practice, which dignifies their natural capacities, is universal in our district."[61] (An ironical conjunction of carnal and maternal love.)

And for those who, to believe anything is happening at all, must see it happening in Paris, there is evidence aplenty. Doctor Menuret de Chambaud wrote in 1786 that while, in general, few Parisian women wet nursed, "some finding in wealth the means and motives for dispensing with this duty, others forced to renounce through misery or the need to work," a new trend towards maternal nursing had commenced among the upper classes: ". . . The wise teachings of Locke about infancy, presented through the eloquent pen of Rousseau, have started to gather fruit in the city. Among the upper orders for several years now an ever greater number of mothers have discovered that the tiresomeness of nursing is compensated by many pleasures and advantages. People are now giving more liberty to children. . . . Pap [*bouillie*] has been banned from their regime and they are given more exercise."[62] Of special interest here is the association between maternal nursing and a renewed concern for the infant's welfare as a whole, evidence that nursing was part and parcel of a larger set of attitudes towards children. One must nonetheless note that the revival of maternal nursing was not just an upper-class Parisian phenomenon, for elsewhere in the Paris region—in the sleepy outlying town of Nemours (Seine-et-Marne), for example— "more prosperous women are nursing their own children. But the infants of the people are put out to mercenaries so that the women may work without hindrance."[63]

Tracing the evolution of breastfeeding among the lower classes is more difficult, partly because when the doctors are not specifically referring to those of their own class, they tend to speak without differentiation of "the people." Thus we may mark specifically proletarian progress only by inferring from statements such as "all mothers have started nursing here . . ." that most of those mothers were from the general populace. In the cities of the Meurthe towards 1796, for example, "the arguments of philosophy against the custom of sending children to mercenary nurses have been well received . . . and today it is rare to see a mother who doesn't nurse, whereas twenty years ago the same was true of one who did. The census taken at the end of 1796 confirms that 98 percent of children on the breast were being fed by their mothers. Without a doubt, this submissiveness to the laws of nature has appreciably diminished mortality."[64] In Mont-Blanc department around 1807 it was said that maternal nursing had made "fortunate progress" in both city and countryside. "And the execution of this duty disposes mothers to another as well, that of taking good care of children during infancy."[65] The local doctor of Châlons-sur-Marne noted, around 1820, that maternal breastfeeding was arriving hand-in-hand with "la tendresse conjugale." Women there were both good mothers and good wives, and "a mood of softness, a happy spirit reigns in households everywhere." This sounds a bit too good to be true, but it is interesting that the writer associated these two realms of affection.[66]

Such chronicles have limits. The authors are maddeningly imprecise about the specific social groups involved, and they are totally silent on the willingness of women who had previously accepted nourrissons from outside to do so in the future. Yet the recitation could be extended well into the nineteenth century, evidence of an onward march of maternal breastfeeding. This transformation in the representative experience of the average baby betokens, I suggest, a revolution in maternal love.

One problem remains, however. Did lower-class women cease to breastfeed other people's children because they themselves had developed a desire for privacy and intimacy within the foyer, as the extreme version of my argument would predict? Or did they cease mercenary nursing simply because the demand was dwindling, because middle-class mothers were refusing to confide their offspring to the undependable mercies of professional nurses?

A different sort of evidence—the changing attitudes of the nurses themselves—suggests that powerful emotional ties between mother and infant were in fact developing among women of the marginal peasantry. Before 1820, indications are rare that anything bound mercenary nurses to infants but the cash nexus; thereafter it becomes ever more frequent for *nourrices* to love and raise their paid nurslings as they would their own children.

Although in matters of this nature exceptions inevitably present themselves, traditional nurses as a rule were indifferent beyond belief to the welfare of the babies they took in. Children were commodities for them, just as, let us say, cocoa futures are commodities for the modern trader. And they acted invariably to maximize their profits, as a trader would with any standardized interchangeable unit in the marketplace. For the commodities dealer, one sack of cocoa is not intrinsically more marvelous or precious than any other given sack. So also for the mercenary nurses of the eighteenth century. We know most about those who took in foundlings and were paid on a quarterly basis by the local foundling home or muncipal hospital. If the first weeks did not go well and the infant's poor physical condition or squalls at night became a problem, the wet nurse would exchange it at the home for another. Thus in the municipal hospital in Limoges, 60 percent of all foundlings changed wet nurses at least once in the first year of life. And all the nurses would return a child to the hospital once it had reached the age of seven, in order to take another infant.[67] Now, the modern mentality is very likely slackjawed at such returns. After having raised a baby for seven years in your home, would you then give it up? Yes, you would, because the hospital paid higher rates for newborn than for older children. Attached though you may be to Cocoa Lot 688, you unload it at the first opportunity if the price drops. And no money at all? No infant care. In the department of the Eure, where unsettled conditions had delayed fee payments during the Revolution, nurses simply stopped coming, and those infants abandoned at the hospitals perished there. Four-fifths of the seven hundred-odd foundlings deposited in the Eure between 1797 and 1801 died within the first months of life, "victims of the putrid fevers which penetrated into the ward where they were assembled."[68]

Perhaps I am unfair. Modern hospital personnel, after all, do not permit themselves passionate attachment to all the babies who pass through their hands; so such commodity mentality need not necessarily be thought of as "traditional." But whereas modern doctors and nurses would feel themselves remiss were their charges to die in great numbers, the death of at least one out of every two infants left the wet nurses apparently unmoved. Here is the report of the General Council of the Aube department on the subject of nurses' care of foundlings in the 1830s: "Many of these unsupervised nurses relegate their charges to some dark and unhealthy nook, cover them scarcely at all, leave them tormented by vermin, tossing in their own ordure and prey to all manner of skin diseases. It is to this lack of care that Monsieur le Préfet attributes the increase in foundling mortality to 67 out of every 100."[69]

To extend this grisly recitation would be pointless. What matters is that traditional *nourrices* seem to have had virtually no intrinsic interest in the welfare of their infants. If one died, they would simply go back to the hospital and be given another. For them the pay was everything, the child—as a tiny spark of life who *might* have been cherished for noneconomic reasons—nothing.

In the course of the nineteenth century, this "economism" on the mercenary nurses' part began to give way to an almost maternal affection. According to Nogent-le-Rotrou's Dr. Brochard, whose mid-nineteenth century criticisms of bad nurses we have listened to already, the majority of nurses were devoted and responsible. "I've spent eighteen years of my medical career among nurses and nurslings. And during these years I've had to hear every day complaints and testimonials from both nurses and parents. I must say that after all the sad things I've recounted, I'm consoled that the number of good nurses surpasses by far the number of bad ones."[70] Contrast this with Dr. Gilibert's judgment, a century earlier, that "there are very few wet nurses sufficiently vigilant to keep their infants passingly clean . . . who wash their clothes, covers, and sheets. The majority do it rarely, dry them poorly, and never change the little mattresses. Through all these forms of negligence the infants are continually surrounded by an atmosphere supercharged with putrid matter."[71] The gap between these two estimates shows one side of the advance of sentiment.

Again, consider what happened when, around 1835, the Guizot government decided to transfer foundlings from the nurses who had been raising them to unknown destinations. This represented an effort to cut down the foundling rate by making it impossible for parents to continue to see, *chez la nourrice*, the children they had formally abandoned.[72] According to one hospital's administrative committee, "the nurses show the greatest reluctance to give up the children. You should have seen the lamentations of the women, and often as well of their husbands who accompanied them. In vain we argued that legitimate children whose nursing the city [Nantes] subsidizes may be withdrawn whenever the parents see fit. 'We know,' the nurses replied, 'that the legitimate babies will be taken back by their families. But the foundlings from the hospitals have no parents. And we become attached to them as to our own. We take them into our hearts. We couldn't imagine that anyone could ever dream of removing them from us.' As proof, many of the women cited foundlings whom they had kept on even after the fees had terminated and who now were good farmers and workers in the area's agriculture."[73] The administrative committee of the hospital in nearby Niort posed the nurses' dilemma even more cogently: "We have seen some of these good women, listening only to their *bon coeur*, declare that they would keep their foundlings for nothing. In their home villages we have been able to verify that these women had no other recourse than to ask for public charity in support of the infants they had just adopted."[74]

Such attachment to the infant foundlings was not confined to the west of France. In the Aveyron, mercenary nurses were making similar decisions when faced with the loss of their nurslings: "At the instigation of the parents a number of nurses declared themselves willing to keep on the infants [cases where the parents had maintained secret ties with the nurse whom the state was paying] . . . but the greatest number of infants were kept on free of charge only as a result of the affection and generosity their nurses dedicated them."[75] Thus, again we see mercenary nurses prepared to put the heart before the pocketbook. The foundling-transfer policy of the Guizot government throws a sharp spotlight onto a historical change whose other parts lie still in darkness: the articulation of maternal love for infant children among the general populace.

By the time of the period between the two World Wars, two important trends had developed fully. First, a general decline in mercenary nursing and a corresponding surge in maternal feeding, either breast or "dry," had set in everywhere. France was adopting the Atlantic pattern of keeping infants at home. Whereas, in 1896, 111,000 legitimate children had been boarded out, by 1913 the figure had fallen to 92,000, and would drop off steadily thereafter.[76] This amounts, to be sure, to a lot of children, with a tenth of all newborn still going *en nourrice* (the great majority of them legitimate infants from cities).[77] But the trend was sharply off. It should be kept in mind that toward the century's end short-lived trendlets came and went, alternating between breast and hand-feeding; pasteurization and scientifically prepared "artificial" food made possible a renewed abandonment of breast-nursing with little observable consequence for infant mortality.[78] Yet however mothers ultimately fed their children, they stopped using paid nurses outside the home. That is one big load that modernization has hauled through the night.

The second major phenomenon was the shift in the mercenary nurse's attitudes from instrumental to expressive, from cash-oriented to love-oriented. Ardouin-Dumazet noted this shift in the 1890s in that classic land of the *nourrice à gages*, the Morvan (Nièvre department): "Formerly the death of an [outside] child was seen as part of exploiting some other family. Today people become attached to such children precisely because of the care they require. We find this sort of adoption above all in the case of foundlings sent out by the Welfare in Paris. They end up with the same status as the families' own sons and daughters. Someone told me about a young nineteen-year-old girl who has control of the keys to the cupboards. And if her "milk brothers" want spending money for the café on

Sunday they have to see her; she has hold of the purse strings."[79] What a long way this is from another story told of the same region a quarter-century earlier! "Two mercenary nurses meet in the village. 'Why are they tolling the bells?' asks the one. 'Oh, it's nothing,' replies the other, 'just the knell of *un Paris* dead this morning.' "[80]

But some international perspectives are in order. Our evidence has been drawn chiefly from France, where in 1920 some 54,000 legitimate children (7 percent of all legitimate births in that year) were still being put out by their parents to mercenary wet nurses.[81] In no other country during the years between the two World Wars did anything like this massive evacuation of the newborn from intact homes take place. It is worth considering, at least briefly, what arrangements other countries made for the care and feeding of infants. There were basically two patterns: maternal breast-feeding and maternal hand-feeding. Nowhere else than in France were mercenaries used around this time, even to live in, on other than an infinitesimal scale. If mothers nursed their own children in England and North America, it was for want of other occupations or pre-occupations, since they had retired from the labor force upon marriage. One mid-1920s investigation tells us that the women of industrial Sunderland in northeastern England "are occupied only with the care of their household." The same study found that the relative absence of digestive disorders among infants in rural Oxfordshire was in part "due to the frequency of maternal nursing, encouraged less by booming economic prosperity than by folkways hostile to the woman working outside the home."[82] This is the famous Anglo-Saxon stay-at-home wife.

Maternal nursing was similarly the rule in Scandinavia and northern Germany, to generalize from the experience of places like Oslo and Cassel; but it happened more because the public health agencies persuaded mothers to take furloughs from work than because of a wife-at-home tradition.[83] Then there were bottle-feeding regions. The miners' wives of Hoensbroek (Netherlands) and the peasant women of Gmunden (Austria) largely handfed their babies during the inter-war years.[84] So did much of southeastern Germany, where artificial feeding had been practiced for at least the previous forty years. (To pluck one statistic from many: in Konstanz County, Baden, 52 percent of all infants had never been breastfed in 1882; 47 percent had not in 1904).[85]

Even within a country, patterns of infant feeding varied considerably. For if a majority of infants in Leyden and Dordrecht (Netherlands) were breastfed, a majority in nearby Maestricht had known only the bottle.[86] And while even in the 1920s the wives of ambitious peasants in France's Seine-Inférieure department boarded out or handfed their babies, rustic women in not-distant Touraine were praised for their attentive nursing.[87]

There are two points to be made here. One is that even by the 1920s the revolution in maternal care had by no means triumphed in many areas of Europe. Granted, many of the women in Germany or Holland who put their babies into day nurseries and went out to earn their bread were forced to do so by sheer necessity. But even so, they worked with the knowledge that their infants' health would thereby be impaired. An international survey noted, in case after case, that women working right up to the time of delivery stood a greater chance of miscarrying. In the same areas (where handfeeding was customary, as well) a high percent of infant loss was due to "inadequate attention" (*mauvais soins*). Thus in Austria's Gmunden County, 17 percent of deaths in the first twelve months came from "poor care," while 33 percent were so caused in the nearby district of Scharding-Engelhartszell.[88]

The second point to be made is that of how poor our ability still remains to place these small pieces into the larger European puzzle. Even though France stays an anomaly within Europe as a whole, we now have some understanding of how swaddling, breastfeeding, and maternal affection fit together there. But where these Croydon (England) or Hedmark County (Norway) mothers came from who in the interwar we discover busily nursing away, is a mystery.[89] Had things been ever so in England and Norway, or did the same shifts take place as had within the relatively well-documented case of France? The following sections offer a tentative answer.

NOTE FOR ESSAY.

Improvements in Mothering

Other evidence besides breastfeeding indicates that a revolution in the quality of mothering began among the middle classes late in the eighteenth century. J. J. Juge, by 1808 a retired natural history teacher in Limoges and an aging nostalgic, described the grim childhood he and his friends had known, boarded out to a wet nurse in the first three years and entrusted to a servant upon returning. At school age parents would exchange their own children for those of friends in Poitiers or Angoulême, "for it was quite correctly believed that an *enfant dépaysé* would lose his accent and behave more docilely."

While at home, the offspring of these middle-class merchants ESSAY could never expect "the slightest caress on the part of father or mother. *Fear* was the principle on which upbringing was founded. Whoever taught the children to read would grab their shirts about the shoulders, then hold the book in one hand, the rod in the other, ready to flail away at the slightest oversight."

How things had changed by 1808 in Limoges, with mothers and infants beaming at each other, the nursery radiant with smiles. "Cheeried up and embraced without end, [the children] will remain unknowing of ill will. Completely unconstrained in their clean sheets and well cared for, their beautiful little bodies develop rapidly. They need merely be of good humor and good health, and they'll draw the eyes of all who come near."[90] Even if we discount by half what is obviously the testimony of a doting grandfather, the change is striking.

Other signs point to an increase in middle-class maternal sentiment in the years before 1860. Bourgeois families snapped up, for example, the child-rearing and infant hygiene literature that began to appear after 1815, a wave that crested with Gustave Droz's bestseller *Monsieur, Madame et bébé* (1866).[91] Mothers agonized about the health of their infants and beleagured the offices of doctors who, until the early nineteenth century, had seemed to have little more to do than make meteorological observations.[92] And finally, towards the mid-nineteenth century, boarding-school attendance began to decline from its eighteenth-century high point. At Paris's Louis-le-

191

Grand *lycée*, the proportion of day boys climbed from 10 percent of total enrollment in 1837–1838 to 69 percent in 1908. "The French family would no longer agree to be separated from its children," writes Philippe Ariès, "even in the interests of their education."[93] All these are waymarks in a middle-class *prise de conscience* of child welfare. We have long known about it because these are the people for whom, after all, the manuals were written and the institutions founded that so preoccupy most histories of childrearing.

We know much less about the lower classes. If the frequency with which lower-class women exposed newborn infants (or reclaimed them once exposed) is in fact a reasonable guide to the lack (or presence) of maternal affection, it was not until the 1860s that the common people of France began to form this same attachment to infants. We have examined above the abandonment of babies as part of the traditional childrearing syndrome. The question now becomes: when did it decline?

There is little evidence from the first half of the nineteenth century to suggest that the attachment of lower-class mothers to newborn infants had crystallized at all. The number of abandoned children continued at a high level and, as the following figures for the Var Department show, the percent taken back by their parents from foundling homes failed to increase:[94]

1810–1814	2.8%
1815–1819	1.9
1820–1824	0.8
1825–1829	0.8
1830–1834	0.3
1835–1839	0.8

Before 1860, whatever improvement did take place in the reclamation of exposed children seems primarily due to administration, such as the odious "transfer" policy of the 1830s, or the granting of small subsidies to unwed mothers willing to retain and nurse their children. Late in the 1840s the French government asked departmental prefects whether there had been any changes since 1835 in the tendency of unmarried mothers to "recognize" their illegitimate offspring (i.e., not to abandon them as foundlings).[95] In some departments there was no change at all in the percent of illegitimate births subsequently "recognized" by the mother (or the father); the Dordogne and the Eure are examples. In others, such as the Ain and Allier, there was an actual decrease in recognitions. But in those departments where recognitions rose and, presumably, maternal attachment therewith, the officials always had a "technical" explanation to offer:

——The Ardennes: "The increase is due to an improvement in the morality of the working class, and it is noteworthy that the number of illegitimate children has decreased at the same time the number of recognitions has risen."

——The Arièges and Basses-Alpes: A breastfeeding subsidy to illegitimate mothers was thought responsible.

——The Gers: Among the causes was the government's night-and-fog policy of removing exposed children from the mother's ken, the suppression of the *tours* (turntables in the doors of foundling homes) in which mothers could place the foundlings unobserved, and increased activity on the part of the mayors to detect the "authors" of the abandonments.

In only two departments were there slight hints of a changing attitude among the unwed mothers themselves:

——The Tarn: Midwives' exhortations to unwed mothers to keep their children were thought principally responsible for the rise in recognitions, and perhaps the monetary subsidy had helped as well. Yet it was also observed that "little by little the recognition of bastard children has become less blameful in the eyes of the population."

——The Maine-et-Loire: After the administrators had exhausted a whole list of explanations redounding to the credit of officialdom, they conceded that "a few decide themselves from the love they bear for these unfortunate children [to keep them], but they're a minority and it's impossible to demonstrate a case where sentiment causes these unwed mothers to act."[96]

If, again, we may assume abandonments, withdrawals, and recognitions to be fair indicators of the degree of maternal sentiment among both the married and unmarried lower classes (after all, abandonment was virtually unknown among the upper orders), the years after 1860 marked a turning point. Thus we note in Figure 5–1:

193

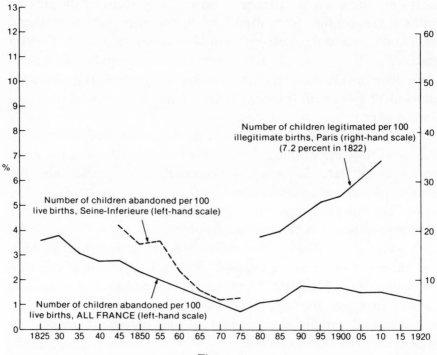

Figure 5-1

Notes: the graph shows the number of exposed and abandoned children as a percentage of all live births in France. Dates on the graph mark the beginning of five-year periods. Data for 1824 and 1825 are from Adolphe-Henri Gaillard, *Recherches . . . sur les enfants trouvés, les enfants naturels et les orphelins* (Paris, 1837), p. 101. Data for 1826–1853 are from Baron de Watteville, *Statistique des établissements de bienfaisance. Rapport a s. exc. le ministre de l'intérieur sur les tours, les abandonnés, les infanticides et les morts-nès de 1826 à 1854* (Paris, 1856), p. 40. Data for 1875–1924 are from annual volumes of the *Statistique annuaire,* and include only *enfants trouvés* and *enfants abandonnés. Orphelins* and *enfants moralement abandonnés* have been excluded. Data were unavailable for 1890 and 1891.

The number of exposed and abandoned children as a percent of all live births in the Seine-Inférieure 1847–1877 is from Ernest Semichon, *Histoire des enfants abondonnés . . .* (Paris, 1880), p. 249. Includes *enfants trouvés and enfants abandonnés.*

The number of children legitimated per 100 illegitimate births in Paris for 1881–1914 is from annual volumes of the *Annuaire statistique de la ville de Paris,* and for 1822 from *Recherches statistiques sur la ville de Paris et le département de la Seine* (Paris, 1826), Tables 23 and 24.

that while the percentage of all newborn children abandoned by their mothers in France as a whole had already begun to turn downwards in the late 1830s, the most dramatic decline occurred between 1850–1854 (2.4 percent) and 1875–1879 (0.9 percent). The figure

194

coasted upwards a bit thereafter, yet without regaining "traditional" levels.

The 1860s marked the definitive downward plunge, if we may let data from the Seine-Inférieure department fill the gap in the national series that extends from 1850 to 1875. And even though the sharpness of that decline is partly owing to the suppression of the foundling turntable in 1860 in the Rouen hospital, the numbers of abandoned children (a separate reporting category from "found-lings" [*enfants trouvés*]) also fell after 1866.

Note that the percentage of illegitimate Parisian children who were *legitimated* by their parents increased steadily from 1885 (when the main time series begins), until the eve of the First World War. Legitimation may be just as much an index of the formation of stable households as of maternal sentiment. Yet the urge to establish these warm little emotional cells, in which one's illegitimate children would be taken in and raised as all others, was precisely the mother's love for her infant.

None of these statistics offer a "definitive" proof of the crystallization of maternal affection. This is a privileged, distant domain, and the people we're dealing with would not have been able to say rightly what they felt, had anyone asked them (which nobody did). Yet the way these mothers *acted* was clearly changing.

By the beginning of the twentieth century, the great transformation of mothering was virtually complete. The indifference towards infant life and death, almost universal a century before, was limited to a few backwaters such as the interior of Brittany, where mothers "scarcely occupy themselves at all with their children. Often unwanted, the Bretons accept them, or sooner tolerate them, and let them grow up with absolutely no attention." Nor were these people much moved by the high infant mortality that such inattentiveness produced; birth and death were received with like placidity.[97] On the Ile de Ré, as well, just off the coast of La Rochelle, traditional patterns continued to reassert themselves towards 1900, with *intérêt* maintaining itself over tenderness. One doctor describes entering peasant cottages during his rounds at harvest time and finding them unlocked and deserted, save for babies "abandoned in their cradles, having alongside only a piece of fruit or a morsel of bread, maybe even a more or less clean rag for the purpose of sucking."[98] Yet we are dealing here with lags in modernization rather than with any enduring differential between peasant and bourgeois life-styles. By the 1950s and 1960s these lags had been overcome and observers were able to describe even the remotest parts of hinterland Brittany in terms that would not have been unfamiliar to a computer programmer in Grenoble.[99]

Elsewhere, even towards 1900, the modern style of mothering had triumphed. Henri Baudrillart was struck by a "softening" of child-rearing modes during his extensive surveys of rural life in the 1880s. "The affection of parents for children seems never to have been so deep, so manifest through care. 'Nowadays children are being infinitely more spoiled than used to be,' is one phrase I hear repeated everywhere. . . ."[100]

Such quotations could be strung together endlessly. Perhaps there is something in the sour world of adult life that causes us always to think children are more "spoiled" now than when we were young. Yet we can be sure that the many eighteenth-century mothers who abandoned their children did not spoil them at all; and that those babies left to squirm and cry for hours in their smelly swaddling clothes, little bottoms red and inflamed, were not spoiled beyond measure either.[101] At some point genuine changes in the way people think and act do occur that cannot be attributed to such historical "constants" as nostalgia. I think that for the popular classes of France, and perhaps by extension for the rest of Western society, the last half of the nineteenth century was one such time.

All this is admittedly less than definitive data. There remains one concrete practice, however, to which we might point as a solid index of a transformation in mothering: infant dress, especially the practice of swaddling. Swaddling is a measure not so much of maternal neglect or indifference—for there is no evidence the practice was physically harmful (provided the baby was changed often enough)— as of motherly *interaction* with the infant. A child lying stiff in swaddling clothes was unable to wave its hands and feet in the air, incapable of reaching out to grasp some dangled object, forbidden by its bonds to respond to maternal playfulness. And if mothers tied

their children from head to feet so that they *couldn't* respond to
tickling, clucking, and cajoling, it must mean the mothers had little
interest in such things in the first place. Liberating the child from
its linen bonds would mean liberating it to interact with newly
playful mothers. This is the principal significance of the progressive
abandonment of swaddling, not just in France but all over the West,
from the mid-eighteenth century onwards. The only point worth
dwelling upon here is the persistence of the class differential in these
changes.

How exactly, was swaddling done? Listen to Dr. Gilibert:[102]

[The nurse] stretches the baby out on a board or straw mattress and
dresses it in a little gown or a coarse, crumpled diaper, on top of which
she begins to apply the swaddling bands. She pins the infant's arms
against its chest, then passes the band under the armpits, which presses
the arms firmly into place. Around and around she winds the band down
to the buttocks, tighter and tighter, pushing the diaper in between the
infant's thighs, then enveloping all these little pits and parts with the
wide swaddling cloth. She takes it clear down to the feet, and after this
neat work, covers the baby's head with a bonnet; a kerchief atop of
this hangs down to the shoulders and is fastened with pins. That's
what swaddling a baby is all about.

The practice enraged Gilibert, as it did so many late-eighteenth- and
early nineteenth-century medical writers. But for all this outrage, there
is no sign that swaddling had begun to lose its hold among the people
before 1850.[103]

In the early years of the nineteenth century, testimony is virtually
universal about the continuation of swaddling in rural areas. In the
Puy-de-Dôme, for instance, Dr. Bertrand tells us how popular swaddling is "among the women of the people. They use it to inhibit the
movements of the infant's body and its lower extremities."[104] The
peasant nurses of Cusset, after choking their charges in swaddling
clothes, would "suspend them from a nail when they want to go
about their work."[105] And Dr. Bérenguier of Rabastens (Tarn) related how "I still see some peasant women garroting their nurslings
in tightly wound swaddling clothes. The torture of this absolute
immobility, which an adult couldn't stand, produces skin excoria-
tions . . ." and other ghastly effects.[106] Well, perhaps not really, for

these doctors were wrong about as often as they were right. What is interesting about Dr. Bérenguier's testimonial, however, is its attribution of swaddling to a shrinking, benighted minority. For by 1850, when he published his treatise, the practice was well on the way out among the common rural folk.

The decline of swaddling had begun perhaps a century earlier among the urban middle and upper classes.[107] Their heads filled with the exhortations of Rousseau, propertied Parisians had fairly early started to liberate their infants "from the tyranny of the *maillot*," according to one doctor's account. And in 1794 "Citizen" Dr. Audin-Rouvière, (although he seems somewhat to have plagiarized his above-cited predecessor), rejoiced that "already infants enjoy the greatest liberty; they've been delivered from the inhibiting confines of their swaddling wraps."[108] In eighteenth-century provincial cities as well, the shift towards the liberation of the infant was underway. We learn of remote Chambéry: "Heeding the counsels of the doctors, women no longer submit their newborn so much to swaddling, and they're no longer bound with bands as was formerly the practice, but rather left much more at ease in their cradles."[109] By the early nineteenth century, full-dress swaddling had become "almost completely proscribed" in Strasbourg; the infants were left with their hands free. Even in rustic Vigan canton the upper classes had, by 1819, begun to loosen their infants' swaddling wraps (although the artisans and peasants continued as before).[110] Such a scattering of quotes is scarcely conclusive, but I have seen no references that the lower orders had begun to unwind their children by 1780, nor that by 1850 the upper orders were still swaddling theirs. Although in the last half of the nineteenth century the practice is everywhere abandoned, the class differential was, I am convinced, quite real before.

Lands outside of France seem to have undergone the same abolition of swaddling, yet with different timing. England was much advanced. By the 1790s, when French urbanites alone had begun abandoning the practice, an English doctor reported that "the barbarous custom of swathing children like mummies is now almost universally laid aside."[111] In Puritan New England, swaddling never seems to have existed, but perhaps that merely reflects the English head start.[112] Germany was the reverse. In the central European cities for which I have seen medical topographies, there are reports of binding children right on into the 1840s. In neither Augsburg nor Hamburg had doctors' protests availed by the late eighteenth century.[113] The practice of "strapping and belting the infants in" evoked much medical hand wringing in Vienna towards 1810, and in Göttingen around 1824 "binding and swathing" were the order of the day.[114]

These bits and pieces permit no inferences about class differences. But they do suggest that an often-remarked difference among countries in the modernization of outlooks crops up in the domain of maternal affection as well: the Anglo-Saxons beginning first (with my suggested possibility that Americans were "born modern"), the French then putting their distinctive national stamp upon the Great Transformation, and the Central Europeans—out there on the perimeter of social change—following distantly behind.

The Decrease in Infant Death

Infant death comes into our lives nowadays like a blinding explosion. Losing a small child is one of the terrible personal disasters of modern times, a scalding that leaves permanent scars. And for about a hundred years, middle-class people generally have thought about infant death in the same way as the people who are likely to read this book. Dr. Jean Jablonski of Poitiers, in a poignant mixture of medical empiricism and parental anguish, tells how he lost his own two-year-old child in a cholera epidemic in 1878.[115]

As for my daughter, one of the last victims of the epidemic, she was of a delicate constitution, nursed at the breast, and weaned at 19 months the preceding May. The change in nourishment didn't seem to have upset her. On the 29th of September, the day when she was seized suddenly with vomiting and diarrhea, a canine tooth and a molar of the first group had yet to arrive (the fourteen other teeth having come without much trouble). She was aired neither in the morning nor the evening, and was warmly clothed. . . . No imprudent steps had been taken, and several hours before the appearance of the first symptoms, which manifested themselves towards two in the morning, she seemed to enjoy perfect health. . . . Thus I have every reason to believe that the ailment to which she succumbed was due to contagion, for each day, despite my repeated prohibitions, people brought in to my consulting room children sick with infantile cholera. But whatever the cause my daughter, whose illness lasted only eight days, had been mortally stricken from the beginning. After the third day there remained no hope of saving her, and all the treatments I attempted with the help of my devoted colleagues were not able to halt for a single moment the progress of the malady.

But infant death was, I think, perceived differently by other social classes, in other times and places. Open beside my typewriter is the genealogy of the Badenese village of Altenheim. As I randomly look through the book, my eye falls upon the family history of Johann Michael Frank, baker, who in October 1729 married Catharina Sutter, a second marriage for her. They had five children:

—Johann Jacob, born August 1730, "a fine lad who was already going to school," died at age six.
—Johann Michael, born October 1732, died at age four.
—Andreas, born December 1735, died at fifteen months.
—Catharina, born March 1738, died at six years.
—Anna Maria, born January 1741, was the sole child to survive to maturity, reaching a ripe old age.

Five years after Anna Maria's birth, Frank's wife Catharina died of typhus and Frank remarried, again to a woman who had already lost one husband.[116] This is a fairly typical family chronicle for an area of Germany where, in general, an infant would have only a one-in-three or one-in-four chance of surviving to adulthood. If the Altenheimers had thought as we do about death, this series of losses would have crippled them psychically and smashed up the social order. That is one way of perceiving the great transition in infant mortality.

What we learn about most from changes in infant mortality, of course, is the history of public health. But public health is not a subject of interest in this book. And the great decline in infant mortality which occurred everywhere in Western society between the end of the nineteenth century and the 1920s and 1930s faithfully mirrors improvements in sterile food, the pasteurization of milk, green soap in the nursery, and other forms of the fight against pathogens.

What does interest us is whether *earlier* declines in infant mortality occurred simultaneously with the improvement in maternal care I have hypothesized in this book. There is no doubt that the quality of mothering plays a role in infant death rates, quite independent of disease and nutrition. The famous survey which found that children in institutional homes died much more often than those in families, even though the two were exposed to the same regimes of feeding and hygiene, is sufficient demonstration.[117] Maternal care affects the quality of infant nutrition; even in traditional times, loving mothers were more likely to exert themselves to obtain cow's milk than to feed their infants pap. And it also affects the level of domestic cleanliness; concerned mothers are again more likely to change their children, wash their bedclothes, keep the pigs away from the cradle, and so forth. Yet even above and beyond this, maternal love operates as an independent variable in the complex equation of infant mortality. As is well known, towards the end of the nineteenth century there occurred a great decline in infant mortality. Yet the data in Appendix V point to two other developments in infant death that are rather less familiar. One is the relative lack of progress *during* the nineteenth century. Indeed, in some places, infant mortality even increased.[118] Whatever improvements in mothering may have taken place by then, the baleful effects of industrialization and urbanization were even stronger, holding a baby's chances of perishing in the first year of life at a high, stable level.

The second trend is the major improvement in infant mortality during the eighteenth century. But this improvement occurred differentially; it was pronounced in England, France, and parts of Scandinavia but nonexistent in central Europe and Italy. The few local series on which these conclusions rest provide an admittedly slim basis for grand conclusions. Still, the uniformity which such minidata show—especially the uniform contrast between France and Germany—is significant. In case after case, mortality in French villages tended downwards in the eighteenth century, declining dramatically in such places as Soudeilles and Mouy and in the small town of Meulan, and slipping at a lesser but nonetheless note-worthy pace in Anjou (Maine-et-Loire and Sarthe departments) and the Moselle. These series drift to a halt in the nineteenth century, and so we cannot be sure if such villages were typical of France as a whole (where nineteenth-century infant mortality changed very little), or if some exceptional feature distinguishes them. But the downward progress of the lines in the graphs for France in Appendix V cannot fail to strike the eye.

English data are much shakier. But to go by the experience of the British Lying-in Hospital in London and the village of Colyton in Devon, the eighteenth century saw a similar improvement. American time series are inadequate, births having been massively under-registered, and trends conflict in the two Massachusetts towns for which eighteenth-century data are available.[119] Yet given the outcry about infant health that resounded in both the colonies and England late in the century, we are probably not too far off the mark in speculating that infant mortality declined at the same time in both France and the Anglo-Saxon world.

In Central Europe the reverse happened. In village after village, from Böhringen in Württemberg, to Bölgenthal in Franconia, to Eibesthal in Lower Austria, infant mortality increased during the eighteenth century. We are not entitled to infer a *worsening* of maternal care from this, for a rise in illegitimacy—bastard infants having much higher death rates than legitimate ones—could have been partly responsible. (Infant death registration might also have improved.) Yet the magnitude and the uniformity of the upward march suggests that deterioration of some kind was taking place in the environment within which these tiny babies found them-selves. Among the German cases known to me, with the sole excep-tion of Leipzig, there is no significant improvement in infant mor-tality until the second half of the nineteenth century, and then only a halting one.

Why this international difference—an eighteenth-century decline in infant mortality in Western Europe, a rise or a high plateau in Central Europe? I am convinced that these differences are linked in some way to the progress of maternal breastfeeding and the gen-eral improvement in maternal care in France and England, noted

above, and to the absence thereof in Germany. Even though the eighteenth-century revolution in mothering was limited to the propertied classes, in France such people were sufficiently numerous to effect a decline in infant mortality rates. In Germany, on the other hand, we encounter no evidence of a new orientation toward infants until the mid-nineteenth century, and even then only in the cities, among middle-class medical patients. The higher level of infant mortality among Germans than among French suggests that, since time out of mind, Central European women had been hand-feeding their babies, and that possibly Germany never experienced a breastfeeding revolution, mothers there simply going over to safe "artificial" foods as they became available towards the end of the nineteenth century.

Let us step back a pace or two. Historians are inclined to account for the lack of parental love for children in traditional times on the basis of high infant mortality; you couldn't permit yourself to become too attached to an infant that you knew death might whisk away. And bear in mind than an infant mortality rate of 25 percent means that one in every four babies will perish before twelve months are up. Furthermore, while we haven't taken up juvenile mortality as a general phenomenon here, the chances were good that another 25 percent of a given crop of babies would not live to twenty-one. Hence there was a fifty-fifty risk that a child would not survive to maturity. Recognizing these probabilities (as people tend to do even without life-expectancy schedules in front of them), parents withdrew emotionally from their children, being—so the argument goes—psychically unable to support loss after heartbreaking loss.

Data on early modern infant mortality suggest that this issue has another dimension. The high rate of infant loss is not a sufficient explanation for the traditional lack of maternal love *because precisely this lack of care was responsible for the high mortality*.[120] At least in part. If children perished in great numbers, it wasn't owing to the intervention of some *deus ex machina* beyond the parents' control. It came about as a result of circumstances over which the parents had considerable influence: infant diet, age at weaning, cleanliness of bed linen, and the general hygienic circumstances that surrounded the child—to say nothing of less tangible factors in

mothering, such as picking up the infant, talking and singing to it, giving it the feeling of being loved in a secure little universe. Now by the late eighteenth century, parents knew, at least in a sort of abstract way, that letting newborn children stew in their own excrement or feeding them pap from the second month onwards were harmful practices. For the network of medical personnel in Europe had by this time extended sufficiently to put interested mothers within earshot of sensible advice. The point is that these mothers did not *care*, and that is why their children vanished in the ghastly slaughter of the innocents that was traditional child-rearing. Custom and tradition and the frozen emotionality of ancien-régime life gripped with deathly force. When the surge of sentiment shattered this grip, infant mortality plunged, and maternal tenderness became part of the world we know so well.

CHAPTER SIX

The Rise of the
Nuclear Family

THE NUCLEAR FAMILY is a state of mind rather than a particular kind of structure or set of household arrangements. It has little to do with whether the generations live together or whether Aunt Mary stays in the spare bedroom. Nor can it be understood with kinship diagrams and figures on family size. What really distinguishes the nuclear family—mother, father, and children—from other patterns of family life in Western society is a special sense of solidarity that separates the domestic unit from the surrounding community. Its members feel that they have much more in common with one another than they do with anyone else on the outside—that they enjoy a privileged emotional climate they must protect from outside intrusion, through privacy and isolation.

In this chapter we shall follow the formation of the nuclear family, that warm shelter of domesticity from the cold, inhospitable night. The French talk of *chacun chez soi*, or "every man has his castle." And the story of this chapter will be the rise of *chacun chez soi*, the building of these precious emotional fortresses into which the modern family has withdrawn. Class differences in this surge of domesticity provide the organizing theme, with the middle classes once again in advance of the lower.

Precisely these class differences reveal the nucleus about which the modern family was to crystallize. The nucleus was not romantic love; for as we have seen, the lower orders were the first to experience the great rush of romance and sexuality that broke in upon the modern consciousness. And for no class, high or low, did romantic sentiments survive more than the first jarring years of marital reality. Rather, the nuclear family would take form about the mother–infant relationship. The *prise de conscience* of infant welfare had first occurred among the middle classes, and domesticity would follow in its train. The emotional web that was spun between mother and baby would reach out to envelop older children and the husband: a sense that the preciousness of infant life required an equally delicate setting for its preservation. Domesticity, the last of the three great eruptions of sentiment, would end up by kindling a cozy fire in the household—and conflagrating the community about it.

The Traditional Pattern: The Family Surrenders Its Members

The family had great difficulty establishing itself as an emotional unit in old-regime Europe, because its members were constantly going off to be with their various peer groups. These peer groups were organized along the lines of age and sex; and while our general ignorance of how things worked in the Bad Old Days leaves the details somewhat vague, it appears that these groups exerted strong claims upon the time and allegiance of their members. I am arguing that these claims were sufficiently powerful to suffocate whatever strivings the traditional family might have felt toward privacy and solidarity.

What exactly were these peer groups, and how did they operate?
Most visible were the organizations of young men. Considerable attention has been paid these in France, where two kinds of youth peer groups seemed to have developed late in the Middle Ages. First came the *confréries*, religious societies of lads whose function it was

to keep up the chapel of the village's patron saint, for example, or to perform other pious tasks of public utility. Second were the local militias (the *guet*), organized along military lines with captains, parade routes, flags, and rifle salvos. With time these two kinds of institutions appear to have merged into a single municipal youth group, losing their military and political functions as the modern state reached in to take command. They instead became responsible for organizing the big blowouts in the annual calendar of village festivities, chief of which was the "village festival."[1] By the eighteenth century, the youth groups had cast off much of the pomp and circumstance with which earlier epochs had endowed them (the authorities now regularly discouraging such antics as firing off rifles in the town square), and contented themselves with tasks like putting together the big parade (*bravade*) at village-festival time, or supervising courtship. After the French Revolution the heart went completely out of the youth "abbeys," and only an annual "king of pleasure" remained to crown over carnival or over the occasional banquet for a year's class of draftees. (Every year *les conscrits* for military service would have a big party at the time of the lottery or the medical examination, and would invite all the girls.)[2]

Here are the youth of Provence, parading in public for the annual festival: "The lads organized themselves into a hierarchical society, on the model of military regiments, which is to say, with a chief who's called "captain," under whose orders there are lieutenants, a color-bearer, in a word everything you need to give a martial appearance to the ceremony and which increases in the eyes of the population its solemnity and glamour . . ." The author goes on to explain how the members of the company presented arms, then paraded about the city, musicians leading the way, to pick up the flag or be greeted by the mayor in front of the town hall. Then there'd be a religious interlude (all going to mass together), some dinner, a bit of shooting, and presumably at the end a good deal of drinking.[3]

Could these youth organizations have been powerful enough to give the conjugal family competition for the allegiance of its sons? Or were they merely a peasant version of the Boy Scouts? In Scandinavia there's no doubt that the former was the case, for as we saw earlier, youth organizations snatched from the family's grasp the vital business of forming marital alliances. Those couples came together whom the peer group rather than the parents found appropriate (or at least it was at the initiative of the group, rather than the family, that boy and girl met). In the Anglo-Saxon world, on the other hand, there's no doubt of the family's triumph, and of the enfeebled state of formal youth organization.

France is a moot case. In view of the many occasions for French youth to come together in an organized way, such as pilgrimages, the hoopla attending marriages, baptisms, and so forth (about which more in a minute), I am inclined to think the peer group exercised considerable claims on the disposable time of the average young man. Apprentices and journeymen in urban crafts had special forms of organization that excluded everyone not a member of the craft. In Lyon, apprentice bakers would gather regularly in particular bars and cafés, go to mass together and perhaps occasionally sue their employers for mistreatment.[4] Urban "prentices" generally lived with their masters but, as one historian of seventeenth-century London has it, owed their allegiance to the "apprentice subculture."[5]

The peer organizations of young women were less visible, yet nonetheless real. For girls, association might mean nothing more than routine get-togethers, without the masculine hierarchy of kings and ensigns. In early modern Finland, for example, the girls would gather for evening parties without the boys, indeed in secret from them. "Because of this rejection the boys came to tease the girls and do mischief: they made a mess or stole the girls' food, spoiled the handiwork, and sometimes turned the entire party room upside down. If the boys were not allowed inside, they made a row outside and tried from there to disturb the girls' work. Especially in the saunas the girls were helpless against the boys' attacks."[6] Nice guys. Or, as in France, the village girls might form organizations parallel to the boys' "youth abbeys," with their own "queens" and *bâtonnières*, to help organize the Saint Catherine's Day festivities or the May Day dance. In some regions, under the aegis of the Church, there were the "Daughters of the Virgin" to decorate the altars and statues, carry banners and relics in processions, and organize Easter egg hunts. Sometimes the girls in these groups would take part in weddings as symbolic delegates of the community. On and on go the varieties of girls' groups—sometimes the province of the church, sometimes merely part of the community.[7] They made claims in time, resources, and money on the lives of young women that a later period would reserve to the nuclear family.

With marriage the formal organizations people belonged to would change. A powerful *informal* set of organizational tentacles would reach out as well to pull them from the bosom of the family. Less apparent because less institutionalized than the youth abbeys, these informal assemblages of adults in the long run probably pried their individual members from the lives of their families with much greater force.

For men, an entire world of social organization pivoted about the bar. There was, for one thing, the whole rich culture of just standing around with your buddies and having a shot, maybe playing cards in between, or in the Midi going out to the square in front to pitch a game of *boules*.[8] The Good Old Boys who do this sort of thing have their own rules and conventions, and they vary little from Harrisburg, Mississippi, where I first came into contact with this world, to the little villages in the Haute-Saône where, in the inter-world war years, men would "seal themselves away in the café to play cards;"[9] or to the small town in the Gard department where, in the 1810s, the men would get together evenings "towards seven in the winter, eight in the summer, at the home of a neighbor or in some common room. They play cards, loser paying the wine, and drink as they go. In the winter they have roasted chestnuts. Others read the paper, talk of business, of what they're doing and going to do, of the hope of a good harvest or the fear of a bad one, and at ten o'clock they retire."[10]

What is interesting is that often Frenchmen didn't just stop at mere elbow-crooking at the village inn from time to time. A group of them would band together, rent a room, put in some furniture, buy wine in bulk (to save money and beverage taxes), and then get together regularly in this impromptu club—called a *chambrée* in the south—to drink, play cards, and shoot the breeze.[11] Sometimes they would even cook, and thus lay in supplies of vegetable oil! Dr. Rouger records disapprovingly how the dissolute artisans of Vigan all take lunch together at the bar, and all turn up evenings at a buddy's house, their dinner "between two plates," to sit, drink, and have a good time; "their male children are at their knees; the womenfolk are sent away."[12] The *chambrée* falls into desuetude late in the nineteenth century, its habitués either returning to the family circle or relocating to public houses.[13] But one can imagine, before that time, the family life of the *chambrée* participant, no sooner home from work than off with his mates in a grown-up version of the Boys' Own Club.

Such systematic male sociability was not confined to small-towners and peasants. In such big cities as Lyon the artisans of the eighteenth century spent part of their non-working hours in "male gatherings," be it "in the numerous cabarets which attract them even on Sunday, or in the occupational associations in which they've been enrolled since bachelor days."[14] In Marseille, "circles" were to urban workers what *chambrées* were to rural folk. Working days were not long, according to Francois Mazuy (himself an ex-tailor). "What to do with those extra hours? Go to the café! But the absence there of privacy with your comrades suggests the idea of getting together and arranging a meeting place where, with a bit of money, you can go every evening, just like home, and without fear of rubbing elbows with people you don't know."[15] In Lille these informal clubs were called *estaminets fermés*, "meetings of drinkers and smokers which ordinarily go on in rented quarters, costs equally divided. Furniture, food, everything belongs to the group and is financed by the members. Look at that good merchant or this office clerk: he arrives at five o'clock, sits down in front of a liter of beer [the preferred drink of the Nord], takes from his pocket his pipe and tobacco pouch, and he's all set to drink and smoke the hours away. Another arrives, and so the hall fills with fifty or sixty men, playing cards and sending clouds of smoke at one another. . . . This is called having a good time."[16]

Even late in the nineteenth century, when the *chambrée* was everywhere giving ground to the public bar, a private club spirit was maintained. In Lille the workers could, for weekly dues of one sou, enter their favorite locale without having to consume anything.[17] The men who frequented these *chambrées* and bars worked long days (save, perhaps for the propertied peasants, who hung out

Essay

*Unlike
Canetti
whore
male
confined
to
Modern*

afternoons at the tavern). If they spent all this time with the boys, when were they with their families? When did they help their wives with the dishes and rock Baby Billy on their knees?

Although bar time was the principal occasion for male sociability in France, it wasn't the only one. For peasants especially, time away from the farm meant time with one's mates, without the women. One observer of Basque country noted how adept the men were at finding excuses to take off, leaving their wives toiling away. "The pretext is buying and selling cattle, but in reality it's a taste for the gathering of men in the village square. On market day, after exchanging news out in the open, they go to the big gathering at the tavern where they remain until closing. Forty years ago [an account of 1909] the men of a village would go in groups to the market . . . those who lived up the mountain forming up with those who lived down, and then all rushing along the road."[18] Gascony's Dr. Labat laid it on the line: all the horse trading the men around there did merely gave them an excuse to leave home two or three days a week. "They don't make money, they lose time and take on unedifying habits." Buying and selling horses was, in other words, "a sort of game of chance."[19] Meanwhile their wives were making the farm go.

Let me just remind the reader that the veillée, the married women's solidarity group, gave the family just as much competition for time, money, and energy as did any of these other groups. Not all veillées were sexually segregated, of course. On many occasions both married men and women convened of an evening in someone's barn for handiwork and storytelling. Or some veillées just included young girls (whom the boys, having suitably prepared themselves at the bar, would then join).[20] But the standard model was married women alongside marriageable daughters, with the suitors at the window.

Although the observers' resolute male chauvinism—which assumes that females just "naturally" drift together to gossip maliciously—erases the detail, we have some notion of the collective life of these women. "In the winter evenings, while the fishermen have assembled in the cabarets of the port [a Breton coastal village], the women get together in the stables where the livestock and the fertilizer pile give off some warmth." Because of the lighting's inadequacy the women are unable to sew; at most they can knit a bit. "One should have liked to hear the stories of yesteryear, the old legends of a region rich in them. But the talk doesn't rise above scandal and chit-chat. The meeting ends towards nine."[21] Or we might take an earlier account of weavers' wives in neighboring Normandy who in the evenings would "assemble by dozens" in dank cellars to spin and talk, "working until midnight, each with her foot warmer or cinderpot filled with coals."[22]

Consider the level of organization required to get these evenings off the ground: someone's barn or cellar had to be chosen, the rotation determined, and all the negotiating and arranging to decide who was in and who out (a formidable task in itself if "dozens" of women were involved). Then there were the evening's logistics, such as who paid for the fuel for the lamp, who brought the collective beverage (if there was one), who decided about letting in the boys who had come to court the girls. In Provence the women would even elect a president.[23] The men who give us our sources weren't interested in such things, and so the level and intensity of married women's organization remains veiled. Yet within those barns on those winter evenings, there must have moved a rich world of social life.

In the end, we can only guess at the answers to the most interesting questions about these various solidarity groups of married and unmarried men and women. How much time during the week would a given person devote to his group, and how much to his family? Did peer-group allegiances surface during work (the veillées were, after all, work occasions) or only in "leisure" time? Did the family occasionally exert counter-tugs upon the various members off in these collective activities—mothers, for example, urging young men who were racing about the countryside to spend more time at home? Or had the family completely absorbed the larger communitarian values that sanctioned these organizations?

How pathetic our present knowledge is! At the moment it is clear only that in traditional Europe—especially France—individual family members spent much more time away from home with peers than was to be the case in modern Europe.

The Traditional Pattern: Family and Community in Birth, Marriage, and Death

In the world we have lost the community was closely involved in the three vital events of a person's life: birth, marriage, and death. Symbolically, this kind of community participation affirms how individual family members were part of a collectivity larger than the family. Practically, the youth of the village—or whomever the community had dispatched as its representatives—had to crank up each time a baptism or wedding took place: to fire off their guns, to put cordons across the road, to have a few beers afterward. And this kind of mobilization strengthed their own solidarity.

A number of nonfamily people participated in a baptism. The mother, of course, couldn't take the child herself to the altar because she hadn't yet been "churched." Sometimes the father would go, sometimes not In Catholic France it was incumbent upon the godparents and neighbors to haul the infant to the parish church; these little corteges would often comprise the midwife, the strong young neighbor's boy (for the church might be a long way away), the families of the godparents, and interested bystanders. The youth of the village, "avid for distraction," would assemble at the church door to fire off rifles and pistols as the group went in and again as it emerged. There would be a final salvo as the cortege filed back to the mother's house, and then the lads would spend the godparents' little token of gratitude in the cabaret.[24] These were older boys. But just as the cortege came out from the church, the little kids of the village, too, drawn by the tolling of the bell, would gather in front to be showered with fruits—a later era would provide sweets and one-franc pieces—that thoughtful godparents had ready in their pockets.[25] So a typical baptism, in fact, reached out to embrace a substantial number of people who were not associated with the infant's family.

Secondly, individual fate and community concern overlapped at death. The intricacies of French village practice supplied three moments in which the death and burial of a person would encompass

213

the nonfamily world. The first was the circulating of the news of a death, done in some places by a crier and in others by the church bells. There would be sixteen rings for a man, twelve for a woman. The bellwork of some churches permitted a range of tolls, making it possible to peal signals announcing the age, sex, and social status of the deceased (as well as how much money he had left to the church). In theory, as the bells tolled, the village's inhabitants would pause to say a prayer. Everyone within earshot of the church bells would therefore, at a minimal level, participate in an individual's passing, if only to see if the church's assessment of the deceased's status diverged from their own view.[26]

Next, the neighbors (not the immediate family) of the deceased would circulate in the village inviting people to the funeral, making sure that relatives in distant communes were notified. Or the church's sacristan would issue the invitations. Here again, community participation in personal fate leaped over the walls of the immediate family.[27]

The wake was the center of the funeral. It was the youth of a village (sometimes the boys in the same military-service class, sometimes the girls in the "Daughters of the Virgin" group or a similar pious association) who helped prepare the room with black cloths, candles, crucifixes, images of the Virgin, ribbons, flowers, and the other sacred accouterments. If the deceased were a young man, his peers would sit the death watch; if a young girl, hers.[28] Often as not, it was drunken clamor and unsteady dancing that crashed in upon the spirit of the deceased. Death in peasant France meant—at least sometimes—partying. People from all over the village would come, have a glass or two, and sit about telling stories and gossiping. In Brittany the invited neighbors thought as much of their stomachs as of the praying and chanting, "above all of having some *crêpes*. Sometimes the crowd is such that a portion of the guests goes off in the barn, and, the same in grief as in gaiety, proceeds to get completely drunk, so that often sobs have been seen to change little by little into cries of joy, and the dancing gets going not far from the cadaver of the friend they had come to mourn." Outraged by such spectacles, Breton curés went so far as to forbid young girls to attend the wakes of anyone save close relatives.

Worse than dancing might break out among the sturdy yeomanry: "A collation towards midnight completed the work which the already well-oiled prayers had begun. Sometimes arguments and veritable battles break out, in which lamp, table, and bottles are hurled across the corpse of the poor deceased." People were more subdued when a young girl or a woman had died, or a father of six children. But unsolemn behavior, laughing, tale-telling, and plotting were all standard in the face of death, the community's contribution to aid the deceased across the bar.[29] Once the nuclear family seized control of funerals in modern times, of course, all this would come to a whimpering end, joining the treasury of lost folklore in Europe and North America.[30]

At the funeral's very end, the community rejoined the family for the post-burial meal. The presumably grief-stricken relatives would slave in the kitchen to accommodate this horde of hungry outsiders; and at the finish, were it a husband who had passed away, dinner would conclude with efforts to marry off the widow.[31] The relationship between the deceased and the community was to become very different in our own dear time: the dying husband secluded behind white hospital doors, with solemn business associates and family friends everywhere whose only concern would be how the Widow Jones was taking it.

It was at weddings, however, that the community thrust itself most forcefully into the "vital" events of personal life. Whereas in our days the wedding is a private party, open only to those invited— save perhaps for passers-by who gawk from the curbstones at confetti showers—in traditional Europe the wedding was open on all sides. Quickest to intervene were the organized youth of the village (*la Jeunesse*). During all the marches back and forth that a wedding was likely to entail, the youth of the place would be on hand to fire off salvos—as the bride left her parental home for the church, during the wedding ceremony, when the cortege left the church, and so on. (Increasingly nervous about revolutionary subversion, the French state discouraged this practice throughout the nineteenth century; it died out entirely after the First World War, when the firing of guns ceased to be associated with merriment.[32] The *Jeunesse* would build at least one barricade to extort drink money from the wedding party, sometimes blocking the trousseau until the ransom was paid, sometimes delaying the wedding party underway to church, or obstructing the happy couple en route to their new home. The barricades might range from a mighty tree, felled across the road, to a simple white ribbon that little children, bribable with candies, would stretch before the church door. The idea was to force the wedding party to pay off the barricade's builders, who would then retire to the tavern until the dancing started. A variant of the barricade was the "honor guard," a band of local youth whom the party would bribe to go ahead and make sure the road was "clear" (and if they weren't bribed enough, it wouldn't be).[33]

On the wedding night, many variations of hide-and-seek took place. The newlyweds would sneak "unobserved" from the wedding dinner to hole up in some villager's borrowed bedroom for a couple of hours, the local *Jeunesse* then setting out on a chase that would terminate in shouts of discovery, many off-color jokes—although determined to keep sex in-limits, these villagers were not at all prudish—and the offering to the couple of a strongly-flavored special "brew" (*la rôtie*) whose purpose was evidently to rekindle their sexual energies. Having run the couple to ground, the *Jeunesse* would hang around, perhaps returning at daybreak in another raucous visit, perhaps posting a guard to make sure the couple didn't have any (more) sex—for in substantial regions of France the "nights of Toby" were still observed, meaning that sexual intercourse was not supposed to commence until the third day after the ceremony. In a bastardized version, the best man in the Morbihan would stay on in the bridal chamber, "back modestly turned," until the candle burned out.[34]

Country weddings would always have dancing after the big dinner. Invariably the entire community was invited, the youth to leap and throw themselves about in the peasant gymnastics that passed for dancing, the older people to sit and watch and drink. The bridal party would pay for the band, were there one (but more often the onlookers would clap or call the time). And in the open field, barn, or tavern where the celebration had been arranged, the newlyweds would start off the first number. Perhaps the wedding party would treat the community to drinks, and to bread as well, though practices varied. The essential was the dancing, and the invitation was to the whole village to join in.[35]

Not every part of France saw all these interventions take place. Different ensembles of customs prevailed in different places, and I have done little more than to sketch the principal activities, the occasions on which the *Jeunesse* would be most likely to go yodeling drunkenly along or to plant themselves oafishly before smiling parents, palms outstretched for payoffs. Here is how events might unfurl in the Trièves district towards mid-nineteenth century, to give a sense of time and place:[36]

When a young girl got married, the youth of the commune came to ask her if she'd like an honor guard, which she almost always accepted.

Then a little row of pine saplings would be placed in front of her door, decorated with wreathes, and a carpet of flowers laid down.

Near the door was placed a similarly decorated table on which were laid out a whole collection of regional liqueurs: *chartreuse, génépi, china, gentiane* . . . that the lads of the guard offered to the parents and their guests.

Of course each guest had to contribute something according to his means.

After the bride appeared on the doorstep to leave for the ceremony, she was saluted by a salvo of rifle shots fired by the lads of the honor guard on each side of the door.

The guard, like the former sappers of our regiments, then led the cortege and charged down the road to clear away any obstacles which might have been present.

In fact, it was customary to place in the route of the party obstacles of all kinds, such as pieces of wood, hunks of iron, carts, pine logs and so forth, especially at spots difficult to detour.

Getting rid of all that was the task of the honor guard.

Salvos of rifle shots were again fired off going and coming from the town hall and the church. Then, their duties over, the lads of the honor guard withdraw to eat at the inn with the contribution the parents had supplied them.

After the wedding meal, as abundant as one might imagine, all these young folks returned to the bride's home and mixed among the guests, then taking part in the dancing that went on all night.

During the dance, the couple was closely surveilled for, to kid them, they had to be stopped from taking off and finding refuge in some neighboring friend's house. Above all, they had to be made to pass a sleepless night. If despite everything they succeeded in escaping, the trail was quickly recovered and they were succored with a "chicory" soup, hot spiced wine poured over slices of toasted bread and served up in a chamber pot.

In birth, marriage, and death, then, the surrounding community was present, intertwining itself about the grief and passion of individuals, separating them from their immediate families, drawing them into a larger world of social interaction. Clearly the nuclear family would have to throw up walls of privacy and seclusion to isolate itself from this kind of interference—these strangers poking about your parlor and putting salt on your dishes as loved ones passed away, these punk kids with their hands out, keeping Billy and Janie from reaching the altar. In traditional society the boundary between conjugal family and community was still quite permeable: where the one flows out, the other rushes in.

The Traditional Pattern: Community Intervention in Family Life

People who know peasants might wonder a bit at these accounts of open-handed distribution of sweets to the village kids, or the generous sponsoring of dances for the community as a whole. Readers aware of the lack of any kind of police or public security forces in early modern Europe might further puzzle at my numerous declarations of "community control" or "forcing individuals to conform" to collective this's or that's. Clearly peasants and small-townsmen were not by nature generous. No noble tradition of largesse informed the backwaters of traditional Europe. The rural gendarmerie was to await the nineteenth century, So if in fact community norms imposed themselves with steely force, how was this done?

The traditional community was able to compel individual family members to follow collective rules through a disciplinary technique called the charivari. We have already touched on it in Chapter 1. The charivari was, in its essentials, a noisy public demonstration to subject wayward individuals to humiliation in the eyes of the community. Sometimes the demonstration would consist of masked individuals circling somebody's house at night, screaming, beating on pans, and blowing cow horns (which the local butchers rented out). On other occasions the offender would be seized and marched through the streets, seated perhaps backwards on a donkey or forced to wear a placard describing his sins. Sometimes the youth would administer the charivari; on other occasions villagers of all ages and sexes would mix together. Many variants were possible; let us look first at France.

Sexual offenders were often the targets of charivaris, such as married men in the village of Vaux (Oise) who got single women pregnant. "The youth assemble with horns, pots, and cowbells, and make a terrible racket at the door of the man and of the girl. Two weeks later they summon all the inhabitants of neighboring villages together in a place of their chosing. The Court of Fools [*La justice des fous*] convenes. Two straw figures representing the man and the girl are juridically condemned to be burned by the master of proceedings, and this is done with a dreadful noise. Then the whole cortege and the accompanying court file through the streets of the village, and in front of the door of the guilty parties."[37]

Cuckolded husbands, too, were singled out for abuse, especially at carnival, on the theory that by permitting his wife to deceive him, he had endangered patriarchal authority in general. On Shrove Tuesday at Bagneux (Hauts-de-Seine), cuckolds were marched about on a chair that then was added to the Mardi-gras bonfire, the husband having been, at the last moment, replaced by a straw mannequin. In the Verberie district (Oise), villagers charivaried deceived husbands with cardboard horns and pots and then, on Mardi-gras, had one of their number dress up as a cuckold (presumably wearing horns)—whose place, after a promenade, "was taken by a straw man that people proceeded to behead."[38]

From time to time, unwed mothers were charivaried as sexual offenders, but over the years they became so numerous that the custom had to be abandoned. In nineteenth-century Walincourt (Nord), however, the youth organization's moral sensitivity still extended to subjecting such women to a "ceremony." "One of the youth carried a straw figure representing the man, another carried an armful of straw covered with wraps depicting the infant. Thereupon everyone danced around the straw man and cradled the 'infant' in front of the house of the incriminated person. The straw forms were then interrogated about their activities in the most abusive term."[39]

The village turned a blind eye to male sexual abuses, and the husband who cheated on his wife with another married woman would be left in peace.[40] What upset the community was not the actual sexual impropriety so much as the threat its consequences posed to the community social order. That is why adulterous wives themselves were not seized and paraded backwards on donkeys (save occasionally in Provence).[41] Their husbands were grabbed because their lack of supervision threatened the structure of authority. That's why masters who slept with their female servants were left undisturbed. Only those couples who dumped bastard children in the village's lap were rebuked. Such selectivity in the charivari's targets shows again that these traditional populations were not prudish, just circumspect.

Marital mismatches offered a second set of targets for the charivari. Marriages between people grossly disproportionate in age, for example, were likely to be attacked. Girls who jilted a suitor of their own group to marry someone much wealthier would be charivaried.[42] Even more castigated were marriages between a widow (or widower) and a single person; the theory on which the villagers operated appears to have been that a widower had to atone for his crime of reducing the pool of eligibles by buying everyone drinks or giving a public dance. And it was the failure to pay tribute to the offended youth group, as much as the act of remarrying, that spawned the charivari. For those who didn't pay in the Saintonge, "the charivari started up every evening for eight consecutive days at almost the same hour, for six or seven hours, lasting until midnight. Moreover, on the day of the wedding the demonstrators followed the nuptial cortege, leading in their midst a straw man or clothed mannequin, and the serenade went on almost the whole day. That evening the straw man was burned in the midst of a deafening uproar."[43] It was possible for re-marriers to buy off the charivari entirely in advance,[44] but a widower who refused to pay the ransom "wouldn't be able to sleep soundly for entire weeks or even months. Around his house boilers, cooking pots, whistles, cowbells, trumpets, and drums went into action, furnishing hellish concerts for hours on end. And above all he couldn't call the gendarmerie [in the nineteenth century], for the authors of the charivari would have escaped and then really let him have it. Finally, weary of war, the victim yields and does what he should have done to start with."[45] Pays. The point was not to prohibit the proposed union, but merely to compensate the young unmarrieds for this body-snatching from their ranks.[46] The rhymes called out by the demonstrators left little doubt about their objective:[47]

> Dis donc vieille carcasse
> Veux-tu pas nous payer
> Les droits de la badôche
> Aux enfants du quartier

> Nous sommes des bons drôles
> Des garcons sans souci
> Il nous faut des pistoles
> Ou bien charivari!

> Fork up, old pal
> The dough that you owe
> We're the boys of the block
> And we want a good show

> We're wild as they come
> And off on a spree
> So out with the cash
> Or charivari!

But just imagine the degree of collective authority over individual autonomy this represents—the power of a bunch of young trouble-makers to force grizzled old farmer Dubois to pay them a dance!

Another category of charivari struck at those who failed to perform some customary obligation such as giving out cakes on "bon-fire" Sunday, or who refused to open their wedding dance to the public. Bridegrooms who declined to admit the bearers of the "brew" to their bedchambers on wedding night would get charivaried, as would visibly pregnant brides who wore white on their wedding days.[48]

The most interesting kind of charivari, from our point of view, was aimed at "disorder" in the household, by which the community meant some kind of deviation from the standard sex roles. Men who did women's work, for example, were charivaried regularly.[49] And husbands who permitted themselves to be beaten by their wives were subject to sharp censure. In old-regime France, where women were prized for their size and strength, it might well happen that a strapping peasant woman would shove her husband about. Folks in the Lot department knew how to handle this violation of the natural order: "When people find out about it, they go hunt for a donkey, and make the husband climb on, outfitted with a distaff. He gets the animal's tail for the reins. Then he's taken around the entire village. If the husband has hidden they take the closest neighbor, to punish him for having permitted, in the vicinity of his dwelling, a woman to forget the respect she owes her husband."[50] No Caspar Milquetoasts the Bretons, either: they grabbed wife-beaten husbands, strapped them to carts, and "paraded them ignominiously through a booing populace."[51] Sometimes the husband-beater herself was punished as well. In one village, for example, the demonstrators would stick the wife backwards upon the donkey, "forcing her to drink wine and then wiping her mouth with the animal's tail."[52]

The community, sensitive to any usurpation of husbandly authority, was especially quick to strike down public manifestations of feminine strength—above all in that haunt of male solidarity, the bar. Women rarely had trouble bringing their mates home from the bar on Sundays at Veynes (Hautes-Alpes), because any husband who permitted himself to be manhandled by women (who, the observer tells us, were "ordinarily a little quick to strike out") would be hustled aboard a donkey and led about the village by a man "disguised as a woman, his friends, similarly dressed in worn-out hats, following behind and feigning intense grief." The ceremony was voluntary, "but no one would think of evading it, at the risk of being exposed to incessant raillery." Because the men were all petrified at being thus charivaried, they all apparently followed their wives home peaceably. "It's true, however, that the home trip is sometimes a bit stormy."[53]

What about men who beat their wives, a more common occurrence than wives who beat their husbands? Were they charivaried as well? The nature of our source material makes quantitative assessments difficult, but it's worth noting that, whereas the community moved against husband-beaters, fallen women, and adulteresses all year round, it struck at *wife*-beaters, if at all, mainly during the month of May. And then, apparently, only at men who in fact beat their wives during that month, traditionally considered the women's month. "During their period of domination, the women of Luxeuil (Haute-Saône) had the right to parade on a donkey husbands who had struck them during May." In the district of the Bresse a straw man was substituted for the husband in the parade, probably because of the nastiness that seizing a flesh-and-blood person might cause.[54] Age-old customs in the Franche-Comté said that "each and every time a husband beats his wife during May, the women of the place must trot him about on a donkey amid joyfulness and gaiety. . . ." In 1816 this right was still being exercised "in a most solemn manner," and then for a final time in 1840. Elsewhere in the region the women's donkey-parade lasted until late in the century, and popular willingness to subject husband-beaters to nighttime "at-home" charivaris extended even later. "But people wouldn't dare to give one to an old, rich libertine from whom something was wanted or feared.[55] The lesson is that either sex's beating of the other could threaten the domestic order and therewith endanger the solidarity of the whole community. But since men were seen as the natural bearers of authority, their abuses met with considerably greater tolerance.

These are all rural events. But in cities, as well, the charivari maintained itself until at least the threshold of the nineteenth century, although we might suspect there were many fewer than in the villages. Still, journeymen in eighteenth-century Paris who married masters' widows were singled out; and we know that, in Lyon, charivaris were launched against marriages with large age discrepancies.[56] At Montpellier a "cuckold's court" was staged for carnival, its masked bailiffs pulling in from around the city "husbands accused of being cheated or beaten by their wives." The tribunal then forced these condemned ones to kiss a large set of ribboned horns.[57] And in late-eighteenth-century Lille, the journeymen brewers had a treat in store for "disorderly" households: "They go masked about the city to the sound of horns and instruments which give off grave, lugubrious noises. One of the participants disguised as a preacher bears in his hands the book of accusations; he's the orator. This masked troupe then shows up in front of houses where according to public rumor there's *mauvais ménage* [domestic discord]. The drums and horns call people together. Then the orator . . . discourses in stentorian tones about the precious advantages of a peaceful household, indirectly apostrophizes the two discordant spouses who are the object of his zeal, and details with astonishing effrontery the personal sins of each, recounting sometimes quite piquant anecdotes. . . ."[58] All this in a bustling provincial metropolis!

Under the names *Haberfeldtreiben*, *Katzenmusiken*, *Schnurren*, skimmingtons, or shivarees, the charivari was known all over Atlantic civilization, from Puritan New England to the mountains of Upper Bavaria.[59] There is little point in merely rehearsing example after example, because, having spent some time now with the case of France, the reader has a clear idea of the custom's forms and purposes. But differences from country to country may tell us something about fundamental differences in family–community relations. Our knowledge here is fragile. The charivari has received almost no systematic scholarly attention, and the wisps of references that have crossed my path may reflect nothing more significant than chance. Yet two themes in England and Germany in particular seem consistent enough to be at least worth noting.

If the English historian E. P. Thompson is correct, English charivaris turned their aim increasingly towards wife-beaters as the eighteenth century gave way to the nineteenth. More and more, English villagers launched noisy demonstrations against men like a certain Joseph Fowler of Waddesdon (Bucks.), who beat his wife because, as he later explained to a Court, she didn't treat his illegitimate son well enough.[60] Or consider this charivari sometime in the 1840s, in a Surrey village: "After night fell a cortege was formed. First came two men with enormous cow horns; then another with a big cauldron suspended from his neck. There followed the orator of the band, and then a motley company outfitted with bells, gongs, cowhorns, whistles, pans, rattles, bones, frying pans. . . . At a given signal they stopped, and the orator began to recite a series of doggerel verses . . . beginning with:

> There is a man in this place
> Has beat his wife!! (forte; a pause)
> Has beat his wife!! (fortissimo)
> It is a very great shame and disgrace
> To all to who live in this place
> It is indeed upon my life!!!

Thereupon all the instruments of the parade broke loose, accompanied by boos and cries." The group then proceeded to dance about the bonfire, "as if they were crazy." They were audible two miles away. "After a half hour of this, silence was called for and the orator advanced once again towards the house, expressing the wish that he would not have to return and inviting the husband to moral improvement."[61] Alongside these wife-beater demonstrations, of course, the English villagers fired skimmingtons at shrewish wives and adulteresses, pregnant maidens, and the whole other gamut of charivari targets we have noted elsewhere.

But of interest to us is the apparent absence in France, and in other lands as far as I know, of this upsurge in community concern over the abuse of women. Van Gennep is certainly silent on such an increase, and in my work I have seen nothing to suggest that charivaris against wife-beaters were more common in 1850 than in 1750. What we may be picking up, therefore, is the early modernization of domestic relationships in England that we have observed at other points. As egalitarian relationships between husband and wife diffused, the community began to perceive as intolerable such vestiges of earlier patriarchal authority as the right to slam one's wife about; and so it moved to rebuke the wife-beaters. In French domestic relations, such egalitarianism arrived so late in time that the charivari was already dead as an active custom—having expired for entirely unrelated reasons—before it could be turned against the violent husband.

In Holland, Germany, Austria, Switzerland, and Scandinavia the charivari was similarly to be found. But so meager is the underpinning of research for these vast stretches that I hesitate even to

comment on international differences. One tentative suggestion however: in perusing Bavarian police dossiers on rural charivaris early in
the nineteenth century, my eye was struck by the large number of
demonstrations against "immoral" unmarried women and libertine
priests. To be sure, this corner of Europe had a very high illegitimacy
rate. There probably was more fooling around before marriage in
Bavaria than in Provence, and so a high proportion of charivaris
against the "village whore" may merely reflect real differences in
behavior. On the other hand, there appears to have been a reso-
luteness among the participants in Bavaria that is lacking in the
more playful French charivarists. In Miesbach County on October
27, 1826, for example, "two fellows came towards eleven at night
to the window of a tavern, knocked, and called out 'Innkeeper!
We're going to charivari your house harlot [*hingeworfene Hur*].
You'd better not do anything. No one's going to get hurt, but if you
set off the alarm, we'll burn your place down.' Thereupon, amidst 'a
horrifying racket' the group proceeded to recite rhymes about whom
the 'above-mentioned female person' was going with, about her
numerous pregnancies, and so forth." Over a hundred shots were
fired in the demonstration. At the end the demonstrators rhymed,
"Now we've got to say good night, or the cops will come and shoot
on sight." ("*Jetzt müssen wir's beschliessen/sonst kommen d'Gen-
darm'n/und thun uns erschiessen.*")[62] This has more the ring of
cops-and-robbers than of earthy folk custom; French peasants didn't
think in terms of shoot-outs with the gendarmes. Other sources
confirm a special Central European preoccupation with sexual
delinquency.[63]

Let me offer this as a suggestion worthy of further exploration:
German charivaris turned more against premarital sexual intercourse
than did the French, because in Germany the community as a whole
was more responsible for the management of mating and dating. In
France, family supervision counted for at least as much as that of
the peer group or surrounding community (as we noted in the relative absence of group nightcourting), and so the community deemed
premarital sexual shortcomings to be essentially family business.
Questions of family authority, such as husband-beating, or matters
affecting marital fidelity (such as the husband's loyalty to his de-

ceased wife), were more likely to arouse the French community to action. Thus more French charivaris struck at the re-marriages of widowers with virgins or at men who did women's work than at the unmarried libertine.

Everywhere the charivari helped the community to maintain order within individual families. It was a powerful solvent of privacy and intimacy in the family circle. It aided a constant collective surveillance of individual behavior and permitted the group to pull individuals back into line, or else—as often happened in England—to drive them entirely from the community. When these traditional assumptions about the community's rights over family affairs changed—that is, when the nuclear family came into life—the charivari became irrelevant.

The Rise of Domesticity

The "companionate" marriage is customarily seen as the hallmark of contemporary family life, the husband and wife being friends rather than superordinate and subordinate, sharing tasks and affection. Perhaps that is correct. But the emotional cement of the modern family binds more than the husband and wife; it fixes the children, as well, into this sentimental unit. The notion of companionship doesn't necessarily say anything about the relationship between the couple and their children. Also, "companionship" implies incorrectly that some form of intense romantic attachment continues to unite the couple. Both ideas are incomplete, and for that reason I prefer the expression "domesticity" in demarcating the modern family from the traditional.

Domesticity, or the family's awareness of itself as a precious emotional unit that must be protected with privacy and isolation from outside intrusion, was the third spearhead of the great onrush of sentiment in modern times. Romantic love detached the couple from communal sexual supervision and turned them towards affection. Maternal love created a sentimental nest within which the modern family would ensconce itself, and it removed many women

227

from involvement with community life. Domesticity, beyond that, sealed off the family as a whole from its traditional interaction with the surrounding world. The members of the family came to feel far more solidarity with one another than they did with their various age and sex peer groups. We know in practical terms when domesticity is present if, like the French, people begin removing their names from the front doors to insure that no one will knock; if, as in Germany, long Sunday walks through the woods begin to tear Papa from his card games; and if, as happens everywhere, people begin spending greater proportions of their time at home.

The development of domesticity displayed the same class differential as did maternal love and, in the reverse way, romance. In France it first took form among the bourgeoisie. Late in the eighteenth century, sources begin to deafen us with the discovery of *maisons très unies* among this class. The first references that I have encountered come from the most modern sectors: those of urban industry. Here, for example, is Doctor Louis Lépecq de la Cloture on the middle classes of Elbeuf in the 1770s: "Unity reigns in the families, and this true solicitousness, which means the sharing equally of trouble and joy, fidelity between the spouses, fatherly tenderness, filial respect and domestic intimacy, are qualities which seem reserved to this happy city. . . ." So Lépecq, who knew Normandy well, thought the textile town of Elbeuf singular for its family life.[64] Menuret de Chambaud, thoroughly at home among the Parisian middle classes, similarly observed for the 1780s "paternal affection, filial piety, fraternal friendship," despite the sullying effects of debauchery among these good people.[65] Thirty years later, Bayonne's P. J. Lesauvage described a veritable idyll of bourgeois family life: "Spouses are united and appear to be mutually affectionate. The men take care of business in the outside world, the wives manage the interior of the home and see the perfection of their happiness in caring for their children and cherishing their husbands."[66] Yet this new domesticity was not confined to the urban middle classes. The Indre's prefect believed his department's entire population "well-matched in marriage: for the most part wedlock is not a yoke but rather a soft exchange of consideration, of kind attentions, and scandalous divorces are uncommon."[67] It remained, however, for prefect Verneilh to lay the crowning praise upon the small-town bourgeoisie of the Savoy: "Husbands have come closer to their wives, mothers to their children. All have felt the need for mutual support, to create for themselves consolations and resources, to give themselves to domestic concerns which formerly they had disdained."[68]

We obviously can not believe all this. The romanticism of these doctors and administrators leaps from the context, and the values they so blithely attribute to the entire bourgeoisie were doubtless to have been found, first of all, in their own households. Yet three comments may be made. One is that these and many similar references confine themselves to the middle classes, normally omitting the lower orders. Secondly, these writers believe themselves living witnesses to a historical change, for they often explicitly compare the Bad Old Days to "our glorious times." Thirdly, I have not encountered similar observations for this class of people in the years before 1775; the clustering of remarks about domesticity in the last quarter of the eighteenth century and first quarter of the nineteenth points quantitatively to an important evolution.

But what did all this rosy beaming actually mean? How had family comportment changed from earlier times? When did the nuclear family begin to resent intrusions from the outside? And when was the collective decision made to spend more time with one another than with nonfamily people?

The prefect of the Bouches-du-Rhône, Christophe de Villeneuve, left the shutter open for a second on the well-to-do of Marseille in the 1820s: "Even before the Revolution people were more outdoors than in, and the men spent much of their time in cafés, in discussion groups, and at entertainments. Today such meeting places are still frequented, but in general, family fathers only rarely attend." This was because family life itself was more attractive than before—harking back, Villeneuve thought, to the ways of one's ancestors: homes were more nicely furnished, the children more genteelly brought up, the fine arts become a new focus of family activity.

Most interesting of all, however, was Villeneuve's account of why bourgeois families no longer went out often in the evening. "The family father, obliged to occupy himself with difficult business problems during the day, can relax only when he goes home. Everyone crowds around him. He beams at the childrens' games; he prides himself on knowing them well and their accomplishments delight him. Family evenings together are for him a time of the purest and most complete happiness." Thus, according to Villeneuve, if middle-class families in Marseille were withdrawing from constant community contact, it was because that outside world—in this case bourgeois commerce—appeared less inviting than formerly. The locus of meaningful ties had shifted from without the family to within. Villeneuve explained: "In former times there was a great distance between husband and wife, between father and children, from family to society. Talk came less easily, human ties were less intimate, relationships more distant." Today, Villeneuve concluded, familiarity was the watchword of family life.[69]

Marseille doubtless led most other places. The whole gamut of traditional rituals that linked family to community survived intact in France for the first half of the nineteenth century (if we are to trust the antiquarians). It was only in the 1860s and 1870s that the small-town and village festivals that fostered so much of this contact started to collapse, ending the St. John's Day fires or the masked carnival celebrations in village after village.[70]

The sources permit us to connect the narrative of *chacun chez soi*, which is of immediate interest, to this tale of perishing folklore at only a few points. One antiquarian tells what happened in the Vosges in the 1860s. Whereas in the mountains the veillées continued as always, the poor folks meeting regularly to do handiwork, play cards, drink, and let the young dance, in the more prosperous valleys the great transformation was already underway. The veillées among these peasants had declined from weekly affairs to just one or two evenings a winter. And their nature had changed from informal sociability in which people brought their own snacks to bourgeois "entertainment." At ten o'clock the hostess would spread out a white tablecloth and produce a late supper of some dimensions. Wine would be served rather than *eau de vie*. This sort of extravagance among the well-off peasants caused the poorer ones who formerly had attended regularly to drop out: "Because a great number of families were not sufficiently fortunate to adopt this mode of partying, it followed that the moment white bread, wine and red

230

meat appeared on the table these people ceased attending the veillées."[71] Thus a bourgeois family style reduced this occasion for community involvement to a rarity among well-to-do peasants, and a bourgeois form of entertainment ensured that the lower classes would have to fall away. In a peasantoid miracle, wine and a white tablecloth had transformed traditional society into modern.

Other straws point in the wind as well to a middle-class withdrawal from the cycle of village ritual. In the small-holding world of Hans-le-Grand (Marne), for example, carnival had ceased by the 1860s to include those "follies and disguises, above all, those get-togethers in which the young would eat in the evening the fruits of a house-to-house search they'd made among all inhabitants of the village, most emerging from the cabaret in a state of complete drunkenness. On that day now families are re-united, each bringing a dish, and the evening passes in gaiety and happiness."[72] And by the 1880s, propertied peasants in the Ile-de-France region had acquired the habit of going into Paris for the wedding ceremony, mass, and banquet. "Therewith vanishes," pontificated Henri Baudrillart, "an occasion for families to get together in those fêtes which sometimes stretched out for three whole days."[73] The perimeter of folklore, and the circulation of intimate life it protected within the entire community, was being remorselessly constricted.

In the case of the working classes, the narratives of domesticity, of *chacun chez soi* and contact with the neighborhood, still lie shrouded in darkness. Here and there are potsherds of understanding—fragments portraying the quality of lower-class life which sooner tantalize than clarify. Contemporary sociological literature tells us that today's working classes in France have taken on many of the forms of bourgeois family life, though not necessarily the substance.[74] In the twentieth century, some rapprochement in the family styles of the two subcultures has gone on. But when did the lower classes begin to turn their backs on the community? Were they merely aping the bourgeoisie, or did the evolution of their family patterns obey a dynamic of its own? Did all groups of the working classes evolve together, agricultural laborers staying home in the evening to listen to the radio and factory workers too? Or did the urban–rural difference remain pronounced? At this stage such questions still await resolution. I wish to give here only a furtive nod at the mid-nineteenth century as the take-off point of worker domesticity.

Let us return to Marseille of the 1830s and 1840s, seen this time through the eyes of the rather proletarian François Mazuy. The seaside shacks of amateur fishermen, called *cabanons*, were the springboard of domesticity among the workers of that city, Mazuy informs us. At first these cabanons served just as a place for fishermen to get out of the sun, have a few glasses of wine, and store their tackle. Then a more regularized male sociability grew up around them, the fishermen banding together in little clubs to buy wine and olive oil in bulk, along the lines of the classical southern French *chambrée*. Then the workers started bringing their wives and children along with them when they went fishing on weekends, and the whole family would stay over in the cabanon from Saturday night until Sunday. Because family mixed in with club members, "indecent language is severely forbidden." The shift from male socializing to family intimacy was now in full swing: little gardens, lawns, and trellises started to be put in about the cabanons. Nor was the final change far behind. "It remains for us to say that *l'amour de chez soi* of the countryside has caused in Marseille an incredible subdivision of property. It is not uncommon to encounter Marseille workers who own their cabanons. This happens slowly. The initial savings go for the purchase of the land, then others for building the cottage, then the ultimate treasure of the worker-proprietor is the acquisition of a buggy and a little corsican pony charged with transporting the family to this happy cottage."[75] Mazuy doesn't tell us what happened to all the drinking buddies, whom the pony was surely not able to haul along as well on weekends.

We cannot know at this stage if these cabanons represented the embourgeoisement of the Marseille workers' family life; nor do we know if what happened in Marseille was typical, in either form or timing, of events elsewhere in France. What is fairly clear, however, is that by the turn of the century this kind of domesticity had become firmly implanted within the lower classes of many different regions. Baudrillart was a gusher, but his testimony cannot have been completely wrong. Of the farmers of the Pas-de-Calais he wrote in the late 1880s: "Morality and affection are the most distinguishing

Modern Family

features of family life. Disharmony between the spouses is quite rare. Callousness from [grown] children towards [retired] parents is unfortunately not unknown, yet represents the exception. And the tenderness on the part of the parents is almost too much of a good thing."[76] Baudrillart trailed such observations behind him as he crisscrossed the provinces of France, delighted with the happy state of peasant family life he encountered. And even though he rocked some distracting hobbyhorses, it is doubtful that he could have written such odes to domesticity had he followed in Arthur Young's footsteps a century earlier.

The struggle between community and domesticity finally ended in the inter-world war years with the triumph of *chacun chez soi*, and only a clutch of misty-eyed old men were left to preside over the interment of the veillée. August Grise, who lovingly chronicled the folkways of his native Isère, was typical: "Because in those days [the 1880s of his youth] people were more open, more frank, less egotistical and self-centered than today, because there was more cordiality and less jealousy, neighbors got together a lot. . . . Nowadays everybody reads his newspaper, in the event that he doesn't have a radio, and *chacun reste chez soi*."[77]

For other countries we do not have sufficient information even to make a beginning. The piecing together of clues from antiquarians, bureaucrats, and doctors has yet to be undertaken for Germany, England, Scandinavia, and North America. So we have no way of knowing whether the hints of seclusion from community life that drift across our view represent a change over time or a permanent condition. Here, for example, is Dr. K. F. H. Marx on the academic population of the university town of Göttingen: "Outsiders complain of formality in social forms here. They believe they encounter the chill of the North first of all in the people. . . ." But there was good reason for this: "Family life must represent a closed-off, joyful and joy-giving whole in and of itself."[78] Richard Sennett argues that an "intensification" of family life took place in the Union Park district of Chicago later in the nineteenth century, by which he means there was a replacement of "the fragmentation and sense of disjointed conglomeration of many private worlds, experienced outside in the city . . . by an overwhelming sense of intimacy within

233

the house."[79] And Robert Roberts is lyrical on the meaning of "home" for a slum child in Edwardian England: "Home, however poor, was the focus of all his love and interests, a sure fortress against a hostile world. Songs about its beauties were ever on people's lips. 'Home, sweet home,' first heard in the 1870s, had become 'almost a second national anthem.' Few walls in lower-working-class houses lacked 'mottoes'—colored strips of paper, about nine inches wide and eighteen inches in length, attesting to domestic joys: EAST, WEST, HOME'S BEST; BLESS OUR HOME; GOD IS MASTER OF THIS HOUSE; HOME IS THE NEST WHERE ALL IS BEST."[80]

Two factors suggest that these fragments may betoken a drift towards domesticity all over Western society. One is the faithfulness with which they echo the French evidence we have already reviewed. And in France, at least, we may state with some confidence that modernization was the tugboat of domesticity. The second is that we know in the contemporary world how the story comes out: the nest has become in fact the norm.

Kinfolk, Community, and the Great Transformation

To understand the contemporary family, one must only keep in mind two simple processes: the couple's almost complete withdrawal from routine community life, and the corresponding strengthening of their ties to parents and close relatives. As the occasions on which the conjugal family come together with neighbors and friends have fallen away, the kin group has taken on a new importance. Everywhere in Western society during our own times, people see their relatives enthusiastically and other members of the social order scarcely at all—socially, that is. People have all kinds of human contacts on the job, and they sustain a variety of memberships in clubs and associations. But they spend almost no time in the rituals of community solidarity that once so diluted intimacy. Yet whereas in traditional society the kin group counted for relatively little in emotional terms, being primarily a reservoir of material support in emergencies, nowadays it's chiefly the parents of the married couple—

and the gaggle of uncles, aunts, and cousins the couple might well find about them—who breach the walls of the nuclear family.

All this is much easier to assert, of course, than to prove. One of the vast unexplored frontiers of historical research is relations with kin. How often did traditional villagers see their relatives, both in absolute terms and in comparison to other kinds of contacts? Did the kin group represent to them a moral comfort, a source of good sense and friendly contact, or was it primarily available for such emergencies as death and court battles? And did people basically like their relatives, or hate them? Let's review country-by-country what meager data are available.

FRANCE

Here and there are hints of how things usually were among kin. Uncordiality and mistrust, indifference and suspicion simply leap to the eye. In eighteenth-century Languedoc, for example, we learn of fathers who conspired with the eldest son to deny the younger their inheritance. The younger siblings then banded together against the eldest, and violent quarrels and murders resulted. Or the father, "seized by the devil," murdered his son. In households where the inheriting son would bring his bride in to dwell with the parents, terrible tensions eventuated between mother and daughter-in-law. For seven long years the widow of a laborer in Escazaux lived with her married son "hating her daughter-in-law and driving the son to mistreat her;" one day the neighbors discovered the both of them whipping the daughter-in-law with a bunch of willow rods.

For these people, out of sight was out of mind. Leaving the village was tantamount to disappearing from the face of the earth. All traces were lost of children who moved away, and a Languedoc doctor was able in 1710 to report of one brother only that he had been "hanged at Nîmes," though he did not know why; of others he had lost track entirely. As long as these relatives stayed in the village together, they were willing to supply one another all kinds of emergency support, the notion of the lineage as a whole being of great importance to them. But all the while, as they battled over inheritance and the patrimony's disposition, they appear to have hated one another; and we must conclude that they found their emotional comrades in the kind of peer groups outlined above. The "solid family cohesion" Nicole Castan reports as characterizing Languedoc was all instrumental, not at all affective.[81]

The contrast with contemporary France is striking. Almost everyone regularly exchanges friendly visits with relatives rather than just rushing in for such emergencies as child birth or job dismissal. Among a sample of people interviewed in Charleroi, Belgium, for example, (which is practically the same as France), almost nine families in ten said they often visited relatives, only four in ten socialized with friends, and only two in ten had contacts from work or the neighborhood. Twice as many declared they preferred to visit relatives than friends when they had a free evening. As for neighbors, while almost all those surveyed knew their names and said hello, steadily decreasing proportions of them were prepared to pass the time of day in the street or borrow sugar. Six in ten refused to allow their neighbors in their homes even for favors, and eight in ten balked at either going out on the town with neighbors or entertaining them at home.[82]

Neighborhood sociability was little better in French villages of the 1960s.

—Of a small village in the Beauce region: "Almost no organized social life exists; each family lives for itself without any real contact with its neighbors, save for relatives." People never go into each other's homes.[83]

—For another village in Lorraine there was a sad little tale to tell: "In the past there were communal laundries, holidays and dances; now social life is limited to the family, or to mutual aid among the farmers. . . . Everyone is aware of this erosion of sociability, above all the young, who find nothing to do in the village at all but are incapable of getting anything together. They had hoped the mayor would undertake something, and reproach him for having transformed the chapel where they played ping-pong into a museum."[84]

—Here was the social composition of a ten-house village in the Marche region during the 1960s: four families of peasants who got along all-right, six other families who didn't speak to each other (including one unemployed family father condemned by the peasants), two municipal workers who were always putting up opposing political posters, a retired veteran living alone, and two sisters who kept a run-down bar. "The social life of the village is characteristic:

without family ties or need for community cooperation, there are no contacts."[85]

—In many hamlets of the Armagnac region there was no borrowing from neighbors and no loaning of farm machinery or equipment, in order to avoid "difficulties." "The veillées where people used to play cards or knit, while shelling corn and eating potatoes or roasted chestnuts, have disappeared; they've been replaced by veillées around the television set."[86]

We could roam through many other French villages and small towns in the 1960s and 1970s.[87] Everywhere the story would be the same: the death of the annual calendar of festivities, or at least of those portions that drew family members into the life of a larger collectivity; the decline of community folklore; the huddling of the kin into a cozy circle about the fire.

BRITAIN

The life of Ralph Josselin, a clergyman in seventeenth-century Essex, provides some modest clues to the force of kinship ties in traditional England. Outside the immediate family and couple's parents, such ties seem to have been nonexistent. Josselin never mentions saying prayers for relatives beyond his own family. There is no evidence that he attended the weddings or funerals of any kinfolk, not even of his sisters. And his copious diary offers no other proof of kin contact, though we know he had relatives living about him. Friends and neighbors were lumped in with relatives among the deaths he "noted and lamented," so that he appears to have grieved equally for his good friend Mary Church and for his daughter Anne, and to have noted with indifference the passing of a host of uncles, cousins, one grandson, and one granddaughter. When it came to emergency help, it was his neighbors and not his relatives who did the midwifing and the bonesetting. There is, in short, no sign whatsoever that any kinfolk outside the immediate family mattered in any way in the exceptionally well-chronicled life of this obscure provincial farmer-pastor.[88]

Against this slender little reed of evidence indicating a triumph of community over kin in seventeenth-century rural England, however, we may offer a mass of evidence indicating the overwhelming importance of mothers and fathers, uncles and aunts, nieces and nephews, brothers and sisters, and in-laws in the life of the average twentieth-century Englishman. It's consistent with my argument that genealogy is *un*important for the contemporary English. Raymond Firth talks of the "general lack of interest" the North Londoners he investigated take in their forbears: they make no effort to learn about their pasts or to teach their children about the lineage. Few are able even to identify their grandparents' siblings.[89] But contrasted with this shallow generational depth of the British kinship system is the stunning intensity of kin contacts in the present.

The key to the network of relatives seems to be the close tie between mother and daughter, as newlyweds make a considerable effort to locate near the wife's family. But links between the married son and his parents are also strong, as are those that embrace brothers and sisters, the closer lateral kin. In Swansea (Wales), for example, in the 1960s, 42 percent of the married daughters had parents living in the same *part* of the city and another 38 percent in some other quarter of Swansea, so that in at least three fourths of the families the wife would have the possibility of visiting her parents regularly. And in fact three fourths of those married daughters had seen their mothers sometime in the week before they were interviewed; the same held for the sons. Four out of five in the sample said they had also seen other kin within the past week.[90] So we may conclude that in Wales, at least, kin ties are very close. And they are in England as well. Over half of the old people (with married children) interviewed in London's middle-class suburb of Woodford and in London's working-class quarter, Bethnal Green, had seen at least one of their offspring *the previous day*, and an additional quarter had done so the previous week.[91] On and on roll these studies, documenting how important the larger kin group is in the life of the British nuclear family in the postwar world.

As someone who sees his parents, and whose friends see their parents, only about once a year, I must confess to a certain bemusement in scanning these statistics. And with my Iowa sense of farm families who help one another to get in the corn, I'm even more surprised by the content of these kin contacts—to have a good time rather than to provide support. If it's true that in traditional society kin figured principally as aids in time of trouble, it seems equally the case that, in modern Britain at least, you see your relatives because you enjoy being with them rather than because they might be able to do something for you. Raymond Firth writes of middle-class society that "the significance of extra-familial kinship is expressive rather than instrumental. Although concrete assistance is of considerable importance—in helping towards choice of school or job . . . it is primarily as a means towards fuller expression of a personality that such kinship ties are maintained."[92]

As kin take the place of friends and community in Britain, and as the state's social service programs take the place of the traditional support that kin once provided, the ties holding the nuclear family to acquaintances and neighborhoods slacken significantly. They sag most of all in the large housing projects which seem the wave of the residential future. One scholar captured the spirit of a housing "estate" in Oxford in talking to residents: "You get to know your next-door neighbour on either side but you don't get much further. I did pass the neighbour next door but one and *gave him the opportunity to greet me* [italics in original] but nothing happened." By way of contrast, St. Ebbe's parish in central Oxford, though scarcely a hotbed of sociability, was considerably friendlier.[93] Even more denuded of neighborly spirit, however was the "Greenleigh" housing project on the edge of London. One woman testified, "When the baby was ill, not a soul knocked at my door to get me an errand." Mrs. Hall opined "I don't think you can go to a neighbour if you want anything personal." And Mrs. Young said simply "my husband doesn't think it right to have neighbours in the place."[94] It was, however, Mr. Stirling, who summed up the case: "I don't mind saying hello to any of them, or passing the time of day with them, but if they don't want to have anything to do with me, I don't want to have anything to do with them. I'm not bothered about them. I'm only interested in my own family. My wife and my two children —they're the people that I care about. My life down here is my home."[95]

It would be unfair to claim that these housing estates are typical of all English society. In older communities people have been around longer and fit into well-established networks of neighborliness. London's district of Bethnal Green illustrates this obvious fact. One half of those interviewed had been born there and another quarter had been resident for at least fifteen years, the practical implication of which is that Mrs. Landon, on a half hour's morning shopping trip, would see a lot of people she knew:[96]

(1) Mary Collins. "She's a sister of Sally who I worked with at the button place before I got married. My Mum knew her Mum, but I sort of lost touch until one day I found myself sitting next to her in Meath Gardens. We both had the babies with us and so we got talking again. I see quite a lot of Mary now. . . ."

(4) Joan Bates is serving behind the counter at the baker's. "She used to be a Simpson. She lives in the same street as my sister. My Mum knows her better than me. . . ."

(8) Richard Fienburgh. "That man over there at the corner. He's a sort of relative. He's a brother of my sister's husband. He lives near them. . . ."

(14) Emma France. This was an elderly, very jolly woman, with grey hair and a loud laugh. She engaged Mrs. Landon in conversation.
—"How's that other sister of yours . . . She's gone to live in Bow, hasn't she?"
—"She's got a place with her mother-in-law there."
—"She doesn't like it? No! It never did work and I don't suppose it ever will."
They both collapsed into laughter at this. Afterwards Mrs. Landon explained that Mrs. France had been her landlady in the first rooms her Mum had got for her.

Over that week Mrs. Landon saw sixty-three people she knew on the street, some a number of times. Over half of them were related to at least one other person among the sixty-three. Multiply Mrs. Landon's experience by a few thousand and you have an urban village, a society that seems almost "traditional," nestled in the heart of postwar London.

Not only do the networks of friends and relatives sprawl widely across Bethnal Green, they produce an intense collective life, each street a little community of one hundred to two hundred people. "The residents of the turning . . . have their own places to meet, where few outsiders ever come—practically every turning has its one or two pubs, its two or three shops, and its 'bookie's runner.' They organize their own parties; nearly every turning had its committee and celebration (and several built wooden stages for the display of local talent) for the Coronation of 1953. Some turnings have little war memorials built on to walls of houses with inscriptions like the following: R.I.P. IN LOVING MEMORY OF THE MEN OF CYPRUS STREET WHO MADE THE GREAT SACRIFICE, 1914–1918. . . ."[97]

Two circumstances discourage the conclusion that such places represent modern versions of the traditional village community. One is that the Bethnal Greens of England, and of Western society in general, are steadily diminishing, with economic development and urban renewal whittling away at their edges. Even as Michael Young and Peter Willmott conducted their classic investigation of that corner of London, many of its residents were outward bound to new suburban housing estates. It's true that as some communities disintegrate, others that had previously been in upheaval begin to congeal. But the overall rate of community disaggregation in the postwar urban world is probably higher than the rate of stabilization.[98] So the Bethnal Greens are in no way archetypical of our own times. The second circumstance is that even though Bethnal Green saw a high rate of participation in community life and strong friend and kin networks, the nuclear family nonetheless represented an inviolable domain into which this thriving, bustling surrounding community did not penetrate. Mr. Jeffreys told the tale:

"I've got plenty of friends around here. I've always got on well with people, but I don't invite anyone here. I've got friends at work and friends at sport and friends I have a drink with. I know all the people around here, and I'm not invited into any one else's home either. It doesn't seem right somehow. Your home's your own."[99] These friendship ties were, in other words, fairly segmented. There was no single, all-embracing network, unlike in the village community of yore. And these relays of friends made not a dent upon the armor of family intimacy.

THE UNITED STATES

It is pointless to review in detail the multitude of American community studies that demonstrate extraordinary degrees of kin contact. In a Detroit study, one half of those polled saw relatives at least once a week, another quarter at least once a month. The same held for Los Angeles and San Francisco. In a study of Cleveland, almost every married couple saw often parents who lived nearby, exchanged services, and so forth. And whereas an investigation of New Haven showed that even though two fifths of all families had no intimate friends outside their kin group, at least their kin interactions were intensive. Another survey of Champaign–Urbana showed that two thirds to three fourths (depending on the social class) of the sample felt close to brothers- and sisters-in-law, and of course to their families of origin.[100] These are all results well known to anyone who has ever taken a first-year sociology course, and we need rehash them no further. Kinship is unquestionably central in the social experience of the average American. Three remarks are worth making:

(1) The American family was probably "born modern" because the colonial settlers seem to have seized privacy and intimacy for themselves as soon as they stepped off the boat. If so, it doesn't matter all that much whether there's been a trend toward withdrawal from the community, or whether Americans have become closer to their kin over the years. The change each produced would be relatively minor, considering the advanced point of departure.

(2) American families have probably tended to cut away some of their ties to past generations, Bernard Farber talks, for example, of the "poverty of genealogical knowledge" among the lower classes of Champaign–Urbana in Illinois, an ignorance of their backgrounds that "serves to make the low socio-economic individual an ahistorical free-floating atom."[101] This lack of time perspective affects the extent to which the young in particular see themselves as continuing a longer lineage. We explore the implications of this in the final chapter.

(3) American families have probably tended to withdraw from whatever community life earlier centuries were able to offer. Research shows a present-day disinvolvement with neighbors that is difficult to reconcile with the peaceable New England kingdoms of the eighteenth century that Michael Zuckerman has described, or the Main Street on the nineteenth-century "middle border" of Lewis Atherton.[102]

How complex these matters are! And how exasperating that their resolution still lies so distant, because of the fixation of the contemporary family-studies industry upon sociological trivia. Even after all the stratified-sample surveys are heaped upon one another, we still don't know if the American family has undergone the same sort of Great Transformation as the European.

But sociability with non-kin does of course exist. And the class differences we observed in the spread of sentiment recur in contemporary patterns. The lower classes, lagging behind the middle in their receptiveness to new, sentiment-oriented values, cling more tightly to their various peer groups. The middle classes, who see in friendship an extension of their domestic bliss, socialize with other couples and avoid the buddies-at-the-bar syndrome.

In the Parisian suburb of Malakoff, for instance, white-collar couples are demonstrated to have more contact with friends than do blue-collar couples.[103] And while in Charleroi two thirds of the managerial types had friends into their homes, only one third of the workers did.[104] On the other hand, the tendency of French workers to hang out at the bar is still much more pronounced than among the bourgeoisie.

In England this class differential in sociability patterns remains quite strong. Working-class couples in the London suburb of Woodford are somewhat less likely to entertain than are middle-class couples.[105] Numerous community studies have established the ongoing importance of the men-only pub for miners, metalworkers, and others.[106] And whereas (in London at least) working-class couples tend to divide up for sociability, middle-class couples see their common friends jointly.[107]

Although the casual closeness of the suburbs and their lack of bars blur class distinctions, American blue-collar workers nonetheless tend much more than white-collar ones to run around with bosom buddies.[108] And while the "Blues" and "Whites," two families in a typical American suburb, have identical incomes, "once every two years the Whites pay off their social debts by having a fairly large outdoor cocktail party; the Blues, pretending with elaborate politeness to be otherwise engaged in their own backyard, watch over the hedge with tolerant amusement."[109]

In short, I would argue that while both classes see much less of friends and neighbors than they used to, the working classes have stuck longer to traditional patterns. And the middle classes have been quicker to devise sociable arrangements for themselves that are in harmony with the nuclear family's taste for sentiment and mirror-gazing. Like romance, when you're gazing into another couple's eyes, what you see is the reflection of your own.

It would be a great temptation to regard the kin group, with its enhanced importance in the contemporary world, as a replacement for the web of community relations. The temptation must be avoided, for in reality the two have different functions. As often as people nowadays see their kin, the intensity of such contact bears no resemblance to the intensity of sociability in traditional times. In terms of viewing oneself as part of a larger social unit, no number of visits with Mom and Dad will add up to the annual cycle of Carnival, Easter, St. John's Day, the harvest home, and so forth—to say nothing of the boys at the bar and the veillées. So, quantitatively, one would have to live with one's kin—and a wide circle of relatives at that—to get anything like the frequency of interaction achieved in village society.

Qualitatively, kin contacts are no replacement for community contacts either. If relatives were available to reinforce one's sense of being part of a larger lineage stretching across the ages, or if relatives were on hand mainly to help out when trouble threatened, that would be one thing—a functional equivalent perhaps of the little community with its rites of solidarity and its sense of a material commonweal. But that's not why people see relatives today. They regard them rather as friends, and come together with them for all the expressive, personality-oriented reasons for which the nuclear family came into being in the first place. Kinfolk today extend and complement the conjugal family's egotistical emotional structure. They don't rival it, or threaten to break it down. So despite the phoenix-like rise of the kin network from the ashes of village society, the nuclear family of the modern world remains in physical and spiritual isolation.

Postscript: Changes in Marital Sexuality

No subject is more forbidding to study in *la vie intime* than marital sexuality. Next to nothing is known about it, because among all the things the popular classes didn't discuss in the Bad Old Days, what they did in bed was foremost (or second only to where they hid their money). And intellectually the subject has the complexity of the Gordian knot: we must untangle quantitative versus qualitative behavior, the frequency of intercourse versus differences in sexual styles, the psychodynamics of intimacy versus a sociological analysis of variation by class and size-of-place, and so on. I have chosen the tactic of a "postscript" in order to veil with modesty my own brief discussion of the subject. The argument of this book suggests a few corollaries for the evolution of sexual behavior among married couples; and the tatters of evidence that clothe our ignorance are not inconsistent with this highly tentative speculation.

One important problem is the extent to which, in traditional society, sex for procreation was unlinked from sex for recreation. Obviously the men in these village populations of yore took pleasure in intercourse. Whether the women did—after the seventh pregnancy—is another matter. But some of the medical literature of the time even argued that a woman had to come to orgasm in order to conceive[110] (although—if the hypothesis of Chapter 2 is right—most men in the popular classes were likely to have been indifferent to their wives' gratification). So we may concede at least that these people liked sex when they engaged in it.

But did either men or women value highly the pleasure side of sexuality? If they thought erotic playfulness important, what I have said about the unaffectionate, ritualistic character of traditional marriage would seem exaggerated, for rigid sex-role divisions could not have survived the tremors of imaginative sex play. If, on the other hand, the average woman accepted the Church's view that sex at least potentially results in conception, the playful side must have seemed marginal to her—something beyond the compass of normal experience. Moreover, spontaneous erotic joy and that sort of thing

245

would seem difficult to come by if she had constantly in the back of her mind the fear of pregnancy.

The logical way to demonstrate that eroticism was unimportant in the life of the traditional couple is to show that they stopped having sex after they had ceased to want children. Various clever statistical demonstrations indicate that they were probably not practicing birth control during the childbearing years.[111] It is unlikely that the couple *then* started contraceiving, after the wife had finally thrown up her hands and cried "Enough kids." A shadow of evidence, perhaps.

Adultery offers a more interesting kind of evidence that marital sexual activity ceased with the end of childbearing. If intercourse counted greatly for either man or woman, we might expect them to seek gratification outside of marriage: if you can't sleep with your wife (or husband) for reasons of family planning, you then go have intercourse with someone else—a man who's willing to take precautions, or a woman whose impregnation won't matter. If, on the other hand, eroticism played a minor role in the lives of these people, we would expect their sexual interest in general to decline once the woman had birthed her last child.

How much adultery actually went on, then, in traditional Europe? What were the chances that the typical married man or woman in a small town or village would brush against an adulterous relationship in the course of married life? Minimal, I should estimate. If we rely upon criminal statistics, our impression of sexual irregularities within marriage will be exaggerated, for by their very nature the courts scoop up the deviant and irregular. The prosecutions for adultery recorded in the criminal tribunals of every part of Western society thus give no hint of *typicality*. The observers of popular life, on whose impressions I rely heavily, suggest that husbandly adultery was minimal and wifely adultery almost nonexistent.[112]

A quantitative assessment of adultery leads inevitably to a quotation war. Some authors carry on about extramarital sex, lamenting the decline of rural morality and onrush of sinfulness; other authors laud the purity of peasant life, the absence of debauchery *à la mode parisienne*. The administrator Joseph Hazzi noted of Griesbach

County in Bavaria, for example: "Almost every peasant has a sweetheart alongside his spouse, and the peasant woman evens things up with one of the servant lads." And Dr. Gilibert complained that "adultery is very frequent in the countryside," the women who sleep around often getting venereal disease and communicating it to their paid nurslings.[113] These are examples of rural-sinfulness quotes. Yet the great bulk of evidence is on the other side. Most writers who bother at all to comment on *marital* rural morality before 1850 praise the absence of fooling around, the universality of fidelity. And we may take as typical Barthélemy Chaix's remark that the village women of the Hautes-Alpes "think only of their households, some perhaps anticipating the natural desires [*rusticité*] their husbands returning from the cabaret will have. . . ."[114]

Although my evidence forces me to speak mainly of France, the "traditional" adultery model which seems to have prevailed at least in that country was that the husband avoided his wife as a birth control measure and slept with one of the servants instead, "fearing to have with his spouse those tender relations which nature inspires."[115] We know how common such master–servant exploitation was in eighteenth-century Nantes.[116] The "modern" adultery model would change this traditional pattern as the wives began sleeping around almost (though not quite) as much as their husbands, and as the motive for seeking extramarital sexual outlets became not just physical release but the search for a soul-mate.

A second big question is the role of eroticism in the formation of conjugal unity. To what extent is sex part of "domesticity?" What, in other words, is the basic tie holding the couple together in modern times: romantic love with a strong component of eroticism, or a sense of household bliss arising from the mother's concern for her small infants? This is not a very practical kind of question, because we have trouble identifying the evidence required to resolve it; and in reality, of course, both sources of domesticity—romance and maternal love—will have to be considered. Yet the available evidence does permit us at least to nudge against one choice as opposed to the other. And the material I have seen from nineteenth-century France suggests that romantic love had relatively little to do with the constitution of the modern nuclear family.

In the 1850–1914 period almost all couples come to be "eroticized," by which I mean merely that coital activity and sexual attraction assumed an independent role in holding man and woman together. The triumph of sexuality in conjugal life may be seen, for example, in the definitive establishment of the wife's right to orgasm.[117] For couples in which the wife never got off could only with difficulty be regarded as eroticized.

But was there a lag, from one social class to another, in the diffusion of this eroticization? We have seen earlier that the middle classes were the first to acquire a sense of domesticity. Therefore, if sexual activity lay at the heart of the new conjugal unit, we should expect middle-class couples to sexualize themselves more rapidly than lower-class ones. But in fact it seems to have been the lower-class couple that first reveled in the newly erotic nature of married life during the nineteenth and twentieth centuries; and this is quite simply because the lower classes were the first to adopt this emotional posture in courtship. What happened in marriage thereafter was just a carry-over. With time, the romanticization of courtship survived farther and farther into married life, until finally the couple would expect to behave affectionately and to be sexually active until the end of its days. While the level of intercourse within lower-class couples was rising (I hypothesize), the middle classes quite independently were pulling tight the shutters and sealing off a domain of intimacy and privacy for themselves. But this process had little to do with sex. It was rather a function of the mother's new concern for her tiny infants.

That's the argument. What evidence exists to back it up? First of all, there are data on how people space their love-making throughout the year. The traditional pattern, one which moreover prevailed for all classes, was to cluster intercourse in the spring and early summer. This may be seen from Appendix IV, where data on the month of probable legitimate conception are presented alongside data on illegitimate conceptions. The diagrams exhibit an abrupt, stairlike up-and-down movement. In the twentieth century, legitimate conceptions in general are much more evenly distributed among the twelve months, a sign that lovemaking has become part of the normal "weekly" experience of married life rather than a special occasion for special times of the year.

But how about class differences in this evening out? We know that married urbanites had coitus more regularly throughout the year than did rural dwellers, and that cottage-industrial workers made love more steadily than did peasants, being at home all the time and relishing the diversion.[118] Yet such data bypass the question of change over time. Sadly, there are no time-series available in the published literature on birth seasonality by class. We know only from a handful of postwar studies that seasonal variation in conception is higher for the upper classes than for the lower.[119] In our own world the lower orders make love more steadily the year through. But these data say nothing, of course, about which class first began to even out the high seasonal fluctuations of traditional society.

As to which couples were more interested in sex—middle class or lower—nineteenth-century opinion was almost unanimous. The lower orders were seen as naturally depraved, creatures of their instincts, at the mercy of whatever animalistic passion happened to seize them at the moment. So naturally they had sex more often than did the middle classes. And more joyfully and unconstrainedly. What can we do with this kind of testimony, which boils to the surface from deep wells of class anxiety and sexual fantasy? In our own days the lower classes are not more imaginative in bed than the middle classes, though perhaps they are more coitally active. (Indeed in North America they appeared once to be considerably *less* inventive with respect to sexual styles, though this class difference is now disappearing.)[120] So we have no a priori reason for crediting such nineteenth-century accounts of married worker depravity. Yet no matter *how* the lower classes made love (the essence of the imagined "depravity"), the intercourse side of conjugal life was probably more important for them than for the middle classes. Or as Dr. Grassl wrote of the Swabian agricultural laborers: "Without the inhibitions of the urbanites and peasants, they succumb to rustic views of body functions. Their choice of wife depends on love, their family size from lust. Too often the feelings of sex are the only thing that can't be taken from them. *Und einen Reiz muss der Mensch haben.*"[121]

If the United States was in fact "born modern," one would look in vain for an eroticization of marriage comparable to the European experience. The marital sex life of the Puritans would be approximately the same as that of the late Victorians, and the latter again the same as that of suburbia in the 1940s. Consider the support for such an hypothesis. Edmund Morgan on "The Puritans and Sex" finds a quite straightforward, approving attitude towards intercourse in the eighteenth century. According to one minister, "the Use of the Marriage Bed is founded in man's Nature," and abstinence from intercourse "Denies all reliefe in Wedlock unto Human necessity. . . ."[122] Sex must not, of course, distract man from adoration of the Lord, but otherwise Morgan was able to discover nothing repressive or anxious about Puritan sexual thought. The Puritans seem to have had, in other words, none of the fearfulness that sexuality would blow community life to pieces that characterized the traditional European attitude.

What subsequent changes, before the 1960s, may we reliably report in American sexual attitudes and behavior *within marriage*? Perhaps a somewhat heightened wifely interest in orgasms took place, if the marriage manuals that Michael Gordon has pored over for the nineteenth and twentieth centuries are any guide.[123] But these were addressed to and consumed by the elite groups from whom I have systematically shied away in this book, and it's unclear that such evidence bears at all on the lives of the popular classes. Kinsey was able to discover no trend in the frequency of intercourse among generations born from 1899 to 1929, a possible index of the couple's joint experience with sexuality.[124] Yet the entire history of American marital eroticism still lies so veiled in darkness that further speculation would be unwarranted. I am impressed by the Puritans' casual acceptance of sexual needs for both men and women; I am equally struck by the lack of sexual variety within marriage during the first half of our own century. These two impressions suggest to me a certain changelessness in American patterns over two hundred years of time—until the 1960s.

One final question: has there been a revolution during the 1960s in marital sexuality similar to the dramatic changes in nonvirginity and sexual styles we noted above for adolescents? A comparison of data assembled by Alfred Kinsey in the 1940s and by Morton Hunt in the early 1970s shows that—in the United States, at least— both sexual activity and sexual styles underwent dramatic altera- tions. If Hunt's data, gathered in a 1972 survey of sample populations in 24 cities, are to be trusted, the sheer level of erotic activity within marriage has soared. Whereas Kinsey found that 40 percent of mar- ried men ages 26–35 masturbated when he polled them in the 1940s, the comparable 1972 figure was 70 percent. And for married women, masturbation rates rose from one third to two thirds. For men, the average frequency of masturbation within marriage climbed from around six times yearly in the 1940s to twenty-four times yearly in 1972.[125]

But if married people masturbated more, suggesting a more thoroughgoing eroticization of their daily lives, they also made love more often. The National Fertility Studies show a 21 percent increase in coital frequencies among married couples between 1965 and 1970; and even after those couples using contraceptive methods not available in 1965 have been removed from the sample, a 14 percent increase remains. Hunt's survey permits explicit comparison with Kinsey's findings from the 1940s:[126]

Marital Coitus in the United States:
Frequency per Week, 1938–1949 and 1972

1938–49		1972	
AGE	MEDIAN	AGE	MEDIAN
16–25	2.45	18–24	3.25
26–35	1.95	25–34	2.55
36–45	1.40	35–44	2.00
46–55	.85	45–54	1.00
56–60	.50	55 over	1.00

Thus not only the young, but couples of all ages, would in the early 1970s have coitus more frequently than in the 1940s. And they would make "longer" love too, for whereas researchers in the 1940s

251

and early 1950s found the median duration of intercourse to be about two minutes, the Hunt survey put it near 10.[127] Finally, the duration of foreplay had risen over time, Kinsey's women mentioning twelve minutes on the average, Hunt's fifteen.[128]

It's not clear that the 1972 data on sexual styles are reliable, for only one person in every five approached agreed to answer Hunt's questionnaire. And if we assume that the refusers would more likely be sexual conservatives, the sexual liberals are probably massively overrepresented among the completed responses. Still, the apparent changes are so striking that I'm inclined to think Hunt has probably seized a part of a significant change, though perhaps overstating its magnitude.

On oral–genital foreplay, the percent of married men reporting that their wives fellated them climbed among the university-educated from 43 percent in 1938–1946 to 61 percent in 1972, and among the high-school graduates from 15 to 54 percent! For women and fellatio, both percentages are less dramatic, but they also increase. Comparable rates were reported for cunnilingus within marriage.[129] So by the 1970s the chances were better than even that normal marital sexuality activity, regardless of social class (for which "educational achievement" is merely a proxy), would include mouth-to-genital contact.

On sexual positions: in the 1940s only one third of the couples ever even experimented with the female-above possibility; by the early 1970s, three fourths had. "Rear-entry vaginal intercourse" was used by only 10 percent of Kinsey's sample, 40 percent of Hunt's.[130]

The last frontier of American marital sexuality appears to be anal intercourse rather than sado-masochism (of which Hunt was able to uncover only traces). Whereas Kinsey found anal intromission to be so infrequent as not even worth recording systematically, Hunt's 1970s data showed it practiced by *one fourth* of the couples thirty-four years and less, with diminishing rates among the older.[131]

But maybe these results represent merely some ghastly new increase in male willingness to exploit women, rather than a hedonistic demolition of barriers to sexual pleasure for both partners. Perhaps female anuses and tongues will have simply been taken advantage of in an eruption of machismo? Hunt believes not. If the fragmentary surveys at our disposal may be credited at all, the early twentieth century saw high rates of orgasm failure among married women. One 1907 study of New York State concluded that as many as three fourths of all women didn't have orgasms. Time then whittled away substantially at these frigidity levels, each cohort of women interviewed by Kinsey routinely achieving more orgasms during intercourse than the previous one. On the whole, around two-thirds of Kinsey's female sample claimed they reached orgasm a third of the time or more. The most interesting Kinsey statistic is that 45 percent of the wives who were in their fifteenth year of marriage almost always had orgasms (more than 90 percent of the time); 53 percent of the wives in a roughly comparable Hunt sample made the same claim.[132] This is not a big increase, but the direction of change is up.

Orgasms, of course, don't necessarily add up to pleasure. Women can have many orgasms and still be sexually exploited and unhappy. But *if* they told the truth to Hunt, they didn't *feel* oppressed or exploited. They just liked all this new sexual activity. Only 5 percent said they wished intercourse were less often, compared to the two thirds of the wives in the 1920s who felt their husbands too demanding.[133] Men, apparently, like it somewhat less, for at this writing male impotence rates are soaring.[134] Perhaps these sudden masculine failures to achieve and maintain erections are a response to the surge of sexual interest among women. And if Vance Packard's notion that it is increasingly women who initiate the foreplay is correct, there must be some wrinkled brows among the Good Old Boys.[135]

Were such changes going on elsewhere in the 1960s? Only for France are systematic data available on sexual styles within marriage. And while we don't have a French baseline comparable to the Kinsey reports to follow change over time, the erotic innovativeness of the average French couple in the 1970s was striking: for one half of the couples polled in a nationwide sample, the woman was often on top; for one fifth the man often entered from behind.[136] This sort of wild stuff was less among older people, so it's apparent that the change shows up mainly among young French couples socialized during the 1960s. For example, 72 percent of men in their twenties reported having oral-genital foreplay, 62 percent of those in their thirties and forties, and 47 percent of those in their fifties (and older). The figures for women closely paralleled those for men. Unlike the liberated Americans, however, the French reported almost no anal intercourse.[137]

This parade of statistics, though important, ends up being mildly depressing. One can conjure up visions of these legions of couples fiddling and fooling with each other in this tremendous forward leap of marital eroticism—and yet, if I am right, one price paid for this new capacity to explore one's sensory responses has been the abandonment of a meaningful emotional life outside the home. Another price is a vastly increased instability in marital relations. A final price of the eroticization of the couple's life, both before marriage and after, is the disintegration of a sense of the lineage of the family. Nothing is free in this world.

CHAPTER SEVEN

The Reason Why

SOME of these trends in family history are not well documented, to say the least. And when our knowledge of even the basic narrative of maternal love or domesticity is so shaky, attempts to explain why such things happened must be speculative indeed. Now in fact, I am fairly confident that the evidence from local doctors, antiquarians, and bureaucrats presented in this book points to important historical changes. And I'm pretty sure as well that the reasons I'm about to suggest for the great transformation of sentiment strike close to the mark. But the reader has no assurance of this.

I can justify my speculations about the reason why on two grounds alone. For one thing, the professional scholar might be sufficiently enraged by my analysis to sally forth and perform the research necessary for refutation; this itself would be an advance, because discovering that Shorter is wrong about the causes of the revolution in sentiment is preferable to neglecting the question entirely. For another, the general reader, who is more interested in understanding where his or her own world comes from than in the intricacies of these scholarly debates, might seize from such a discussion some small added insight into what's happening to family life in the 1970s.

Market capitalism was probably at the root of the revolution in sentiment. At the same time that mentalities were undergoing the historic shift toward individualism and affection, the economic sub-structure of the world in which village people lived was in upheaval as well. It was most likely the replacement of this traditional "moral" economy with a modern marketplace economy that changed so thoroughly values and behavior.[1]

Consider for a moment what "capitalism" entailed for traditional Europe. There was, first of all, the smelting of countless little economically self-sealed units into great nation- or region-wide market-places. During the eighteenth century, political economists every-where urged that the flow of labor and goods from one place to the next be unimpeded by the customs barriers, dues, taxes, and local privileges that had so hampered long-distance commerce in the old regime. Formerly, of course, the local guilds had guaranteed that commodities produced elsewhere would not invade their towns. The complex system of grain-trade regulation saw to it as well that food produced locally would be sold locally. Finally, the price of most hired labor, from fieldhands to live-in servants, was regulated by administrative decree. So, in effect, each district would represent a hermetically sealed economic unit, transactions within which were run more by custom than by the free workings of the law of supply and demand. And the trickle of outside foodstuffs or peddler-born commodities that managed to penetrate this seal nowhere near righted the balance. The traditional economy was a local economy, where moral notions about how much people were entitled to charge or earn in order to support a family replaced market transactions.

But the political economists' war on the guilds and the state ad-ministrators' anxiety about feeding such great, potentially turbulent, cities as Paris punctured these watertight seals. Far-flung markets in grain were opened up in France, for example, so that speculators could come into a grain-producing district and use the leverage their cash gave them to pry the local grain supply away for resale in some distant area of shortage. And the scholar-bureaucrats who ran Prussia or Austria were equally concerned to abolish the guilds' fair-price restrictions which were keeping output at a minimum. For them national power was tied closely to industrial production; so they stripped the coopers and tanners and locksmiths of their tra-ditional police powers, and ensured that the law of supply and demand would coax upward the production of barrels and hides and door hinges. Finally, the administrators abandoned their efforts to enforce traditional master–servant regulations, and let employee wages and labor mobility be set by the free working of the economy. All these are often-told stories, and I wish merely to remind the reader that by 1830, most West Europeans would find themselves competing for wages or profits in a free market whose circumference was many times larger than those of the traditional economies in which their grandfathers had found themselves.

Secondly, "capitalism" carried the material standard of living upward. This rise began in England sometime in the second half of the eighteenth century, and on the continent at some point in the 1830–1850 period. Whether the early days of the factory system brought an absolute immiseration in the lives of industrial workers remains a moot point. But few would dispute that after the machine's enormous increases in productivity had begun, real wages climbed— and began to shift the fundamental material conditions of life. Outside the factory system similar changes took place, as agricultural capitalism boosted the productivity of the fields: new crop rotations, drainage, and fertilizing made available a better-balanced diet to the average person at less cost. Almost none of this happened on the continent before the 1840s, but thereafter the improvement was so quick as to be one of the great dramas of the social history of the popular classes. This story, too, is well known to specialists, and I merely remind the reader that most of the improvement stemmed from capitalist entrepreneurs' technological innovations.

A third consequence of "capitalism" was the recruitment of an industrial proletariat, clearly differentiated in cultural and material terms from the surrounding traditional populations. Economic historians are only now beginning to appreciate the rural origins of this development; for it was first in the countryside, as a result of cottage industry, that a modern industrial work force began to form. The great demand for cotton cloth, fashionable gloves, or lace doilies motivated urban entrepreneurs to buy up raw materials that would be sent to rural outworkers. Peasant women would spin raw cotton into yarn, and other peasants (or at least people who had formerly been peasants) would weave this yarn into cloth. The cloth would be turned into garments, probably in an urban sweatshop; tailors and seamstresses in some dismal loft would be hunched over their own small contribution to this far-flung industrial system coordinated by these capitalist entrepreneurs.

In textiles, small-scale ironmongery, wickerware, and a host of other popular consumer goods, the cottage-industrial system made giant strides during the late eighteenth and early nineteenth centuries. At a reasonable estimate, one in every three rural dwellers was caught up in it. Some were traditional peasants who, in the veillées or dreary winter days, would take advantage of these new earning opportunities. Others were landless laborers—or peasants who had made themselves landless by selling off their holdings—who were able to wrench themselves up from absolute misery through this form of domestic industrial work. Unlike the other two above-mentioned spearheads of capitalism, the "domestic system" still lies in darkness. We are only beginning to discover how widespread it was and what changes it effected in the lives of its work force.[2] What is important for our purposes is that popular involvement with the market economy—rustic outworkers were subject to all the mercurial price fluctuations and competitiveness of the market system—commenced during the eighteenth century, even as the first of the great revolutions in sentiment was getting underway.

Is there a direct causal relationship between the two? May we argue that the illegitimacy explosion or the surge of sentiment in courting was propelled upward by these economic changes? Although any satisfactory explanation must ultimately be complex, and incorporate many different kinds of variables, I believe that laissez-faire marketplace organization, capitalist production, and the beginnings of proletarianization among the work force were more important than any other factors in the spread of sentiment.

Analytically, the relationships are not complicated. So let's take up the argument. How did capitalism help cause that powerful thrust of sentiment among the unmarried that I have called the romance revolution? To what extent may sleeping around before marriage and choosing partners on the basis of personal attraction rather than wealth be associated with economic change? The principal link here is the increased participation of young unmarried people, especially women, in the free-market labor force. The logic of the marketplace positively demands individualism: the system will succeed only if each participant ruthlessly pursues his own self-interest, buying cheap, selling dear, and enhancing his own interests at the cost of his competitors (i.e., his fellow citizens). Only if this variety of economic egoism is internalized will the free market come up to the high expectations of its apologists, for if people let humanitarian or communitarian considerations influence their economic behavior, the market becomes inefficient; the weak cease to be weeded out. Thus, the free market engraves upon all who are caught up in it the attitude: "Look out for number one."

I am arguing that, among the common people whom the eighteenth century had forced into the marketplace, this egoistical economic mentality spread into various noneconomic domains of life, specifically into those ties that bind the individual to the surrounding community. Egoism that was learned in the marketplace became transferred to community obligations and standards, to ties to the family and lineage—in short, to the whole domain of cultural rules that regulated familial and sexual behavior. In this book I have suggested a "teeter-totter" relationship between community obligation and individual self-fulfillment. In traditional society, the balance was very heavily tilted toward the community, toward adhering to the rules and standards of those about you and away from pursuing your own desires and pleasures. Capitalism tilted this balance the other way. And once the rules of marketplace individualism had been learned, they easily took control of the whole arena of conscious attitudes. It is this *prise de pouvoir* that Fred Weinstein and Gerald M. Platt call "the wish to be free."[3] My argument is that for young people in late eighteenth-century Europe, the sexual and emotional wish to be free came from the capitalist marketplace.

In the domain of men–women relations, the wish to be free emerges as romantic love. The desire to find personal happiness, to commence that long voyage of personality development and self-discovery that constitutes the Inner Search, rises to the conscious surface as romance: you look into another person's eyes in the hope that you'll find yourself. And even if we believe that these eighteenth-century lower-class young people were about eight pegs below this level of self-awareness (an assumption I'm not automatically willing to concede), there still remains the simple force of sexual desire. Sexual experience is part of all this self-fulfillment, and people cut loose by individualism from the mooring of community allegiance would quickly drift towards fooling around. So capitalism exerted its impact upon romantic love through involvement in the market labor force: economic individualism leads to cultural egoism; private gratification becomes more important than fitting into the common weal; the wish to be free produces the illegitimacy explosion.

This is an old argument—a favorite, in fact, of conservative nineteenth-century social theorists who never tired of calling the wish to be free *l'amour déreglé du plaisir*.[4] Two modifications encourage me to bring it forth anew.

In the first place, we should note that this wish to be free affected women more than men. We can probably assume that men have always been avid for intercourse, that a male desire to get women into bed is probably a historical constant. But how do we explain this new, eighteenth-century willingness on the part of women to climb into the sack with them? How may we account for this historical reversal in the willingness of young, unmarried women to abandon traditional chastity and instead go out with different men, have sex before marriage, and preoccupy themselves generally with personal happiness? I believe it was the new access to paid employment. In 1803, Prefect Colchen of the Moselle department supplied a plausible explanation:[5]

As for women, they were never entirely strangers to hard work, but today they take on almost as much as the men, above all in the vineyards. The losses caused by the war have contributed to this. Moreover these rustic women have strong constitutions and are able to perform the hardest jobs. But this kind of life changes in them the modest bearing of their sex, and the habitual frequentation with the opposite sex it necessitates gives their morals a certain libertineness that causes the premature loss of their innocence.

Not only did paid work give young women an inclination to escape the sexual restrictions of their parents and the town fathers, it also gave the *possibility* of doing so. Economically independent women have greater liberty than economically dependent ones, for paid work makes it possible to ignore parental admonitions and to shrug off the parson's scolding. During the eighteenth century the industrial town of Annonay (Ardèche) saw illegitimacy increase much more rapidly than did the neighboring traditional *bourg* of Serignan. And while in Serignan only one fifth of the unwed mothers were economically independent (most of them servants), in Annonay fully one half were, a mixture of servants and workers. Alain Molinier concludes: ". . . having used the advantages of their job to escape the moral constraints of the family milieu, these mothers were able to adopt a freer style of life. More numerous in the cities, above all in the eighteenth century, these women might have contributed to the increase in the illegitimacy ratio."[6]

A second modification of the classic notion that economic individualism means sexual experimentation is that it seems to have happened mainly among the lower classes. The new proletarians of the eighteenth century were the vanguard of the sexual revolution because they were the first to be caught up in the market economy. Oh, to be sure, the upper bourgeoisie—the bearers of Max Weber's famous capitalist rationality and religious anxiety—were the class that gave these lower orders work. But the capitalists themselves escaped being caught in the sexual revolution because for them family values overrode everything else. The lower classes who labored in the laundries and sweatshops of the bourgeoisie, on the other hand, didn't have any property to preserve. They owned no great patrimonies to be transmitted, and so they were free to pursue individual rather than family objectives once the idea of doing so had occurred to them—which is to say, once they were able to shake free of *communal* controls upon their intimate lives. Although we don't normally think of things in this way—so firmly has our collective historical gaze been riveted on the upper orders—it was the lower classes who first were fully socialized in the ways of the market economy. The people whom the budding proletarian laborforce scooped up were marginal farmers, agricultural laborers, and the noninheriting or miserably-dowered daughters of propertied peasants.

Did these women seek out capitalism because the dawning wish to be free had aroused within them a desire for personal independence and sexual adventure? Or were they driven by hardship from their traditional nests into this uncongenial new economic setting, there to be sexually exploited? The former possibility seems more generally applicable. From one end of Europe to the other, young unmarried women in the nineteenth century were rejecting traditional occupations in favor of paid employment within a capitalist setting. The tailors of Bavaria's Wolfstein county, for example, complained that many girls, avoiding the "unpleasantness" of domestic service and wishing for themselves instead "a free and comfortable life," were becoming seamstresses.[7] In France's Tarn department, children were repaying, by leaving home, the patriarchal fathers who "treat them as minors even after they reach adulthood, seeing in them mere fieldhands to whom nothing is owed and who themselves own nothing. . . . One may admire this abnegation and devotion that gives a family so much solidarity, but it's unlikely this situation will be maintained without some protest."[8] By the interwar years of the twentieth century, complaints were heard from all sides in France about young women who no longer wanted to marry peasants and were taking off for the city in droves.[9]

Nor was England different. One observer explained the enormous migration of young people to late-nineteenth-century London as the result of "the contagion of numbers, the sense of something going on, the theaters and the music halls, the brightly lighted streets and busy crowds—all, in short, that makes the difference between the Mile End fair on a Saturday night and a dark muddy country lane, with no glimmer of gas and with nothing to do. Who could wonder that men are drawn into such a vortex, even were the penalty heavier that it is." And not only men, for J. A. Banks argues that young women in particular who left home to accept work in London were not so much responding to economic opportunity as to "a means of independence from the often severe restraints on behavior inherent in rural family life, dominated by the Victorian paterfamilias." Once in the city, these young women "copied the example of the young men, becoming lodgers . . . or fending wholly for themselves where they did not marry early."[10] Such testimony, unless entirely unrepresentative, points to a close interaction between capitalist work, escape from traditional controls, and the wish to be free. It is the argument of this book that these things came together late in the eighteenth century and that they made, for young women especially, "romantic love" a codeword for personal autonomy.

Capitalism was also linked to maternal love. Because the great articulation of sentiment for infant children began first among the middle classes, who were the last group to be caught up in the capitalist market for labor, we cannot employ the same chain of argumentation that carried us from proletarian work to the wish to be free. In fact, the old middle class of husband–wife store owners, small artisans, and peasants managed to retain *anti*capitalist values and cling to the traditional economic matrix longer than any social group save the nobility. How, then, can we argue that "capitalism" had anything at all to do with the affection of mothers for infants among these people?

The logic of the argument relates to the standard of living. The defining characteristic of these "old middle classes" was their economic independence. As owners of the "means of production," pitifully small though their share may have been, they found themselves increasingly producing for the market. And because they had their small capital investments to give them leverage, they profited more handsomely from the staggering economic growth of the nineteenth century than did the workers, who had only the sweat of their brows to invest. Hence the living standards of the old middle classes rose more rapidly than did those of the new proletarians, and the Mom-and-Pop store owners became the first group to be subjected to the new social outlooks that higher living standards entailed. Foremost among these new values was maternal love.

But, the reader may object, involvement in the market economy is approximately the same for a "capitalist" as for a worker. Both obey the same principles and should in consequence develop the same kind of egoism. How, then, can I ascribe values to the newly capitalistic petty producers that differ fundamentally from those of the newly-recruited proletarians?

Here the family intervenes. The petty-bourgeois capitalists—the small peasant who found himself grappling with region-wide grain markets, for example, or the struggling master tinsmith who had managed to take on a few extra journeymen in order to wrestle with a cooking-pot order from Rennes larger than his colleagues had ever seen—continued to value prudence and circumspection, because the desire to transmit their property to following generations remained as strong as ever. They clung to the whole array of anti-erotic, communitarian personal values of traditional society, because their need to guarantee the lineage ruled out the experimentation with life-styles and the following of heartstrings that the Inner Search entailed. Thus even though their marketplace situation might have awakened in them stirrings of the wish to be free, familistic values effectively drowned out such siren calls. The traditional family demanded allegiance to the ancestors of the past and to the inheritors of the future. And as long as inheritable property remained to be transmitted, the Inner Search would stay on the shelf among these people.

But keep in mind that the new profit opportunities of this large-holding peasant and this master tinsmith were raising their living standards. What, then, is the relationship between greater material prosperity and improved mothering? The reader will remember that the traditional mother performed indifferently and without affection, not necessarily because she wanted to be that way but because other demands on her time were so heavy that infant care had to take a back seat. The traditional mother was first committed to helping make the farm or craftshop go, because without her help all would perish. It was this absolutely pressing need to invest her time elsewhere that took her away from child care and of necessity stamped an indifferentist cast upon her attitudes. The traditional mother failed the "sacrifice" test (refusing to sacrifice other objectives to infant welfare) because the stakes were too high to risk on the life of a single child; and in any event there were plenty more where that child came from.

Economic growth liberated mothers from this desperate need to employ their time elsewhere. As the craftsman took on more journeymen, he would need his wife's help less; as the peasant engaged more fieldhands, he could more easily dispense with his wife's aid. As these traditional settings became permeated by capitalism, the division of labor between the sexes became more elaborated (though sex *roles* became less segregated—which is why I have rigorously distinguished the two throughout this book), and women could now devote themselves more to mothering and less to production. Not all Mom-and–Pop store owners became capitalists, of course, nor all peasants market-gardeners, nor all artisans small-scale entrepreneurs. Many went under. But then they and their children would begin following proletarian rules.

So improved material conditions made better mothering possible. As family income increased, women could exchange the grim pressures of production for the work of infant care—which would be no less pressing and no less tedious, for washing and swabbing and infant-food preparation in the pre-Similac days was taxing drudgery. But in the end their children would live.

The dramatic decline of infant death at the end of the nineteenth century reflects, of course, not only new attitudes to mothering (born of better well-being) but also the medical assault upon the terrible infectious killers. And that in turn was as much the work of public health officers and hygiene specialists as it was the result of the half-formed awareness among these millions of anonymous mothers that diapering and washing their infants regularly, and feeding them at the breast rather than with street-vendor's milk, would keep them around longer.

Manifestly, not all of the important developments in the history of childhood are reducible to "capitalism." What I am arguing is that the transformation of child care *within the family* came about as a direct result of the economic growth that nineteenth-century capitalism produced; and that the middle classes profited sooner than the proletarians from the higher personal incomes this growth entailed, and so were the first to modify their infant-care practices.

The free market was like an acid bath for the traditional village and small town. In the name of agricultural individualism, common lands were apportioned out, jointly-farmed and collectively-administered fields were broken up into individual plots, and common herds disaggregated into family livestock. In the name of private enterprise the guilds were shattered, so that individual producers might compete against one another rather than collectively administering their monopoly. Individual masters were freed to take on as many journeymen as they wished, to adopt new machinery as they saw fit, and to undercut the prices of their colleagues as necessary for profit. "Corporate" production thus gave way to free enterprise.

We can get a hint of the agony that this intrusion of the market economy into the traditional moral order caused in an 1843 petition of the town council of Bayreuth to the Bavarian government. The prosperity of the town had badly declined, the petitioners explained, because of free competition among the local craftsmen. The market sufficed to support nobody adequately, and because trade and industry had generally expanded, even those crafts not threatened by local "overcrowding" were menaced by the competition of foreign imports. The same spirit had also corrupted the morality of the local inhabitants, "for as in other cities, so in Bayreuth do the citizen and craftsman exceed the borders of simplicity and modesty; the craze for vanity and pleasure among the burghers and their wives no longer bears any relationship to their means; the children are led astray by the example of their parents, follow in their footsteps, and further increase expenditures."[11]

The Bayreuth town council's petition put its finger on a relationship between social change and cultural values that has been the principal organizing theme of this book: contact with the marketplace gave local people a new sense of individual gratification and a corresponding unwillingness to conform to traditional community values of self-abnegation and self-denial. What the town council perceived as vanity and the lust for pleasure would come across a hundred and fifty years later as the wish to be free. Even less would the children want to conform to the example of the town fathers. More and more, the proletarians and "strangers" whom social change was shipping through the town would show their indifference to the Good Old Ways, and Bayreuth would begin its long journey into the modern world.

The disintegration of a collective way of life in thousands of Bayreuths across Europe shifted the balance of family–community relations from community involvement to intimacy. The withdrawal of the nuclear family into the hearth's cozy circle came about not only because notions of egoism and individualism had given self-gratification a priority over community allegiance, but also because these communities were less and less able to pull individuals from the household and maintain their allegiance. There was a reciprocal relationship between the family's striving for privacy and the community's insistence upon surveillance. Just as capitalism accelerated the former by quickening egoism, it diminished the latter, as well, by cutting through the web of community ties.

Other powerful factors were also at work. While I shall have nothing substantive to say about them, let me allude to the rich literature that links state-making to a decline in communal autonomy, for example, or associates higher rates of migration with individual disaffiliation from the surrounding community.[12] The more the central states' forestry agents and tax officials, court justices, and health officers intervened in local situations, the more these traditional communities surrendered their autonomy—and therewith their sense of solidarity. The more the sullen proletarians poured in, and the more an individual's chance of being born in the same place as his grandfather decreased, the less the population as a whole was interested in learning about all the established ways of doing cultural business.

A familiar story, but it has two final implications for family history. First, even though the balance between community involvement and intimacy tilted at about the same speed for all social classes, it was. initially the middle classes who acquired that privileged sense of nuclear-family solidarity I have termed "domesticity." This is because the emotional center of the intimacy was the tiny infant. The middle classes were the first to pick up this new attitude towards children.

Second, I mean to suggest that the sexual revolution of the late eighteenth and early nineteenth centuries was not only a matter of young women newly acquiring the sense that personal autonomy meant sexual autonomy; it meant taking the lid off, as well. Before women would undertake sexual experimentation in large numbers, the matrix of the community controls that had hitherto struck them with such severe "fornication penalties"—humiliation for premarital pregnancies, mocking dolls on the name-day of one's patron saint, and the like—would have to be weakened. As the guilds declined, they lost their power to punish people for premarital intercourse.

With the expansion of central-state power and the secularization of church property came a diminution in the moral authority of the local clergy. Accompanying large-scale migration was an indifference to whatever the established families of Oberbooblesbach thought about one's personal life. I feel uneasy with the metaphor of collapse and disintegration in describing the collective experience of communities. But just as new, sexually-permissive subcultures did take form atop the repressive traditional culture—a positive development, smacking of organization and integration—the old ways *did* end up in ruins. It's just like my mother said: nothing comes free in this world.

CHAPTER EIGHT

Towards the Postmodern Family (or, Setting the Course for the Heart of the Sun)

WHEN Captain Video told Ranger to set the course for the heart of the Sun, he thought he was undertaking a voyage that no one had ever made before. The Pink Floyd, who brought this aging television artifact up to date in a song title, give us a clue to where the contemporary family is heading: the unknown. For if the argument of this book is right, three different aspects of family life today are evolving in directions that have no historical precedent—or none, at any rate, in the three recent centuries of Western history that have concerned us here.

One of these aspects is the definitive cutting of the lines leading from younger generation to older—an adolescent indifference to the family's identity, to what it stands for, that shows up in the discontinuity of values from parents to children. A second aspect is the new instability in the life of the couple, which is mirrored in skyrocketing divorce rates. A third is the systematic demolition of the "nest notion" of nuclear family life that a new liberation for

269

women has meant: for much of the female population of the Western world, it is turning out that the nest is not best after all. We
glance briefly at each of these developments in turn.

It is fairly clear that a major shift in relations between the generations has taken place in the late 1960s and early 1970s. The chances
that adolescent children will have the same views as their parents
about love and sex, or politics and economics, are significantly poorer
now than before. Young children, of course, continue as always to
learn the basic contours of the world as they are shaped within the
family circle. And patterns of child socialization have changed
relatively little. The new development is that *adolescent* children
have begun to manifest a massive uninterest in their parents' values
and in their own identities as guardians-apparent of the family line.

This discontinuity of values and interests is *not* the much heralded
"generation gap," which seems to exist only in the minds of magazine editors and in the undergraduate sociology courses at Berkeley
from which so much scholarly hysteria about Youth's New Way
has come. No serious person who has investigated representative
samples of regular youth—as opposed to the politically visible cam-
pus radicals—has been able to uncover widespread adolescent hostility to parents. The generations are not "in conflict," nor is the
typical young person likely to find himself seething with rage towards
his mother and father. Everything we know about how often young
couples continue to visit their parents suggests the ludicrousness of
generation-gap alarmism.[1]

The real discontinuity is more subtle, though nonetheless sharp.
For a century now in Europe, and possibly longer in North America,
the nuclear family has clasped its children until they left the nest,
taking from the community the role of forming them by keeping
them around for Sunday walks and family-night dinners and visits
to Grandma's grave. Historically, the defining characteristic of the
nuclear family has been precisely this privileged relationship between
parents (especially the mother) and children, a relationship that
endured through adolescence to the threshold of marriage. Now
the peer group is again taking up the task of adolescent socialization;
and as the children move through puberty, parental thoughts about

good and bad, right and wrong, and which way is up are becoming ever more irrelevant to them.

This resurgence of the peer group and slackening of family influence comes through in a number of studies of adolescent–parent relations. Unfortunately, despite masses of surveys (such as asking the 186 students in your undergraduate family-relations course whether they like their parents), the giant sociology-of-the-family industry has left us feebly equipped to answer any questions that concern international comparisons, change over time, or indeed any intellectual problem lying beyond the swamp of trivia in which this subject has bogged down. Yet there are usable findings. To go by the data that do exist for the post-1965 period, adolescents are escaping with increasing frequency into a subculture that is not so much in opposition to the dominant culture as independent of it. And the typical posture of young people in generational relations is not so much rejection as indifference.

One mid–1960s study in the Paris region, of boys and girls aged fifteen to twenty, documented a strong adolescent preference for the companionship of friends as opposed to family. Strong minorities felt they had insufficient liberty from their parents, which is not surprising. But among the post-seventeen students (adolescents at work were also included), strong majorities declared they'd prefer to live away from home, which is—to those who know the French family historically—a big change. More interesting were the reasons many gave for wanting more freedom: a rejection in principle of the whole idea of parental tutelage. One student of seventeen declared, "I'm old enough to know what I should do, to see right and wrong. I listen to my parents' advice but I want to take only those parts that I choose." At stake was not affection for the parents but a sense of autonomy and independence born of the desire to be free, to be different. Most of these young Parisians felt their worlds were in flux; and while adolescents, as people en route from childhood to adulthood, are always sensitive to such notions, what is new is the desire on the part of the most restless to identify with their close friends. "I believe that between my parents and me the lack of understanding is total," explained another boy. "Except perhaps on the subject of schoolwork, I think about life completely differently than they do." And precisely these adolescents try to find refuge, not in some kind of romantic isolation (the classical historical pattern), but in the company of the youth group, as I shall suggest in a moment.[2]

The author of another Parisian youth study argues expressly that the indifference of young people to whatever lessons their parents might have to teach is an important historical change. One of the fellows he interviewed—a fifteen-year-old—made the point clearly:[3]

> I'll have my job certificate and I'll work at night to have pocket money [and continue in school]. With the money I'll buy a motorcycle to go see my fiancée in the suburbs. With a pal I'll rent a room, preferably a garret because it's more poetic. That'll be the realization of my biggest dream, liberty. . . . I won't have to haggle any more with my mother for hours on end to be able to stay out one hour extra. Nobody'll say to me, 'Do you realize how late it is,' or 'This is the last time you're going out.' I'll be able to paint without worrying about the walls, in bed or anywhere. However, I'll spend Saturday evening with my parents. [!] It wasn't clear though, what the pal would say about painting in bed.

Now, Paris is not necessarily representative of France as a whole, and young people in the provinces tend to poke along far behind this advanced St. Germain lycée crowd.[4] But since the great revolt of May 1968, it appears that French youth everywhere have turned much more from the parental nest and toward the subculture. The observation has not been systematically documented, but most French writers believe it to be true, and the merchants of bluejeans and motorcycles have cause to think so as well.

Almost nothing is known in a systematic way about German youth. Revulsion from the Nazi horrors of the parents' generation has given a peculiar stamp to generational relations in that country. So aspects of the staggering discontinuity in political and social values from old to young may be *sui generis*. Only 12 percent of the boys polled in 1954, for example, deemed their parents and adult acquaintances to be worth modeling oneself after (as opposed to 41 percent around 1905).[5] Yet more than a rejection of the Third Reich was at stake, for a sample of boys interviewed in the late 1950s declared themselves "often unrightfully restricted" by parental limitations. One eighteen-year-old trade student said:[6]

When I chose my occupation my parents put all kinds of obstacles in my path. Originally I wanted to be an auto mechanic in order to take part in car and motorcycle racing. In short, I wanted to become a racing driver. But my parents explained to me that this was not a proper occupation, and that I'd always have one foot in the grave. They made clear to me in various ways how wonderful the civil servant's life would be. I finally surrendered in this sort of cold war. To be sure I have some interest in the civil service, but still, I'll think of it as just a job. And when I'm twenty-one I'll buy a racing bike and start hitting the tracks.

If Denmark is typical of the continent as a whole, the adolescent shift from parents to peer group is much more advanced in Europe than in the United States. In a comparative study of America and Denmark, adolescents ages fourteen to eighteen were asked on whose opinions they would rely for various things. In both countries the advice of peers on what to read was more important than that of parents, showing who it is that triumphs in the contest of intellectual guidance. And Danish youth get considerably more useful advice from peers than from parents in the realm of values and personal problems. In fact, to go by this survey, American teenagers seem rather pokey.[7]

But what about the United States? Are American youth still relatively *un*detached from parental views? Scholarly opinion is badly divided over whether American adolescents learn their basic beliefs and morals from their parents or from their friends, and whether those beliefs, however learned, differ significantly from the ideas and values of the parents. From one camp we have comforting assurances that nothing has changed and that kids absorb just about everything from their parents except how to prevent venereal disease; from the other we have frantic armwaving about how youth-in-search will lead us to the Promised Land. Much of this research is poorly designed and based on small, unrepresentative samples. But even the reliable data are directly in conflict.

The 1950s studies point to a delightful harmony between parents and children: nobody challenges or rejects, and sample after sample of high school students or college freshmen declare how much they like their mother and father, agree with the way they were brought up, and so forth.[8] Even in the 1960s, tranquility continued to reign in many places, as in those Chicago high schools where only "mentally healthly adolescents . . . well integrated into the value system of their culture" were able to be discovered. "They were middle-of-the-roaders," explains the author. "They used to like President Kennedy and now they liked President Johnson. If they or their families were Republicans, they would mention the current Republican leader. The vast majority of the subjects liked their communities and were proud of them. They agreed with their parents that the open-space suburban life was good and felt sorry for anyone living in the city. They were interested in family life, found it pleasant and gratifying, and when grown up wanted to have a family similar to the one in which they grew up. . . ."[9]

Yet some contradicting voices sounded in the late 1960s and 1970s. One survey of Philadelphia adolescents, together with their parents and grandparents, found that the breach in attitudes was considerably greater between the children and their parents than between the parents and grandparents. In politics there had been a slow liberalization across all three generations; in religion, sex, and the "role of women" dramatic lurches had occurred. Among the generations in each family, more continuity turned up than was apparent between each generation as a whole; yet especially in sexual matters, the third generation seemed to be much more socialized by the peer group than was the case for the older generations.[10]

Another author, in a reanalysis of much of this complacent literature on the political socialization of youth, found a fairly high "group correspondence" (i.e., one generation, as a whole, agreeing on most points with the older generation) but a low "pair correspondence" (individual children in agreement with their own parents). Indeed, "it appears from a substantial body of evidence that processes within the family have been largely irrelevant to the formation of specific opinions. It appears that older and younger generations have developed their opinions in parallel rather than in series, by similar experiences in a common way of life."[11] Which is precisely what an independent youth culture is all about.

But if mechanisms of political socialization are breaking down, other types of continuity between generations are in collapse as well. The way people dress and present themselves, for example. A 1970 survey of seventh- and eighth-grade girls from Catholic working-class families in Cincinnati—not exactly an *outré* population—found that ideas of fashionableness came much more from other girls, especially older ones, than from mothers. Mothers approved only of two items of sixteen on the fashion list: maxicoats and tunics. Crocheted vests and eye makeup were explicitly rejected by the older generation, yet the girls' friends wore them and so they wanted to also.[12] We have no historical data for comparison, yet I would bet that within the Cincinnati families of an earlier time, whom Frances Trollope describes in her *Domestic Manners of the Americans*, eighth-grade girls dressed just as their mothers told them to.

Two larger points remain to be clarified.

First, if youth are switching from parental guidance to the tutelage of an adolescent subculture, what exactly are the values of this subculture? To what extent do they diverge from those of the dominant adult culture the parents represent? A recent study of the "language of adolescence" in the United States gives some hints. Although teenagers go along with their parents on the desirability of being educated—or at least certified as educated—and on ending up in a career that will guarantee some measure of security, in the vital area of how you act toward other people, adolescent values seem remarkably unlike parental ones. It is the characteristics that supposedly "reveal a person's masculinity or femininity" that are salient in the teen subculture. "For boys, the crucial external signs of inner manhood are physical strength, athletic talent, courage in the face of aggression, a willingness to defend one's honor at all costs, and sexual and drinking prowess. According to girls, the most admirable feminine traits are physical attractiveness, personal vivacity, and the ability to delicately manipulate various sorts of interpersonal relationships."[13] If a similar portrait had been attempted around 1900 for a comparable population—let us say the bourgeoisie of Dijon—I am confident that different traits would have emerged: the filiopiety, prudence, thrift, and aesthetic sensibility that the nuclear family worked so hard to transmit.

Second, does the adolescent subculture in the 1960s and 1970s represent a return to earlier patterns in which the traditional village youth group grabbed people from parental homes? Are there cycles in the history of adolescence, whereby peer group and family alternately prevail in the competition for the allegiance of the fifteen to twenty-three-year-olds? Probably not. The distinguishing feature of the traditional youth group was its complete integration into the larger structure of community life. All the adults sanctioned the *jeunesse* because it served certain essential functions, particularly the organization of mating, sexual surveillance, and the control of anti-social behavior. So there was a basic harmony between youth as a collectivity (I'm reluctant to call it a subculture) and the surrounding adult world. It's tempting to think that adolescents in the 1960s and 1970s are returning to past patterns, but in fact the new teenage subculture is independent of adult values rather than being closely integrated with them. The subculture is not oppositional but stand-offish. In what Kenneth Keniston calls a "gentleman's agreement," neither generation interferes with the other.[14] Schwartz and Merten explain that "the cultural categories which shape adolescent orientations to their own social milieu are largely autonomous inasmuch as they are embodied in a system of meanings whose implications are not immediately apparent to adults."[15] So the adults who press their noses against the glass from outside really don't understand what they see; nor do the adolescents care.

What larger significance may we attach to these generational skirmishes over maxicoats and motorcycles? They suggest to me a fundamental shift in the willingness of adolescents to learn from their parents. In the 1960s, relations between the generations started to undergo the same evolution that kinship had earlier undertaken: from function to friendship. In the heyday of the modern nuclear family, the prime burden of transmitting values and attitudes to teenage children fell upon the parents, and the rules of the game were learned in the cloistered intimacy of countless evenings about the hearth. But as the post-modern family rushes down upon us, parents are losing their role as educators. The task passes instead to the peers, and with its transfer passes as well a sense of the family as an institution continuing over time, a chain of links across the generations. The parents become friends (an affective relationship), not representatives of the lineage (a functional relationship). If this is so, we are dealing with an unprecedented pattern.

A second harbinger of the post-modern family is a growing instability of the couple. Since the mid-1960s, divorce rates have accelerated dramatically in every country in Western society. To be sure, ever since the mid-nineteenth century when divorce first started to be eased, the rates have been inching upwards. But that long, gradual climb (interrupted in the 1950s by a plateau in most places) gave way in the 1960s to an unprecedented explosion.[16] Save for France and Portugal, divorce rates accelerated sharply everywhere around the mid-1960s.[17]

Now, data of this nature are subject to all kinds of "technical" explanations; for example, if divorce rates seem to rise, it may be just because more people are marrying early, and young marriages tend to have high breakdown rates. The best measure is to compare changes in the number of divorces among different groups ("cohorts") of people, each group being composed of people who got married around the same time. Such group data reflect the same rapid acceleration in divorce during the 1960s. In Britain, for example, among those who married in 1960, fourteen of every 1,000 had divorced within three years, seventeen per 1,000 of those married in 1962, and 22 per 1,000 of those married in 1965. Projecting these trends, one English researcher speculates that "one sixth to one fourth of all contemporary marriages may ultimately experience some form of breakdown." By 1969 the English marriage breakdown rate had almost doubled from ten years earlier.[18]

The same divorce take-off in the United States turns up among different age groups of women. Among married women born in 1915–1919, for instance, only 2 percent had been divorced by 1940, when they were in their early twenties. But among those born in 1945–1949, 6 percent were divorced by their early twenties in 1970. One scholar infers from a 1971 census study that "between 1 in 4 and 1 in 3 women around 30 years old today are likely to experience divorce during their lifetime," and 5 to 10 percent will probably end up divorced twice.[19]

I believe that behind these dry statistics lies a major upheaval in the life of the couple. Marital breakup has crept from the marginal, disgraceful position it had in the nineteenth century to become a strong possibility in our own times. People are coming to have the normal expectation of not spending their entire lives together. Why?

The conventional explanations for increases in the divorce rate are all inadequate. The upthrust has simply been too powerful and universal to be dismissed as a result of more liberal divorce laws. There was, for instance, no change in English divorce legislation over the period of the postwar increase, until 1971. And although the end of the Vietnam War may have caused some marital disruption in the United States, divorce rates in currently war-free Europe have gone up as well.

We may also reject the hysterical proposition that "the family" is breaking up, for the fact is that all these divorcing people turn right around and marry again. Rates of remarriage have followed closely the rates of marital dissolution; and even though, in the 1970s, younger women are marrying somewhat less than they used to, the number of divorced women remarrying has reached historic heights (almost tripling since the 1930s).[20] So the legal institution of marriage isn't coming to an end at all, just the idea that you have to stay with the same person all your life.

Two developments in the 1960s and 1970s have weakened the force of the permanent union—if the ideas set forth in this book are right. First, the intensification of the couple's erotic life that we discussed above has injected a huge chunk of high explosive into their relationship. Because sexual attachment is notoriously unstable, couples resting atop such a base may easily be blown apart. To the extent that erotic gratification is becoming a major element in the couple's collective existence, the risk of marital dissolution increases. The nuclear family was built on the mother's affection for her infants. But that platform is being displaced by eroticism in the post-modern family, and the chances that the family will not stay together are now threatening to become staggeringly high. The rocks on which these couples run aground, as Big Mama noisily explained in *Cat on a Hot Tin Roof*, are on the bed.

Second, women are becoming more independent economically, and can afford to extract themselves from undesired unions. We have observed throughout this book the importance of outside work for power relationships inside the family. And working women, by virtue of their ability to import resources into the family circle, have considerably more influence—and a greater sense of personal autonomy—than do nonworking women. In the 1960s a sharp increase occurred in the percent of married women employed. Among twenty to twenty-four-year-old married women, for example, only 31 percent had jobs in 1957; 43 percent had jobs in 1968.[21] Similar rises occurred in other countries and among other age groups.[22] With the ability to support themselves came the ability to be free. So if sexual dissatisfaction among millions of women newly alert to their own rights to fulfillment was prying them emotionally from their husbands, gainful employment was giving them the possibility of escaping.

A final way in which the nuclear family has been giving way to the post-modern family we might call "the destruction of the nest." The nuclear family was a nest. Warm and sheltering, it kept the children secure from the pressures of the outside adult world, and gave the men an evening refuge from the icy blast of competition. And as the nuclear family rose in the nineteenth century, women liked it too, because it let them pull back from the grinding exactions of farm work, or the place at the mill, and devote themselves to child care. So everyone huddled happily within those secure walls, serene about the dinner table, united in the Sunday outing.

In the 1960s things started to go bad for the nest, not merely in North America but all over Western civilization. An outside adolescent subculture began to pull away the children—or was it that they were forced away by internal changes in the family? In any event, teenagers began withdrawing from the family circle. A generation of men whose gospel on relationships between the sexes is *Playboy* magazine contributed also to the abrading of the nest. They wanted to see sex bunnies in their wives as well as earth mothers, and only awakened resentment and anxiety when, after repeated taps with the magic wand, the sex bunny refused to leap from the station wagon.

But the major unsettlers of the nest have been the women themselves. You know, there *is* something unrewarding about a life devoted to childcare, without any other form of personal fulfillment. In the Bad Old Days, raising infants meant a semiheroic struggle against death and dirt, and the mother whose sons survived diphtheria to take a job in the post office could count her life's work well done. But in the twentieth century, public health has battered down the risk of infant death to levels that put it outside the average mother's consciousness. And the peer group will soon snatch her sons and daughters for a separate life in the private world of adolescence. So not a great deal remains.

Towards the end of the eighteenth century, a transformation in domestic life occurred, the shift from traditional to nuclear family. I argued that "capitalism" was the driving force behind that change. What master variable is at work today though, I must say, is unclear.

We conventionally refer to this complex of changes in the couple's erotic life, in the experience of adolescence, and in the likelihoood of wives working, as "women's liberation." But I think that things are much more complex than just the "wish to be free" suddenly plopping itself into the consciousness of the millions and millions of anonymous women about whom this book has mainly been. In the 1960s and 1970s the entire structure of the family has begun to shift. The nuclear family is crumbling—to be replaced, I think, by the free-floating couple, a marital dyad subject to dramatic fissions and fusions, and without the orbiting satellites of pubertal children, close friends, or neighbors . . . just the relatives, hovering in the background, friendly smiles on their faces.

Notes

Appendixes

Index

NOTES

Publishers' names have been omitted for books published before 1945.

Chapter 1

1. M. Sévegrand, "La Section de Popincourt pendant la Révolution française," in Commission d'histoire économique et sociale de la Révolution française, ed., *Contributions à l'histoire démographique de la Révolution française*, 3rd series: *Etudes sur la population parisienne* (Paris: Bibliothèque nationale, 1970), pp. 9–91, esp. p. 86, children 15 or under; Adeline Daumard, *La Bourgeoisie parisienne de 1815 à 1848* (Paris: SEVPEN, 1963), p. 337; Christiane Klapisch, "Household and Family in Tuscany in 1427," in Peter Laslett and Richard A. Wall, eds., *Household and Family in Past Time* (New York: Cambridge University Press, 1972), pp. 274, 277.

2. Suzanne Dreyer-Roos, *La Population strasbourgeoise sous l'Ancien Régime* (Strasbourg: Istra, 1969), p. 170; Inger Ernst Momsen, *Die Bevölkerung der Stadt Husum von 1769 bis 1860: Versuch einer historischen Sozialgeographie* (Kiel: Selbstverlag des Geographischen Instituts der Universität Kiel, 1969), pp. 160–171; Emil J. Walter, "Kritik einiger familiensoziologischer Begriffe im Lichte der politischen Arithmetik des 18. Jahrhunderts," *Schweizerische Zeitschrift für Volkswirtschaft und Statistik*, 97 (1961), 64–75, esp. pp. 72–73.

3. Bernard Farber, *Guardians of Virtue: Salem Families in 1800* (New York: Basic Books, 1972), pp. 46, 48.

4. Roger Smith, "Early Victorian Structure: A Case Study of Nottinghamshire," *International Review of Social History*, 15 (1970), 69–84, esp. pp. 73–74. (Propertied, 6.0; laborers, 4.5.)

5. Michael Anderson, *Family Structure in Nineteenth Lancashire* (New York: Cambridge University Press 1971), p. 51.

6. On the short duration of the average union see, for example, Gérard Bouchard, *Le Village immobile: Sennely-en-Sologne au XVIIIe siècle* (Paris: Plon, 1972), p. 232. The average marriage in the American colonies would, however, last considerably longer. John Demos, in a letter to me, puts it at 20–30 years.

7. Micheline Baulant estimates that during the early modern period in one part of the Paris region, a fifth of all households would contain children of different marriages. A third of all unions were remarriages for one of the partners. Baulant, "La famille en miettes: Sur un aspect de la démographie du XVIIe siècle," *Annales: Economies, Sociétés, Civilisations*, 27 (1972), 959–968. For an Austrian example of children from previous marriages in numerous households, see Michael Mitterauer, "Zur Familienstruktur in ländlichen Gebieten Österreichs im 17. Jahrhundert," in Heimold Helczmanovski, ed., *Beiträge zur Bevölkerungs- und Sozialgeschichte Österreichs* (Vienna: Verlag für Geschichte und Politik, 1973), pp. 168–222, esp. p. 175.

8. Western France: Bouchard, *Village immobile*, p. 231; Languedoc: Nicole Castan, "La Criminalité familiale dans le ressort du Parlement de Toulouse, 1690–1730," in A. Abbiateci *et al.*, eds., *Crimes et criminalité en France sous l'Ancien Régime, 17e-18e siècles* (Paris: Colin, 1971), pp. 91–107, esp. p. 96; for an English example: Roger

Schofield, "Age-Specific Mobility Is an Eighteenth-Century Rural English Parish," in *Annales de démographie historique*, 1970, pp. 261–274.

9. C. Viry, *Mémoire statistique du département de la Lys* (Paris, 1812), p. 57. The author was prefect of the department. In two Salzburg County parishes the children's exodus would commence towards nine, accelerate sharply towards twelve, and climb thereafter; by age twenty, all those who were going to enter service had already done so. Boys left earlier than girls; the children of *Inwohner* remained servants longer than the children of the propertied peasantry. See Mitterauer, "Familienstruktur Österreichs," p. 205.

10. Schofield, "Age-specific mobility," *passim*.

11. Alan Macfarlane, *The Family Life of Ralph Josselin, A Seventeenth-Century Clergyman: An Essay in Historical Anthropology* (New York: Cambridge University Press, 1970), p. 93.

12. In the highlands around Zurich this custom was called *Rast geben*, and children would leave as early as six to earn their bread in the homes of cottage weavers. See Rudolf Braun, *Industrialisierung und Volksleben: Die Veränderungen der Lebensformen in einem ländlichen Industriegebiet vor 1800 (Zürcher Oberland)* (Erlenbach–Zurich: Eugen Rentsch, 1960), pp. 81–89.

13. Peter Laslett proposes a slightly different typology for classifying kin in households:

————The simple conjugal family (or CFU—conjugal family unit): the couple plus offspring.

————The "extended family household:" the conjugal family plus additional relatives, whose spouses and children (if any) do not cohabit. If a widowed parent happens to be present, Laslett calls the household "extended upwards," but in the context of early modern Europe, where the inheriting son brings his bride into the parents' living space, I prefer the phrase "stem family."

————The "multiple family household:" two or more conjugal family units connected by kinship or marriage. Cases where both members of the senior couple remain alive as the inheriting son arrives with his bride I should prefer to lump in the "stem family" box. Cases where the senior couple retains authority over several cohabiting junior couples, all related by kinship or marriage, are manifestly distinct from the "stem family" and deserve to be the core of this category "multiple family household." See Laslett and Wall, *Household and Family in Past Time*, pp. 28–31.

14. The writer I take so severely to task here is of course my good friend Peter Laslett, who states in the preface of his magisterial *Household and Family in Past Time*, "What I have called the null hypothesis in the history of the family, which is that the present state of evidence forces us to assume that its organization was always and invariably nuclear unless the contrary can be proven, is an outcome of [a special conference on the subject]," not all the papers of which prove congenial to Laslett's case (p. xi). Further down the page Laslett continues: "It is simply untrue as far as we can tell, that there was ever a time or place when the complex family was the universal background to the ordinary lives of ordinary people." Now, to scholars familiar with the social history of the Balkans, the Baltic countries, Alpine Europe, central Germany, and central and southern France (to take some documented regions), it is sooner Laslett's lack of balance that needs correction. For another instance of overbalancing the extended family fantasy, see Helmut Schwägler, *Soziologie der Familie: Ursprung und Entwicklung* (Tübingen: J.C.B. Mohr, 1970), pp. 141–145, who believes the "stem family" was little widespread in pre-industrial society.

15. David H. Flaherty, *Privacy in Colonial New England* (Charlottesville: University of Virginia Press, 1972), pp. 48–50, 60.

16. See in Laslett and Wall, *Household and Family in Past Time*, the quite convincing discussions on pp. 46–62 and pp. 125–203.

17. Anderson, *Family Structure in Lancashire*, pp. 56–62.

18. See, for example, Philip J. Greven, Jr., *Four Generations: Population, Land, and Family in Colonial Andover, Massachusetts* (Ithaca: Cornell University Press, 1970), pp. 139–141 and *passim*.

19. Netherlands: A. M. van der Woude, "Variations in the size and structure of the household in the United Provinces of the Netherlands in the Seventeenth and Eighteenth Centuries," in Laslett and Wall, *Household and Family in Past Time*, pp. 299–318, esp. the table on p. 309; Norway: Michael Drake, *Population and Society in Norway, 1735–1865* (New York: Cambridge University Press, 1969), p. 116; Austria: Mitterauer, "Familienstruktur Österreichs," pp. 198–202, 213; Isbergues: Christian Pouyez, *Une communauté rurale d'Artois: Isbergues, 1598–1826*, thèse de 3e cycle, Université de Lille III, 1972, p. 90; Périgord: Jean-Noël Biraben, "A Southern French Village: The Inhabitants of Montplaisant in 1644," in Laslett and Wall, *Household and Family in Past Time*, pp. 237–254, esp. p. 241.

20. Lutz Berkner, "The Stem Family and the Developmental Cycle of the Peasant Household: an Eighteenth-Century Austrian Example," *American Historical Review*, 77 (1972), 398–418.

21. Michael Z. Brooke, *Le Play: Engineer and Social Scientist: The Life and Work of Frédéric Le Play* (London: Longman, 1970), pp. 78–88, provides a convenient introduction; a basic Le Play text is *L'Organisation de la famille* (Paris, 1871).

22. Good descriptions of the extended family's operation are in Lutz Berkner and Franklin Mendels, "Inheritance Systems, Family Structure, and Demographic Patterns in Western Europe (1700–1900)," in Charles Tilly and E. A. Wrigley, *Population Growth and Early Industrialization* (Princeton: Princeton University Press, 1975); and John W. Cole, "Estate Inheritance in the Italian Alps," University of Massachusetts Department of Anthropology, *Research Reports*, No. 10 (1971).

23. Paul Ourliac, "La Famille pyrénéene au Moyen Age," in Paul Ourliac, ed., *Recueil d'études sociales à la memoire de Frédéric Le Play* (Paris: Picard, 1956), pp. 257–263, esp. p. 259.

24. Berkner, "The Stem Family and the Development Cycle of the Peasant Household," song from p. 403.

25. Abel Hugo, *La France pittoresque*, 3 vols. (Paris: 1835), I, p. 266.

26. Upper Provence: Alain Collomp, "Famille nucléaire et famille élargie en Haute Provence au XVIIIe siècle (1703–1734)," *Annales: ESC*, 27 (1972), 969–975; Aveyron: Raymond Noel, "L'Etat de la population de Mostuejouls (Aveyron) en 1690," in Société de démographie historique, *Sur la population française au XVIIIe et au XIXe siècles: Hommage à Marcel Reinhard* (Paris: SDH, 1973), pp. 505–522, esp. p. 512. A recent article by William Parish and Moshe Schwartz, admirable at least for its ingenuity if not for its persuasiveness, suggests that multiple family households were widespread in France's rural departments toward the mid-nineteenth century, "Household Complexity in Nineteenth Century France," *American Sociological Review*, 37 (1972), 154–173.

27. On the chances of parents surviving into grandparenthood, see Hervé Le Bras, "Parents, Grand-Parents, Bisaïeux," *Population*, 28 (1973), 9–38.

28. On the zadruga, see Joel Halpern, *A Serbian Village*, rev. ed., (New York: Columbia University Press, 1967), pp. 134–150; and, with Barbara Kerewsky Halpern, *A Serbian Village in Historical Perspective* (New York: Holt, Rinehart and Winston, 1972); see also E. A. Hammel, "The Zadruga as a Process," in Laslett and Wall, *Household and Family in Past Time*, pp. 335–373. Halpern also has a contri-

Notes

bution in that volume, on the census of 1863, pp. 401–428. Also important is Joel M. Halpern and David Anderson, "The Zadruga, A Century of Change," *Anthropologia*, New Series, 12 (1970), 83–97.

29. Andrejs Plakans, "Peasant Farmsteads and Households in the Baltic Littoral, 1797," *Comparative Studies in Society and History*, 17 (1975), 2–35.

30. Plakans, "Peasant Farmsteads," table 6.

31. Mary Matossian writes of the Russian peasant family that "there must have been frequent tensions arising from the presence of an eighteen-year-old female and a forty-year-old male, no blood kin to each other, living in a tiny room together for many months," and ascribes to this the "notoriously hostile mother-in-law and daughter-in-law relationship." Matossian, "The Peasant Way of Life," in Wayne S. Vucinich, ed., *The Peasant in Nineteenth-Century Russia* (Stanford: Stanford University Press, 1968), pp. 1–40, esp. p. 18.

32. A nominal list of Neudroschenfeld's population in 1836 is in the Bavarian Hauptstaatsarchiv, Ministerium des Innern (MI) 53272. The mean age of both kinds of family fathers was close (45.2 years for the houseowners, 42.8 for the tenants), which means we're not rubbing against some variation in·life style whereby young fathers whose families aren't yet completed are still tenants.

33. Drake, *Population and Society in Norway*, pp. 107–119; see also Erik Gronseth, "Notes on the Historical Development of the Relation between Nuclear Family, Kinship System and the Wider Social Structure in Norway," in Reuben Hill and René König, eds., *Families in East and West: Socialization Process and Kinship Ties* (The Hague: Mouton, 1970), pp. 225–247.

34. N. L. Tranter, "The Social Structure of a Bedfordshire Parish in the Mid-Nineteenth Century," *International Review of Social History*, 18 (1973) 90–106, esp. pp. 93–94.

35. Bouchard, *Village immobile*, p. 231.

36. Bayerisches Hauptstaatsarchiv, Neudroschenfeld nominal list, MI 53272. On Sarcelles, see John Ardagh's savage sketch, *The New French Revolution* (New York: Harper & Row, 1968), pp. 212–222.

37. Rudolf Virchow, *Die Noth im Spessart. Eine medizinisch-geographisch-historische Skizze*, first delivered as a lecture in 1852, reprinted by the Wissenschaftliche Buchgesellschaft (Darmstadt, 1968), p. 12. The Würzburg example is from Bayerisches Hauptstaatsarchiv, MI 46556, letter of 30 February 1839.

38. Cited by Lothar Schneider, *Der Arbeiterhaushalt im 18. und 19. Jahrhundert, dargestellt am Beispiel des Heim- und Fabrikarbeiters* (Berlin: Duncker & Humblot, 1967), pp. 68–69.

39. *Ibid.*, p. 135.

40. Antje Kraus, *Die Unterschichten Hamburgs in der ersten Hälfte des 19. Jahrhunderts* (Stuttgart: Fischer, 1965), p. 68; Helmut Möller, *Die kleinbürgerliche Familie im 18. Jahrhundert* (Berlin: de Gruyter, 1969), pp. 121–122.

41. On the custom of young girls spending at least the summer nights in stables and outbuildings, see, for Scandinavia: Drake, *Population and Society in Norway*, p. 144; Matti Sarmela, *Reciprocity Systems of the Rural Society in the Finnish–Karelian Area, with Special Reference to Social Intercourse of the Youth* (Helsinki: Suomalainen Tiedekatemia, 1969), p. 159; K. Rob. V. Wikman, *Die Einleitung der Ehe: Eine vergleichende ethno-soziologische Untersuchung über die Vorstufe der Ehe in den Sitten des Schwedischen Volkstums* (Abo: Abo Akademi, 1937), pp. 77–81.

42. On farm hands lodging in stables see, for example, Amans-Alexis Monteil, *Description du département de l'Aveiron* (Rodez, 1802), I, 121; A. Bernard-Langlois, *Etudes topographiques, historiques, hygiéniques, morales . . . sur le canton de Bourbon-*

Lancy (Moulins, 1865), p. 87. On western France, see François Lebrun, *Les Hommes et la mort en Anjou aux 17e et 18e siècles: Essai de démographie et psychologie historiques* (Paris: Mouton, 1971), p. 269, whose account is based on descriptions of 1803 and 1843. Dr. E. Bogros speaks of peasants sleeping "entassé par groupes de trois ou quatre dans le même lit." *A travers le Morvand* (Chateau-Chinon, 1873), p. 35.

43. Maurice Garden, *Lyon et les Lyonnais au XVIIIe siècle* (Paris: Les Belles-Lettres, 1970), pp. 159, 405; on Paris, see, for example, Jeffry Kaplow, *The Names of Kings: The Parisian Laboring Poor in the Eighteenth Century* (New York: Basic Books, 1972), pp. 68–69.

44. W. G. Hoskins, *Provincial England: Essays in Social and Economic History* (London: Macmillan, 1963), p. 144.

45. Alan Everitt, "Farm Labourers," in Joan Thirsk, ed., *The Agrarian History of England and Wales*, vol. IV: *1500–1640* (New York: Cambridge University Press, 1967), pp. 442–443; see also the floor plans of yeoman farmhouses in M. W. Barley's article in the same volume, pp. 736–738.

46. Flaherty, *Privacy in Colonial New England*, pp. 36–42.

47. *Ibid.*, p. 42.

48. Lewis Mumford, *The City in History* (New York: Harcourt Brace & World, 1961), pp. 286, 382–385.

49. Adeline Daumard, *Les Bourgeois de Paris au XIXe siècle* (Paris: Flammarion, 1970), p. 70.

50. On the hallway question, and on the general relationship between house form and upper-class family life, see Philippe Ariès, *Centuries of Childhood: A Social History of Family Life*, Eng. trans. by Robert Baldick (New York: Vintage, 1965), pp. 398–399 and *passim*.

51. On settlement, see C. T. Smith, *An Historical Geography of Western Europe before 1800* (London: Longmans, 1967), pp. 260–295; and J. M. Houston, *A Social Geography of Europe*, rev. ed. (London: Duckworth, 1963), p. 103 and *passim*.

52. On communal ties and settlement patterns see Jerome Blum, "The European Village as Community: Origins and Functions," *Agricultural History*, 45 (1971), 157–178.

53. Pierre Chaunu, *La Civilisation de l'Europe classique* (Paris: Arthaud, 1970), pp. 196–197.

54. According to the Bavarian government, charivaris had been almost entirely stamped out in the hamlets and farms of Oberbayern by 1850 (Bayerisches Hauptstaatsarchiv, MI 46557-46559, "Das sogenannte Haberfeld-Treiben"); similarly in the French Alps, where settlement is also dispersed, charivaris against the remarriage of widows were declining by 1807 (de Verneilh, *Statistique générale de la France . . . département du Mont-Blanc* (Paris, 1807), p. 295. In the Franche-Comté, however, a land of more nucleated settlement, the charivari was still going strong in the 1880s (see Charles Perron, *Les Franc-Comtois: leur caractère national, leurs moeurs, leurs usages* (Besançon, 1892), pp. 139–142; and in the villages of the Brabant the charivari was to revive after the Second World War, police repression having driven it underground in the interwar years. See A. Doppagne, "Enquête en Brabant Wallon: Fréquentation et fiançailles," Institut de sociologie de l'Université libre de Bruxelles, *Document de travail* No. III/1 (March 1970), 2–16.

55. See the map of "Régression des feux de Brandons et des feux de la St. Jean" at the end of André Varagnac, *Civilisation traditionnelle et genres de vie* (Paris: Albin Michel, 1948).

56. See Wikman's map of "Nachtfreierei" in *Die Einleitung der Ehe*, p. 264.

57. In the English village of Clayworth, for example, a good 40 per cent of the population present in 1676 were absent twelve years later, excluding those known to have died in the interim. See Peter Laslett and John Harrison, "Clayworth and Cogenhoe," in H. E. Bell and R. L. Ollard, eds., *Historical Essays, 1600–1750, presented to David Ogg* (London: Adam and Charles Black, 1963), pp. 157–184, esp. p. 184. See also E. A. Wrigley, "A Simple Model of London's Importance in Changing English Society and Economy, 1650–1750," *Past and Present*, 37 (July, 1967), 44–70.

58. The local studies on which this impression rests are too numerous to cite here. Pierre Goubert, who probably knows the hundreds of theses and microstudies better than anyone, concludes that the early modern French were "a rooted, sedentary, stable population." Goubert, *The Ancien Régime: French Society, 1600–1750,* trans. Steve Cox (London: Weidenfeld and Nicolson, 1973), p. 42 *et seq.* Mack Walker's important study of early modern Germany finds that "not only was it hard to get into a community, it was hard to get out," and that with such *Bürgerrecht* policies, migration approached zero. Walker, *German Home Towns: Community, State, and General Estate, 1648–1871* (Ithaca: Cornell University Press, 1971), pp. 140–141. Population turnover in traditional Swedish society was similarly low. Kurt Agren *et al., Aristocrats, Farmers, Proletarians: Essays in Swedish Demographic History* (Uppsala: Scandinavian University Books, 1973), p. 74.

59. See, for example, Michel Terrisse, " 'Prolétariat flottant' et 'migrations temporaires' à Marseille," *Dh: Bulletin d'information,* 4 (Oct. 1971), pp. 2–7; or de Verneilh, *Mont-Blanc,* p. 288.

60. It's from the wrong time and setting, but I was impressed anyway with Robert Roberts' testimony on what composed "respectability" in the eyes of the English working classes. Roberts, *The Classic Slum: Salford Life in the First Quarter of the Century* (Manchester: Manchester University Press, 1971), pp. 1–25.

61. Tina Jolas and Françoise Zonabend, "Gens du Finage, gens du bois," *Annales: ESC,* 28 (1973), 285–305, esp. p. 292.

62. Karl Sigismund Kramer, *Die Nachbarschaft als bäuerliche Gemeinschaft* (Munich–Pasing: Verlag Bayerische Heimatforschung, 1954), pp. 16–17.

63. Bayerisches Hauptstaatsarchiv, MI 52135. I came across this example, and much additional evidence, in the course of preparing my doctoral dissertation "Social Change and Social Policy in Bavaria, 1800–1860" (Harvard, 1967).

64. Joseph Hazzi, *Statistische Aufschlüsse über das Herzogthum Baiern . . .,* 11 vols. (Nürnberg, 1801–1808), III (2), p. 633. For a general review of "Fornikationsstrafen" see Wilhelm Wächtershauser *Das Verbrechen des Kindesmordes im Zeitalter der Aufklärung* (West Berlin: Schmidt, 1973), pp. 129–137, 159–160.

65. On the edict of 1556 see, recently, Marie-Claude Phan, "Introduction à l'étude des déclarations de grossesse et autres series documentaires concernant la sexualité illégitime dans la France des XVIe, XVIIe et XVIIIe siècles," Mémoire de maîtrise, Université Paris VIII, 1972.

66. On this arsenal in Bavaria see Shorter, "Social Change and Social Policy," pp. 518–519.

67. See Mack Walker's tale of the efforts of the tinsmith Flegel, whose prospective bride's *father* was illegitimately born, to marry and become a master craftsman against the wishes of the Hildesheim tinsmith's guild. *German Home Towns,* pp. 73–75.

68. Bayerisches Hauptstaatsarchiv, MI 54844, 1836.

69. *Verhandlungen der Kammer der Abgeordneten des Königreichs Bayern,* March 1840, Vol. IV, p. 428.

Notes

Chapter 2

1. Alexandre Bouët, *Breiz Izel, ou vie des Bretons dans l'Armorique*, 2nd ed. (Quimper, 1918; first ed. 1835), p. 278.
2. K. Rob, V. Wikman, *Die Einleitung der Ehe* (Abo: Abo Akademi, 1937), p. 348.
3. Brieude, *Topographie médicale de la Haute-Auvergne*, rev. ed. (Aurillac, 1821, first published 1782–1783), pp. 110–111.
4. Abel Hugo, *France pittoresque*, 2 vols. (Paris, 1835), II, p. 29, for the Finistère department.
5. A. Bernard-Langlois, *Etudes topographics . . . sur le canton de Bourbon-Lancy* (Moulins, 1865), p. 123.
6. Hughes Maret, *Mémoire dans lequel on cherche à déterminer quelle influence les moeurs des Francois ont sur leur santé* (Amiens, 1772), p. 149.
7. Micheline Baulant, "La famille en miettes," *Annales: ESC* (1972), 967.
8. Louis Texier-Olivier, *Statistique générale de la France, département de la Haute-Vienne* (Paris, 1808), p. 99.
9. Archives nationales, F20 172 ms. "Statistique de la Charente, an IX."
10. Adrien Berénguier, *Topographie physique, statistique et médicale du canton de Rabastens (Tarn)* (Toulouse, 1850), p. 101.
11. François Lebrun, *Les Hommes et la mort en Anjou aux 17e et 18e siècles* (Paris: Mouton, 1971), p. 428.
12. Martine Segalen, ed., *Mari et femme dans la France rurale traditionnelle* [catalogue of exposition at the Musée national des arts et traditions populaires, 22 September–19 November 1973] (Paris: Ministère des Affaires culturelles, 1973), p. 73.
13. Anon., *La Ciotat au XVIIIe siècle d'après un manuscrit de l'époque par Antisthène* (La Ciotat, 1877), p. 17.
14. C. Dupin, *Mémoire statisque du département des Deux-Sèvres* (Paris, 1804), p. 210.
15. Bossi, *Statistique générale de la France: département de l'Ain* (Paris, 1808), p. 311.
16. D. Monnier, *Moeurs et usages singuliers du peuple dans le Jura* (Lons-le-Saunier, 1823), p. 49.
17. E.-J. Savigné, *Moeurs, coutumes habitudes (il y a plus d'un siècle) des habitants de Sainte-Colombe . . .* (Vienne, 1902), p. 11.
18. Hugo, *France pittoresque*, II, p. 203.
19. Brieude, *Haute-Auvergne*, 2nd ed., p. 75.
20. Maurice Garden, *Lyon et les Lyonnais au XVIIIe siècle* (Paris: Les Belles-Lettres, 1970), p. 436.
21. Louis-Sebastien Mercier, *Tableau de Paris*, rev. ed., 12 vols. (Amsterdam, 1782–1788), vol. I, p. 86.
22. Curt Gebauer, "Studien zur Geschichte der bürgerlichen Sitten reform des 18. Jahrhunderts," *Archiv für Kulturgeschichte*, 15 (1920), 100.
23. Helmut Möller, *Die kleinbürgerliche Familie im 18. Jahrhundert* (Berlin: de Gruyter, 1969 pp. 300–307.
24. Josef Brückl, *Zolling, aus Vergangenheit und Gegenwart*, vol. 2 (Zolling: Gemeinde Selbstverlag, 1968), pp. 320–336.
25. Peter Laslett, *The World We Have Lost*, rev. ed. (London: Methuen, 1971), p. 22.
26. Alan MacFarlane, *The Family Life of Ralph Josselin, A Seventeenth-Century Clergyman* (New York: Cambridge University Press, 1970), pp. 106–110.

27. Frank Huggett, *A Day in the Life of a Victorian Farm Worker* (London: Allen & Unwin, 1972), p. 64.

28. Roger Thompson remarks, "There seems little doubt from the available evidence that the portion or dowry was rather less crucial in the colonies than it was in England, in all classes." Thompson, *Women in Stuart England and America: A Comparative Study* (London: Routledge, 1974), pp. 122–123.

29. John Demos, *A Little Commonwealth: Family Life in Plymouth Colony* (New York: Oxford University Press, 1970), p. 99; Edmund Morgan, *The Puritan Family: Religion and Domestic Relations in Seventeenth-Century New England*, rev. ed. (New York: Harper & Row, 1966), pp. 46–64. In an analysis of the periodical fiction aimed at the upper-middle classes of the northeastern United States, Herman R. Lantz et al., have found the literature of the late-eighteenth century abundant with references to romantic love, and especially to what they term "the glorification of emotions." Lantz, "The Preindustrial Family in America: A Further Examination of Early Magazines," *America Journal of Sociology*, 79 (1973), 566–588, esp. p. 577.

30. Edmund S. Morgan, *Virginians at Home: Family Life in the Eighteenth Century* (Charlottesville: University Press of Virginia, 1952), p. 50.

31. Charles Perron, *Les Franc-Comtois*, Besançon, 1892), p. 88.

32. Luc Thoré, "Langage et sexualité," in Centre d'études laènnec, ed., *Sexualité humaine* (Paris: Aubier-Montaigne, 1970), pp. 65–95, esp. p. 77.

33. How much "power" the conventional wisdom ascribes to "women" depends, of course, on the time and place being discussed. A common argument is that in traditional society women had high rates of labor force participation, doing important jobs within agriculture and industry such as the running of farms or tanning shops; it was in the course of modernization that they were forced out of the world of work and into the cloister of the household, to languish in dependency. For this viewpoint see Gerda Lerner, *The Woman in American History* (Menlo Park, California: Addison Wesley, 1971), pp. 16–19, and *passim*. Other writers see women as powerless in economic matters since, basically, the dawn of time.

34. Mme. Charles d'Abbadie d'Arrast, *Causeries sur le pays Basque: la femme et l'enfant* (Paris: 1909), pp. 53–56. I am uneasy about this source, partly because its author belongs to the upper-middle classes, whose testimony I customarily reject systematically, and partly because the Basque country was atypical for France as a whole.

35. Abbadie, *Pays Basque*, pp. 50–57; Paul Ourliac, "La famille pyrénéenne au Moyen Age," in Paul Ourliac, ed., *Recueil d'études sociales à la mémoir de Frédéric Le Play* (Paris: Picard, 1956), "Famille pyrénénne," p. 261. In my three main series of evidence, there occasionally appear rather vague remarks about the peasant's wife living in subjection, being his first servant, and so on. I infer from these that in other regions of France husbands consulted little with their wives on strategic resource decisions, yet I have seen no hard information on this subject, a matter clearly of capital importance in assessing the "power" of peasant women in traditional times.

36. Henriette Dussourd, *Au même pot et au même feu: étude sur les communautés agricoles au Centre de la France* (Moulins: Pottier, 1962), p. 43.

37. On female participation in field work, by type of agricultural system, see the numerous observations of Henri Baudrillart, scattered throughout his three-volume survey of French rural life, *Les Populations agricoles de la France*, Vol. I: *Normandie et Bretagne* (Paris, 1885), Vol. II: *Maine, Anjou . . .* (1888), Vol. III: *Les Populations du Midi* (1893). For other observations see also Bossi, *Ain*, pp. 294; Beauvais de St.-Paul, *Essai historique et statistique sur le canton et la ville de Mondoubleau*

(Le Mans, 1837), p. 45; Guy Thuillier, "Pour une histoire des travaux ménagers en Nivernais au XIXe siècle," *Revue d'histoire économique et sociale*, 50 (1972), 238–264, esp. p. 239.

38. André Varagnac, *Civilisation traditionnelle et genres de vie* (Paris: Albin Michel, 1948), p. 188.

39. See the photographs in Segalen, *Mari et femme*, p. 61.

40. Observers thought fishing households different from peasant ones primarily because control over money was allocated differently. In Boulogne, fishermen turned over profits from the catch directly to their wives, keeping back only pocket money. P.-J.-B. Bertrand, *Précis de l'histoire . . . de la ville de Boulogne-sur-Mer* (Boulogne, 1829), p. 331. And in the Eure's Quillebeuf, the authority of fishermen's wives extended even to the power to buy and sell property without their husband's consent, a custom which had originated with the perilousness of seafaring, but which with time had been adopted by the town's nonfishing population as well. Jean-Baptiste-Victoire Boismare, "Mémoire sur la topographie et les constitutions médicales de la ville de Quillebeuf . . ." *Extrait des Actes de l'Academie des sciences de Rouen, pour l'anée 1811* (n.p., n.d.), p. 25.

41. Eugene Hammel, "The Jewish Mother in Serbia, or Les Structures alimentaires de la parenté," in *Kroeber Anthropological Society*, Special Publications No. 1 (1967), pp. 55–62, and esp. p. 57.

42. In parts of Normandy, according to J.-M. Gouesse, it was wives who had the principal responsibility for marketing and "taking care of exterior relations," yet I know of no similar cases elsewhere. Gouesse, "Parenté, famille et mariage en Normandie aux XVIIe et XVIIIe siècles: Présentation d'une source et d'une enquête," *Annales: ESC*, 27 (1972), 1139–1154, esp. p. 1148.

43. Yves Castan, "Mentalités rurale et urbaine à la fin de l'Ancien Régime dans le ressort du Parlement de Toulouse d'après les sacs à procès criminels, 1730–1790," in A. Abbiateci, *et al.*, eds., *Crimes et criminalité en France sous l'Ancien Régime, 17e-18e siècles* (Paris: Colin, 1971), pp. 109–186, esp. p. 141.

44. Segalen, *Mari et femme*, p. 72.

45. Hugo, *France pittoresque*, II, p. 234.

46. *Ibid.*, II, p. 234.

47. Segalen, *Mari et femme*, pp. 72–73.

48. Hugo, *France pittoresque*, II, p. 234. (Mayenne department.)

49. G. Maillet's article on "Fêtes de Dames," which appeared in *La Croix*, 24–25 October 1937, cited in Varagnac, *Civilisation traditionnelle*, p. 195.

50. Varagnac, *Civilisation traditionnelle*, p. 196.

51. Möller, *Kleinbürgerliche Familie*, pp. 305–311. While some of the evidence Möller offers on "domesticity" at the end of the eighteenth century seems to foreshadow the whole family's withdrawal from the community, perhaps contemporaries imagined this cozy retreat as an extension of behavior expected hitherto only of women.

52. Pierre Chaunu finds the territorial effect much stronger than the class effect in explaining fertility differences, from which might be inferred the operation of community norms in setting target family sizes. Chaunu, "Malthusianisme démographique et malthusianisme économique: Réflexions sur l'échec industriel de la Normandie à l'époque du démarrage," *Annales: ESC*, 27 (1972), 1–19, esp. pp. 15–16; see also his "Réflexions sur la démographie normande," in Société de démographie historique, ed., *Sur la population francaise au XVIIIe et au XIXe siècles: Hommage à Marcel Reinhard* (Paris: SDH, 1973), pp. 97–117, esp. pp. 108–110.

53. See the citations to Rétif in Etienne and Francine van de Walle, "Allaitement, stérilité et contraception: les opinions jusqu'au XIXe siècle," *Population*, 27 (1972), 685–701, esp. p. 693.

54. Balme, ". . . Quelques réflexions critiques sur la question, si la grossesse est une exclusion à l'alaitement," *Journal de médecine*, 47 (1777), 402–423, 494–507. ". . . le paysan, chez qui nous mettons le nourrisson, ne mene pas ordinairement une vie assez oiseuse ou assez délicieuse pour qu'elle puisse l'exciter à des caresses capables de lui nuire ainsi qu'à son épouse. Le mari revenant de son travail, harrassé de fatigue & de misere, porte tous ses desirs vers une nourriture necessaire, & le plus souvent peu abondante. Le repos, dont il a le plus grand besoin, le détourne ensuite des plaisirs, qui ne pourroient le délasser. La femme, de son côté, fatiguée des soins & des peines de de la journée, après un repas frugal, dont le nourrisson emporte tout le fruit, cherche le sommeil à côté de son mari plutôt que dans ses bras. Je le dis avec certitude, leurs caresses ne font que le pur effet de la nature, qui s'explique sur de vrais besoins, & plutôt au soulagement du corps qu'a son détriment." (p. 411)

55. Möller, *Kleinbürgerliche Familie*, p. 287.

56. "Bey dem Zanken der Eheleute machte oft die Frau dem Manne den Vorwurf, dass er ihr nicht ehelich beywohne und doch von ihr verlange, dass sie ihm ————." Respondent unnamed, cited in Christian Gotthilf Salzmann, *Ueber die heimlichen Sünden der Jugend*, 2nd ed. (Frankfurt, 1794), p. 54.

57. Louis Bandy de Nalèche, *Les Maçons de la Creuse* (Paris, 1859), p. 34.

58. Academie de Médecine, SRM 181, ms. "Topographie médicale de St. Malo," 1790.

59. Academie de Médecine, SRM 142, ms. of 12 July 1788.

60. Brieude, *Haute-Auvergne*, p. 305.

61. V. Stoeber and G. Tourdes, *Topographie et histoire médicale de Strasbourg* (Paris, 1864), p. 381.

Chapter 3

1. Peter Laslett has shown me much as yet unpublished English data in which this late sixteenth-century rise is unmistakable, and on the basis of which he argues that illegitimacy moves in long oscillations.

2. Preliminary documentation in Edward Shorter, "Illegitimacy, Sexual Revolution and Social Change in Modern Europe," *Journal of Interdisciplinary History*, 2 (1971), 237–272.

3. Illegitimate fertility series for major western nations after 1850 are presented in Edward Shorter, John Knodel and Etienne van de Walle, "The Decline of Non-Marital Fertility in Europe, 1880–1940," *Population Studies*, 25 (1971), 375–393, esp. 377. For a discussion of post-1850 premarital pregnancy series see appendix II.

4. Curves showing the parallelism in the decline are presented in *ibid.*, p. 378.

5. Among recent treatments of the antimasturbation and anti-intercourse literature of mid-nineteenth century America are Ben Barker-Benfield, "The Spermatic Economy: A Nineteenth-Century View of Sexuality," *Feminist Studies*, 1 (1972), 45–74; John S. Haller and Robin M. Haller, *The Physician and Sexuality in Victorian America* (Urbana: University of Illinois Press, 1973); Stephen Nissenbaum, "Careful Love: Sylvester Graham and the Emergence of Victorian Sexual Theory in the United States, 1830–1840" (Ph.D. dissertation, University of Wisconsin, 1968); Charles E. Rosen-

Notes

berg, "Sexuality, Class and Role in 19th-Century America," *American Quarterly*, 25 (1973), 131–153; and Daniel Scott Smith, "Family Limitation, Sexual Control, and Domestic Feminism in Victorian America," *Feminist Studies*, 2 (1973), 40–57. A selection of readings is Ronald Walters, ed., *Primer for Prudery: Sexual Advice to Victorian America* (Englewood Cliffs, N.J.: Prentice-Hall, 1974). On Canada see Michael Bliss, "Pure Books on Avoided Subjects: Pre-Freudian Sexual Ideas in Canada," Canadian Historical Association, *Historical Papers*, 1970 (Ottawa: CHA, 1970), pp. 89–108. These themes have been less pursued by students of Europe, but see Jean-Louis Flandrin's various works.

6. On increases in the fecundability of the unmarried see Phillips Cutright, "The Teenage Sexual Revolution and the Myth of an Abstinent Past," *Family Planning Perspectives*, 4 (1972), 24–31. For sources on postwar out-of-wedlock conceptions see chapter 3, note 81.

7. The sole merit of G. Rattray Taylor, *Sex in History*, rev. ed. (New York: Vanguard Press, 1970) is to state clearly the "pendulum" theory of sexuality: "In the past two thousand years the pendulum has swung twice from matrism to patrism and back, and it is now swinging towards matrism for the third time." (p. 285) The one-shot theory of sexual change has passed into the conventional wisdom on modernization, but most students of the question have gotten the story wrong, believing in a passage from free and easy traditional eroticism to cramped repression in modern times. Philip Slater's otherwise admirable book, for example, recapitulates the conventional left-psychoanalytic doctrine that links modern capitalism to repressiveness and associates whatever went before (unspecified, but vaguely alluded to as "primitive society") with sexual liberality. Slater, *The Pursuit of Loneliness: American Culture at the Breaking Point* (Boston: Beacon Press, 1970); see chapter 4, "Putting Pleasure to Work."

8. Beatrice Gottlieb's paper, "The Problem of Clandestine Marriage," delivered in 1972 to the American Historical Association's annual meeting in New Orleans, is most enlightening. On the Lutheran Church and "marriage" which begins with engagement see Matti Sarmela, *Reciprocity Systems of the Rural Society in the Finnish-Karelian Area* . . . (Helsinki: Suomalainen Tiedekatemia, 1969), p. 86. On the church's struggle against betrothal license and "informal" marriage in Denmark, see P. Hertoft, "Le Comportement sexuel des jeunes danois," in Maj-Briht Bergström-Walan *et al.*, eds., *L'expérience scandinave: La sexualité, l'état et l'individu*, French trans. (Paris: Laffont, 1971), pp. 60–143, esp. pp. 65–72.

9. J. M. Tanner has recently reviewed the menarche (first menstruation) literature in *Growth at Adolescence*, 2nd ed. (Oxford: Blackwell, 1962), pp. 143–155. The most careful compilation of historical sources is Gaston Backman, "Die beschleunigte Entwicklung der Jugend: Verfrühte Menarche, verspätete Menopause, verlängerte Lebensdauer," *Acta Anatomica*, 4 (1948) 421–480. Although Backman puts the definitive decline of the age at puberty in France around 1890, my own investigations suggest the 1850s or 1860s would be more correct. I culled references to menarche from over a hundred "topographies médicales" and special surveys in the years after 1750. Most commonly before 1850 the doctors only bracket the modal ages, saying "puberty begins here between fifteen and seventeen," or some such formulation. I then added up the midpoints of all these brackets (or took more precise data, when given) and computed half-century averages. Preliminary results for the average age at which menstruation begins are:

Notes

	ALL OBSERVATIONS	IMPRESSIONISTIC OBSERVATIONS	CLINICAL SURVEYS
1750–1799	15.9	15.9	—
1800–1849	15.7	15.7	15.2
1850–1899	15.1	15.2	15.0
1900–1949	14.4	—	14.4
1950 and after*	13.5	—	13.5

* Mainly the Paris region.

10. There is little variation in the age of the mother at the birth of the first illegitimate child. Peter Laslett and Karla Oosterveen, "Bastardy in Colyton (Devon) and Hawkshead (Lancs): A Comparison," put it in the late twenties for the whole period 1540–1839, with little change over the years (table 7 of their 1974 circulated paper); for 18th-century Béziers and Annonay (Ardèche), the age was mid- to late-twenties, Alain Molinier, "Enfants trouvés, enfants abandonnés et enfants illégitimes en Languedoc aux XVIIe et XVIIIe siècles," in Société de démographie historique, ed., *Sur la population française au XVIIIe et au XIXe siècles: Hommage à Marcel Reinhard* (Paris: SDH, 1973), pp. 445–473, esp. p. 455; Alain Lottin suggests twenty-four to twenty-five for northern France in "Naissances illégitimes et filles-mères à Lille au XVIIIe siècle," *Revue d'histoire moderne et contemporaine*, 17 (1970), 278–322, esp. p. 306; and Jacques Depauw's frequency distributions for Nantes point to the mid- to late twenties, "Amour illégitime et société à Nantes au XVIIIe siècle," *Annales: ESC*, 27 (1972), 1155–1182, esp. table following p. 1166. Figures for late nineteenth- and early twentieth-century Germany indicate a slightly lower mean age. On the basis of Auguste Lange's data, I computed it at 23.6 for Baden in 1898—see Lange, *Die unehelichen Geburten in Baden: eine Untersuchung über ihre Bedingungen und ihre Entwicklung* (Karlsruhe, 1912), pp. 86*–87*; for Dresden in 1899–1910, the modal age group was twenty to twenty-four, a group having over half the cases—see Georg Prenger, *Die Unehelichkeit im Königreich Sachsen* (Leipzig, 1913), p. 72; for Zurich just before the Great War, T. R. Speich finds twenty to twenty-five the modal age group, with only 8 percent of all unwed mothers younger—see Speich, *Die unehelichen Geburten der Stadt Zürich* (Glarus, 1914), p. 33. A time series has been established for Sweden, where the mean age drops one year from 27.9 in 1868–70 to 26.8 in 1891–1900; see Gustav Sundbärg, *Bevölkerungsstatistik Schwedens, 1750–1900* (Stockholm: Statistika Centralbyran reprint, 1970; Urval nr. 3), p. 126.

11. Phillips Cutright, *Illegitimacy in the United States: 1920–1968* (Washington: Government Printing Office, 1972), pp. 18–19 and table 3.7. In a 1971 paper to the American Historical Association, Daniel Scott Smith and Michael S. Hindus expressed reservations about the possibility of charting historical trends in fecundity, "since infecundity is measured through observed infertility in the population, it cannot be empirically measured except in a non-contracepting population. In any case, the proportion of women sterile before age thirty is too low . . . for historical variations in biological potential at a given interval from menarche to have had much influence on variation in premarital pregnancy ratios." Smith and Hindus, "Premarital Pregnancy in America, 1640–1966" (p. 76). While it's true that variations in absolute sterility might not have amounted to much, they may, however, serve as an index to variations in sub-fecundity, and such *partial* impairments in the ability to conceive may have varied considerably.

Notes

12. See Emmanuel Le Roy Ladurie, "L'aménorrhée de famine (XVIIe–XXe siècles)," *Annales: ESC,* 24 (1969), 1589–1601.

13. This evidence is reviewed in Edward Shorter, "Female Emancipation, Birth Control, and Fertility in European History," *American Historical Review* 78 (1973) 629–630.

14. Balguerie, préfet, *Tableau statistique du département du Gers* (Paris, 1802), p. 48. On coitus interruptus among the Vendées youth, see Marcel Baudouin's classic *Le Maraichinage: Coutume du Pays de Monts (Vendée),* 5th ed. (Paris, 1932; first ed., 1900), pp. 131–132; the practice is also mentioned in Dr. Boismoreau, *Coutumes médicales et superstitions populaires du Bocage vendéen* (Paris, 1911), pp. 45–46.

15. In a 1971 poll, John F. Kantner and Melvin Zelnik discovered that a half of unmarried adolescent Americans failed to use any contraceptive technique the last time they had intercourse, and that only 20 percent contraceived consistently. Kantner and Zelnik, "Contraception and Pregnancy: Experience of Young Unmarried Women in the United States," *Family Planning Perspectives* 5 (1973), pp. 21–35 esp. 21–22. Michael Schofield found similar results for British teenagers in the mid-1960s: only 20 per cent of the girls regularly took precautions; 60 per cent left contraception entirely to the boy, and only 43 per cent of the males "always" employed some technique, mostly the sheath. Schofield, *The Sexual Behaviour of Young People* (Harmondsworth: Pelican, 1968), pp. 88–89. Gunter Schmidt and Volkmar Sigusch, finally, were appalled that the "overwhelming majority" of the young unmarried workers they polled in Germany in 1968 "either used an inefficient contraceptive means or none at all." Schmidt and Sigusch, *Arbeiter-Sexualität: Eine empirische Untersuchung an jungen Industriearbeitern* (Neuwied: Luchterhand, 1971), p. 54. Only in Denmark and Sweden did a majority of teenagers practice contraception effectively, relying upon methods more sophisticated than withdrawal. P. Hertoft, "Le Comportement sexuel des jeunes danois," and Joachim Israel *et al.,* "Formes de comportements sexuels chez la jeunesse suédoise des grandes villes," in Maj-Briht Bergström-Walan, *L'Expérience scandinave: La sexualité, l'état et l'individu,* pp. 101, 185.

16. Cutright, *Illegitimacy in the United States,* table 4.6; data for 1940.

17. David Glass, *Population Policies and Movements in Europe* (Oxford, 1940), p. 429.

18. Louis Lépecq de la Cloture, *Collection d'observations sur les maladies et constitutions épidémiques* (Rouen, 1778), p. 273.

19. Alain Molinier, *Une paroisse du bas Languedoc: Serignan, 1650–1792* (Montpellier: Imp. Déhan, 1968), pp. 199–202, attributes the higher marital fertility of the post-1750 period to a lower fetal-loss rate. Thomas McKeown et al., in a recent conspectus of the literature, explicitly reject the possibility that the big improvements in English diet which did take place during the eighteenth century could have caused a "spontaneous increase" in fertility. McKeown, "An Interpretation of the Modern Rise of Population in Europe," *Population Studies,* 26 (1972), 345–382, esp. p. 350.

20. See David Glass's discussion of abortion in the German fertility decline, for example. Glass, *Population Policies,* p. 61. Jean Sutter argues that French anti-abortion legislation at the end of the nineteenth century increased the number of women willing to undertake "autoavortement." Sutter, "Sur la diffusion des méthodes contraceptives," in Hélène Bergues, ed., *La Prévention des naissances dans la famille: ses origines dans les temps modernes* (Paris: INED, 1960), pp. 341–359, esp. p. 347.

21. Jean-Louis Flandrin, "L'attitude à l'égard du petit enfant et les conduites sexuelles dans la civilisation occidental: structures anciennes et évolution," *Annales de démographie historique,* (Paris: Morton: 1973), pp. 143–210.

Notes

22. Vienna's Dr. D. Z. Wertheim wrote in 1810, for example, that tougher laws had possibly reduced abortion, and that the abolition of the fornication penalties had probably lessened the incidence of infanticide as well. Wertheim, *Versuch einer medicinischen Topographie von Wien* (Vienna, 1810), pp. 87, 112.

23. Coutèle, *Observations sur la constitution médicale de l'année 1808 à Albi*, 2 vols. (Albi, 1809), II, pp. 60–61.

24. Adrien Bérenguier, *Topographie physique, statistique et médicale du canton de Rabastens (Tarn)* (Toulouse, 1850), p. 99.

25. Archives nationales, F^{15} 3897.

26. The Paris example from Roger-Henri Geurrand, *La Libre maternité, 1896–1969* (Paris: Casterman, 1971), p. 30; Berlin example from Max Nassauer, *Der moderne Kindermord und seine Bekämpfung durch Findelhäuser* (Leipzig, 1919), p. 16. On Belgium, see J. Stengers, "Les Pratiques anticonceptionnelles dans le mariage au XIXe et au XXe siècle: Problèmes humains et attitudes religieuses," *Revue belge de philologie et d'histoire*, 49 (1971), 403–481, 1119–1174, esp. pp. 1152–1153.

27. Andre Cachois, *Démographie de la Seine-Inférieure* (Rouen, 1929), pp. 273–274.

28. See, for example, the reference to the "alleged high frequency of abortion" and the opinions of J. J. Spengler in Norman E. Himes, *A Medical History of Contraception*, repr. (New York: Gamut Press, 1963; first ed., 1936), p. 374.

29. For local cases in which the illegitimacy and premarital pregnancy ratios rose simultaneously in the late eighteenth century, see the graphs for Sainghin, Meulan, Troarn, Durlach, "an Oldenburg town," Boitin, Volkshardinghausen, and Kreuth in the appendix of Shorter, "Illegitimacy, Sexual Revolution and Social Change . . ." pp. 266–269.

30. G. Cless, *Versuch einer medicinischen Topographie . . . Stuttgart* (Stuttgart, 1815), p. 54; Karl Kisskalt, "Die Sterblichkeit im 18. Jahrhundert," *Zeitschrift für Hygiene und Infektionskrankheiten*, 93 (1921), 429–511, esp. pp. 448–451; Otto Konrad Roller, *Die Einwohnerschaft der Stadt Durlach im 18. Jahrhundert* (Karlsruhe, 1907), p. 111.

31. Bernard-Benoît Remacle, *Rapport . . . concernant les infanticides et les mort-nés dans leur relation avec la question des enfants trouvés* (Paris, 1845), p. 21.

32. A generation of French historical demographers has by now submitted the eighteenth-century parish registers of that country to exacting tests. They find almost no change, until the Revolution, in the quality of the reporting or in the probable proportion of births slipping unnoticed through the official screen. English illegitimacy data for the early nineteenth century are suspicious because of incompleteness in the registration, as are those for the time of the Civil War in the seventeenth century. If the Germans err, it is in the direction of recording too much, sometimes noting as illegitimate the children conceived outside of wedlock but born *legitimately*. The transition of birth registration from clerical to civil changes on occasion the quality of the reporting; yet the illegitimacy explosion commenced everywhere considerably before this administrative innovation, and lasted for decades.

33. I discussed in detail such evidence for Bavaria in Edward Shorter, "Towards a History of *La Vie Intime*: The Evidence of Cultural Criticism in Nineteenth-Century Bavaria," in Michael R. Marrus, ed., *The Emergence of Leisure* (New York: Harper and Row, 1974), pp. 38–68.

34. See, for example, Bayerisches Hauptstaatsarchiv, MI 46556, 1837.

35. Joseph Hazzi, *Statistische Aufschlüsse über das Herzogthum Baiern*, 11 vols. (Nürnberg, 1801–1808), III, pp. 193, 657.

36. Bayerisches Hauptstaatsarchiv, MI 15396.

37. Bayerisches Hauptstaatsarchiv, MI 46556, 1839.

Notes

38. Bayerisches Hauptstaatsarchiv, MI 52137.

39. Howls about declining morality were, of course, heard elsewhere than just Germany and France. See, for example, Henry Fielding's diatribe against the corruption of the lower orders through voluptuousness and luxury, within the discussion "Of too frequent and expensive diversions among the lower kind of people." See also the subsequent section, "Of drunkenness, a second consequences of luxury among the vulgar," in "An Enquiry into the Causes of the Late Increase of Robbers . . .," *The Works of Henry Fielding*, 10 vols. (London, 1806), X, pp. 349–367 *et seq*. Edgar S. Furniss cites numerous eighteenth-century English opinions on rising debauchery, immorality, indolence, and intemperance; see pp. 99–109 and appendix II ("The Moral Life Conditions of the English Laborer, 1660–1775") of Furniss, *The Position of the Laborer in a System of Nationalism: A Study in the Labor Theories of the Later English Mercantilists*, repr. (New York: Augustus Kelley, 1965; first ed., 1918).

40. Lépecq de la Cloture, *Collection d'observations sur les maladies*, p. 189.

41. Gabriel-Antoine-Joseph Hécart, *Précis historique et statistique sur la ville de Valenciennes* . . . (Valenciennes, 1825), p. 91.

42. Louis-René Villermé, *Tableau de l'état physique et morale des ouvriers employés dans les manufactures de coton, de laine et de soie*, 2 vols. (Paris, 1840), I, pp. 291–292.

Though complaints of this order were common, they were not universal. In some countrysides purity seems to have prevailed. "*L'amour* in rural communes is generally confined to marriage. Here the heart is much less hasty. Work in the fields holds back the girls' imaginations and the dangers of seduction. Being freer than the married women, young girls are permitted to go out a bit [*la fréquentation des garçons*] with boys, yet this does not give rise to the commonplace regrets of those countries where the roll of illegitimacy is so long, even though rural parents here commit the imprudence of letting their daughters take the cows to water.

"Love talk [*le langage galant*] in the countryside is as chaste as the behavior, and you wouldn't be any more likely to crack dirty jokes with our girls than with the daughters of the bourgeois.

"As a consequence, for every thousand girls in a rural canton, there probably aren't ten who don't preserve their virginity up to the altar." Barthélemy Chaix, *Préoccupations statistiques, géographiques, pittoresques et synoptiques du département des Hautes-Alpes* (Grenoble, 1845), p. 269; the author was subprefect from 1800–1815, thereafter a member of the *conseil général* of the department.

43. Jean-Louis Flandrin, "Mariage tardif et vie sexuelle: discussions et hypothèses de recherche," *Annales: ESC*, 27 (1972), *passim*.

44. Both Flandrin and E. H. Hare argue for an increase in masturbation in the seventeenth and early eighteenth centuries owing to the Catholic Church's repression of premarital intercourse in France and to Puritanism's austere morality in England. Hare mentions as well possible anxiety over venereal disease. Hare, "Masturbatory Insanity: the History of an Idea," *Journal of Mental Science*, 108 (1962), 1–25, esp. p. 12.

45. Hughes Maret, *Mémoire dans lequel on cherche à déterminer quelle influence les moeurs des François ont sur leur santé* (Amiens, 1772), pp. 61, 87.

46. Joseph Daquin, *Topographie médicale de la ville de Chambéry* (Chambéry, 1787), p. 89.

47. For overviews of the antimasturbation literature see Hare, "Masturbatory Insanity," *op cit.*, and Robert H. MacDonald, "The Frightful Consequences of Onanism: Notes on the History of a Delusion," *Journal of the History of Ideas*, 28 (1967), 423–431.

Notes

48. The 2nd edition of Salzmann's book is dated 1794, but its preface, bearing the location Schnepfenthal, was written in 1787. Christian Gotthilf Salzmann, *Ueber die heimlichen Sünden der Jugend*, (Frankfurt, 1794), p. 54. On the purity of the country-side versus the masturbatory cities, see also Dr. Moulet's ms., "Mémoire sur la topographie médicale de Montauban," 1786, Académie de médecine, SRM 181, and Louis Caradec, *Topographie médico-hygiénique du département du Finistère* (Brest, 1860), pp. 84–85.

49. Dr. Grassl, "Bäuerliche Liebe," *Zeitschrift für Sexualwissenschaft*, 13 (1927), 369–380, esp. p. 372.

50. Salzmann, *Ueber die heimlichen Sünden*, pp. 11, 14, 24, 54, 101, 103, 105, 107, 122.

51. Guillaune Daignan, *Tableau des variétés de la vie humaine* (Paris, 1786), pp. 328–329.

52. Wertheim, *Wien*, pp. 105–106, 120–121.

53. This portrait of nightcourting combines the accounts of K. Rob. V. Wikman, *Die Einleitung der Ehe* . . . (Abo: Abo Akademi, 1937), *passim*, and Sarmela, *Reciprocity Systems of the Rural Society*, pp. 155–180.

54. We know that nightcourting meant betrothal license for many couples if only because, in traditional Sweden and Denmark, up to half of all first legitimate children were conceived before marriage. Hertoft, "Le Comportement sexuel des jeunes danois," p. 71, and Wikman, *Einleitung der Ehe*, p. 287. But Wikman points out that, whereas the daughters of poorer peasants would begin intercourse with engagement, those of wealthier peasants could lie chastely for years next to their fiancés (pp. 285–287).

55. Wikman discusses German and Slavic nightcourting practices, *ibid.*, pp. 216–257; in these regions "individual" nightcourting tended to predominate over the collective variety, however. For a summary of the system in Denmark see Hertoft, "Le Comportement sexuel des jeunes danois," pp. 66–67. Michael Drake reprints the ethnographer Eilert Sundt's account of individual nightcourting in Michael Drake, *Population and Society in Norway, 1735–1865* (New York: Cambridge University Press, 1969), pp. 138–145.

56. Wikman, *Einleitung der Ehe*, p. 284.

57. Sarmela, *Reciprocity Systems of the Rural Society*, p. 164.

58. *Ibid.*, pp. 135–144.

59. Hertoft, "Le Comportement sexuel des jeunes danois," p. 72.

60. Baudouin *Le Maraichinage*, pp. 105–121 and *passim*; see also Boismoreau, *Coutumes médicales du bocage vendéen*, pp. 45–46; and Henri Baudrillart, *Les Populations agricoles de la France: Maine, Anjou* . . . (Paris, 1888), p. 186.

61. I am indebted to Etienne van de Walle for these data on illegitimate fertility.

62. Leon Kaczmarek and Guy Savelon, "Problemes matrimoniaux dans le ressort de l'officialité de Cambrai, 1670–1762: Les séparations de corps et de biens," mémoire de maîtrise under the direction of P. Deyon (Univ. de Lille 1971), p. 141; available through Microeditions Hachette.

63. Elard Hugo Meyer, *Badisches Volksleben* (Strasbourg, 1900), p. 193.

64. C.-H. Machard, *Essai sur la topographie médicale de la ville de Dole* [Jura] (Dole, 1823), p. 58.

65. See, for example, Leon Bernard, *The Emerging City: Paris in the Age of Louis XIV* (Durham: Duke University Press, 1970), pp. 180–183; P. Martell, "Zur Geschichte der Prostitution der Stadt Berlin," *Zeitschrift für Sexualwissenschaft*, 16 (1929–30), 133–145; and Jacques Solé, "Passion charnelle et société urbaine d'Ancien Régime: Amour vénal, amour libre et amour fou à Grenoble au milieu du règne de

Notes

Louis XIV," in *Annales de la Faculté des lettres et sciences humaines de Nice*, Nos. 9–10 (1969), pp. 211–232.

66. Such as is presented in Shorter, Knodel, van de Walle, "Decline of Non-Marital Fertility," p. 387.

67. The most sophisticated debunker, Phillips Cutright, has forced me to reflect at length about the "second sexual revolution" idea. Yet in this case I think the demographer's professional reflex of seeking first the most *un*spectacular explanation is inappropriate. Cutright, "The Teenage Sexual Revolution and the Myth of an Abstinent Past," pp. 24–31.

Other pooh-poohers, however, have been caught more flat-footed by recent trends. Ira Reiss, for example, has consistently represented the viewpoint that sexual behavior has not been changing, only people's willingness to talk about it. Reiss, "The Sexual Renaissance: A Summary and Analysis," *Journal of Social Issues*, 22 (1966), 123–137, esp. 126. And Erwin O. Smigel and Rita Seiden could still write in 1968, ". . . we have not had a recent or current sexual revolution in terms of behavior." Smigel and Seiden, "The Decline and Fall of the Double Standard," *Annals of the American Academy of Political Science*, March 1968, pp. 6–17, quote from p. 17.

68. United States Public Health Service, *Trends in Illegitimacy: United States, 1940–1965*, National Center for Health Statistics, Series 21, No. 15 (Washington: GPO, 1968), p. 3. Data from Kinsey's Institute of Sex Research show a slightly more rapid increase in premarital conceptions.

*Females with conception experience
before marriage (before age 25)*

DECADE OF BIRTH	PER CENT
1890–1899	3.3
1900–1909	7.0
1910–1919	9.4
1920–1929	10.9

See Paul H. Gebhard *et al.*, *Pregnancy, Birth and Abortion* (New York: Wiley, 1966; first published 1958), p. 70.

69. Prebridal pregnancies, as well as the general risk of out-of-wedlock conception, dropped off during the Depression to around a fourth of all births, increasing again after the Second World War. Sydney H. Croog, "Premarital Pregnancies in Scandinavia and Finland," *American Journal of Sociology*, 57 (1952), 358–365, esp. p. 361; Phillips Cutright, "Illegitimacy: Myths, Causes and Cures," p. 40.

70. See the string of references in C. Rauhe, *Die unehelichen Geburten als Sozialphänomen: Ein Beitrag zur Bevölkerungsstatistik Preussens* (Munich, 1912), p. 19; on Dresden for 1890–1894, Dr. Schneider, "Ueber voreheliche Schwängerung," *Jahrbücher für Nationalökonomie und Statistik*, 3rd ser., 10 (1895), 554–561, esp. p. 555, where 31 per cent of the wives of supervisors and small clerks were premaritally pregnant, 49 per cent of the wives of workers and apprentices. Thirty years later, among a roughly comparable population of Kiel shipyard workers, 44 per cent of the supervisors' wives were pregnant before marriage, 50 per cent of the skilled workers' wives, and 61 per cent of the unskilled workers' wives. Karl Heinz Koch, "Die Kinderzahlen der Arbeiter und Angestellten von Kieler Werften: Ein Beitrag zur Frage der unterschiedlichen Fortpflanzung," *Archiv für Rassen- und Gesellschaftsbiologie*, 31 (1937), 245–263, esp. p. 260. Within less "modern" settings, such as the village

of Remmesweiler, prebridal pregnancy advanced more rapidly, from 15 percent in 1900–1929 to 28 percent in 1930–1959. Jacques Houdaille, "La Population de Remmesweiler en Sarre aux XVIIIe et XIXe siècles," *Population*, 25 (1970), 1183–1191, esp. p. 1185.

71. Shorter, Knodel, van de Walle, "Decline of Non-Marital Fertility," p. 382.

72. Alfred C. Kinsey *et al.*, *Sexual Behavior in the Human Female* (New York: Bantam, 1965; first ed., 1953), pp. 298–301, esp. figure 50.

73. *Ibid.*, pp. 31–37.

74. This point is made in Daniel Scott Smith, "The Dating of the American Sexual Revolution: Evidence and Interpretation," reprinted in Michael Gordon, ed., *The American Family in Socio-Historical Perspective* (New York: St. Martin's Press, 1973), pp. 321–335.

75. Data collected in 1934 by Lewis Terman suggest that the swing towards non-virginity among both men and women had begun considerably sooner than the 1920s. Of the women who came of age towards 1900, 86 per cent said they had postponed sex until marriage; of those who matured towards 1910, 74 per cent, and so forth down the hill. Yet Terman's sample suffered the same middle-class–professional biases as Kinsey's. Terman, *Psychological Factors in Marital Happiness* (New York, 1939), p. 321.

76. The results of these surveys are conveniently drawn together in Gerald R. Leslie, *The Family in Social Context* (New York: Oxford University Press, 1967), pp. 388–389.

77. Virginity at marriage data from the French Institute of Public Opinion (L'Institut francais d'opinion publique–IFOP), *Patterns of Sex and Love: A Study of the French Woman and her Morals*, trans. Lowell Bair (New York: Crown, 1961), p. 109, "Simon" data from Pierre Simon *et al.*, *Rapport sur le comportement sexuel des francais* (Paris: Julliard-Charron, 1972), p. 224; survey conducted in 1970. Pre-bridal pregnancy data from J. Deville, *Structure des familles: enquête de 1962* série démographie et emploi, nrs. 13–14 (Paris: INSEE, 1972), p. 91.

During the 1960s the mean age of first female intercourse in France fell from twenty-two, where it had stayed in the 1930s, 1940s and 1950s, to around twenty. Simon, *Rapport sur le comportement sexuel des francais*, p. 201. Among the cohort of twenty to twenty-nine year-olds interviewed, 19.1 was the mean age at first coitus for women. Yet 20 per cent of this cohort was still virginal at the time of the survey, so the cohort's true mean age will turn out to be somewhat higher.

78. Cross-national illegitimacy rates for the years 1950, 1960, and 1965 are given in Phillips Cutright, "Economic Events and Illegitimacy in Developed Countries," *Journal of Comparative Family Studies*, 2 (1971), 33–53, esp. pp. 51–53. The rate represents the number of illegitimate births per 1,000 unmarried women age 15 to 44. Annual French illegitimacy rates for 1962–1969 are presented in the *Annuaire statistique de la France*, 1972 (Paris: INSEE, 1973), p. 29. The increase in the total rate is almost entirely the result of a rise in teenage illegitimacy.

79. Cutright, "Teenage Sexual Revolution," *passim*. On the balance between intercourse and fecundability in Australia, see K. G. Basavarajappa, "Pre-marital Pregnancies and Ex-nuptial Births in Australia, 1911–66," *Australian and New Zealand Journal of Sociology*, 5 (1969), 126–145, esp. p. 135.

80. Annual illegitimate fertility rates to 1968 are available in the *Statistical Abstract of the United States*, 1972, p. 51. In 1968 women 15 to 19 produced 47 per cent of all illegitimate live births. Age-specific illegitimacy rates to 1967 have been graphed in Abbott L. Ferriss, *Indicators of Change in the American Family* (New York: Russell Sage Foundation, 1970), p. 57, figure 25.

Notes

81. The number of prebridal pregnancies per 100 marriages for 1955, 1960, 1965, and 1970 is given in France Prioux-Marchal, "Les Conceptions prenuptiales en Europe occidentale depuis 1955," *Population*, 29 (1974), 61–88, esp. table 1, p. 63, and observations about Swedish and Danish illegitimate fertility, p. 66. Daniel Scott Smith presents premarital pregnancy data from the 1965 Current Population Survey in "The Dating of the American Sexual Revolution," table 3, p. 326. Of the women polled, 9.3 per cent of the 1940–1944 marriage cohort were pregnant at the time of wedlock, 20.4 per cent of the 1960–1964 cohort.

82. The French "Rapport Simon" and H. L. Zetterberg's *Om sexuallivet i Sverige* (Stockholm: Nordiska Bokhandeln, 1969) are exceptional in asking different age groups of the population about their premarital sexual experiences.

83. Birgitta Linnér, *Sex and Society in Sweden* (New York: Harper & Row, 1972; first ed. 1967), p. 19. Zetterberg found that of the generation of women born in 1905–1935, 68 per cent were nonvirginal before marriage, of those born in 1935–1950 fully 86 per cent were nonvirginal, cited in Hertoft, "Le Comportement sexual des jeunes danois," p. 81. In an across-the-board survey of the Stockholm population done in 1966–1967, Maj-Briht Bergström-Walan and collaborators discovered a trend in the 1960s towards earlier ages at first coitus: whereas only 2 per cent of the twenty-five-year-olds had experienced intercourse at age fourteen, 7 per cent of the sixteen-year-olds had done so (but 11 per cent of the seventeen-year-olds). Almost 80 per cent of the less-educated women in the sample had been sexually active by age eighteen, about 55 per cent of the better-educated ones. Bergström-Walan, "Jeunesse suédoise des grandes villes," pp. 177–180.

84. Harold T. Christensen and Christina F. Gregg, "Changing Sex Norms in America and Scandinavia," *Journal of Marriage and the Family*, 32 (1970), 616–627, esp. p. 621.

85. John F. Kantner and Melvin Zelnik, "Sexual Experience of Young Unmarried Women in the United States," *Family Planning Perspectives*, Vol. 4, No. 4 (October, 1972), pp. 9–19, esp. p. 10, table 1; Kinsey, *Sexual Behavior in the Human Female*, p. 286.

86. Vance Packard, *The Sexual Wilderness: The Contemporary Upheaval in Male-Female Relationships* (New York: David McKay, 1968), pp. 160–162.

87. Cited in F. Ivan Nye and Felix M. Berardo, *The Family: Its Structure and Interaction* (New York: Macmillan, 1973), p. 196.

88. Robert R. Bell and Jay B. Chaskes, "Premarital Sexual Experience Among Coeds, 1958 and 1968," *Journal of Marriage and the Family*, 32 (1970), 81–88, esp. p. 83. A more recent study of attitudes shows continuing liberality, James W. Croake and Barbara James, "A Four Year Comparison of Premarital Sexual Attitudes," *Journal of Sex Research*, 9 (1973), 91–96.

89. Christensen-Gregg, "Changing Sex Norms," p. 621.

90. Reported in the *Hartford Courant*, 12 August 1973, p. 24; I am indebted to Daniel Scott Smith for this reference.

91. These data have been kindly supplied by F. M. Barrett, from his unpublished paper, "Sexual Experience, Birth Control Usage, and Sex Education: A Study of Students at the University of Toronto" (1974). Female non-virginity was almost identical 44 (per cent) in a comparable Scottish undergraduate population surveyed in 1971. C. McCance and D. J. Hall, "Sexual Behaviour and Contraceptive Practice of Unmarried Female Undergraduates at Aberdeen University," *British Medical Journal*, 17 June 1972, 694–700.

92. Worker story from Robert P. Neuman, "Industrialization and Sexual Behavior: Some Aspects of Working-Class Life in Imperial Germany," in Robert Bezucha, ed.,

Modern European Social History (Lexington, Mass.: D.C. Heath, 1972), pp. 270–298, esp. p. 280. Toilet walls and hands in pockets from A. Wolff, *Untersuchungen über die Kindersterblichkeit: medicinisch-statistischer Beitrag zur öffentlichen Gesundheitspflege unter Berücksichtigung der Verhältnisse in Erfurt* (Erfurt, 1874), pp. 63–64.

93. Schmidt and Sigusch, *Arbeiter-Sexualität*, pp. 80, 123; the authors interviewed some students as a control group.

94. Kinsey, *Sexual Behavior in the Human Female*, p. 180; *Sexual Behavior in the Human Male* (Philadelphia: Saunders, 1948), p. 96.

95. Kinnér, *Sex and Society in Sweden*, p. 24; in Denmark 93 per cent of all boys polled in a 1963–1964 survey said they masturbated, four fifths of them having begun before age sixteen. Hertoft, "Le Comportement sexuel des jeunes danois," p. 77. In postwar Finland, 90 per cent of "educated" youth masturbated; only 60 per cent, however, of those who had received only an elementary-school education. Yrjo Raivio, "Masturbation and Premarital Intercourse among Present-day Finnish Male Youths," *International Journal of Sexology*, 7 (1953), 73–74.

96. Simon, *Rapport sur le comportement sexuel des français*, p. 262.

97. Kinsey, *Sexual Behavior in the Human Female*, p. 151; Simon, *ibid.*, p. 263.

98. The "little finger" reference is from Dr. E. Bogros, *A Travers le Morvan: moeurs, types, scènes et passages* (Château-Chinn, 1873), p. 43. Jean-Louis Flandrin brought this work to my attention.

99. Kinsey, *Sexual Behavior in the Human Male*, p. 370; *Sexual Behavior in the Human Female*, pp. 257–258.

100. Schmidt and Sigusch, *Arbeiter-Sexualität*, pp. 55, 127.

101. Schofield, *Sexual Behaviour of Young People*, pp. 45, 50.

102. Eleanore B. Luckey and Gilbert D. Nass, "A Comparison of Sexual Attitudes and Behavior in an International Sample," *Journal of Marriage and the Family*, 31 (1969), 364–379, esp. p. 374.

103. Christian Pouyez, *Une Communauté rurale d'Artois: Isbergues (1598–1826)*, Lille III thesis, 1972, p. 95.

104. Lottin, "Naissances illégitimes," p. 310.

105. K. F. H. Marx, *Göttingen in medicinischer . . . Hinsicht* (Göttingen, 1824), p. 173.

106. William Acton, "Observations on Illegitimacy in the London Parishes of St. Marylebone, St. Pancras, and St. George's, Southward, during the Year 1857," *Journal of the Statistical Society of London*, 22 (1859), 491–505, esp. p. 493, For eighty-nine women no occupation was stated, yet we have no cause to assume that such women clustered in the upper orders.

107. Marie-Hélène Jouan, "Les Originalités démographiques d'un bourg artisanal normand au XVIIIe siècle: Villedieu-les-Poëles (1711–1790)," *Annales de démographie historique*, 1969, 87–124, esp. p. 103; Molinier, "Enfants trouvés Languedoc," p. 457; Camille Bloch, *L'Assistance et l'état en France à la veille de la Révolution* (Paris, 1908), p. 104.

108. Dr. Schneider, "Ueber voreheliche Schwängerung," *Jahrbuch für Nationalökonomie und Statistik*, 3rd ser., 10 (1895), 554–561, esp. p. 555. Figures include both prebridal pregnancy and illegitimacy.

109. Lange, *Unehelichen Geburten in Baden*, pp. 95*–97*.

110. For example, Beth Berkov and Paul W. Shipley, *Illegitimate Births in California, 1966 and 1967* (State of California Department of Public Health pamphlet, 1971), p. 23; Daniel Scott Smith and Michael S. Hindus, "Premarital Pregnancy

in America, 1640–1971: An Overview and Interpretation," *Journal of Interdisciplinary History*, 5 (1975), 537–570, tables 2 and 3.

The number of premarital pregnancies per 100 marriages in France for all age groups of women combined ran as follows in a 1962 survey:

Peasants	11
Farm laborers	20
Shopowners and employers	11
Free professions and executives	8
Supervisers (cadres moyens)	11
Employees	14
Workers	20
Overall	15/100

Jean-Claude Deville, *Structure des familles: Enquête de 1962*, No. 66 des Collections de l'INSEE, série D (Paris: INSEE, 1972), table 36, pp. 92–93.

Chapter 4

1. For descriptions see Joseph Schaible, *Geschichte des badischen Hanauerlandes, nebst einer medizinisch-statistischen Topographie* (Karlsruhe, 1855), p. 200; Elard Hugo Meyer, *Badisches Volksleben* (Strasbourg, 1900), p. 164.

2. The account from Marcel Badouin, *Le Maraichinage* (Paris, 1932), pp. 51–52.

3. Xavier Thiriat, *La Vallée de Cleurie,* (Mirecourt, 1869), p. 309.

4. Matti Sarmela, *Reciprocity Systems of the Rural Society in the Finnish–Karelian Area* . . . (Helsinki: Suomalainin Tiedekatemia, 1969), pp. 114–127.

5. General observations about Europe based on K. Rob. V. Wikman, *Die Einleitung der Ehe* . . . (Abo: Abo Akademie, 1937), esp. the map on p. 264. For a French youth-group example see Arnold Van Gennep, *Manuel de folklore francais*, I(1) (Paris: A. Picard, 1937–58), pp. 199–200.

6. The veillée has, to my knowledge, never been studied systematically by historians, and the few folkloric studies that attempt general statements are inadequate. This account is based on numerous French and German local studies.

7. See for example, Van Gennep, *Manuel de folklore francais*, I(1), p. 252.

8. Sarmela, *Reciprocity Systems of the Rural Society*, pp. 64–70.

9. Emile Violet, *Les Veillées en commun et les réunions d'hiver* (Macon, 1942), pp. 7–8.

10. Cambry, *Description du département de l'Oise*, 2 vols. (Paris, 1803), I, p. 260; describes commune of Anseauvilliers.

11. de Verneilh, *Statistique générale de la France* . . . *département du Mont-Blanc* (Paris, 1807), p. 301.

12. C. Dupin, *Mémoire statistique du département des Deux-Sevres* (Paris, 1804), pp. 210–211.

13. For an example of veillées, the purpose of which seems more dancing than working, see "Statistique de la Charente, 1801," Archives nationales F20 172.

14. Varagnac states explicitly: "the principal attraction of the veillées was to stimulate or promote *relations courtoises* between young men and women." André Varagnac, *Civilisation traditionnelle et genres de vie* (Paris, Albin Michel, 1948), pp. 96–97.

15. On Russia and Finland, Sarmela, *Reciprocity Systems of the Rural Society,* pp. 114–121.

16. See Rudolf Braun, *Industrialisierung und Volksleben* . . . (Erlenbach–Zurich: Eugen Rentsch, 1960), for an account of "Lichtstubeten," pp. 120–122.

17. Marx, *Göttingen,* p. 174.

18. Violet, *Veillées en commun,* p. 13.

19. Abel Hugo, *La France pittoresque,* 3 vols. (Paris, 1835), I, p. 170.

20. Richard Weiss, *Volkskunde der Schweiz: Grundriss* (Erlenbach-Zurich: Eugen Rentsch, 1946), p. 216.

21. The old ways haven't disappeared entirely, for among peasant families of the Wallonian Brabant, girls aged fourteen to twenty are still today accompanied by a relative when they go out dancing. Yet such cases are rare enough to be curiosities. A. Doppagne, "Enquête en Brabant Wallon . . ." Institut de Sociologie de l'Université libre de Bruxelles, *Document de Travail* No. III/1 (March 1970), 8.

22. The following discussion owes much to Arnold Van Gennep's great compilation, *Manuel de folklore francais.* And though Van Gennep is at times distressingly ahistorical, his work is nonetheless indispensable for historical ethnography in France.

23. *Ibid.,* I(3), pp. 1105–1107.

24. *Ibid.,* I(3), p. 1070.

25. *Ibid.,* I(3), pp. 1113–1114.

26. Henri Lepage and Ch. Charton, *Le Département des Vosges: Statistique, historique et administrative* (Nancy, 1845), I, p. 713.

27. Van Gennep, *Manuel de folklore français,* I(4), p. 2035.

28. *Varagnac, Civilisation traditionnelle,* pp. 62–63, 74.

29. Sarmela, *Reciprocity Systems of the Rural Society,* table on p. 131; Anton Birlinger, *Aus Schwaben: Sagen, Legenden, Sitten,* Vol. II (Aalen: Scientia reprint, 1969; first ed. 1874), pp. 62–65.

30. Jacques-Antoine Delpon, *Statistique du département du Lot* (Paris, 1831), I, p. 208; See also Dieudonné, *Statistique du département du Nord* (Douai, 1804), I, p. 98.

31. Van Gennep, *Manuel de folklore français,* I(4), pp. 1564–1565.

32. *Ibid.,* pp. 1686–1687.

33. *Ibid.,* p. 1866.

34. *Ibid.,* p. 1907. The account is from 1909.

35. Alain Molinier, "Enfants trouvés, enfants abandonnés et enfants illégitimes en Languedoc aux XVIIe et XVIIIe siècles," in Société de démographie historique, ed., *Sur la population française au XVIIIe et au XIXe siècles: Hommage à Marcel Reinhard* (Paris: SDH, 1973), p. 464.

36. Meyer, *Badisches Volksleben,* p. 229.

37. Delpon, *Lot,* I, p. 206.

38. Auguste Grise, *Coutumes du Trièves au XIXe siècle: souvenirs de ma jeunesse* (Grenoble, 1939), p. 28; Account of the 1880s.

39. For examples see Edward Shorter, "Towards a History of *La Vie Intime*: The Evidence of Cultural Criticism in Nineteenth-Century Bavaria," in Michaèl R. Marrus, ed., *The Emergence of Leisure* (New York: Harper & Row, 1974), pp. 38–68.

40. Sarmela takes full note of the evolution in Finland, *Reciprocity Systems of the Rural Society,* pp. 33–44.

41. Sapin-Sylvoz, "Les Rapports sexuels illégitimes au XVIIIème siècle à Grenoble d'après les déclarations de grossesses," travail d'études under the direction of J. Solé, Université Grenoble," n.d., pp. 96–97; and Annie K. Thivollier and Pierre Laroque,

"Filles-mères à Lyon au XVIIIe siècle," mémoire de maîtrise, under the direction of Maurice Garden (Université Lyon, 1970–1971), p. 61.

42. Sapin-Sylvoz, "Rapports sexuels Grenoble," pp. 77, 82.

43. Dupont, *Arrondissement de Lille*, pp. 79–80.

44. Sapin-Sylvoz, "Rapports sexuels Grenoble," pp. 71–73.

45. Van Gennep doubts that arranged marriage ever occurred widely in France, which fits with his larger argument that romance is a traditional posture. He sees intimacy draining from nineteenth-century courtship with the diffusion of the dogma of Immaculate Conception. ". . . dans les moeurs françaises, même avant la période romantique, l'amour a toujours été regardé comme respectable. . . . Il faut admettre l'existence d'une atmosphère sentimentale qui s'oppose à la prétendue domination absolue des parents, et plus spécialement du père." I(1), 236. Immaculate Conception argument I(1), 288.

46. Monnier, *Moeurs et usages singuliers du peuple dans le Jura* (Lons-le-Saunier, 1823), p. 10.

47. Louis Guibert, *La Famille limousine d'autre fois d'après les testaments et la coutume* (Limoges, 1883), p. 89.

48. Henriette Dussourd, *Au même pot et au même feu . . .* (Moulins: Pottier, 1962), p. 89.

49. Camille Ragut, *Statistique du département de Saône-et-Loire*, 5 vols. (Macon, 1838), I, p. 291.

50. Lascoulx-Germignai, "De la topographie médicale . . . du bas limousin," 1787, ms. in Académie de Médecine, SRM 181; see also Louis Texier-Olivier, *Statistique générale de la France, département de la Haute-Vienne*, (Paris, 1808), p. 88.

51. Yet in 1831 the Haute-Vienne department had one of the lowest mean female ages at marriage in France (21.7 years), so the custom clearly had some importance. I am obliged to Etienne van de Walle for this information.

52. Henri Pourrat, *Ceux d'Auvergne, types et coutumes* (Paris, 1928), p. 68. I owe this reference and an eloquent warning to watch out for my own cultural blinkers to Jean-Louis Flandrin.

53. For instances of go-betweens see Martine Segalen, *Nuptialité et alliance* (Paris: Maisonneuve, 1972), p. 114; Van Gennep, *Manuel de folklore français*, I(1) pp. 269–271; E. Bogros, *A travers le Morvand* (Château-Chinon, 1873), p. 44, on "croque-avoine."

54. Hugo, *France pittoresque*, II, 50.

55. "Statistique de la Charente," ms. of 1801, Archives nationales F20 172.

56. Bogros, *Morvand*, p. 45.

57. Van Gennep, *Manuel de folklore francais*, I(1) pp. 272–273.

58. de Caila, "Recherches sur les moeurs des habitans des Landes de Bordeaux . . . dans le Captalat de Buch," *Mémoires de l'académie celtique*, 4 (1809), 70–82, esp. 78. Jean-Louis Flandrin kindly supplied this reference.

59. Dupin, *Deux-Sevres*, p. 77.

60. Bogros, *Morvand*, p. 44.

61. The list from Van Gennep, *Manuel de folklore francais*, I(1), pp. 264–265.

62. I'm dubious that even this evidence represents a solidly "traditional" orientation, because it borrows so heavily from the nineteenth century. Before that time appropriate ethnographic descriptions are simply not available.

63. Déribier-du-Chatelet, *Dictionnaire statistique ou histoire Cantal, du département du Cantal*, 5 Vols. (Aurillac 1852–1857), II, pp. 134–135; for an account of the manure-pile inspection in Germany, called the "B'schau," see Meyer, *Badisches Volksleben*, p. 256.

64. Pourrat, *Auvergne*, p. 72.

65. See, for example, the story Susan Carol Rogers tells of Christine Motelet, a farmer's daughter in the eastern French village of "St. Martin of today." She decided to drop the young peasant who was courting her (of whom her father greatly approved) for a factory worker whom she liked but to whom her father was "violently opposed." Nor did the father want to pay for more than one wedding banquet. Aided by her mother, the daughter rode right over the father's opposition and ended up with the worker and two banquets to boot. Rogers, "Female Forms of Power and the Myth of Male Dominance: A Model of Female/Male Interaction," circulated paper, 1973, p. 31.

66. Meyer, *Badisches Volksleben*, p. 193.

67. Charles Perron, *Les Franc-Comtois* . . . (Besançon, 1892), p. 85.

68. Theodore Zeldin points out, on the basis of medical examinations for induction into military service, that around one-third of all marriageable men were in some way physically deformed, so the women had some eye-closing to do too. Zelden, *France, 1848–1945*, vol. 1: *Ambition, Love and Politics* (Oxford: Clarendon Press, 1973), p. 304.

69. Perron, *Franc-Comtois*, p. 84.

70. Hugo, *France pittoresque*, II, p. 82; Ille-et-Vilaine department.

71. Joseph Hazzi, *Statistische Aufschlüsse über das Herzogthum Baiern*, 11 vols. Nürnberg, 1801–1808), III(3), p. 1130.

72. Bayerische Staatsbibliothek, Handschrift. Cod. Germ. 6874(2), Beilage 2, 1859.

73. Sarmela, *Reciprocity Systems of the Rural Society*, pp. 188–190.

74. Boniface Breton, *Le village, histoire, morale, politique et pittoresque de Courrières* [Pas-de-Calais] (Arras, 1857), pp. 410–411.

75. Ange Guépin and Charles-Eugène Bonamy, *Nantes au XIXe siècle: Statistique, topographique, industrielle et morale* (Nantes, 1835), pp. 478–479.

76. Louis-Sébastien Mercier, *Tableau de Paris*, rev. ed., 12 vols. (Amsterdam, 1782–1788), I, pp. 80–82.

77. Sapin-Sylvoz, "Rapports sexuels Grenoble," p. 78.

	1677–1735 PER CENT	1735–1790 PER CENT
Friendship (*amitié*)	33	5
Tenderness (*tendresse*)	23	11
Inclination-*penchant*	23	20
Love (*amour*)	16	25
Passion	0	27
Affection	6	11
TOTAL	100	100
	(N = 31)	(N = 44)

78. Gérard Bouchard, *La Village immobile* . . . (Paris: Plon, 1972), p. 375. "Ma très cher ami je tens brass le tous mon quiar je ne saurez pas tou bliez tous les joure je pense a tois je souète que tus soit de mem poure moy Marque mois ta fason de panser Si tus me veux faire plaisir je suis ton bonamis jacques gepien."

79. Etienne-Michel Massé, *Mémoire historique et statistique sur le canton de la Ciotat, département des Bouches-du-Rhône* (Marseille, 1842), p. 240.

Notes

80. Emmanuel Labat, *En Gascogne: L'Abandon de la terre (Extrait de la Revue des Deux-Mondes, 1er août 1910)* (Agen, 1911), p. 27.

81. Charles Tilly, *The Vendée* (Cambridge: Harvard University Press, 1964), p. 94, table 10.

82. Nels W. Mogensen, "La Stratification sociale dans le pays d'Auge au XVIIIe siècle," *Annales de Normandie*, 23 (1973), pp. 211–249, esp. pp. 218–219.

83. See Hubert Charbonneau, *Tourouvre-au-Perche au XVIIe et XVIIIe siècles* (Paris: PUF, 1970), p. 88; Marcel Couturier, *Recherches sur les structures sociales de Châteaudun, 1525–1789* (Paris: SEVPEN, 1969) pp. 138–139. Donald Macleod, in an unpublished University of Toronto seminar paper on the Baden village of Wollbach, finds a "clear propensity for farmers to marry farmers' daughters." Macleod, "A Report on the Wollbach Ortssippenbuch: The Farmer and Birth Control," (1972), p. 7. Within various Norwegian villages towards the mid-nineteenth century, propertied peasant bridegrooms took the daughters of other propertied farmers three fourths of the time; propertyless crofters ended up with propertyless brides four fifths of the time. Michael Drake, *Population and Society in Norway, 1735–1865* (New York: Cambridge University Press, 1969), table 6.1, p. 135.

84. Segalen, *Nuptialité et alliance*, table 34, pp. 77–78.

85. Leslie, *The Family in Social Context* (New York: Oxford University Press, 1967), pp. 364–365 and 425–427, offers an excellent review of this literature.

86. Girard, *Le Choix du conjoint: Une enquête psycho-sociologique en France*, new edition (Paris: PUF, 1974), p. 79; Claude Henryon and Edmond Lambrechts, *Le Mariage en Belgique: Etude sociologique* (Brussels: Editions Vie duvrière, 1968), p. 57.

87. G. A. Harrison *et al.*, "Social Class and Marriage Patterns in Some Oxfordshire Populations," *Journal of Biosocial Science*, 3 (1971), 1–12, esp. p. 7.

88. Macleod, "Ortssippenbuch Wollbach," p. 6.

89. The numerous American local studies that might have contributed to this question persist in taking overly short time periods, thus making it impossible to separate the waves from the ripples. For example, see the contributions in Stephan Thernstrom and Richard Sennett, *Nineteenth-Century Cities: Essays in the New Urban History* (New Haven: Yale University Press, 1969).

90. R. F. Peel, "Local Intermarriage and the Stability of Rural Populations in the English Midlands," *Geography*, 27 (1942), 22–30, esp. p. 27, figure 2.

91. P. J. Perry, "Working-Class Isolation and Mobility in Rural Dorset, 1837–1936: A Study of Marriage Distances," Institute of British Geographers, *Transactions*, No. 46 (March, 1969), 121–141, esp. p. 124.

92. David Sabean, "Household Formation and Geographical Mobility: A Family Register Study for a Württemberg Village, 1760–1900," *Annales de démographie historique* (1970), 274–294, esp. p. 280, table 3.

93. Couturier, *Châteaudun*, pp. 132–136, for example; but in Lyon during the first half of the eighteenth century only a third of the men born in the parishes of Saint-Pierre and Saint-Saturnin seem to have married there, if I read correctly the figures Maurice Garden presents in *Lyon et les Lyonnais . . .* (Paris: Les Belles-Lettres, 1970), p. 89. As for the countryside. Fresel-Lozey reports of a Bearnais village that almost all local men married local women. Michel Fresel-cozey. *Histoire démographique d'un village en Bearn: Bilheres-d'Ossau, XVIIIe-XIXe siècles* (Bordeaux: Eds. Bière, 1969), p. 76; Pierre Valmary, *Familles paysannes au XVIIIe siècle en Bas-Quercy* (Paris: PUF, 1965), pp. 109–111. Valmary finds some outsiders marrying into villages in Bas-Quercy, but from nearby, *Familles paysannes*, pp. 109–111; yet Jean Ganiage reports of the Ile-de-France substantial numbers of women who didn't marry locally, *Trois villages de l'Ile-de-France au XVIIIe siècle* (Paris: PUF, 1973), p. 60.

Notes

94. Alain Gintrac, "Histoire démographique d'un village corrénzien:: Soudeilles (1610–1859)," [summary of thesis], *Dh: Bulletin d'information*, no. 6 (April, 1972), 9–11; Segalen, *Nuptialité et alliance: Vraiville*, p. 92.

Such statistics are not perfect. Because their compilers often neglect to tell us how the percentage of locally-born men (or women) marrying people who lived outside changed, we may be cutting into changes in migration, seasonal labor, or other circumstances that affect the sheer number of non-locally born available in a place for acquaintanceship. These proportions are also subject to the vagaries of changing age distributions among men and women, so that if at one time a number of men reach outwards for women, it may simply be because the scythe of mortality had spared too few potential brides. One would expect such shifts in the sex ratio to wash out over the very long haul, but the matter belongs to that long agenda still awaiting investigation.

95. Leslie, *Family in Social Context*, pp. 449–452.

96. Girard, *Choix du conjoint*, p. 64.

97. See the explanation offered by the Norwegian ethnologist Eilert Sundt, quoted in Drake, *Population and Society in Norway*, pp. 139–140.

98. Van Gennep cites Paul Sébillot's explanation of younger men marrying older women in Brittany: "Il n'est pas rare de voir de tout jeunes gens épouser des filles qui ont quinze ans de plus qu'eux. De cette façon, ils sont moins exposés à avoir beaucoup d'enfants." *Manuel de folklore francais*, I(1), p. 247.

99. "Il arrive aussi, qu'après vingt ans de service, une servante se trouve avoir quelques épargnes. Elle passe pour un bon parti; les beaux yeux de sa cassette donnent dans la visière d'un jeune artisan yvrogne, débauché, qui vient lui en conter. La vieille servante se met l'amour en tête, le jeune homme lui plait, le mariage est d'abord conclu." Then things fall to pieces. Jean-Louis Murat, *Mémoire sur l'état de la population dans le pays de Vaud* [canton of Berne] (Yverdon, 1766), p. 91.

100. A petition of the Nurnberg joiners, tinsmiths, and instrument-makers in 1848 complained that many journeymen were able to become master craftsmen only by marrying the aged widows of their colleagues. "There could be no talk of love, of mutual respect. Young journeymen perhaps twenty years of age married sixty-year-old widows, hoping to be rid of these creatures soon through death. And if their plans went awry, these unhappy marriages would be plagued by personal mistreatment and such." Bayerisches Hauptstaatsarchiv, MH 6133, 31 March.

101. For recent trends in France and Britain see P. R. Cox, "International Variation in the Relative Ages of Brides and Grooms," *Journal of Biosocial Science*, 2 (1970), 111–121.

102. Jacques Solé, "Passion charnelle . . . a Grenoble . . .," *Annales de la Faculté des lettres et sciences humaines de Nice*, Nos. 9–10 (1969), p. 226.

103. An abbreviated version of Jacques Depauw's "Amour illégitime et société à Nantes au XVIIIe siècle," appeared in *Annales: ESC*, 27 (1972), 1155–1182; the paper was made available in fuller form by Microéditions Hachette (Paris, 1973). Seducer data from Hachette edition, p. 191; "repeater" data from the article, p. 1175; "promises of marriage" data from article, p. 1166.

104. Several other studies present data on the social distance between the "illegitimate" couple, without however making time series available. See Alain Molinier, "Enfants trouvés . . . en Languedoc . . .," in Société de démographie historique, ed., *Sur la population française au XVIIIe et au XIXe siècles: Hommage à Marcel Reinhard* (Paris: SDH, 1973), p. 467, for eighteenth-century Annonay; Sapin-Sylvoz, "Rapports sexuels illégitimes au XVIII siècle à Grenoble," p. 59 of ms. And for Norwegian

Notes

data (1897–1898) see Theodor Geiger, "Zur Statistik der Unehelichen," *Allgemeines Statistisches Archiv*, 11 (1918–1919), pp. 212–220, esp. pp. 216–218.

105. Amic, *Considérations médico-topographiques sur la ville de Brignoles* (Brignoles, 1837), pp. 47–48.

106. Meyer, *Badisches Volksleben*, pp. 171–172.

107. Boismoreau, *Bocage vendée*, p. 46.

108. Grise, *Triéves*, pp. 26–29. Renate Reiter describes how the car has transformed courtship in southern France since World War II by creating a region-wide market. Reiter, "Modernization in the South of France: The Region and Beyond," *Anthropological Quarterly*, 45 (1972), 35–53, esp. p. 47.

109. Readers who wish to verify this proposition might look through three or four years of the family–sociology industry's house organ, *The Journal of Marriage and the Family*.

110. Birgitta Linnér, *Sex and Society in Sweden*, (New York: Harper & Row, 1972; first ed. 1967), p. 26; Girard, *Choix du conjoint*, pp. 98ff.: Robert C. Sorensen, *Adolescent Sexuality in Contemporary America* (New York: World, 1973), p. 53.

111. On the basis of research conducted early in the 1960s, Ira Reiss has described one widespread pattern of American premarital behavior as "permissiveness with affection," in which intercourse is accepted as long as romantic love is involved. We may infer from this account that women who change partners frequently are deemed to lack attachment to any given partner and are thus considered "promiscuous." Reiss presented this analysis in *Premarital Sexual Standards in America: A Sociological Investigation of the Relative Social and Cultural Integration of American Sexual Standards* (New York: Free Press, 1960), pp. 126–145, and supplied supporting data in *The Social Context of Premarital Sexual Permissiveness* (New York: Holt, Rinehart and Winston, 1967), pp. 25–26, 74–88. Eugene Kanin writes, in a 1960s study of university men, "The definition of a female as being sexually experienced is sufficient in some male groups—particularly where the double standard prevails—to render her a legitimate target for any type of sexual approach." Kanin, "Reference Groups and Sex Conduct Norm Violations," *Sociological Quarterly*, 8 (1967), 495–504, esp. p. 502.

112. P. Hertoft, "Le Comportement sexuel des jeunes danois," in Maj-Briht Bergström-Walan *et al.*, eds., *L'éxperience scandinave*, French trans. (Paris: Laffont, 1971), p. 100. Although it was probably true before that time, the proposition that young people bend easily to peer-group pressures in their sexual lives did not find strong support from survey data in the 1960s and 1970s. Michael Schofield did discover that sexually experienced English adolescents were more likely to subscribe to the "teenage mythology" and to go out in groups than the unexperienced (*The Sexual Behaviour of Young People*, [Harmondsworth: Pelican, 1968], pp. 80, 204), but other research failed to uncover a very cohesive subcultural matrix for teenage sexual adventure. Kanin found that sexually aggressive young men were more likely to report peer-group pressures than nonaggressive men, but the differences were slight, and the sample small (32 per cent of the nonaggressive experienced "little" pressure from their friends "for new sex experience," 33 percent of the aggressive did so; variation was noticeable only at the ends of the scale.) Peter Davis concluded, of a sample of patients in a V.D. clinic in Christchurch, New Zealand, that "individuals with unusually high levels of sexual activity are less likely to have been exposed to a sex-salient peer group environment," yet the peer group remained more important than the family in shaping the sexual attitudes of his respondents. Davis, "Contextual Sex-Saliency and Sexual Activity: The Relative Effects of Family and Peer Group in the Sexual Socialization Process," *Journal of Marriage and the Family*, 36 (1974), 196–202, quote from p. 196.

113. Daniel Scott Smith, "Parental Power and Marriage Patterns: An Analysis of Historical Trends in Hingham, Massachusetts," *Journal of Marriage and the Family*, 35 (1973), 419–428, esp. p. 425.

114. Marvin R. Koller, "Some Changes in Courtship Behavior in Three Generations of Ohio Women," *American Sociological Review*, 16 (1951), 366–370, esp. p. 367, table 1.

115. Sorensen, *Adolescent Sexuality in Contemporary America*, p. 388.

116. *Ibid.*, p. 69.

117. *Ibid.*, p. 76.

118. Alfred E. Kinsey *et al.*, *Sexual Behavior in the Human Female*, (New York: Bantam, 1965; first ed., 1953), p. 336, table 78.

119. Sorensen, *Adolescent Sexuality in Contemporary America*, p. 433, table 343, p. 441, table 404.

120. *Ibid.*, p. 198 and p. 405, table 168.

121. Pierre Simon *et al.*, *Rapport sur le comportement sexuel des francais* (Paris: Juillard-Charron, 1972), p. 224.

122. Gunter Schmidt and Volkman Sigusch, *Arbeiter-Sexualität* (Neuwied: Luchterhand, 1971), pp. 85, 99.

123. Harold T. Christensen and Christina F. Gregg, "Changing Sex Norms in America and Scandinavia," *Journal of Marriage and the Family* 32 (1970) p. 624; note that this survey found no change in the cumulative number of partners among undergraduates at a midwestern American university, but discovered a drift towards serial monogamy among the Mormons!

124. Schofield, *Sexual Behaviour of Young People*, pp. 79, 231, 259.

Chapter 5

1. See especially Philippe Ariès, *L'Enfant et la vie familiale sous l'ancien régime*, rev. ed. (Paris: Seuil, 1973), ch. 2; Jean-Louis Flandrin, "L'Attitude à l'égard du petit enfant et les conduites sexuelles dans la civilisation occidentale: Structures anciennes et évolution," *Annales de démographie historique*, 1973, pp. 143–210; and Lloyd deMause, "The Evolution of Childhood," *History of Childhood Quarterly*, 1 (1974), 503–575. DeMause and Ariès find themselves, however, in sharp disagreement on several points.

2. Ariès, *L'Enfant et la vie familiale*, the first edition of which was translated into English as *Centuries of Childhood: A Social History of Family Life* (London: Jonathan Cape, 1962).

3. See, for example, Wertheim, *Versuch einer medicinischen Topographi von Wien*, (Vienna, 1810), p. 103, and Jean-F. Deffis, *Hygiene de l'arrorndissement de Pau* (Pau, 1848), p. 102, for peasants.

4. Christian Pfeufer, "Ueber das Verhalten der Schwangeren, Gebährenden und Wöchnerinnen auf dem Lande, und ihre Behandlungsart der Neugeborenen und Kinder in den ersten Lebensjahren," *Jahrbuch der Staatsarzneikunde*, 3 (1810), 43–74, esp. p. 63.

5. Wertheim, *Wien*, p. 101.

6. G. Cless, *Versuch einer medicinischen Topographie . . . Stuttgart* (Stuttgart, 1815), p. 40, "heftiges Hin- und Herschaukeln."

7. Documented in Pfeufer, "Verhalten der Schwangeren," pp. 67–69, and in Emile Bancel, *Topographie médicale et hygiène de l'arrondissement de Toul* (Toul, 1866), p. 78.

Notes

8. Didelot, "Description topographique et médicale des montagnes de la Vôge," in Société royale de médicine, *Histoire [et Mémoires] de la S.R.M.*, 1777–1778 (Paris, 1780), pp. 107–138, esp. p. 138.

9. J. A. Mourgue, *Essai de statistique* [Montpellier] (Paris, 1801), p. 27, n. 2. "Le tems auquel on élève les vers à soie, est le tems auquel on peuple le plus le paradis."

10. Cambry, *Description du département de l'Oise*, 2 vols. (Paris, 1803), II, p. 142.

11. I. Schlesinger, *Medicinische topographie . . . Pesth-Ofen* (Pesth, 1840), p. 92.

12. J.-B.-Denis Bucquet, *Topographie médicale de la ville de Laval: Manuscrit inédit de 1808* (Angers, 1894), p. 43.

13. Nicole Castan, "La Criminalité familiale dans le ressort du Parlement de Toulouse, 1690–1730," in A. Abbiateci *et al.*, eds., *Crimes et criminalité en France sous l'Ancien Régime, 17e–18e siècles* (Paris: Colin, 1971).

14. deMause, "Evolution of Childhood," p. 531.

15. Both examples from Ivy Pinchbeck and Margaret Hewitt, *Children in English Society*, vol. 1: *From Tudor Times to the Eighteenth Century* (London: Routledge, 1969), p. 301.

16. Nicole Castan, "Criminalité familiale," p. 97.

17. François Lebrun, *Les Hommes et la mort en Anjou aux 17e et 18e siècles* (Paris: Mouton, 1971), p. 424.

18. Micheline Baulant, "La famille en miettes," *Annales: ESC*, 27 (1972), 964.

19. Joseph Hazzi, *Statistische Aufschlüsse über das Herzogthum Baiern . . .*: 11 vols. (Nürnberg, 1801–1808), IV(2), p. 85. "Sie sind gut aufgehoben."

20. Lebrun, *Mort en Anjou*, p. 423.

21. Leon Kaczmaretk and Guy Savelon, *Problèmes matrimoniaux dans le ressort de l'officialité de Cambrai 1607–1762: Les séparations de corps et de biens* (Université de Lille, mémoire de maîtrise, 1971); directed by P. Deyon and A. Lottin, p. 116.

22. Dr. Meyer claimed that, for the women factory workers of Ober-Ehnheim at least, abandonment had replaced infanticide. *Ober-Ehnheim am Fusse der Vogesen in medizinisch-topographischer Rücksicht* (Strasbourg, 1841), p. 213. For the general argument that exposing infants amounted to infanticide, see William L. Langer's two articles "Checks on Population Growth, 1750–1850," *Scientific American*, 226 (February, 1972), 93–99, and "Infanticide: A Historical Survey," *History of Childhood Quarterly*, 1 (1974), 353–365.
Outright child murder probably played little role in overall infant mortality and is more interesting as an index of parental attitudes to children. Reliable time series on infanticide are rare, yet the few available indicate a decline during the eighteenth century. In Surrey, for example, about one case a year came up before 1720, but in the forty-two years studied by John Beattie between 1722 and 1802 only fifteen bills of indictment for infanticide were presented to grand juries. Beattie emphasizes "the decline from the earlier level . . . is made all the clearer when it is remembered that the population of the county more than doubled in the eighteenth century." Beattie, "The Pattern of Crime in England, 1660–1800," *Past and Present*, No. 62 (February, 1974), pp. 47–95, quote from p. 61.

23. Alain Molinier, "Enfants trouvés . . . en Languedoc . . .," in Société de démographie historique, ed., *Sur la population française au XVIIIe et au XIXe siècles: Hommage à Marcel Reinhard* (Paris: SDH, 1973), p. 446.

24. Jean-Claude Peyronnet, "Recherches sur les enfants trouvés de l'hôpital général de Limoges au XVIIIe siècle." Thèse de 3e cycle, Université de Poitiers, 1972, p. 186.

25. René Lafabrègue, "Des Enfants trouvés à Paris," *Annales de démographie internationale*, 2 (1878), 226–299, esp. 229. But N.B., data on the department of the Seine show the percentage fluctuating early in the nineteenth century beneath 10 percent of the total. Adolphe-Henri Gaillard, *Recherches . . . sur les enfants trouvés . . .* (Paris, 1837), p. 135. Gaillard showed that in nearby Poitiers the percent of legitimate foundlings ran from 1806 to 1836 between 6 and 30 percent of the total, 11 percent on the average (pp. 140–141).

26. Peyronnet, "Enfants trouvés Limoges," pp. 106–109, 177–187.

27. *Ibid.*, 144–149, 179–186, quote from p. 146. Around a seventh of all found-lings were taken back by their parents, and perhaps a tenth of those were legitimate, according to Watteville's estimate for France as a whole in 1838–1845. See his *Statistique des établissements et services de bienfaisance* (Paris, 1849), pp. 25–26. Yet another administrator thought that most children withdrawn from foundling homes were probably legitimate. See Archives nationales, F 15 3896, Saône-et-Loire to Paris, October 1838. Peyronnet puts at one-fourth the surviving children abandoned at the hospital of Limoges in 1739–1740 who were taken back by their parents, both legitimate and illegitimate (p. 149). In Lyon between 1830 and 1847, an estimated 460 of the 1,400 abandoned children returned to their parents were legitimate; to their number must be added a further 100 legitimated after birth. But compare this 1500 who returned to family life, an annual average of 170, to the total number of foundlings deposited at the Charité hospital in Lyon, an annual average of around 2,000. Jean-Francois Terme and J.-B. Monfalçon, *Nouvelles considérations sur les enfants trouvés* (Lyon, 1838), pp. xxix-xxxi.

28. Dieudonné, I, *Statistique du département du Nord* (Douai, 1804) 79.

29. Terme-Monfalcon, *Nouvelles considérations*, p. xxviii.

30. Alan Macfarlane, *The Family Life of Ralph Josselin, a Seventeenth-Century Clergyman* (New York: Cambridge University Press, 1970), p. 86, n. 1.

31. On class differences in wet-nursing in England see Ian G. Wickes, "A History of In-fant Feeding," *Archives of Diseases in Childhood*, 28 (1953), pp. 151–502, esp. p. 239, and Pinchbeck and Hewitt, *Children in English Society*, II, pp. 519–526, 612–620. On the conditions in which foundlings were wet-nursed, see the two Langer articles cited above in n. 22.

32. Claire E. Fox, "Pregnancy, Childbirth and Early Infancy in Anglo-American Culture, 1675–1830" (University of Pennsylvania, unpublished American Civ. Diss., 1966), p. 224.

33. Johann Peter Süssmilch, *Die göttliche Ordnung in den Veränderungen des menschlichen Geschlechtes*, 2nd rev. ed., 2 vols. (Berlin, 1761–1765), I, pp. 103, 509–513.

34. See for example Schlesinger on Budapest, *Pesth-Ofen*, p. 75, "die Milch eines Miethlings."

35. Roger Mercier, *L'Enfant dans la société du XVIIIe siècle (Avant l'Emile)* (Paris: thèse complémentaire pour le doctorat, Université de Paris, 1961), p. 33.

36. Jean Ganiage has estimated that virtually every peasant household in the Beauvais region which did not send its children out to be nursed accepted other children from the outside, with the result that there were about as many little Parisians *en nourrice* in the region as there were native children. Ganiage, "Nourrissons parisiens en Beauvaisis" in Société de démographie historique, *Sur la population francaise au XVIIIe et au XIXe siècles: Hommàge à Marcel Reinhard* (Paris: SDH, 1973), pp. 271–287, esp. pp. 273, 287. On mercenary wet-nursing in Normandy see Pierre-Marie Bourdin, "La Plaine d'Alençon et ses bordures forestières: Essai d'histoire

Notes

démographique et médicale," in a volume which Bourdin edited together with Michel Bouvet, *A travers la Normandie des XVIIe et XVIIIe siècles* (Caen, 1968; Cahier des Annales de Normandie, nr. 6), pp. 253–254. If we assume that similar densities of mercenary wet-nursing existed elsewhere within a sixty-kilometer radius of Paris, we have already encompassed a substantial proportion of the rural population of northern France. (In fact the density of *Petits-Paris*, as the infants from Paris being wet-nursed in the provinces were called, was high in areas considerably beyond this 60 km. radius, such as the Nièvre department.) And if we further assume that other cities and towns saturated their surrounding rural areas with *nourrissons* as did the Parisians, we end by concluding that perhaps a majority of the peasant households of France in which a nursing mother lived accepted outside nurslings. The regional density of mercenary wet-nursing must have varied considerably, strongly implanted in some areas such as Lyon's Bugey, sparsely in others such as the Vendée. In the absence of local studies, these figures remain purely speculative. For our purposes it is important only to note that sending infants to mercenary nurses—and its counterpart, willingness to accept other people's children in one's own home—was a phenomenon of vast dimensions in eighteenth-century France, reaching surely into the daily life of the average person.

37. For example ". . . que des femmes mariées, spéculant sur leur fecondité et du consentement de leurs époux, apportaient aux hospices leurs nouveaux nés, afin de se faire ensuite un revenu du lait maternel qu'elles vendaient en donnant leur sein à des enfans étrangers." Report of prefect to Conseil Général of Gard, 1838. Archives nationales F 15 3898. Charles Monot describes the women of the Morvan who get pregnant in order to have milk, then go off to Paris to work as resident wetnurses, either leaving their infants behind, or shipping them home after arriving. Monot, *De l'industrie des nourrices et de la mortalité des petits enfants* (Paris, 1867), pp. 34–46. See also Karl Kisskalt, "Die Sterblichkeit im 18. Jahrhundert," *Zeitschrift für Hygiene und Infektionskrankheiten*, 93 (1921), 438–511, esp. p. 469, and Süssmilch, *Göttliche Ordnung*, I, 103–104: "Die Kinder der Ammen kommen mehrentheils um, wenn ihre Pflegekinder noch gerettet werden. Diese müssen um einen weit geringern Lohn, als die Amme selbst empfängt, augsethan werden. Die Erfahrung lehret es, dass die meisten Hurenkinder aus dieser Ursache verhungern, oder durch gleich liederliche Personen, denen sie gegeben werden, unverantwortlich verabsaumet werden."

38. Joseph Daquin, *Topographie médicale de la ville de Chambéry*, (Chambéry, 1787), p. 82. On Lyon, see Maurice Garden, *Lyon et les Lyonnais, au XVIIIe siècle* (Paris: Les Belles-Lettres, 1970), pp. 116–140; on Montpellier, Mourgue, *Essai de statistique* p. 26; on Puy, Ms. "Mémoire sur la topographie médicale du canton de Puy" [date illeg.], Dr. Arnaud, Paris, Academie de médecine, SRM 176. On the phenomenon among small merchants and artisans, Alain Bideau, "L'Envoi des jeunes enfants en nourrice: L'exemple d'une petite ville. Thoissey-en-Dombes, 1740–1840," in Société de démographie historique, *Sur la population francaise*, pp. 49–58, esp. 52.

39. Margaret Hewitt, "The Effect of Married Women's Employment in the Cotton Textile District on the Organization and Structure of the Home in Lancashire, 1840–1880" (University of London diss., 1953), p. 181.

40. Dumont, *Essai sur la natalité dans le canton de Lillebonne (Seine-Inférieure)* (Paris, 1892), p. 41; Karl Paul Brandlmeier, *Medizinische Ortsbeschreibungen des 19. Jahrhunderts im deutschen Sprachgebiet* (Berlin medical diss., 1942), p. 35.

41. On the "Direction municipale des nourrices," see André-Théodore Brochard, *De la mortalité des nourrissons en France, specialement dans l'arrondissement de Nogent-le-Rotrou (Eure-et-Loir)* (Paris, 1866), *passim*. Statistic from p. 94. Recently

there has been George D. Sussman's informative article, "Wet-Nursing Business in Paris," *Proceedings of the First Annual Meeting of the Western Society for French History, 1974* (University Park: New Mexico State University Press, 1974).

42. Brochard, *Mortalité des nourrissons*, p. 64.

43. F 15 3898, 1841, report of a commission on foundlings.

44. Charles Monot, *De la mortalité excessive des enfants pendant la première année de leur existence* (Paris, 1872), pp. 39–40.

45. F 15 3898, 1841, Eure-et-Loir.

46. Letter from Dr. Jousset, Bellème (Orne), reprinted in Brochard, *Mortalité des nourrissons*, pp. 51–52.

47. *Ibid.*, p. 57.

48. Monot, *Mortalité excessive des enfants*, p. 41.

49. On these narcotics in England see Hewitt, "Married women's employment," pp. 307–308, in France, Monot, *Industrie des nourrices*, p. 43.

50. See for example F 15, 3898, Eure-et-Loir, 1841.

51. Schlesinger, *Pesth-Ofen*, p. 106.

52. Ph. Heineken, *Die freie Hansestadt Bremen und ihr Gebiet in topographischer, medizinischer und naturhistorischer Hinsicht* (Bremen, 1836), I, p. 72. The reference is to illegitimate children.

53. Sir William Fordyce in 1773, cited in Wickes, "Infant Feeding," p. 238.

54. J.P. Bardet, "Enfants abandonnés et enfants assistés à Rouen dans la seconde moitié du XVIIIe siècle," in Société de démographie historique, *Sur la population française au XVIIIe siècle* (Paris: SDH, 1973), pp. 27–29. Data on legitimate children were available only for those whose boarding out was subsidized by the city. The mortality of those infants whose parents made private arrangements with the nurses is unknown.

55. Brochard, *Mortalité des nourrissons*, p. 112.

56. A. Wolff, *Untersuchungen über die Kindersterblichkeit* (Erfurt, 1874), p. 44. Some of the wet nurses were resident.

57. George D. Sussman, "Wet-Nursing Business in Paris," pp. 179–194, esp. table I, p. 193.

Etienne van de Walle and Samuel H. Preston infer from census and mortality data that the recourse by Parisians to rural and urban wet nurses increased in the years 1800–1850. Van de Walle and Preston, "Mortalité de l'enfance au XIXe siècle à Paris et dans le département de la Seine," *Population*, 29 (1974), 89–106, esp. pp. 96–97. Yet Sussman's direct data appear to me more convincing.

58. On the whole question of what people thought about breastfeeding see Roger Mercier's thorough study, *L'Enfant du XVIIIe siècle*, and recently Etienne and Francine van de Walle's "Allaitement, sterilité et contraception: Les opinions jusqu'au XIXe siècle," *Population*, 27 (1972), 685–701.

59. Manuscript, "Mémoire sur la topographie du pays d'Aulnis, envoyé à la correspondance des hopitaux militaires en 1766 par M. Destrapierre"; sent to Paris from La Rochelle 15 October 1777, in SRM 178.

60. Bideau, "L'Envoi des jeunes enfants," p. 54, n. 16.

61. Manuscript "Topographie médicale de St. Malo," 19 Jan. 1790, by M. Mallet de la Brossière, DM. SRM 181.

62. Menuret de Chambaud, *Essais sur l'histoire médico-topographique de Paris* (Paris, 1786), pp. 99–100.

63. Dr. Rose, "Description de l'épidémie qui a régné . . . 1783 . . . dans la ville de Cheroi, élection de Nemours, avec la topographie de ces deux villes," in *Description*

Notes

des épidémies qui ont régné en 1783 dans la généralité de Paris, vol. II (Paris, 1785), p. 34.

64. Marquis. *Mémoire statistique du département de la Meurthe* (Paris, 1805), p. 104.

65. de Verneilh, *Statistique générale de la France . . . département du Mont-Blanc* (Paris, 1807), pp. 277, 287. See also Graffenauer, *Topographie physique et médicale de la ville de Strasbourg* (Strasbourg, 1816), pp. 66–67.

66. Jolly. *Essai sur la statistique et la topographie médicale de la ville de Châlons-sur-Marne* (Châlons, 1820), p. 54.

67. Peyronnet, "L'hôpital général de Limoges au XVIIIe siècle," pp. 225, 229.

68. Masson-Saint-Amand, *Mémoire statistique du département de l'Eure* (Paris, 1805), p. 59.

69. F15 3896. Report from the Commission d'Instruction publique du Conseil Général de l'Aube to Conseil as a whole. Session 1836 pour 1839.

70. Brochard, *Mortalité des nourrissons,* p. 78.

71. Jean-Emmanuel Gilibert, *L'Anarchie médicinale, ou la médacine considérée comme nuisible à la société* (Neuchâtel, 1772), III, p. 292.

72. Léon Lallemand says the policy of *déplacement* was initiated with a ministerial circular of 27 July 1827. *Histoire des enfants abandonnés et délaissés* (Paris, 1885), p. 286. But the major effort centered in the mid-thirties, as may be seen from the correspondence in F 15 3896–3898. Watteville summarizes the results of the *déplacement* policy to 1845 in *Statistique des établissements et services de bienfaisance,* pp. 22–23 and table 27.

73. F15 3896. Communication of 17 August 1838 from Commission Administrative des hospices de Nantes to préfet de la Loire-Inférieure.

74. F15 3896. Communicaiton of 10 August 1838 from Commission Administrative de l'hospice civil et militaire to préfet des Deux-Sevres.

75. F15 3896. Extrait du rapport du préfet du département de l'Aveyron au Conseil Général dans la session de 1837.

76. Fernand Ledé, "La Protection des enfants du premier âge," *Journal de la société de statistique de Paris,* 63 (1922), 261–301, and 64 (1923), 59–68, esp. 265. Data are limited to those 43 departments having in 1913 more than a thousand nurslings.

The trend towards keeping infants at home did not begin in Paris until the eve of the First World War, and indeed Parisians slightly *increased* the dispatching of their babies to rural nurses in the years 1884–1909.

Percent of Paris-born infants sent
en nourrice, either within
the city or outside

1885–1889	29.9 percent
1890–1894	31.2
1895–1899	32.1
1900–1904	32.6
1905–1909	32.7
1910–1914	29.7

Figures computed from data presented in Etienne van de Walle and Samuel H. Preston, "Mortalité de l'enfance au XIXe siècle à Paris," p. 103.

Notes

77. Babies to one year old sent to mercenaries in 1897 amounted to 9 per cent of all live births in that year. Less than half were wet-nursed, which helps explain why the mortality of boarded-out infants continued to be much higher than that of infants kept by their mothers. In 1897, fully 45 per cent of all newborn in Lyon were boarded out and 32 per cent of those in Paris, in both cases almost all to homes outside the city. Only in Marseille were more infants put *en nourrice* within the city than without. Jacques Bertillon, "Du Degré d'efficacité de la loi du 24 décembre 1874 (Loi Théophile Roussel)," *Journal de la société de statistique de Paris*, 43 (1902), 289–342, esp. pp. 325–326.

78. Although the grim distance between the mortality of hand- and breastfed infants had narrowed over time, it had not disappeared. Mid-nineteenth century French data are reviewed in Paul Chaulet, *Etude démographique sur l'arrondissement d'Agen* (Agen, 1880), pp. 27–28, where in case after case thirty or forty percentage points separate the two. The same distance appears in the German statistics summarized by Wolff, *Kindersterblichkeit*, pp. 42–43. On closing the gap see H. Selter, "Die Ursachen der Säuglingsterblichkeit unter besonderer Berücksichtigung der Jahreszeit und der sozialen Lage," *Zeitschrift für Hygiene und Infektionskrankheiten*, 88 (1919), 234–250, following table from p. 237:

Deaths per 100 infants age 0–1 in Berlin

	BREASTFED	HANDFED (ANIMAL MILK)
1885–1886	8.4	54.1
1895–1896	6.0	35.8
1906	6.3	23.6

79. Victor-Eugène Ardouin-Dumazet, *Voyage en France*, 20 vols. (Paris, 1893–1899), I, p. 39.

80. Charles Monot, *De l'industrie des nourrices*, p. 87.

81. Ledé, "Protection des enfants du premier age," p. 296. The real percentage would be a little higher because only seventy-nine departments reported nursling data. Yet the others were likely to have had few cases, however, and the discrepancy is minor.

82. Robert Debré *et al.*, *La Mortalité infantile et la mortinalité: Résultats de l'enquête poursuivie en France et dans cinq pays d'Europe sous les auspices du comité d'hygiène de la Société des Nations* (Paris, 1933), pp. 252, 267–268.

83. *Ibid.*, pp. 225, 245.

84. *Ibid.*, pp. 294, 306.

85. John Knodel and Etienne van de Walle, "Breast Feeding, Fertility and Infant Mortality: An Analysis of some Early German Data," *Population Studies*, 21 (1967), 109–131, esp. p. 120 and map on 119.

86. Debré, *Mortalité infantile*, pp. 219, 222, 237.

87. *Ibid.*, pp. 58, 95.

88. *Ibid.*, pp. 306, 312.

89. *Ibid.*, pp. 229, 269.

90. J. J. Juge, *Changemens survenus dans les moeurs des habitans de Limoges depuis une cinquantaine d'années*, 2nd ed. (Limoges, 1817; first ed., 1808), pp. 34, 84.

91. Mentioned in Theodore Zeldin, *France, 1848–1945*, vol. I: *Ambition, Love and Politics* (Oxford: Clarendon Press, 1973), p. 328. The accumulation of infant-

care titles after 1815 may be seen from the Bibliothèque Nationale's collection of works on both children's hygiene and children's diseases. In each case there is an initial flurry of publication in the 1770s, and then a grand nineteenth-century wave beginning in the Napoleonic years. Bibliothèque Nationale, *Catalogue des sciences médicales*, I, pp. 488–494, for series Tc³¹ and pp. 637–641 for series Td³⁶.

92. I'm alluding to the eighteenth-century doctors' preoccupation with weather and climate. Early in the nineteenth century, clinical observation and systematic collection of medical data replace meterology almost entirely in the doctors' world-view.

93. Ariès, *Centuries of Childhood*, pp. 282–284.

94. Anon. [chef de division à la préfecture du Var], *Statistique du département du Var* (Draguignan, 1838), p. 178. The denominator of the percentage was computed by adding to the number of abandoned children on hand at the beginning of the year the number admitted during the year, then subtracting the number who left the welfare system upon attaining age twelve and the number who died. The numerator was simply the number of children withdrawn by their parents during the period in question.

Watteville's data on the percent withdrawn for France as a whole between 1838 and 1845 show no change whatsoever. *Statistique des établissements et services de bienfaisance*, p. 25. In Lyon some increase took place between 1830 and 1837 in the number of children withdrawn by their parents from the Hospice de la Charité, but the number of abandoned children was rising as well. On withdrawals, Terme-Monfalcon, *Nouvelles considérations*, p. xxxi. On expositions in Lyon, Watteville, p. 7.

95. Reports of departmental prefects, F 20 135².

96. All this from *ibid.*, correspondence of 1847.

97. Henry Roger, *Le Finistère: Ses habitants, leurs moeurs* . . . (Montpellier, 1919), pp. 48–49.

98. A. Drouineau, *Géographie médicale de l'Ile de Ré* (Paris, 1909), p. 72.

99. Edgar Morin writes of the commune of Plodémet, at the southwestern tip of Brittany: "La nouvelle mère qui accouche toujours en clinque désormais, consacre, à la manière urbaine, de multiples attentions d'hygiène, de diététique, de toilette à ses enfants. A l'âge scolaire, elle surveille leçons et devoirs, tire vanité des succès, jalouse de ceux du petit voisin, et va parfois jusqu'à récriminer auprès des maîtres." Morin, *Commune en France: La Métamorphose de Plodémet* (Paris: Fayard, 1967), p. 171.

100. Henri Baudrillart, *Les Populations agricoles de la France*, vol. I: *Maine, Anjou* . . . (Paris, 1885), quotation about Picardy, p. 385; see also his remarks on childrearing in Provence, vol. III: *Les Populations du Midi* (Paris, 1893), p. 113.

101. See Gilibert's vivid description, *Anarchie médicinale*, III, pp. 290–291.

102. *Ibid.*, pp. 304–305.

103. Among other testimony, see P.-S.-E. de Smyttère, *Topographie* . . . *de Cassel* (Paris, 1828), p. 101; Barthèlemy Chaix, *Préoccupations statistiques* . . . *des Hautes-Alpes* (Grenoble, 1845), p. 232; and Bancel, *Toul*, p. 79.

104. Bertrand, *Mémoire sur la topographie médicale du département du Puy-de-Dôme* (Clermont, 1849), p. 84.

105. Alex Giraudet, *Topographie physique et médicale de Cusset* (Paris, 1827), p. 113.

106. Adrien Bérenguier, *Topographie* . . . *medicale du canton de Rabastens (Tarn)* (Toulouse, 1850), p. 129.

107. See Mercier, *L'enfant du XVIIIe*, pp. 110, 160–161.

108. Menuret de Chambaud, *Essai Médico-Topographique de Paris*, p. 100; Joseph-Marie Audin-Rouvière, *Essai sur la topographie physique et médicale de Paris*, (Paris, 1794), p. 77.

109. Daquin, *Chambéry*, p. 82.

110. Graffenauer, Strasbourg, p. 65; François-Alexandre Rouger, *Topographie statistique et médicale de la ville et canton du Vigan* (Montpellier, 1819), pp. 100, 106, 111.

111. Fox, "Pregnancy, Childbirth in Anglo-American Culture," p. 210.

112. John Demos, A *Little Commonwealth* (New York: Oxford University Press, 1970), p. 133, citing Alice M. Earle, *Child Life in Colonial Days* (New York, 1927), 21ff. and 34ff.

113. Helmut Möller, *Die kleinbürgerliche Familie im 18. Jahrhundert* (Berlin: de Gruyter, 1969), pp. 37–38.

114. Wertheim, *Wien*, p. 100; K. F. H. Marx, *Göttingen in medicinischer . . . Hinsicht* (Göttingen, 1824), p. 141; see also Schlesinger, *Pesth-Ofen*, p. 76.

115. Jean Jablonski, *Etude médicale sur l'arrondissement de Poitiers pendant l'année 1878–1879* (Poitiers, 1880), pp. 26–27.

116. Albert Köbele, ed., *Ortssippenbuch Altenheim, Gemeinde Neuried, Ortenaukreis/Baden* (Grafenhausen bei Lahr/privately published by author, 1973), p. 275, entry 1631.

117. René A. Spitz, "Hospitalism: An Inquiry into the Genesis of Psychiatric Conditions in Early Childhood," *Psychoanalytic Study of the Child*, I (1945), 53–74, esp. pp. 53–54, 59.

118. Few industrial cities do not evidence some increase in infant mortality at some time during the nineteenth century. See, for example, Pierre Pierrard, *La Vie ouvrière à Lille sous le Second Empire* (Paris: Bloud & Gay, 1965), p. 127, for a large increase in perinatal mortality, 1851–1870, or Aline Lesaege, "La Mortalité infantile dans le département du Nord de 1815 à 1914," *Revue du Nord*, 52 (1970), 238–243, esp. p. 240. For a comparable German example, Kisskalt, "Sterblichkeit," p. 465, gives infant mortality in Königsberg, 1781–1913 (an increase from 22 per 100 in 1781 to 1802 to 26 in 1894 to 1903). Yet in nonindustrial reaches of Central Europe, as well, the nineteenth century saw large increments in the infantile mortality rate; cf. the decennial series for Saxony, Bavaria, and Prussia that Gustav Sundbärg gives in *Aperçus statistiques internationaux* (Stockholm, 1908; Gordon and Breach reprint), p. 142.

119. Infant mortality increases from 11 to 16/100 in Andover, Mass., over 1670–1759, Philip J. Greven, Jr. *Four Generations* (Ithaca: Cornell University Press, 1970), p. 189, but declines in Salem, Mass., from 31 per cent in the "17th century" to 18 per cent in the "18th century." The latter are the findings of James K. Somerville, "A Demographic Profile of the Salem Family, 1660–1770," unpublished paper, cited in Maris Vinovskis, "Mortality Rates and Trends in Massachusetts Before 1860," *Journal of Economic History*, 32 (1972): 184–213, esp. p. 199.

120. To my knowledge, Jean-Louis Flandrin is the first to have argued the case, for early modern Europe, that parental insouciance was a main cause of high infant mortality, rather than the other way round. ". . . Pour des raisons culturelles et non pas seulement matérielles, les parents d'autrefois étaient moins soucieux de leurs enfants que ceux d'aujourd'hui." Flandrin, "L'attitude à l'égard de l'enfant," p. 176.

Chapter 6

1. This description of prerevolutionary youth organizations draws heavily upon Maurice Agulhon's two books, *Pénitents et Francs-Maçons* (Paris: Fayard, 1968), pp. 43–64, and *La Vie sociale en Provence intérieure au lendemain de la Révolution*

(Paris: Société des études robespierristes, 1970), pp. 222–223, and on Arnold Van Gennep, *Manuel de folklore français contemporain*, I(1) (Paris: A. Picard, 1943), pp. 201–206.

These *abbayes de la jeunesse* or *rois d'amour* may have been more widespread in southern France than northern. Natalie Davis has argued that they even served as springboards for popular political protest, but the evidence supporting such an interpretation seems thin to me. Davis, "The Reasons of Misrule: Youth Groups and Charivaris in Sixteenth-Century France," *Past and Present*, 50 (February, 1971), 41–75.

2. For later descriptions see Dieudonné, *Statistique du département du Nord* (Douai, 1864), I, 82–83; Xavier Thiriat, *La Valleé de Cleurie* (Mirecourt, 1869), pp. 333–334; Henri Pourrat, *Ceux d'Auvergne, types et coutumes* (Paris, 1928), p. 67.

3. L.-J.-B. Bérenger-Féraud, *Reminiscences populaires de la Provence* (Paris, 1885), pp. 81–83.

4. Maurice Garden, *Lyon et les Lyonnais au XVIIIe siècle* (Paris: Les Belles-Lettres, 1970), pp. 555–571.

5. Steven R. Smith, "The London Apprentices as Seventeenth-Century Adolescents," *Past and Present*, 61 (November, 1973), 194–161, esp. p. 157.

6. Matti Sarmela, *Reciprocity Systems of the Rural Society in the Finnish-Karelian Area* . . .(Helsinki: Suomalainen Tiedekatemia, 1969), p. 116.

7. For these French examples, Van Gennep, *Manuel de folklore français*, I(1), pp. 207–213, I(4) pp. 1589–1595.

8. Described, for example, in Laurence Wylie, *Village in the Vaucluse: An Account of Life in a French Village*, rev. ed. (Cambridge: Harvard University Press, 1964), chapter 11.

9. *Enquête sur l'habitation rurale en France*, 2 vols. (Paris, 1939), II, p. 187.

10. François-Alexandre Rouger, *Topographie statistique et médicale de la ville et canton du Vigan* (Montpellier, 1819), p. 103.

11. For a description of *chambrées* in Provence see Maurice Agulhon, *La République au village* (*Les populations du Var de la Révolution à la Seconde République*) (Paris: Plon, 1970), pp. 219–245. On the *chambrée's* persistence even into the contemporary world, see Lucienne A. Roubin's rich study, *Les Chambrettes des Provençaux: Une Maison des hommes en Méditerranée septentrionale* (Paris: Plon, 1970), *passim*.

12. Rouger, *Vigan*, p. 110.

13. See Maurice Agulhon, "Les Chambrées en Basse-Provence: histoire et ethnologie," *Revue historique*, 498 (1971), 337–368.

14. Garden, *Lyon*, p. 432.

15. Francois Mazuy, *Essai historique sur les moeurs et coutumes de Marseille au 19e siècle* (Marseille, 1853), p. 197; see also C. Viry, *Mémoire Statistique du département de la Lys* (Paris, 1812), for the early nineteenth century; rural-dwellers went less, yet whenever they had the chance.

16. Jean-Baptiste Dupont, *Topographie historique* . . . *de l'Arrondissement de Lille* (Paris, 1833), p. 75.

17. Henri Baudrillart, *Les Populations agricoles de la France*, vol. II: *Maine-Anjou* . . . (Paris, 1888), p. 287.

18. Mme Charles d'Abbadie d'Arrast, *Causeries sur le pays Basque* (Paris, 1909), pp. 109–110.

19. Emmanuel Labat, *En Gascogne* (Agen, 1911), p. 32.

20. Pierre Caspard distinguishes clearly between work-bee veillées in which two or three families—or just married women—would get together, and courtship veillées including just the young people. Caspard, "Conceptions prénuptiales et développement

Notes

du capitalisme dans la Principauté de Neuchâtel (1678–1820)," *Annales: ESC*, 29 (1974), 989–1008, esp. pp. 993–994.

21. A. Carlier, *Un village breton en 1895 (Saint-Pierre de Quiberon)* (Cannes: Imprimerie à l'école, 1949), p. 13.

22. Lepécq de la Cloture, *Collection d'observations sur les maladies et constitutions épidémiques de la Normandie* (Rouen, 1778), p. 126.

23. Roubin, *Chambrettes des Provençaux*, p. 164.

24. For a typical description see J. Chalette, *Précis de la statistique générale du département de la Marne* (Chalons, 1844), I, p. 115.

25. Van Gennep, *Manuel de folklore français*, I (1), pp. 139–140.

26. For the above see *ibid.*, I(2), pp. 689–699.

27. *Ibid.*, p. 689.

28. *Ibid.*, p. 699.

29. On wakes see *ibid.*, pp. 688–710, examples from pp. 704, 705.

30. Philippe Ariès surveys this larger transformation in *Western Attitudes Towards Death from the Middle Ages to the Present*, trans. Patricia M. Ranum (Baltimore: Johns Hopkins University Press, 1974).

31. Van Gennep, *Manuel de folklore français*, I(2), p. 783.

32. *Ibid.*, p. 431.

33. Grise, *Trièves*, pp. 19–20. See also Elard Hugo Meyer, *Badisches Volksleben* (Strasbourg, 1900), p. 251, Van Gennep, *Manuel de folklore français*, I(2), pp. 437–441.

34. On the best man's presence in the bedroom, see Jacques Chambry, *Voyage dans le Finistère* (Brest, 1836), p. 41; on the "brew" (*rotie*) and hide-and-seek traditions see Van Gennep, I(2), pp. 555–557; E. Deliège, *Pays d'Argonne* (Reims, 1907), p. 168; Marquis, *Mémoire statistique du département de la Meurthe* (Paris, 1805), p. 140; J.-B. Frion, *Description . . . de la ville de Chaumont-en-Vexin* (Beauvais, 1867), p. 128, where the *rotie* was said to be in decline; Xavier Thiriat, *La vallée de Cleurie* (Remiremont, 1869), p. 313; Charles Perron, *Les Franc-Comtois* (Besançon, 1892), p. 166, where the drink was called the "trempotte."

35. On wedding dancing, see Van Gennep, *Manuel de folklore français*, I(2), pp. 541–550.

36. Auguste Grise, *Coutumes du Trièves au XIXe siècle* (Grenoble, 1939), pp. 19–20.

37. Cambry, *Description du département de l'Oise*, 2 vols. (Paris, 1803), I, p. 257.

38. Both examples from Van Gennep, *Manuel de folklore français*, I(3), p. 1075.

39. *Ibid.*, p. 1074.

40. *Ibid.*, p. 1077.

41. H. Barre *et al.*, *Les Bouches-du-Rhône, Encyclopédie départementale*, vol. XIII: *La Population* (Marseille, 1921), p. 398.

42. For illustrations, Thiriat, *Cleurie*, p. 250; Van Gennep, *Manuel de folklore français*, I(2), p. 619.

43. J. L. M. Noguès, *Les Moeurs d'autrefois en Saintonge et en Aunis* (Saintes, 1891), p. 16.

44. For instance, J. Quenin, *Statistique de canton d'Orgon* (Arles, 1838), p. 76.

45. Grise, *Trièves*, pp. 20–21.

46. Sometimes, however, the charivari was intended actually to punish the remarriers. In Languedoc their door was broken in. Nicole Castan, "La Criminalité familiale dans le ressort du Parlement de Toulouse, 1690–1730," in A. Abbiatecci *et al.*, eds. *Crimes et criminalité en France sous l'Ancien Régime, 17e–18e siècles* (Paris: Colin, 1971), p. 106.

47. Van Gennep, *Manuel de folklore français*, I(2), p. 626.
48. Perron, *Franc-Comtois*, p. 142; Van Gennep, *ibid.*, I(2), pp. 572, 619.
49. Van Gennep, *ibid.*, I(2), p. 618.
50. Delpon, *Lot*, I, p. 207.
51. Alexandre Bouët, Breiz Izel, 2d ed. (Quimper, 1918; first ed., 1835), p. 278; on seizing the nearest neighbor see also J.C.F. Ladoucette, *Histoire . . . des Hautes-Alpes*, 3rd ed. (Paris, 1848), p. 578.
52. Ladoucette, *Hautes-Alpes*, commune of Saint-Julien-en-Champsaur, p. 578.
53. *Ibid.*, p. 578.
54. Van Gennep, *Manuel de folklore français*, I(4), p. 1702.
55. Perron, *Franc-Comtois*, pp. 139–143.
56. Jeffry Kaplow, *The Names of Kings* (New York: Basic Books, 1972), p. 109; Garden, *Lyon*, p. 441.
57. Van Gennep, *Manuel de folklore français*, I(3), pp. 1075–76.
58. Dieudonné, *Nord*, I, pp. 97–98.
59. For a recent review of the international literature see Roger Pinon, "Qu'est-ce q'un charivari? Essai en vue d'une définition opératoire," in *Kontakte und Grenzen. Probleme der Volks-, Kultur- und Sozialforschung. Festschrift G. Heilfurth* (Göttingen: Schwartz, 1969), pp. 393–405.
60. E. P. Thompson, " 'Rough Music,' Le Charivari anglais," *Annales: ESC*, 27 (1972), 285–312, esp. p. 297.
61. *Ibid.*, p. 297. I have retranslated some quotes from the French text.
62. Bayerisches Hauptstaatsarchiv, MI 46557.
63. See the articles "Haberfeldtreiben" and "Katzenmusik," in E. Hoffmann-Krayer and Hanns Bächtold-Stäubli, eds., *Handwörterbuch des deutschen Aberglaubens* (Berlin, 1930–1932), III, p. 1291 and IV, pp. 1125–1132; Karl Meuli, "Charivari," in Horst Kusch, ed., *Festschrift Franz Dornseiff* (Leipzig: VEB Bibliographisches Institut, 1953), pp. 231–243; P. T. Meertens, "Die Katzenmusik in den Nieder-landen," in *Die Nachbarn: Jahrbuch für vergleichende Volkskunde*, 3 (1962), 126–139, esp. pp. 130–132.
64. Lépecq de la Cloture, *Maladies de Normandie*, p. 205.
65. Menuret de Chambaud, *Essais sur l'histoire médico-topographie de Paris* (Paris, 1786), p. 112.
66. P. J. Lesauvage, *Essai topographique et médical sur Bayonne et ses environs* (Paris, 1825), pp. 115–116.
67. Dalphonse, *Mémoire statistique du département de l'Indre* (Paris, 1804), p. 111.
68. de Verneilh, *Statistique générale de la France . . . département du Mont-Blanc* (Paris, 1807), p. 287.
69. Christophe de Villeneuve, *Statistique du département des Bouches-du-Rhône*, 4 vols. (Marseille, 1821–1829), III, pp. 277–278; the author had been prefect. For a similar account see Rame, *Essai historique et médical sur Lodève* (Lodève, 1841), p. 41.
70. See at the end of André Varagnac, *Civilisation traditionnelle et genres de vie* (Paris: Albin Michel, 1948), "Carte de regression des feux de brandons et des feux de la St. Jean," for the period "pre-1880" to 1937.
71. Thiriat, *Cleurie*, pp. 330–331.
72. Richez-Adnet, *Recherches historiques sur Hans-le-Grand* (Châlons-sur-Marne, 1867), p. 79.
73. Baudrillart, *Populations agricoles de la France* (1888), p. 512.
74. Andrée Michel, for example, in a study of contemporary family planning atti-tudes, finds that "emotional" factors such as husband-wife interaction are more power-

ful predictors than socio-economic factors such as class, a hypothesis which a scholar who believed subcultural differences strong even today would not have expected. Michel, "Interaction and Family Planning in the French Urban Family," *Demography*, 4 (1967), 615–625. In Jean Labbens' account of proletarian family life, *Le Quart monde: La pauvreté dans la société industrielle: étude sur le sous-prolétariat francais dans la région parisienne* (Paris: Editions science et service, 1969), pp. 107–156, the reader has the impression of people whose values are fundamentally petty bourgeois. From the articles of Robert Boudet ("La Famille bourgeoise") and Jacques Doublet ("Parents et enfants dans la famille ouvrière"), written in the 1950s, a certain convergence in the family styles of the two classes may be inferred; both pieces appeared in M. Sorre, ed., *Sociologie comparée de la famille contemporaine* (Paris: CNRS, 1955), pp. 141–151 and 157–168. Finally Alain Girard, while discovering slight interclass differences in attitudes to premarital intercourse and significant differences towards contraception, concludes that on the whole, "Les normes à l'égard du marriage seraient très générales à l'intérieur de la culture francaise, et s'il y a des 'sous-cultures,' celles-ci participent au mouvement d'ensemble, mais à un rythme plus ou moins rapide, les milieux plus attardés n'étant pas loin cependant de rejoindre ceux qui sont en tête." *Le choix du conjoint*, new ed. (Paris: PUF, 1974), p. 179. The reader will conclude from both my desperate scramble for contemporary evidence, and from Andrée Michel's inclusion in her new reader of principally Anglo-Saxon material, what a disaster area the sociology of the current French family has become. See Michel, *La Sociologie de la famille: recueil de textes présentés et commentés.* (Paris: Mouton, 1970).

75. François Mazuy, *Marseille*, pp. 191–193.

76. Baudrillart, *Populations agricoles*, vol. II (1888), pp. 340–341.

77. Grise, *Trièves*, pp. 22–24.

78. K. F. H. Marx, *Göttingen*, p. 175; for similar testimony see Ph. Heineken, *Die freie Hansestadt Bremen* . . . (Bremen, 1836), I, p. 84.

79. Richard Sennett, *Families Against the City: Middle Class Homes of Industrial Chicago, 1872–1890* (Cambridge: Harvard University Press, 1970), p. 195.

80. Robert Roberts, *The Classic Slum* (Manchester: Manchester University Press, 1971), p. 35.

81. All this Languedoc material from Castan, "Criminalité familiale," pp. 98–104.

82. Jean Rémy, "Persistance de la famille étendue dans un milieu industriel et urbain," *Revue francaise de sociologie*, 8 (1967), 493–505, esp. pp. 498–500.

83. M. Jollivet and H. Mendras, eds., *Les Collectivités rurales francaises: Etude comparative de changement social* (Paris: Colin, 1971), I, p. 86; "Orchains en Beauce."

84. *Ibid.*, pp. 96–97; "Grand-Frault en Lorraine."

85. *Ibid.*, p. 113; "Beaufort en Marche."

86. *Ibid.*, p. 139; "Montbois en Armagnac."

87. See, for example, Tina Jolas and Françoise Zonabend on Minot (Cote d'Or), where present-day residents testify "chacun reste chez soi," "Gens du finage, gens du bois," *Annales: ESC*, 28 (1973), 285–305, esp. p. 286; Placide Rambaud and Monique Vincienne discuss "religion et désagrégation des communautés humaines" for a rural arrondissement in southeastern France, *Les Transformations d'une société rurale: La Maurienne (1561–1962)* (Paris: Colin, 1964), pp. 208–210; and Robert T. Anderson and Barbara Gallatin Anderson speak of "a revolutionary breakdown of communal solidarity" in Wissous (Essonne), *Bus Stop for Paris: The Transformation of a French Village* (Garden City, N.Y.: Doubleday, Anchor, 1966), p. 144.

88. Alan Macfarlane, *The Family Life of Ralph Josselin, A Seventeenth-Century Clergyman* (New York: Cambridge University Press, 1970), pp. 153–160. Michael Anderson provides no information on kin network obligations in his discussion of

village society in nineteenth-century Lancashire, aside from data on the co-residence of aging parents and married children, *Family Structure in Nineteenth Century Lancashire* (New York: Cambridge University Press, 1971), p. 84.

89. Raymond Firth, *Families and their Relatives: Kinship in a Middle-Class Sector of London* (London: Routledge, 1969), p. 166.

90. Colin Rosser and Christopher Harris, *The Family and Social Change: A Study of Family and Kinship in a South Wales Town* (London: Routledge, 1965), pp. 212–221.

91. Peter Willmott and Michael Young, *Family and Class in a London Suburb* (London: Routledge, 1960), p. 38.

92. Firth, *Families and Their Relatives*, p. 462.

93. John Mogey, *Family and Neighbourhood: Two Studies in Oxford* (London: Oxford University Press, 1956), pp. 83–88.

94. Michael Young and Peter Willmott, *Family and Kinship in East London* (London: Routledge, 1957), p. 142 of Pelican ed.

95. *Ibid.*, p. 149.

96. *Ibid.*, pp. 106–107.

97. *Ibid.*, p. 109.

98. As far as I know, nobody has ever estimated net "congealment rates." These are guesses on my part.

99. Young and Willmott, *Family and Kinship in East London*, p. 108.

100. Some of the literature is reviewed in Gerald R. Leslie, *The Family in Social Context* (New York: Oxford University Press, 1967), pp. 323–325; see also Ivan Nye and Felix Berardo, *The Family* (New York: Macmillan, 1973), pp. 412–413. Bernard Farber described Champaign-Urbana in *Kinship and Class: A Midwestern Study* (New York: Basic Books, 1971), p. 79. See also Robert P. Stuckert, "Occupational Mobility and Family Relationships" [Milwaukee], *Social Forces*, 41 (1962–63), 301–307; Scott Greer, "Urbanism Reconsidered: A Comparative Study of Local Areas in a Metropolis" [Los Angeles], *American Sociological Review*, 21 (1956), 19–25; and C. Edward Noll and Michael Gordon, "Urban Kinship Interaction: A Test of Two Hypotheses," paper presented at the annual meeting of the American Sociological Society, Denver, Colorado, August, 1971.

101. Farber, *Kinship and Class*, p. 112.

102. Once such clearly exceptional communities as Boston's downtown Italians are put to the side—Herbert Gans, *The Urban Villagers* (New York: Free Press, 1962)— Paul Craven's and Barry Wellman's assessment seems appropriate that "it is rare to find a neighborhood which constitutes the major setting of informal interaction for the majority of its residents." Craven and Wellman, "The Network City," *Sociological Inquiry*, 43 (1973), 57–88. Michael Zuckerman's book is entitled *Peaceable Kingdoms: New England Towns in the Eighteenth Century* (New York: Knopf, 1970), and Lewis Atherton's is *Main Street on the Middle Border* (Bloomington: Indiana University Press, 1954).

103. Pierre Feugeyrollas, "Prédominance du mari ou de la femme dans le ménage: Une enquête sur la vie familiale," *Population*, 6 (1951), 83–102, esp. pp. 92–93; Andrée Vieille's investigation of working-class families who were thrust into furnished hotel rooms after the Second World War found very high degrees of neighboring, not just boys-at-the-bar social contacts of the traditional sort. But I'm inclined to think these results are the product of exceptional circumstances. Vieille, "Relations parentales et relations de voisinage chez les ménages ouvriers de la Seine," *Cahiers internationaux de sociologie*, 17 (1954), 140–153.

104. Rémy, "Persistance de la famille étendue," p. 503.

105. Willmott and Young, *Family and Class in a London Suburb*, p. 109.

106. See, for example, Norman Denis *et al.*, *Coal is Our Life: An Analysis of a Yorkshire Mining Community* (London: Tavistock, 1956), pp. 142–156; Brian Jackson, *Working Class Community: Some General Notions Raised by a Series of Studies in Northern England* (London: Routledge, 1968), ch. 4, "At the Club," pp. 39–68.

107. Michael Young and Peter Willmott, *The Symmetrical Family: A Study of Work and Leisure in the London Region* (London: Routledge, 1973), pp. 229–230.

108. Arthur B. Shostak, *Blue-Collar Life* (New York: Random House, 1969), pp. 190–192.

109. From John Brooks, *The Great Leap*, cited in Shostak, *ibid.*, p. 120.

110. Natalie Davis assures me this opinion was common among sixteenth-century doctors.

111. The numerous French "family reconstitution" studies converge on the view that birth control was not practiced to any significant extent in marriage before the last quarter of the eighteenth century.

112. A study of marital separations in the diocese of Cambrai makes it evident that, however infrequent adultery may have been on the whole, it was more acceptable for men than for women. Some wives were prepared to suffer their husbands' misbehavior long in silence, whereas the husbands had no tolerance at all for their wives' adultery. Indeed, the husbands seem to have even thought it morally acceptable to bed their servants if their wives refused sex. Léon Kaczmarek and Guy Savelon, *Problèmes matrimoniaux dans le ressort de l'officialité de Cambrai, 1670–1762: Les séparations de corps et de biens* (Université de Lille, mémoire de maitrise, 1971; directed by P. Deyon and A. Lottin), pp. 94, 112.

113. Joseph Hazzi, *Statistische Aufschlüsse uber das Herzogthum Baiern . . . 11 vols.* (Nürnberg, 1801–1808), III(3), p. 1129; Jean-Emmanuel Gilibert, *L'Anarchie médicinale . . .* (Neuchâtel, 1772), III, p. 276.

114. Barthélemy Chaix, *Préoccupations statistiques, géographiques, pittoresques et synoptiques du département des Hautes-Alpes* (Grenoble, 1845) p. 275.

115. Balguerie, *Tableau statistique du département du Gers*, (Paris, 1802), p. 45.

116. See Jacques Depauw, "Amour illégitime et société à Nantes au XVIIIe siècle," *Annales: ESC*, 27 (1972), 1155–82.

117. Theodore Zeldin shows that the woman's right to orgasm had been generally accepted in French marriage manuals by the beginning of World War I. *France, 1848–1945: vol. I: Ambition, Love and Politics* (Oxford: Clarendon Press, 1973), pp. 295–297. On the growing acceptance of female orgasm in the United States see Michael Gordon, "From Procreation to Recreation: Changes in Sexual Ideology, 1830–1940," in James Henslin, ed., *The Sociology of Sex* (New York: Appleton-Century-Crofts, 1971), pp. 53–77.

On the basis of medical textbooks and marital manuals, John S. Haller and Robin M. Haller argue that American sexuality passed from a free-and-easy early modern phase to a prudish repressiveness in the nineteenth century. But I am fundamentally mistrustful of such general texts, not anchored liked the medical topographies in specific contexts of time and place, and accordingly I believe the question still to be open. Haller and Haller, *The Physician and Sexuality in Victorian America* (Urbana: University of Illinois Press, 1974), pp. 92–97 and *passim*.

118. François-Emmanuel Foderé, *Voyage aux Alpes Maritimes* (Paris, 1821), II, 207–208; Louis René Villermé, "De la distribution par mois des conceptions et des naissances de l'homme," *Annales d'hygiène publique*, 5 (1831), p. 29; Jean-César Vincens, *Topographie de la ville des Nismes* (Nimes, 1802; ms. finished in 1790), p. 127.

119. W. H. James, "Social Class and Season of Birth," *Journal of Biosocial Science,* 3 (1971), *passim.*

120. Morton Hunt reached this conclusion in his 1972 survey of American sexual practices, *Sexual Behavior in the 1970s* (New York: Playboy Press, 1974), p. 202 and *passim.* Although it pains me to cite this imprimatur, the study is not badly done.

121. Dr. Grassl, "Bäuerliche Liebe," *Zeitschrift für Sexualwissenschaft,* 13 (1927), p. 378.

122. Edmund Morgan, "The Puritans and Sex," *New England Quarterly,* 15 (1942), 591–607, esp. pp. 592–593.

123. Gordon, "Procreation to Recreation."

124. Alfred E. Kinsey, *Sexual Behavior in the Human Female* (New York: Bantam, 1965), pp. 356–358.

125. Hunt, *Sexual Behavior,* p. 32. All Kinsey data reported in this section are taken from Hunt.

126. Charles F. Westoff, "Coital Frequency and Contraception," *Family Planning Perspective,* 6 (1974), p. 141. The Kinsey–1972 comparative data from Hunt, *Sexual Behavior,* p. 191. The English median frequency was about twice weekly in the late 1960s. See Geoffrey Gorer, *Sex and Marriage in England Today: A Study of the Views and Experience of the Under-45s* (London: Nelson, 1971), p. 115.

127. Hunt, *Sexual Behavior,* p. 205.

128. *Ibid.,* p. 201.

129. *Ibid.,* p. 198.

130. *Ibid.,* p. 202.

131. *Ibid.,* p. 204.

132. Kinsey, *Female,* pp. 356–358. Hunt, *Sexual Behavior,* p. 212, where the 1907 New York Study is also cited.

133. Hunt, *Sexual Behavior,* p. 216, on wifely discontent. There is, according to Hunt's data, a strong correlation between sexual pleasure and affection in marriage, pp. 231–232.

134. See George L. Ginsberg *et al.,* "The New Impotence," *Archives of General Psychiatry,* 26 (1972), 218–220; the authors write: "the male concern of the 1940s and 1950s was to satisfy the woman. In the late 1960s and early 1970s, it seems to be 'Will I have to maintain an erection to maintain a relationship?'" (p. 219).

135. Vance Packard, *The Sexual Wilderness* (New York: David McKay, 1968), p. 275.

136. Pierre Simon *et al., Rapport sur le comportement sexuel des français* (Paris: Julliard-Charron, 1972), p. 240.

137. *Ibid.,* pp. 246, 249–251.

Chapter 7

1. I have tried elsewhere to explain in greater detail how capitalism affected intimate life. Shorter, "Illegitimacy, Sexual Revolution and Social Change in Modern Europe," *Journal of Interdisciplinary History,* 2 (1971), 237–272; "Capitalism, Culture, and Sexuality: Some Competing Models," *Social Science Quarterly,* 53 (1972), 338–356; and "Female Emancipation, Birth Control, and Fertility in European History," *American Historical Review,* 78 (1973), 605–640.

2. The few data which permit a systematic comparison of cottage-industrial and nearby agricultural regions show dramatic differences in sexual behavior and courtship patterns. For example, in those parishes of the principality of Neuchâtel where

cottage weaving flourished, prebridal pregnancy increased threefold, from 21 per cent of all unions in 1745 to 1755 to 64 per cent in 1800 to 1810. In neighboring parishes where husbandry was practiced, however, the percentage of brides pregnant at marriage actually declined over that time (albeit only 1 point, from 40 to 39 per cent). Pierre Caspard, "Conceptions prénuptiales et développement du capitalisme dans la Principauté de Neuchâtel (1678–1820)," *Annales: ESC* 29 (1974), 999–1008, esp. table 1, p. 992.

3. Fred Weinstein and Gerald M. Platt, *The Wish to be Free: Society, Psyche, and Value Change* (Berkeley: University of California Press, 1969).

4. See for example Henri Baudrillart, *Populations rurales*, vol. II: *Maine, Anjou* . . . (Paris, 1888), p. 383.

5. Colchen, *Mémoire statistique* . . . *Moselle*, p. 52.

6. Alain Molinier, "Enfants trouvés . . .," in Société de démographie historique, ed., *Sur la population française au XVIIIe et au XIXe siècles* (Paris: SDM, 1973), pp. 465–467.

7. Bavaria. Kammer der Abgeordneten. *Verhandlungen*, 1831, appendix, vol. VII, pp. 197–202.

8. Baudrillart, *Populations rurales* . . . *Midi*, p. 426.

9. *Enquête sur l'habitation rurale en France*, II, p. 153 for Hautes-Alpes, p. 187 for Haute-Saône, p. 304 for Vosges, p. 429 for Indre-et-Loir.

10. J. A. Banks, "The Contagion of Numbers," in H. J. Dyos and Michael Wolff, eds., *The Victorian City*, 2 vols. (London: Routledge, 1973), I, pp. 105–122, esp. pp. 113–114; the "observer" was H. L. Smith.

11. Kreisarchiv Bamberg, K3 735. Letter sent to Kreisregiervng of Mittelfranken.

12. An important new addition to the literature on centralization is Benjamin R. Barber's *Death of Communal Liberty: A History of Freedom in a Swiss Mountain Canton* (Princeton: Princeton University Press, 1974), pp. 207–220 and 248–255. And Maurice Crubellier has recently recalled our attention to the impact of migration upon local culture. *Histoire culturelle de la France, XIXe–XXe siècle* (Paris: Colin, 1974), pp. 142–149.

Chapter 8

1. For one guide to the enormous "generation gap" literature, see Vern L. Bengston, "The Generation Gap: A Review and Typology of Social-Psychological Perspectives," *Youth and Society*, 2 (1971), 7–32. For a characteristic piece of academic overwroughtness, see Edgar Friedenberg, "Current Patterns of Generation Conflict," *Journal of Social Issues*, 25 (1969), 21–38.

2. Bianka Zazzo, *Psychologie différentielle de l'adolescence*, 2nd ed. (Paris: P.U.F., 1972), quotes from pp. 255, 259; see also pp. 261, 281–289.

3. Gérard Vincent, *Les Lycéens: Contribution à l'étude du milieu scolaire* (Paris: Colin, 1971; FNSP, cahier nr. 179), pp. 542, 558; quote from p. 561.

4. See, for example, Suzanne Frère, *La jeunesse bagnolaise: Enquête sociologique* (Paris: Pailhé, 1968), pp. 113–123.

5. Friedhelm Neidhart, *Die junge Generation* (Opladen: Leske, 1967), p. 61, citing a 1966 study by Uno Undeutsch.

6. Hermann Bertlein, *Das Selbstverständnis der Jugend Heute*, 2nd ed., (Hanover: Schroedel, n.d. [ca. 1965]), p. 228, quote from p. 249. On the basis of 1964 survey data, Viggo Graf Blücher rejects the view that tensions exist between the generations in Germany. Yet it seems likely that even at that time a major historical change had

already progressed, and that by the 1970s such findings are simply no longer applicable. Blücher, *Die Generation der Unbefangenen: Zur Soziologie der jungen Menschen Heute* (Düsseldorf: Diedrichs, 1966).

7. Denise B. Kandel and Gerald S. Lesser, *Youth in Two Worlds: United States and Denmark* (San Francisco: Jossey-Bass, 1972), p. 119, table 18 (2,300 American and 1,600 Danish youth were interviewed). The book as a whole rejects the view that young people are turning from parents to a peer subculture. Yet the data fall short of the authors' expectations, indicating only that participation in the peer group is largely independent of participation in family life.

	United States	Denmark
Morals and values		
Parents	51%	34%
Friends	17	49
Personal problems (not involving parents)		
Parents	42	33
Friends	33	49
What books to read		
Parents	14	22
Friends	27	52

8. See, for example, the 1955 and 1956 national surveys of adolescents reported by Elizabeth Douvan and Joseph Adelson, in which only one-fourth of the 2,000 girls interviewed in grades 6 to 12 reported "*any* reservations, however mild, about their parents' rules, and only 5 per cent consider them to be unjust or severe." Douvan and Adelson, *The Adolescent Experience* (New York: Wiley, 1966), pp. 107–115.

9. Daniel Offer, *The Psychological World of the Teen-Ager: A Study of Normal Adolescent Boys* (New York: Basic Books, 1969), p. 200; quote from p. 206.

10. Bernard J. Gallagher, "An Empirical Analysis of Attitude Differences between Three Kin-Related Generations," *Youth and Society*, 5 (1974), 327–359, esp. 335–343.

11. R. W. Connell, "Political Socialization in the American Family: the Evidence Re-Examined," *Public Opinion Quarterly*, 36 (1972), 322–333, esp. p. 330.

12. Jerome B. Kernan, "Her Mother's Daughter? The Case of Clothing and Cosmetic Fashions," *Adolescence*, 8 (1973), 343–350.

13. Gary Schwartz and Don Merten, "The Language of Adolescence: An Anthropological Approach to the Youth Culture," *American Journal of Sociology*, 72 (1967), 453–468, quote from p. 460.

14. Kenneth Keniston, *The Uncommitted: Alienated Youth in American Society* (New York: Harcourt, Brace, 1960), p. 397.

15. Schwartz and Merten, "Language of Adolescence," p. 458.

16. For long series, see Griselda Rowntree and Norman H. Carrier, "The Resort to Divorce in England and Wales, 1858–1957," *Population Studies*, 11 (1958), 188–233; National Center for Health Statistics, U.S. DHEW, "100 Years of Marriage and Divorce Statistics, United States, 1867–1967," *Vital and Health Statistics*, series

21, nr. 24 (1973); Louis Roussel, "Les Divorces et les séparations de corps en France (1936–1967)," *Population,* 25 (1970) 275–302; graph on p. 279 has 1885–1939 data.

17. Data to 1970 are available in the *Statistisches Jahrbuch der Schweiz,* 1973, p. 590.

18. Robert Chester, "Contemporary Trends in the Stability of English Marriage," *Journal of Biosocial Science,* 3 (1971), 389–402, esp. table 2, p. 393, and table 3, p. 396.

19. Paul C. Glick and Arthur J. Norton, "Perspectives on the Recent Upturn in Divorce and Remarriage," *Demography,* 10 (1973), 301–314, esp. figure 3, p. 307.

20. *Ibid.,* pp. 302–303.

21. Abbott L. Ferriss, *Indicators of Change in the American Family* (New York: Russell Sage Foundation, 1970), p. 126, series nr. 210.

22. For 1940–1960 data, see Valerie Kincade Oppenheimer, *The Female Labor Force in the United States: Demographic and Economic Factors Governing Its Growth and Changing Composition* (Berkeley: University of California Population Monograph Series, No. 5, 1970), table 1.4, p. 11, which shows substantial increases among married women of all age brackets. For a tour of the international data see Evelyne Sullerot, *Histoire et sociologie du travail féminin: essai* (Paris: Gonthier, 1968), p. 201 *et seq.* For Canadian data, Canada, Department of Labour, *Women in the Labour Force, 1970: Facts and Figures* (Ottawa: Information Canada, 1971), table 10, p. 21; Ontario, Department of Labour, "Working Women in Ontario," p. 4 (multilithed pamphlet, n.p., n.d., available from Women's Bureau of the DL).

APPENDIX I

Fertility Rates for the Pre-1850 Period by Social Class

Village studies finding higher fertility for the landed than the landless

G. Heckh, "Unterschiedliche Fortpflanzung ländlicher Sozialgruppen aus Südwestdeutschland seit dem 17. Jahrhundert," *Homo*, 3, iv (1952), 169–175. In 1650–1799 the *Bauern* and *Landwirte* averaged 6.4 children per marriage, *Handwerker* and *Gewerbetreibende* 5.8, and *Taglöhner* 5.0. These differentials are partially explicable by differences in the age at marriage, which was several years higher for laborers than for landed peasants (p. 170).

Marcel Lachiver, "Fécondité légitime et contraception dans la région parisienne," in Société de démographie historique, ed., *Sur la population française au XVIIIe et au XIXe siècles: Hommage à Marcel Reinhard* (Paris: SDH, 1973), pp. 383–401. In Suresnes between 1735 and 1785 the "descendance des femmes mariées à 20 ans" was 11.6 for the rich, 10.4 for the "classes moyennes," and 9.8 for the poor, p. 398.

Raymond Deniel, "La Population d'un village du Nord de la France: Sainghin-en-Mélantois, de 1665 à 1851," *Population*, 20 (1965), 563–602. Farmers and artisans married between ages 20–24, in those unions contracted before 1790, had 8.5 children per completed family; day laborers and weavers married at the same age had 8.3. Farmers and artisans married between 25 to 29 had 6.8 children, day laborers only 5.6. These gaps were narrowed somewhat for marriages contracted in 1790–1829 (p. 582).

Michel Terrisse, "Un Faubourg du Havre: Ingouville," *Population*, 16 (1961), 285–300. For those marriages joined in 1730–1770, women from the peasant farmer (*laboureur*) class had at all ages higher fertility than those from the "artisans et ouvriers" class (p. 290).

Hubert Charbonneau, *Tourouvre-au-Perche aux XVIIe et XVIIIe siècles: Etude de démographie historique* (Paris: PUF, 1970); for those couples married 1665–1765 women of all ages among the "laboureurs," "marchands," and "artisans"—the propertied groups—had higher fertility than women among the "sabotiers" and "manoeuvres," the disadvantaged (p. 108).

Appendix I

Studies finding no difference in the fertility of the landed and the landless

John Knodel, "Two and a half Centuries of Demographic History in a Bavarian Village," *Population Studies*, 24 (1970), 353–376, esp. pp. 370–371.

Marcel Lachiver, *La Population de Meulan du XVIIe au XIXe siècle (vers 1600–1870): Etude de démographie historique* (Paris: SEVPEN, 1969), p. 165.

David Gaunt, "Family Planning and the Preindustrial Society: Some Swedish Evidence [the parish of Alskog]," in Kurt Agren *et al.*, *Aristocrats, Farmers, Proletarians: Essays in Swedish Demographic History* (Uppsala: Scandinavian University Books, 1973), pp. 28–59; for the age groups in which the number of women was sufficient to analyze, Gaunt reports "nearly identical" fertility rates between the nonfarm and the total population (p. 57).

Several studies of English towns, done with the census of 1851, have found slightly larger numbers of children resident in lower-class than in middle- and upper-class homes. Yet the confidence limits of these means (computed from sample data) overlap, which makes the difference only apparent. And these studies provide no control for infant mortality because they are based on census data. See W. A. Armstrong, "The Interpretation of the Census Enumerators' Books for Victorian Towns," in H. J. Dyos, ed., *The Study of Urban History* (London: Arnold, 1968), pp. 67–85; Roger Smith, "Early Victorian Household Structure: A Case Study of Nottinghamshire," *International Review of Social History*, 15 (1970), 69–84.

Studies finding larger family sizes (no fertility rates computed) for the landless than the landed

David J. Loschky and Donald F. Krier, "Income and Family Size in Three Eighteenth-Century Lancashire Parishes: A Reconstitution Study," *Journal of Economic History*, 29 (1969), 429–448; whereas the mean completed size of farmers' families was 3.8 children, that of poor families was 4.6. The poor married several years earlier than the farmers, doubtless a partial explanation of the difference (pp. 436, 442).

Pierre Guillaume, *La Population de Bordeaux au XIXe siècle* (Paris: Colin, 1972); for those marriages contracted in 1822–1824, an average of 1.4 children were born to the "bourgeoisie," 1.8 to the "peuple" (p. 301).

Literature on social-class variation in other variables affecting fertility

Class and fecundability. There's no doubt that middle-class girls became pubertal sooner than lower-class girls, a result of their better diet. And if diet accelerated the onset of menstruation, it probably raised the capability of middle-class women of all ages to conceive. On these class differences in age at menarche see, for example, the section on Nemours (Seine-et-Marne) in *Description des épidémies qui ont régné depuis quelques années dans la généralité de Paris* (Paris, 1783), p. 44: "celles [the girls] du peuple un peu plus tard que les filles aisées"; anon., "Statistique. Description de la France . . . Département de la Drôme," *Annales de Statistique*, 2 (an X–1802), "celles . . . qui tiennent à la classe des citoyens doués de la fortune, le sont [pubertal] un peu plutôt" (p. 490); according to A. Brierre de Boismont, upper-class Parisian girls began to menstruate at thirteen years, seven months on the average in the 1830s; daughters of Parisian textile workers, on the other hand, were not normally pubertal until fourteen years five months (yet middle-class "demoiselles" preceded them by an average of only one month), *De La Menstruation* (Paris, 1842), pp. 13–22; A. Raciborski reports, finally, that in Marseille (presumably during the 1860s) the "classe aisée" began menstruating at 13.3 years on the average, the "classe ouvrière" at 13.9. *Traité de menstruation* (Paris, 1868), p. 222.

Class and contraception. I have attempted elsewhere to demonstrate that it was the propertied, rather than the propertyless, who first adopted contraception in eighteenth- and nineteenth-century Europe: Edward Shorter, "Female Emancipation, Birth Control, and Fertility in European History," *American Historical Review,* 78 (1973), 605–640, esp. p. 629.

Class and fetal mortality. There tends to be an inverse correlation between socio-economic status and incidence of fetal loss, but it is neither invariable nor very pronounced. Whereas poor sections of early-nineteenth century Brussels had proportionally more stillbirths than wealthy sections, the same was not true of Paris, as Bernard-Benoît Remacle pointed out in *Rapport . . . concernant les infanticides et les mort-nés dans leur relation avec la question des enfants trouvés* (Paris, 1845), pp. 32–33; and in industrial Abbeville only 4.4 per cent of the children of the "pauvres" were stillborn, 5.9 per cent of those of the "riches." L. Brion, *Recherches statistiques sur la population et sur l'industrie d'Abbeville* (Joigny, 1846), p. 67. In contemporary times, a negative correlation between class and fetal mortality appears regularly though not strongly; Dugald Baird discovered that in Britain of the 1940s, the lower classes experienced higher stillbirth rates than did the upper classes for the first birth, and that lower-class rates climbed more rapidly for subsequent children than did upper-class rates. "Social Class and Fetal Mortality," *The Lancet,* 253 (Oct. 11, 1947), 531–535. Within an upstate New York population in the early 1950s, professional and managerial workers suffered both lower incidences of neonatal mortality and fetal loss than did sales and clerical workers and craftsmen; operatives and service workers had the highest rates. Sam Shapiro *et al., Infant, Perinatal, Maternal, and Childhood Mortality in the United States* (Cambridge: Harvard University Press, 1968), pp. 64–65.

APPENDIX II

Problems and Statistical Sources in the Measurement of Illegitimacy and Premarital Pregnancy, Seventeenth to Twentieth Centuries

The best indicator of bastardy is the *illegitimacy rate*, the number of illegitimate births per 1,000 unmarried women, ages fifteen to fourty-four. The illegitimacy rate measures propensity: the likelihood that in any given year a single woman within that age range will bear a bastard child. The rate is most suitable for our purposes because, ultimately, we are trying to find out the average woman's chances of brushing against sex in the years before her marriage. Unfortunately, to compute the rate, we need to know the number of unmarried women in the population, which means a census. And before 1840 there were very few censuses. In those scattered cases where census data have been available to demographers, and where illegitimacy rates have been calculated, the trend turns out to be in the expected direction: in Sweden after 1750 and in Belgium after 1830, illegitimate fertility goes up. But these are exceptional time series.[1]

We normally content ourselves with a much inferior measure of bastardy, the *illegitimacy ratio*, or the number of illegitimate births per 100 total births. The ratio is less desirable than the rate, because it is subject to influence by two outside factors: changes in the number of unmarried women in the population, and changes in the number of legitimate births. If, for example, the unmarried female population of a given city increases substantially as a result of an inrush of servants or young seamstresses, that city's illegitimacy ratio could go up sharply, there being more women around to produce illegitimate children. Yet the propensity of these individual women to sleep around before marriage and thus become pregnant might not have changed at all. It is the composition of the place's population that has altered, not the behavior of its inhabitants. A change in the marriage rate could similarly affect the number of unmarried women. Or let us say the number of legitimate births in the city drops off substantially, while the number of illegitimate ones stays the same. This reduces the births in the ratio's denominator (the total number of births), so that even if the ratio's numerator (the number of illegitimate births) does not move, the ratio will appear to have increased. The ratio, therefore, is an indicator that we must approach with great caution, making sure that any change is not the result of one of the above-mentioned artifacts before we start drawing grand conclusions from it.

Unfortunately, the ratio is the only measurement of illegitimacy available for the most fascinating part of our period, 1750–1800. Swarms of local historians have been burrowing away in parish registers, counting up births and publishing the annual tabulations, which is one key source of data. And the official tabulations of national statistical offices commonly make available the annual number of legitimate and illegitimate births. So we have a good supply of illegitimacy ratios.

Do these two possible sources of distortion—changes in the population at risk (number of unmarried females) for illegitimacy, and changes in the number of legitimate births—qualify the inference that it was rising levels of intercourse that caused increases in illegitimacy ratios? The first one may have done so; the second almost certainly did not. Beyond a doubt, the increasing illegitimacy ratios we encounter in big European cities after 1750 stem partly from a "compositional effect." Numbers of unmarried females in these cities were growing as ever more women quit the farm and the humdrum of small towns to go where the action was. Yet illegitimacy ratios weren't just rising in the towns, although perhaps it was there they took off first; illegitimacy was going up almost everywhere around this time, in isolated hamlets, large villages, market towns, and provincial centers alike. There are cases where illegitimacy does not climb in the years 1750–1800, but in those communities premarital pregnancy was increasing, which means that local courtship customs had managed to accommodate the new pattern of premarital sexual activity.[2] Now, the population of unmarried women couldn't have been rising in all these places simultaneously, at least not owing to migration; the average age at marriage for women in this period does go up a year or two, but it seems unlikely that this slight lengthening in the time women had to wait for wedlock could have propelled them in such huge numbers into the arms of their suitors and seducers. So a change in the composition of the unmarried population at risk probably did not cause the explosion in the illegitimacy ratio.

As for a shift in the number of legitimate births, we may rule that out even more speedily as a factor in a changing illegitimacy ratio. The legitimate birth rate was going *up* in many places during this half century; or, if not rising, it was certainly not falling. With higher proportions married, and indeed with an increase in the marital fertility of younger women (or, in some places, women of all ages), more children were being born inside marriage as well as outside.[3] Thus changes in this factor would sooner have deflated than inflated the illegitimacy ratio.

One unresolved problem is the course of premarital pregnancy during the nineteenth century. Data available to me indicate that no decline took place. During the general 1850–1930 period, most European and several American prebridal pregnancy series remained at a high, stable level. Now, it's true that illegitimacy does fall off over that time, probably the result of contraception. But we may assume that contraception influenced prebridal pregnancy less than it did illegitimacy because engaged women (which a good share of the prebridally pregnant are) tend generally to contraceive less often and less efficiently than unengaged women. So if it's true that the engaged didn't take precautions, and got pregnant at the same rate as previously, we might infer that "Victorianism" did not diminish the level of premarital intercourse.

Premarital pregnancy data that even run through part of the nineteenth century are available for only five American communities, and in three of them there is a sharp rise towards the century's end:[4]

Appendix II

Per cent of first legitimate children
born within eight and one-half months of marriage

Hingham, Mass.	
1801–1820	25
1821–1840	16
1841–1860	8
1861–1880	16
Coventry, Conn.	(9 months)
1771–1800	25
1801–1840	5
Mansfield, Conn.	
1770–1799	21
1800–1819	12
1820–1849	6
Lexington, Mass.	
1854–1866	4
1885–1895	19
Willimantic, Conn.	
1850, 1870	19
1890	32
1910	25

Within Europe, only in Medmenham (Bucks.) and Kreuth (Bavaria) does a nineteenth-century downturn take place, among the series that are known.[5] In Anhausen (Bavaria), Remmesweiler (Saar), Boitin (Mecklenburg), Volksharding-hausen (Hesse), and in an unnamed Oldenburg town, the nineteenth century saw either constant or rising prebridal pregnancy.[6] I feel therefore that the downward nineteenth-century curve which Daniel Smith and Michael Hindus draw in their graph of seventeenth to twentieth century prenuptial conceptions overrepresents the experience of a few New England towns,[7] the results for which moreover are ambiguous, and exaggerates a possible prebridal pregnancy decline. As for their argument that premarital intercourse decreased in the nineteenth century, I don't believe that at all.

Series of premarital pregnancy and illegitimacy are as follows for the period 1550–1650:

England
P.E.H. Hair, "Bridal Pregnancy in Rural England in Earlier Centuries," *Population Studies*, 20 (1966–67), 233–243, and Hair, "Bridal Pregnancy in Rural England further examined," *Population Studies*, 24 (1970), 59–70, esp. p. 60. Higher levels of pregnancy at marriage clearly prevailed in the sixteenth than in the seventeenth and early eighteenth centuries. Thereafter, however, the Hair data point to an enormous increase.

Peter Laslett and Karla Oosterveen, "Long-term Trends in Bastardy in England A Study of the Illegitimacy Figures in the Parish Registers and in the Reports of the Registrar General, 1561–1960," *Population Studies*, 27 (1973), 255–286, especially the graph on p. 260. A marked rise and fall in the illegitimacy ratio occurs from 1561 to 1651.'

Appendix II

France

Alain Croix, who found illegitimacy ratios up to 6 per cent for the 1500s, calls it "the century of illegitimacy," without however presenting data for subsequent epochs. "La Démographie du pays nantais au XVIe siècle," *Annales de démographie historique*, 1967, pp. 63–90, esp. p. 72.

One student, in an unpublished study of the Bresse district, discovered the ratio at 5 percent in 1560–1562, dropping steadily thereafter until 1680. Jean-Louis Flandrin communicated this information to me in a letter.

The illegitimacy ratio in Isbergues (Pas-de-Calais) experienced a bumplet in 1626–1650, but otherwise was minimal until late in the eighteenth century. Christian Pouyez, "Une communauté rurale d'Artois: Isbergues, 1598–1826," Thèse de 3e cycle, Université de Lille III, 1972, p. 94. Microéditions universitaires, 73 944 37.

Germany

For Weiden/Oberfalz there's an early seventeenth-century peak in the ratio, then a great rise after 1740. Roger Mols, *Introduction à la démographie historique des villes d'Europe du XIVe au XVIIIe siècle*, 3 vols. (Louvain: Bibliothèque de l'Université, 1955), II, p. 302.

The half-century aggregates that Julius Gmelin presents show no crest before the late nineteenth century, and a steady upward movement from 1601 to 1870. "Bevölkerungsbewegung im Hällischen seit Mitte des 16. Jahrhunderts," *Allgemeines Statistisches Archiv*, 6 (I) (1902), 240–283, esp. p. 248.

For a large farm village in Oldenburg, the illegitimacy ratio falls from 3.8 in 1607–1700 to 1.5 in 1701–1750. Premarital pregnancy remains constant in those years, however. Erich Meyer, "Beiträge zum Sexualleben der Landjugend," *Zeitschrift für Sexualwissenschaft*, 16 (1929–30), 106–111.

With 3 percent, the Strasbourg illegitimacy ratio is higher in 1600–1611 than late in the seventeenth century. After 1806, however, it regularly runs between 20 and 30 percent. Adolph Kriesche and Joseph Krieger, *Beiträge zur Geschichte der Volksseuchen zur medicinischen Statistik und Topographie von Strassburg im Elsass* (Strasbourg, 1878), p. 84.

Italy

There are crests in the illegitimacy ratio of Siena throughout the early modern period, and no tendency to increase after 1750. Mols, *Démographie des villes*, II, p. 301.

Space does not permit listing of the local studies on which observations about prebridal pregnancy for 1750–1850 rest. Series for Britain, France, and the United States are reviewed in Daniel Scott Smith and Michael S. Hindus, "Premarital Pregnancy in America, 1640–1971: An Overview and Interpretation," *Journal of Interdisciplinary History*, 5 (1975), 537–570. A preliminary list of illegitimacy series, from which the parellelism of the illegitimacy and premarital pregnancy ratios may be noted, appeared in Edward Shorter, "Illegitimacy, Sexual Revolution, and Social Change in Modern Europe," *Journal of Interdisciplinary History*, 2 (1971), 237–272. For additional time series on prebridal pregnancy in Germany and elsewhere, see Shorter, "Female Emancipation, Birth Control, and Fertility in European History," *American Historical Review*, 78 (1973), 605–640, esp. p. 637. Several little-known series of illegitimacy ratios are given in Helga Seibel, "The Illegitimacy Trend in 18th and 19th Century Germany," Princeton graduate research paper prepared in 1971 under the direction of John Knodel. Other French prenuptial pregnancy series not included in Smith-Hindus are: F. Desjardins, "Etude démographique du pays d'Arthies aux XVIIe et XVIIIe siècles (1668–1819) [summary of] mémoire de maîtrise," *Dh: bulletin d'information,* nr. 3 (April, 1971), pp. 5–11; Pouyez, "Isbergues," pp. 94, 208; premarital pregnancy available from 1620; Martine Segalen, *Nuptialité et alliance: le choix du conjoint dans une commune de l'Eure* (Paris: Maisonneuve, 1972), p. 41.

The simultaneous increase of premarital pregnancy in colonial New England poses certain problems for my "born-modern" hypothesis about American sexuality. May we argue that seventeenth-century Puritan society was in fact "traditional," but that the ice broke up much sooner in the colonies than in Europe, giving us the true-love testimony we saw in chapter two at a time when French marriage candidates were still inspecting each other's manure piles? Or did an essentially "modern" romantic temperament, inherent within American puritanism from the beginning, merely advance a step or two from hand-holding to love-making in the eighteenth century? Daniel Smith and Michael Hindus, whose statistics show premarital pregnancy climbing in case after American case, argue for an increase in intercourse as part of the wish to be free from the parents. Yet within what larger setting of mentalities this sexual behavior occurred remains nonetheless obscure.

Notes

[1] *Annuaire Statistique de la Belgique et du Congo Belge,* 34 (1903), 109–111; Gustav Sundbärg, *Bevölkerungsstatistik Schwedens, 1750–1900* (Stockholm: Statistiska Centralbyran reprint, 1970; Urval nr. 3), p. 117.

[2] For communes where illegitimacy fell or stayed level while premarital pregnancy rose in the 1750–1800 period, see Alain Molinier, *Une paroisse du bas Languedoc: Serignan, 1650–1792* (Montpellier: Imp. Déhan, 1968), p. 164, and Philippe Wiel, "Une grosse paroisse du Cotentin aux XVIIe et XVIIIe siècles," *Annales de démographie historique,* 1969, pp. 136–189, esp. p. 161.

[3] Data on this eighteenth-century age-specific rise in marital fertility have been drawn together in Edward Shorter, "Female Emancipation, Birth Control, and Fertility in European History," *American Historical Review,* 78 (1973), 633–635.

[4] I have taken all these series from Daniel Scott Smith and Michael S. Hindus, "Premarital Pregnancy in America, 1640–1971: an Overview and Interpretation," *Journal of Interdisciplinary History,* 5 (1975), 561–570.

[5] Medmenham data in P.E.H. Hair, "Bridal Pregnancy in Earlier Rural England further examined," *Population Studies,* 24 (1970), p. 60; Kreuth data in Jacques Houdaille, "Quelques résultats sur la démographie de trois villages d'Allemagne de 1750 à 1879," *Population,* 25 (1970), 649–654.

[6] On Anhausen, see John Knodel, "Two and a Half Centuries of Demographic History in a Bavarian Village," *Population Studies,* 24 (1970), 353–376, esp. 369. On Remmesweiler, see Jacques Houdaille, "La Population de Remmesweiler en Sarre aux XVIIIe et XIXe siècles," *Population,* 25 (1970), 1183–91. On Boitin and Volkshardinghausen, see Houdaille, "Trois villages d'Allemagne."

[7] Smith and Hindus, "Premarital Pregnancy in America."

APPENDIX III

Age Differences Between Spouses, Seventeenth to Twentieth Centuries

	PERCENTAGE OF WIVES MORE THAN FIVE YEARS OLDER THAN THEIR HUSBANDS	PERCENTAGE OF HUSBANDS MORE THAN FIVE YEARS OLDER THAN THEIR WIVES
	FRANCE (FIRST MARRIAGES)	
Tourouvre (Orne) 1665–1770[1]	14	54
Troarn (Calvados) 1668–1792[2]	20	50
Crulai (Orne) 1674–1742[3]	16	51
Dole (Jura) 1710–1789[4]	22	44
Lyon, 1714–1740[5]	18	36
Azereix (Hautes-Pyr.) 1732–1792[6]	20	57
Three villages (Oise) 1740–1792[7]	23	43
Sotteville (Seine-Mar.) 1760–1790[8]	16	25
Syndicat de St. Amé (Vosges)[9]		
1760–1790	23	46
Meulan (Yvelines)[10]		
1660–1739	21	42
1740–1789	20	40
1790–1839	13	53
1840–1869	8	66
Saumur (Maine-et-Loire)[11] 1888–1896	9	61

All France	First marriages	All marriages	First marriages	All marriages
1856–1860[12]	11	11	57	58
1899[13]	9	10	62	61
1909	8	9	60	60
1920		11		55
1929		10		50

BELGIUM (ALL MARRIAGES)		
Chièvres (Hainault) 1720–1795[14]	20	51
Grosage (Hainault) 1720–1795[14]	17	60
All Belgium[15]		
1841–1850	21	49
1851–1860	19	51

CENTRAL EUROPE (ALL MARRIAGES)			
Eibesthal (Austria)[16]			
1801–1850	22		50
1851–1890	15		49
Trier[17]			
1802	35		59
1961/62	15		33
East Germany, 1971[18]	3		20
Switzerland, 1971[19]	10(8*)	46	48(46)*
Netherlands, 1970[20]	6		27

SCANDINAVIA (ALL MARRIAGES)		
Denmark, 1970[21]	7	45
Norway, 1970[22]	6	46
Sweden, 1972[23]	8	38

OTHER (ALL MARRIAGES)		
Italy[24]		
1865–1871 (excl. Rome province)	6	65
1872–1877 (incl. Rome province)	10	63
Canada, 1970[25]	6	44

° First marriages only.

Notes

Statistical sources normally present these data in large tables that cross-classify, in five-year aggregates, the age of the bride by the age of the groom. Thus for grooms twenty to twenty-four, we may learn how many brides were ages fifteen to nineteen, twenty to twenty-four, twenty-five to twenty-nine, and so on. To compute the percentage of mates five years or more older than their spouses, I have simply kept track of the number of marriages in which one partner was in a higher age bracket than the other partner.

[1] *Tourouvre.* Hubert Charbonneau, *Tourouvre-au-Perche aux XVIIe et XVIIIe siècles: Etude de démographie historique* (Paris: PUF, 1970), p. 77.

[2] *Troarn.* Michel Bouvet, "Troarn: Etude de démographie historique (XVIIe-XVIIIe siècles), *Cahier des Annales de Normandie*, nr. 6 (1968), 241.

[3] *Crulai.* Etienne Gautier and Louis Henry, *La Population de Crulai: Paroisse normande, étude historique* (Paris, PUF, 1958), p. 85.

Appendix III

4 *Dole.* Anne Lefebvre-Teillard, *La Population de Dole au XVIIIe siècle: Etude d'histoire économique et sociale* (Paris: PUF, 1969), p. 53.

5 *Lyon.* Maurice Garden, *Lyon et les Lyonnais au XVIIIe siècle* (Paris: Belles-Lettres, 1970), p. 91. Standard: six years or older. Data from parishes of Saint-Pierre and Saint-Saturnin for years 1714–1718 and 1733–1740.

6 *Azereix.* Anne Zink, *Azereix: La Vie d'une communauté rurale à la fin du XVIIIe siècle* (Paris: SEVPEN, 1969), p. 79.

7 *Three villages.* Jean Ganiage, *Trois villages d'Ile-de-France au XVIIIe siècle: Etude démographique* (Paris: PUF, 1963), p. 59.

8 *Sotteville.* Pierre Girard, "Aperçus de la démographie de Sotteville-lès-Rouen vers la fin du XVIIIe siècle," *Population*, 14 (1959), p. 490.

9 *St-Amé.* Xavier Thiriat, *La Vallée de Cleurie: Statistique, topographie . . .* (Mirecourt, 1869), p. 246.

10 *Meulan.* Marcel Lachiver, *La Population de Meulan du XVIIIe au XIXe siècle (vers 1600–1870): Etude de démographie historique* (Paris: SEVPEN, 1969), pp. 142–143.

11 *Saumur.* Simon, (le docteur), *Etude médicale sur la ville de Saumur* (Saumur, 1898), p. 67.

12 *France, 1856–1860.* Ad. Quetelet and Xav. Heuschling, *Statistique internationale (Population)* (Brussels, 1865), pp. 236–238.

13 *France, 1899–1929.* Annuaire statistique (France), vols. for 1901, 1911, 1927, 1932.

14 *Chièvres and Grosage.* Pierre Bauwens, "La Population des paroisses de Chièvres et de Grosage aux XVIIe et XVIIIe siècles (1607–1798), *Annales du cercle royal d'histoire et d'archeologie d'Ath*, 42 (1967–69), 93, 135.

15 *Belgium 1841–1860.* Quetelet, *Statistique internationale*, p. 123.

16 *Eibesthal.* "Bevölkerungsbewegung im Orte Eibesthal in Nieder-Oesterreich in den Jahren 1683–1890." [Austria] *Statistiches Monatschrift*, N.F. 4 (1899) p. 261.

17 *Trier.* Heinz Monz, "Die Bevölkerungsstruktur einer mitteleuropäischen Stadt und ihrer Region im Jahre 1802 im Vergleich zu den Jahren 1961/64," *Archiv für Sozialgeschichte*, 5 (1965), 171.

18 *East Germany.* Statistisches Jahrbuch der Deutschen Demokratischen Republik, 1973, pp. 486–487. Data are given in yearly intervals.

19 *Switzerland.* Statistisches Jahrbuch der Schweiz, 1972, p. 60.

20 *Netherlands.* Statistical Yearbook of the Netherlands, 1971, p. 29.

21 *Denmark.* Statistisk Arbog, 1972, p. 42.

22 *Norway.* Statistik arkbok, 1972, p. 18.

23 *Sweden.* Statistisk arsbok, 1973, p. 73.

24 *Italy.* Alexander von Oettingen, *Die Moralstatistik in ihrer Bedeutung für eine Socialethik*, 3rd ed. (Erlangen, 1882), end table 10.

25 *Canada.* Vital Statistics, 1970, p. 226.

APPENDIX IV

Probable Month of Conception, Selected Places, Seventeenth to Twentieth Centuries

Seasonality in Illegitimate Conceptions, Seventeenth to Twentieth Centuries

	INDEX OF SEASONALITY
Grenoble, 1680–1790[1]	14.8
Niort (Deux-Sevres), 1774–1793[2]	19.5
Ostend (Belgium), 1780–1800[3]	25.0
Montpellier (Herault),	
1772–1792[4]	15.6
1793–1805[5]	9.6
Liège (Belgium),[6]	
1720–1744	14.1
1745–1769	12.6
1770–1794	7.4
Abbeville (Somme), 1818–1842[7]	13.3
Netherlands, 1850–1859[8]	8.7
Austria, 1851–1864[9]	7.9
Sweden, 1901–1961[10]	6.9
England and Wales, 1939–1961[11]	5.4
Germany	
1905[12]	7.4
(West) Germany 1967[13]	4.9
United States, 1963[14]	4.6

Appendix IV

The "index of seasonality" is the average standard deviation of the monthly seasonal index of illegitimate conceptions. The probable months of conception correspond, of course, to illegitimate births nine months later.

The "seasonal index" for each month is simply the average number of illegitimate conceptions per day in that month, divided by the daily average for that year. The standard deviation of each month is then computed to give a single indicator of variation for the year as a whole.

Among several possible indexes of seasonal fluctuation, the average standard deviation is preferable because it takes into account the deviation of each month from the annual mean. An alternative index proposed by W. H. James (the sum of the average number of illegitimate births per day for each month from February to May, divided by the sum of average births per day for November and December) has the disadvantage of considering the data for only six months in the year, and those months will not necessarily be in every country the major peaks and troughs. "Social Class and Season of Birth," *Journal of Biosocial Science*, 3 (1971), pp. 309–320.

The national Center for Health Statistics of the United States Public Health Service employs the average standard deviation to compute the magnitude of seasonal fluctuations in births. See *Seasonal Variation of Births: United States, 1933–1963* (PHS publication No. 1000, Series 21, No. 9, 1966), p. 4.

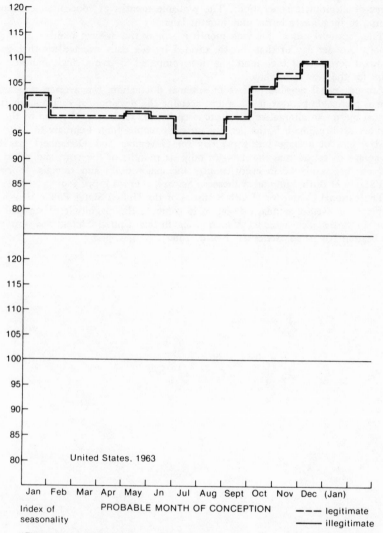

Index of
seasonality

PROBABLE MONTH OF CONCEPTION

- - - legitimate
—— illegitimate

*The scale on these graphs is the average number of births per day each month expressed as a percentage of the yearly average. Thus 100 is in each case the yearly average.

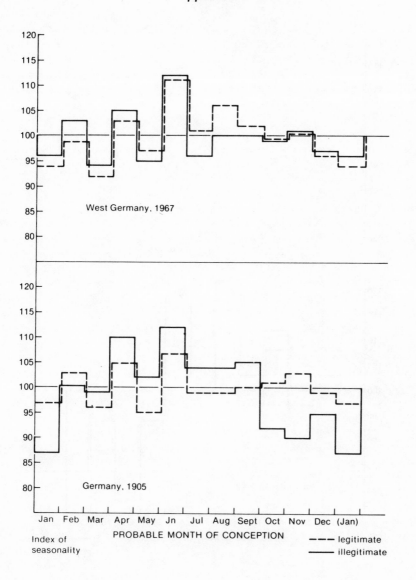

West Germany, 1967

Germany, 1905

Jan Feb Mar Apr May Jn Jul Aug Sept Oct Nov Dec (Jan)

Index of
seasonality

PROBABLE MONTH OF CONCEPTION

- - - - legitimate
———— illegitimate

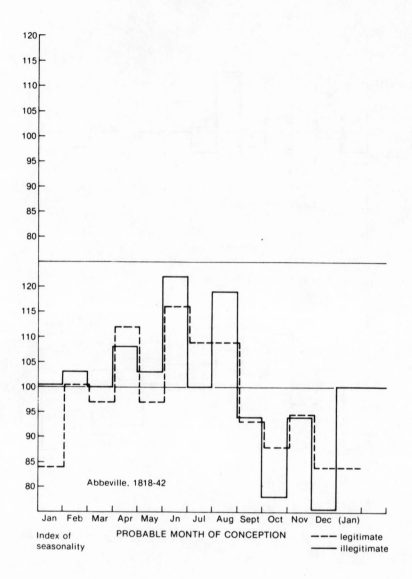

Abbeville, 1818-42

Index of
seasonality

PROBABLE MONTH OF CONCEPTION

- - - legitimate
—— illegitimate

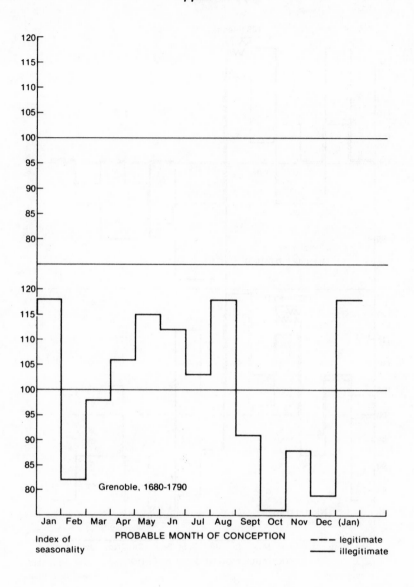

Grenoble, 1680-1790

Index of
seasonality

PROBABLE MONTH OF CONCEPTION

- - - legitimate
——— illegitimate

345

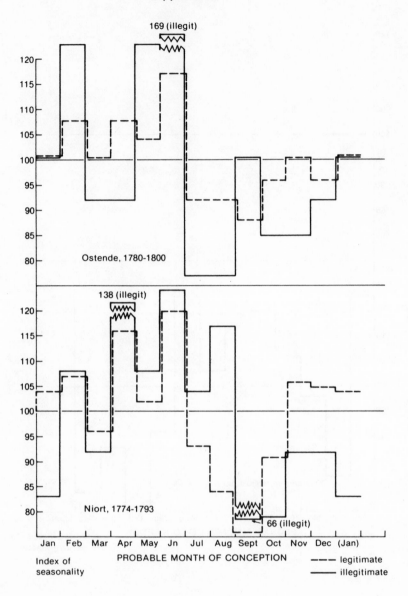

169 (illegit)

Ostende, 1780-1800

138 (illegit)

Niort, 1774-1793

66 (illegit)

Index of
seasonality

PROBABLE MONTH OF CONCEPTION

- - - - legitimate
———— illegitimate

Jan Feb Mar Apr May Jn Jul Aug Sept Oct Nov Dec (Jan)

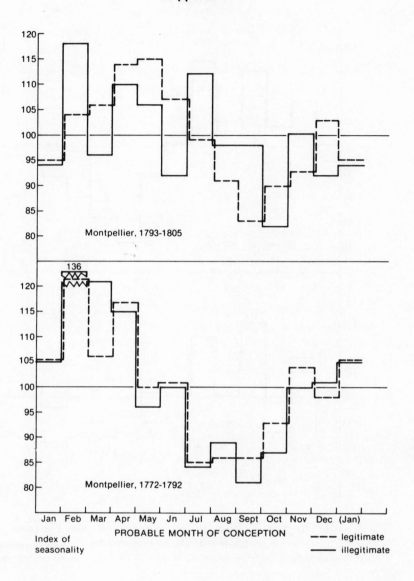

Index of
seasonality

PROBABLE MONTH OF CONCEPTION

- - - - legitimate
——— illegitimate

347

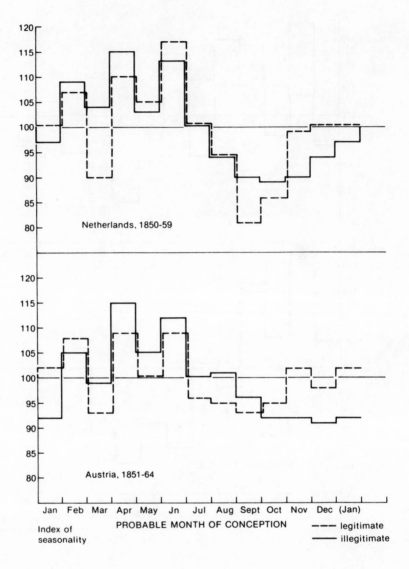

120 —
115 —
110 —
105 —
100
95 —
90 —
85 —
80 —

Netherlands, 1850-59

120 —
115 —
110 —
105 —
100
95 —
90 —
85 —
80 —

Austria, 1851-64

Jan Feb Mar Apr May Jn Jul Aug Sept Oct Nov Dec (Jan)

Index of
seasonality

PROBABLE MONTH OF CONCEPTION

- - - - legitimate
———— illegitimate

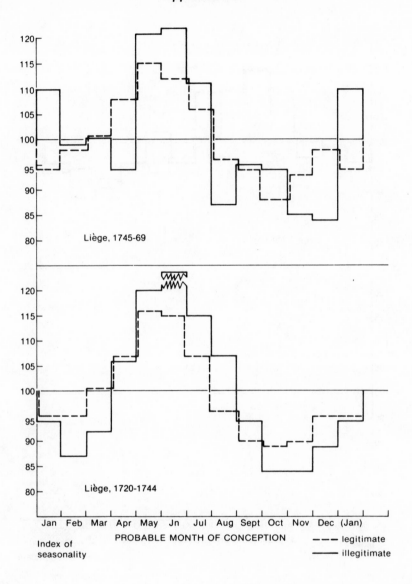

Liège, 1745-69

Liège, 1720-1744

Index of
seasonality

PROBABLE MONTH OF CONCEPTION

- - - - legitimate
———— illegitimate

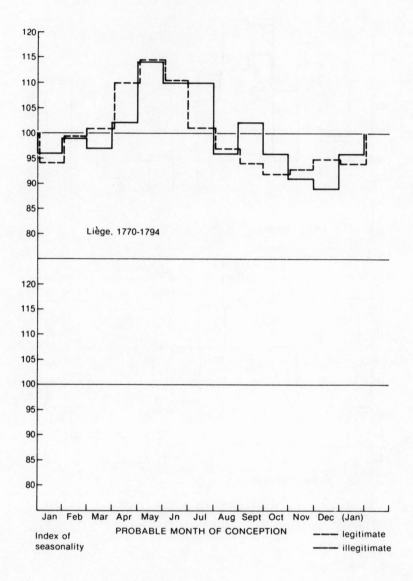

Liège, 1770-1794

Jan Feb Mar Apr May Jn Jul Aug Sept Oct Nov Dec (Jan)

Index of
seasonality

PROBABLE MONTH OF CONCEPTION

- - - - - legitimate

———— illegitimate

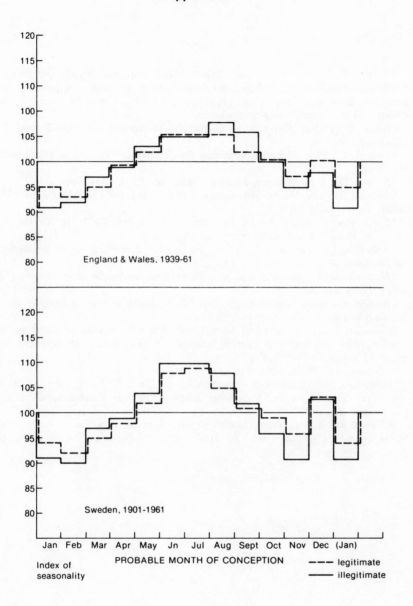

England & Wales, 1939-61

Sweden, 1901-1961

Index of
seasonality

PROBABLE MONTH OF CONCEPTION

- - - legitimate
——— illegitimate

Appendix IV

Notes

[1] *Grenoble.* Melles. Sapin and Sylvoz, "Les Rapports sexuels illègitimes au XVIIIème siècle à Grenoble d'après les déclarations de grossesses," unpublished paper under the direction of Jacques Solé (1971), p. 26. Data are based on pregnancy declarations and not monthly illegitimate births.

[2] *Niort.* C. Dupin, *Mémoire statistique du départment des Deux-Sevres* (Paris, 1804), pp. 189–190.

[3] *Ostend.* C. Viry, *Mémoire statistique du département de la Lys* (Paris, 1812), pp. 28–29.

[4] *Montpellier.* J. A. Mourgue, *Essai de statistique* (Paris, 1801), pp. 3–5.

[5] *Montpellier.* J.-A. Murat, *Topographie médicale de la ville de Montpellier* (Montpellier, 1810), table 37.

[6] *Liège.* Etienne Hélin, *La Démographie de Liège aux XVIIe et XVIIIe siècles* (Brussels: Palais des académies, 1963), pp. 158–159.

[7] *Abbeville.* L. Brion and C. Paillart, *Recherches statistiques sur la population et sur l'industrie d'Abbeville* (Joigny, 1816), p. 39.

[8] *Netherlands.* Ad. Quetelet and Xav. Heuschling, *Statistique internationale (Population)* (Brussels, 1865), p. 293.

[9] *Austria.* Alexander von Oettingen, *Die Moralstatistik in ihrer Bedeutung für eine Socialethik*, 3rd ed. (Erlangen, 1882), p. 305.

[10] *Sweden.* Index figures taken from Ursula Cogwill, "Season of Birth in Man. Contemporary Situation with Special Reference to Europe and the Southern Hemisphere," *Ecology*, 47 (1966), 619.

[11] *England and Wales. Ibid.*, 619.

[12] *Germany, 1905. Statistisches Jahrbuch für das Deutsche Reich*, 1907, p. 17.

[13] *West Germany, 1967. Statistiches Jahrbuch für die Bundesrepublik Deutschlands*, 1969, p. 44.

[14] *United States.* U.S. Public Health Service, *Seasonal Variation of Births, United States, 1933–63* (National Center for Health Statistics, Series 21, No. 9, 1966), p. 9.

APPENDIX V

Infant Mortality Rates— Seventeenth to Twentieth Centuries

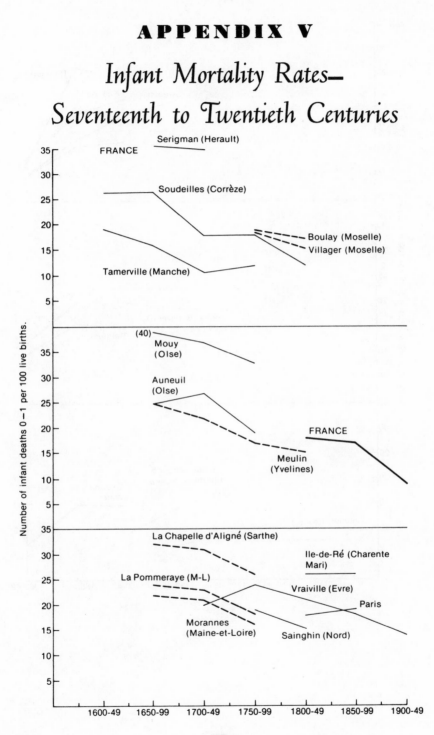

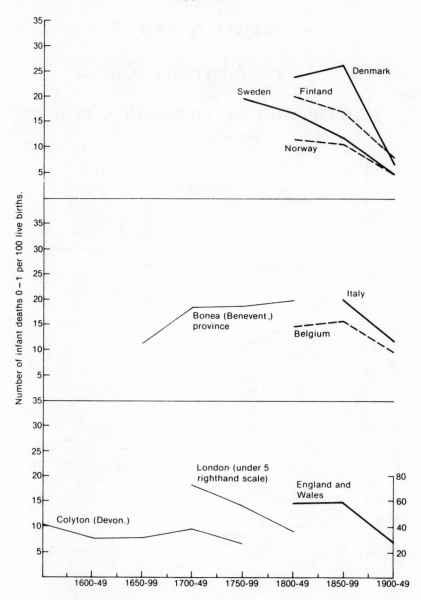

Appendix V

Germany-I

Eibesthal (Lower Austria)

Geroda-Platz (Franc.)

Largenleiten (Franconia)

Sigmaringen

(48)   (48)   (48)

Leipzig

Bölgenthal (Franconia)

Kreuth (Bav.)

Stuttgart

Bortin (Meckl.)

Volkshardinghaven (Hesse)

Böhringen (Württ.)

Three communes in Württemberg

Number of infant deaths 0 – 1 per 100 live births.

1600-49   1650-99   1700-49   1750-99   1800-49   1850-99   1900-49

Appendix V

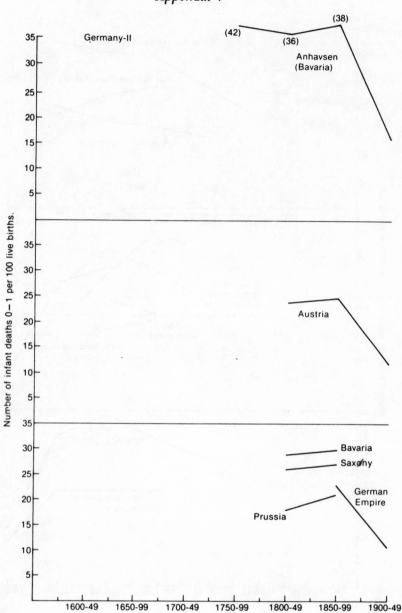

Appendix V

Notes

Unless otherwise specified, all figures are the averages of rates given in the secondary sources. Writers customarily present infant mortality series as the number of deaths 0–1 year per 100 live births over ten- or twenty-year periods. To get fifty-year figures I have averaged together these already-computed rates.

National-level data have been taken from the following:

Gustav Sundbärg, *Aperçus statistiques internationaux* (Stockholm, 1908; Gordon and Breach reprint), p. 142. Data in ten-year blocs, beginning for Norway in the 1840s, Denmark 1840s, Finland 1810s, England-Wales 1830s, Belgium 1840s, Prussia 1810s, Bavaria 1820s, Saxony 1830s, and Austria 1820s. The national series for Sweden have been taken from Sundbärg, *Bevölkerungsstatistik Schwedens, 1750–1900* (Stockholm: Statistiska Centralbyran reprint, 1970), p. 131, for the period to 1900. The entire series for France comes from the *Annuaire statistique, 1966*, p. 13*. And the entire Italian national series was computed from decennial rates presented in Stefano Somogyi, *La Mortalità nei primi cinque anni di eta in Italia, 1863–1962* (Palermo: Editioni Ingrana, 1967), p. 42, table 11, deaths 0–12. Data on Saxony, Bavaria and Prussia taken from Sundbärg, *Aperçus*; data on the German Empire from F. Prinzing, "Die Entwickelung der Kindersterblichkeit in den europäischen Staaten," *Jahrbücher für Nationalökonomie und Statistik*, 3rd ser., 17 (1899), 583, years 1872–1880, 1892–1895.

(1900–1949) *Annuaire statistique de la France*, 1966, p. 13*. This source omitted the years 1911–1919, but the results for 1900–1949 should not thereby be greatly affected.

Local-level data were drawn from the following:

France

Ile de Ré. A Drouineau. *Géographie médicale de l'Ile de Ré* (Paris, 1909), p. 69. Data in five-year intervals.

Soudeilles. Alain Gintrac, "Histoire démographique d'un village corrézien: Soudeilles (1610–1859)" [summary of a *thèse*], *Dh: bulletin d'information*, No. 6 (April, 1972), p. 10. 1610–1699, 1700–1779, 1780–1819, 1820–1859.

Auneuil and Mouy. Pierre Goubert, *Beauvais et le Beauvaisis de 1600 à 1730*, 3 vols. (Paris: SEVPEN, 1960), III, p. 64. Data 1657–1696, 1697–1756, 1757–1790. Figures estimated from source graph.

Boulay. Jacques Houdaille, "La Population de Boulay (Moselle) avant 1850," *Population*, 22 (1967), 1076. 1750–1779, 1780–1809, 1810–1889.

Seven villages around Boulay. Jacques Houdaille, "La Population de sept villages des environs de Boulay (Moselle) aux XVIIIe et XIXe siècles," *Population*, 26 (1971), 1071. Same groups of years as above.

Meulan. Marcel Lachiver, *La Population de Meulan du XVIIe au XIXe siècle (vers 1600–1870)* (Paris: SEVPEN, 1969), p. 195. 1668–1714, 1715–1764, 1765–1814, 1815–1839.

Three communes in Anjou (Morannes, La Pommeraye, La Chapelle d'Aligné). François Lebrun, *Les Hommes et la mort en Anjou aux 17e et 18e siècles: Essai de démographie et de psychologie historiques* (Paris: Mouton, 1971), p. 182. 1670–1709, 1710–1749, 1750–1789: note that towards the end of the Old Regime, the infant mortality rates turn sharply upwards.

Appendix V

Sérignan. Alain Molinier, *Une Paroisse du bas Languedoc: Sérignan, 1650–1792* (Montpellier: Déhan, 1968), p. 204. 1650–1715, 1716–1782.

Sainghin. Raymond Deniel, "La Population d'un village du Nord de la France: Sainghin-en-Mélantois, de 1665 à 1851," *Population*, 20 (1965), 589. Ten-year blocs.

Vraiville. Martine Segalen, *Nuptialité et alliance: Le choix du conjoint dans une commune de l'Eure* (Paris: Maisonneuve, 1972), p. 41. Ten-year blocs, 1706–1962.

Tamerville. Philippe Wiel, "Une grosse paroisse du Cotentin aux XVIIe et XVIIIe siècles," in Société de démographie historique, *Annales de démographie historique*, 1969, p. 157. In twenty-year blocks, 1624–1792.

Paris. Etienne van de Walle and Samuel H. Preston, "Mortalité de l'enfance au XIXe siècle à Paris et dans le département de la Seine," *Population*, 29 (1974), 89–106, esp. 100. A definitive downturn begins around 1880. Data on graph represent averages of five-year figures for girls in 1811–1850 and 1851–1905.

Central Europe

Sigmaringen. Karl Paul Brandlmeier, *Medizinische Ortsbeschreibungen des 19. Jahrhunderts im deutschen Sprachgebiet* (Berlin medical diss., 1942), p. 38; 1658–1680, 1680–1705, 1705–1730, etc. Rates per 100 total births. Data apparently taken from F. X. Mezler, *Versuch einer medicinischen Topographie von Sigmaringen* (Freiburg, 1822).

Böhringen. G. Heckh, "Bevölkerungsgeschichte und Bevölkerungsbewegung des Kirchspiels Böhringen auf der Uracher Alb vom 16. Jahrhundert bis zur Gegenwart," *Archiv für Rassen- und Gesellschaftsbiologie*, 33 (1939–1940), 141. In decades from 1720 to 1936. Rates per 100 total births. I averaged together figures for male and female.

Boitin, Volkshardinghausen, and Kreuth. Jacques Houdaille, "Quelques résultats sur la démographie de trois villages d'Allemagne de 1750 à 1879," *Population*, 25 (1970), 654. "Before 1810," 1810–1869.

Anhausen. John Knodel, "Two and a Half Centuries of Demographic History in a Bavarian Village," *Population Studies*, 24 (1970), 359. 1750–1799, 1800–1849, 1850–1899, 1900 onwards.

Three communes in Württemberg. Ilse Müller, "Bevölkerungsgeschichtliche Untersuchungen in drei Gemeinden des württembergischen Schwarzwaldes," *Archiv für Bevölkerungswissenschaft und Bevölkerungspolitik*, 9 (1939), 198. In decades, 1680–1937. I averaged together the rates for male and female.

Bölgenthal. Ulrich Planck, "Hofstellenchronik von Bölgenthal, 1650–1966: Strukturwandlungen in einem fränkischen Weiler," in Heinz Haushofer, and Willi A. Boelcke, eds., *Wege und Forschungen der Agrargeschichte* (Frankfurt/M: DLG Verlag, 1967), p. 248. Per 100 total births, in half-century intervals from 1650.

Stuttgart. F. Prinzing, "Entwickelung der Kindersterblichkeit," p. 623. For 1812–1822, 1846–1856, 1858–1866, 1875–1881, 1885–1894.

Leipzig. *Ibid.*, pp. 595–596. Per 100 total births, in decades from 1751 to 1870.

Eibesthal. Franz Riedling, "Bevölkerungsbewegung im Orte Eibesthal in Nieder-Oesterreich in den Jahren 1683–1890," (Austria) *Statistische Monatschrift*, N.F., 4 (1899), 263. By decade.

Langenleiten and Geroda-Platz. Ludwig Schmidt-Kehl, "Wandel im Erb- und Rassengefüge zweier Rhönorte, 1700–1936," *Archiv für Bevölkerungswissenschaft*, 7 (1937), 182. I averaged together the rates for males and females.

Appendix V

Other

London. M. W. Beaver, "Population, Infant Mortality and Milk," *Population Studies*, 27 (1973), 246. Children under 5, 1730–49, 1750–69, 1770–89, 1790–1809, 1810–29. Use right-hand scale to interpret in graph.

Colyton. E. A. Wrigley, "Mortality in Pre-Industrial England: The Example of Colyton, Devon, Over Three Centuries," *Daedalus* (Spring, 1968), p. 558. 1538–1599, 1600–1649, 1650–1699, 1700–1749, and 1750–1837.

Bonea. Gerard Delille, "Dalla Peste al Colera: La Mortalita' in un Villaggio del Beneventano, 1600–1840," *Quaderni Storici*, 17 (1971), p. 407. Eleven-year blocks.

Suggestions for Further Reading

The "history of the family" has only recently become a recognized field of research, and the few books about it are not very good. The suggestions which follow, therefore, are distributed among themes essential to the history of the family.

The History of Women

J. A. and Olive Banks, *Feminism and Family Planning in Victorian England* (New York: Schocken, 1964).

J. A. Banks, *Prosperity and Parenthood: A Study of Family Planning among the Victorian Middle Classes* (London: Routledge, 1954).

William H. Chafe, *The American Woman: Her Changing Social, Economic, and Political Roles, 1920–1970* (New York: Oxford, 1972).

Mary Hartman and Lois W. Banner, eds., *Clio's Consciousness Raised: New Perspectives on the History of Women* (New York: Harper & Row, 1974); reprints some important articles.

William L. O'Neill, *Everyone Was Brave: A History of Feminism in America* (Chicago: Quadrangle, 1969).

Joan W. Scott and Louise A. Tilly, "Women's Work and the Family in Nineteenth-Century Europe," *Comparative Studies in Society and History* 17 (1975) 36–64; a useful antidote to Shorter.

Edward Shorter, "Female Emancipation, Birth Control, and Fertility in European History," *American Historical Review*, 78 (1973), 605–640.

Robert W. Smuts, *Women and Work in America* (New York: Columbia, 1959).

Evelyne Sullerot, *Histoire et sociologie du travail féminin* (Paris: Gonthier, 1968); the standard work.

Roger Thompson, *Women in Stuart England and America: A Comparative Study* (London: Routledge, 1974); draws overmuch on literary sources for my taste, but rich.

Suggestions for Further Reading

Martha Vicinus, ed., *Suffer and Be Still: Women in the Victorian Age* (Bloomington: Indiana University Press, 1972); original essays on many aspects of women's
lives; see especially Peter Stearns on "Working-Class Women."

The History of Childhood and Adolescence

Philippe Ariès, *Histoire des populations francaises et de leurs attitudes devant la vie
depuis le XVIIIe siècle* (Paris: Seuil, 1971); one of the old masters at building bridges
between statistics and culture.
————*Centuries of Childhood: A Social History of Family Life*, trans. Robert Baldick
(London: Cape, 1962) (French rev. ed. 1973 from 1960 French ed., *L'Enfant et
la vie familiale sous l'Ancien régime*); the classic work.
Lloyd de Mause, ed., *The History of Childhood* (New York: Psychohistory Press,
1974); de Mause's introductory essay is especially stimulating; unfortunately, the
other contributions, which treat specific countries and periods, are mediocre.
Claire E. Fox, *Pregnancy, Childbirth and Early Infancy in Anglo-American Culture,
1675–1830* (Univ. of Pennsylvania, American Civilization dissertation, 1966); available from University Microfilms.
John Gillis, *Youth and History* (New York: Academic, 1974); not boring.
Michael Gordon, ed., *The American Family in Social-Historical Perspective* (New
York: St. Martin's, 1973); see especially the reprinted essays by John and Virginia
Demos on the history of adolescence, and the two contributions on illegitimacy and
colonial demography by Daniel Scott Smith.
Jean-Louis Flandrin, "L'Attitude à l'égard du petit enfant et les conduites sexuelles
dans la civilisation occidentale: structures anciennes et évolution," *Annales de
démographie historique*, 1973, pp. 143–210; fundamental.
Oscar Handlin and Mary F. Handlin, *Facing Life: Youth and the Family in American
History* (Boston: Atlantic and Little Brown, 1971); irritating, but contains some
interesting ideas.
David Hunt, *Parents and Children in History: The Psychology of Family Life in Early
Modern France* (New York: Basic, 1970); already a classic study in psychohistory.
William L. Langer, "Infanticide: A Historical Survey," *History of Childhood Quar-
terly*, 1 (1974), 353–365; a good introduction to the literature.

Demographic History

Annales: Economies, Sociétés, Civilisations, Numéro spécial: "Famille et Société," 27
(1972); the last word in research, and moreover a good introduction to the
"Annales" school of history.
M. W. Beaver, "Population, Infant Mortality and Milk," *Population Studies*, 27
(1973), 243–254.
Pierre Goubert, *Cent Mille Provinciaux au XVIIe Siècle: Beauvais et le Beauvaisis de
1600 à 1730* (Paris: Flammarion, 1968) a condensed version of one of the great
local studies that helped open up the history of popular life.
John E. Knodel, *The Decline of Fertility in Germany, 1871–1939* (Princeton: Prince-
ton University Press, 1974).
Marcel Lachiver, *La Population de Meulan du XVIIe au XIXe siècle* (Paris: SEVPEN,
1969); what a local community looks like through the eyes of a demographer.
Peter Laslett, ed., *Household and Family in Past Time* (New York: Cambridge Uni-

versity Press, 1972); original essays, mainly on household size, but that at least raise the important issues.

Theodore K. Rabb and Robert I. Rotberg, eds., *The Family in History: Interdisciplinary Essays* (New York: Harper & Row, 1971); see especially Robert Wells, "Demographic Change and the Life Cycle of American Families."

Martine Segalen, *Nuptialité et alliance: le choix du conjoint dans une commune de l'Eure* (Paris: Maisonneuve, 1972); a fine example of studying kinship with quantitative historical data.

E. A. Wrigley, *Population and History* (New York: McGraw-Hill, 1969); the introduction to historical demography for people who want, ultimately, to find out about larger issues.

Families and Communities

Michael Anderson, *Family Structure in Nineteenth Century Lancashire* (New York: Cambridge University Press, 1971).

Gérard Bouchard, *Le Village immobile: Sennely-en-Sologne au XVIIIe siècle* (Paris: Plon, 1972); in the outpouring of French local studies, the most successful effort to link family structures and mentalities.

John Demos, *A Little Commonwealth: Family Life in Plymouth Colony* (New York: Oxford Press, 1970); a small tour de force.

Philip J. Greven, Jr., *Four Generations: Population, Land, and Family in Colonial Andover, Massachusetts* (Ithaca: Cornell University Press, 1970); the only work of its kind for North America.

Peter Laslett, *The World We Have Lost*, rev. ed. (London: Methuen, 1971); the book that started up interest in the family life of common people among British and North American scholars.

François Lebrun, *Les Hommes et la mort en Anjou aux 17e et 18e siècles* (Paris: Mouton, 1971).

Helmut Möller, *Die kleinbürgerliche Familie im 18. Jahrhundert: Verhalten und Gruppenkultur* (Berlin: deGruyter, 1969); the only work on Germany.

Robert Roberts, *The Classic Slum: Salford Life in the First Quarter of the Century* (Manchester: Manchester University Press, 1971).

Michael Young and Peter Willmott, *The Symmetrical Family: A Study of Work and Leisure in the London Region* (London: Routledge, 1973); on how the story comes out.

Laurence Wylie, *Village in the Vaucluse: An Account of Life in a French Village*, rev. ed. (Cambridge: Harvard University Press, 1964); a masterpiece.

Michael Zuckerman, *Peaceable Kingdoms: New England Towns in the Eighteenth Century* (New York: Knopf, 1970).

INDEX

Index

Collomp, Alain, 35

Communes, 37

Communication, 6

Community, 5, 6, 7, 14, 17, 18–21, 44–53; agriculture and, 46; baptism and, 213; charivari, 218–227; courtship and, 122–138, 159–161, 167; development of domesticity and, 227–234; funerals and, 214–215; kinfolk and, 234–244; market economy and, 266–267; morality, 46, 50–53; settlement patterns, 45–46; stability, 47–49; weddings, 215–218

Companionship, 227

Conception, 86–87, 158, 248–249, 340–352

Confréries, 206–207

Conjugal family, 29, 30, 31; baptism, 213; bar time, 209–211; charivari, 218–227; funerals, 214–215; veillées, 211–212; weddings, 215–218; youth organizations and, 207–209

Contraception, 10, 38, 81, 84, 87–88, 109, 111, 112, 113, 118, 155–156, 246

Coram, Thomas, 172

Cottage industry, 6, 69–70, 71, 257–258

Cottager class, 23, 25–26

Courtship, 5, 14, 73, 120–167; arranged marriages, 138–139; bonfires, 46–47, 130, 132, 133; bundling, 47, 102, 124; carnaval, 129–130, 231; community and, 122–138, 159–161, 167; in contemporary world, 161–167; dancing, 95, 127–128, 130; dônages, 130–132, 137; eroticism in, 80, 89, 103, 105–107; festivals, 72, 74, 96–97, 129–137, 158; lack of romance in, 121, 140–148; night courting, 41, 102–105, 124; parish holiday, 135–136; property-oriented, 120; traditional, 120–148; transformation of, 148–161; veillées, 69, 124–127, 160, 211–212, 230–231, 258

Coutèle, Dr., 90

Creativity, 19

Cunnilingus, 252

Daignan, Guillaume, 101

Dancing, 95, 127–128, 130

Death, 8, 57–59, 172, 213–215

Demos, John, 65

Denmark, see Scandinavia

Destrapierre, Dr., 183

Diet, improvement in, 86

Divorce, 7, 173, 269, 277–279

Domestic groups, see Households

Domesticity, 6, 17–18, 57, 168, 205, 206, 267; rise of, 227–234

Dônages, 130–132, 137

Dowries, 139, 140, 147, 148, 150

Drake, Michael, 37

Droz, Gustave, 191

Dumont, Arsène, 177

Economy, 4, 255–267

Education, 191–192

Emile (Rousseau), 182

Empathy, 15–16, 60, 65, 148–149, 168, 169

Endogamy, 150–154

Engagement, 105–106

England: charivaris, 224–225; children in labor force, 26–28; development of domesticity, 233, 234; divorce, 277, 278; endogamy, 153; household size, 25, 37; illegitimacy, 82, 84, 112, 117–118; infant mortality, 201–204; kinfolk, role of, 237–241; kinless domestic unit, 30; living space, 42; marital affection in, 64–65; maternal breastfeeding, 189, 190; mobility of population, 47; premarital sexual activity, 81, 84, 117, 165; sociability patterns, 243; standard of living, 257; swaddling, 198; wet nurses, 176, 177, 181; women in labor force, 262

Eroticism, 80, 98, 103, 105–107, 245–247, 254, 278

Extended family, 29, 30, 31, 35

Extramarital sexual behavior, 98, 246–247

Factory system, 71, 257

Famille souche, 31

Family size, see Households

Famines, 87

Farber, Bernard, 242

Fecundity, 82, 86–87, 89

Fellatio, 252

Fertility, 26, 38, 83, 329–331

Festivals, 72, 74, 96–97, 129–137, 158, 207, 230

Fetal mortality, 26, 38, 82, 88–89

Index

Individualism, 21

Infant mortality, 15, 26, 38, 172–173, 176, 181, 183, 186, 190, 195, 280, 353–359; decrease in, 199–204, 265

Infanticide, 51, 89, 92

Infants, *see* Mother-infant relationship

Instrumental sexuality, 16

Intimacy, 17, 20, 39, 44, 57, 168, 267

Intrabuccal kissing, 106, 123, 160

Jablonski, Jean, 199–200

Josselin, Ralph, 27, 64, 237

Juge, J. J., 191

Keniston, Kenneth, 276

Kinfolk, 4, 7, 25, 234–244; patterns of domestic groups, 29–39

Kinless conjugal family, *see* Conjugal family

Kinsey, Alfred, 109–110, 116, 164, 250–253

Kurland, 35–37

Labat, Emmanuel, 211

Labor, division of, 66–72, 149, 264

Labor force: children in, 26–28; women in, 6–7, 259–262, 279, 280

Laborers, 23–25, 51

Laslett, Peter, 30, 64

Le Play, Frédéric, 31, 47

Lebrun, François, 58, 173

Legitimacy requirement, 51–52

Lent, 129, 130

Leonard, Ann, 43

Lépecq de la Cloture, Louis, 96, 228

Lesauvage, P. J., 228

Lineage, 5, 7, 9, 19, 55

Living space, 39–44

Locke, John, 183

Macfarlane, Alan, 64

Maconnais, 125–126

Maraichinage, 106–107, 123, 160

Mardi gras, 129

Maret, Hughes, 57, 99

Marriage: affection in, 55–65; age at, 15, 138–139, 154–156, 337–339; arranged, 138–139; endogamy, 150–154; halting of, 52; honor-saving, 91, 109; parental approval, 142–144, 162–163; proposals, 140–141, 143; remarriage, 26, 220, 278

Marx, K. F. H., 233

Masturbation, 76, 98–102, 106, 114–116, 251

Maternal love, 17, 169, 184, 227; capitalism and, 263–265; *See also* Mother-infant relationship

May Day, 132, 134

Mazuy, François, 210, 232

Meals, 59, 60, 67

Medical doctors, as source, 11

Men: labor, division of, 66–72; marital affection, 55–65; sexual roles, 65, 66, 73–78; social organizations, 209–211; subordination of women, 54, 56, 59, 62–63; *See also* Sexuality

Menstruation, 86, 139

Menuret de Chambaud, 183, 228

Merchants, 24, 25

Mercier, Louis-Sebastien, 61, 147–148

Merten, Don, 276

Migration, 49

Miscarriages, 38, 81, 89

Modern society, defined, 18–19

Modernization, 13, 14, 17, 21, 28

Möller, Helmut, 61–62, 76

Monnier, D., 59

Monsieur, Madame et bébé (Droz), 191

Morality, 46, 50–53, 95–98

Morgan, Edmund, 65, 250

Mortality rates, 31, 32, 59

Mother-infant relationship, 5, 17, 168–204, 267; breastfeeding, maternal, 181–185, 188, 189, 190, 202; improvements in mothering, 191–199, 203; infant mortality, decrease in, 199–204; nuclear family and, 206; swaddling, 170, 196–199; traditional indifference, 169–175; wet nurses, 76, 175–183, 185–189

Mourning, 59

Multiple family household, 29

Municipal government, 49–53

Murat, Jean-Louis, 155

Netherlands: charivaris, 225; infant feeding, 189, 190; kinless domestic unit, 31; premarital sexual activity, 113

Index

Night courting, 41, 102–105, 124
Noel, Raymond, 35
Nongenital sexual activity, 102–105
Norway, *see* Scandinavia
Nuclear family, 14, 30, 33, 38, 205; adolescent-parent relations, 270–277; changes in marital sexuality, 245–254; divorce and, 277–279; domesticity, rise of, 227–234; kinfolk, role of, 234–244; mother-infant relationship, 206

Onania (Tissot), 99–100
One-person household, 29
Oral-genital contact, 116–117, 252
Orgasm, 75, 245, 248, 253
Out-of-wedlock pregnancy, *see* Premarital pregnancy
Overcrowding, 40–41

Packard, Vance, 114, 253
Parish holidays, 135–136
Patriarchal rule, 19, 29
Peasantry, 23, 25–26; labor, division of, 66–71; lack of romance, 140–142; marital affection, 55–60; sexual roles, 72–75; sexuality, 76–78
Peer groups, 4, 6, 161, 162, 167, 206–209, 212, 271, 273, 275–276, 280
Perron, Charles, 66, 144–145
Petting, 102–105
Petty bourgeoisie, 23, 24; lack of romance, 146–147; marital affection, 60–63; sexual roles, 74; sexuality, 76
Physical attractiveness, 144–145
Plakans, Andrejs, 36
Platt, Gerald M., 259
Postmodern family, 269–280
Premarital pregnancies, 51, 80, 83, 85, 97, 108–109, 110, 111, 112–113, 118, 332–336
Premarital sexual activity, 80–119; multiple partners, 163–165; seasonal patterns, 158; second sexual revolution, 108–119; serial monogamy, 164–165; *See also* Illegitimacy; Premarital pregnancies
Privacy, 5, 17, 20, 39–44, 48, 149, 168
Property, 5, 7, 25, 55, 58

Prostitutes, 107–108
Prudence, 146, 148
Public health, 200–201, 265, 280

Reformation, 85
Relatives, *see* Kinfolk
Remacle, Bernard-Benoît, 92
Remarriage, 26, 220, 278
Roberts, Robert, 234
Romantic love, 5, 6, 7, 17, 19, 57, 60, 149, 227, 247–248; age at marriage and, 156; capitalism and, 259–260; defined, 15; seasonal sexual patterns and, 157–159; *See also* Courtship
Rouger, Dr., 209–210
Rousseau, Jean-Jacques, 182, 183, 198
Russia, courtship, 127

St. John's Day (Midsummer), 134, 135
Salem, Massachusetts, 24–25
Salzmann, Christian, 100
Scandinavia, 14; adolescent-parent relations, 273; charivaris, 225; communes, 37; courtship, 41, 123–124, 127, 145–146, 162; development of domesticity, 233; engagement, 105–106; festivals, 135; illegitimacy, 84, 112; infant mortality, 201; kinless domestic unit, 31; maternal breastfeeding, 189, 190; night courting, 41, 102–105; premarital sexual activity, 84, 105, 109, 113, 162, 165; prostitution, 107; settlement, 45; stillbirths, 92; youth organizations, 207–208
Schofield, Roger, 27
Schwartz, Gary, 276
Self-realization, 19, 167
Sennett, Richard, 233
Sentiment, 5–7, 9, 17, 138, 148, 227, 255, 258
Serial monogamy, 164–165
Servants, 24, 25, 28, 51, 134–135
Settlement patterns, 45–46
Sexual revolution, 16, 79–119, 166, 267; masturbation, 76, 98–102, 106; petting, 102–105; second, 16, 84, 108–119, 161, 166–167; *See also* Illegitimacy
Sexual roles, 16, 65, 66, 73–78, 149, 264